The concepts and theories of modern democracy
3rd edition

This highly acclaimed and popular academic text is now available in a new edition, having revised and updated the analyses of the use and abuse and ambiguity of many essential concepts used in political discourse and political studies. These include basic concepts such as liberty, democracy, rights, representation, authority and political power.

New to this edition are three sections of great topical interest:

- Entirely original analysis of global terrorism, which puts the recent development of Islamic terrorism into perspective by comparing it with earlier examples of terrorist tactics by a variety of state agencies, revolutionary groups and minority nationalist movements.

- Extended discussion on multiculturalism, which supplements theoretical arguments with succinct summaries of the differing ways in which ethnic and cultural minorities have been dealt with in Canada, Britain, France and the Netherlands.

- A section on democratization that focuses on the problems, social and political and even theological, involved in turning authoritarian regimes into stable democracies in the Middle East and elsewhere.

The Concepts and Theories of Modern Democracy is a stimulating guide to current world problems as well as essential reading for university politics.

Anthony H. Birch is Emeritus Professor at the University of Victoria, Canada. He has London degrees and pursued postdoctoral studies at Harvard and the University of Chicago. He has taught political science at universities in England, the United States, Australia and Canada, has published eight books and numerous articles, has served for three years as Vice-President of the International Political Science Association and is Fellow of the Royal Society in Canada.

The concepts and theories of modern democracy
3rd edition

Anthony H. Birch

Routledge
Taylor & Francis Group

LONDON AND NEW YORK

To Dorothy Madeleine Birch

First published 1993
Second edition, 2001
Third edition, 2007
by Routledge
2 Park Square, Milton Park, Abingdon, Oxon OX14 4RN

Simultaneously published in the USA and Canada
by Routledge
270 Madison Ave, New York, NY 10016

*Routledge is an imprint of the Taylor & Francis Group,
an informa business*

© 1993, 2001, 2007 Anthony H. Birch
Typeset in Garamond by Graphicraft Limited, Hong Kong

Printed and bound in Great Britain by TJ International Ltd, Padstow, Cornwall

British Library Cataloguing in Publication Data
A catalogue record for this book is available from the British Library

Library of Congress Cataloging in Publication Data
A catalog record for this book has been requested

ISBN10: 0-415-41463-6 (pbk)
ISBN10: 0-415-41462-8 (hbk)
ISBN10: 0-203-96365-2 (ebk)

ISBN13: 978-0-415-41463-0 (pbk)
ISBN13: 978-0-415-41462-3 (hbk)
ISBN13: 978-0-203-96365-4 (ebk)

Contents

Part IV Styles of political analysis

Acknowledgements

I am grateful to Cambridge University Press for permission to reprint (in Chapter 16) several paragraphs from my article entitled 'Economic models in political science: the case of "exit, voice, and loyalty"' that first appeared in 1975 in the *British Journal of Political Science*, 5(1): 69–82.

For assistance in preparing this edition, my thanks go again to my good friend Bernie Wainewright. I am also grateful to the staff of the University of Victoria library, whose helpfulness has made it the most agreeable of the many academic libraries in which I have worked. And my thanks go to my secretary, Catriona Kaufman, who has coped with my untidy manuscript with great patience and efficiency.

Finally, and as ever, I am grateful to my wife, Dorothy, for her support and encouragement.

A.H.B.

Chapter 1

Introduction

This is a book about the concepts and theories that are invoked when people discuss politics and government in modern democracies. It examines a variety of theories, both analytical and evaluative, and approaches them by analysing some basic political concepts because ideas about politics can only be expressed by using concepts.

A concept is defined by the *Oxford English Dictionary* as 'an idea of a class of objects, a general notion or idea', and by *Webster's Dictionary* as 'an abstract or generic idea generalized from particular instances'. A political concept is an abstract idea about politics and people who discuss political matters use political concepts all the time. They cannot avoid doing so, because, as a British philosopher has said, 'our idea of what belongs to the realm of reality is given for us in the language that we use. The concepts that we have settle for us the forms of the experience we have of the world' (Winch 1958: 15). An American political theorist has said much the same with particular reference to politics, observing that in political life 'our language is not just a neutral medium from some independent reality but instead is partly constitutive of that reality' (Herzog 1991: 111).

The problem for all those who observe, study or participate in politics (and in modern societies that means most people) is that many political concepts are ambiguous, value-laden and subject to more than one meaning or interpretation. The object of this book is to examine some of the basic concepts of modern politics so as to clarify their meaning or meanings, to indicate the implications of using them in one sense rather than another, and to discuss their utility in political analysis.

In the course of doing this various familiar theoretical controversies will be thrown into a new light and examined from a relatively detached viewpoint. These include controversies about the power of the national state, the bases of political authority within the state, the nature of democratic ideals, the relationships between economic and political power, the case for extending popular participation in government, and the nature of minority rights. Because students of politics have varied widely in their methods of analysis, as well as in the nature of their political values, the final two chapters of the book will discuss the main methods adopted by political scientists and make suggestions about their relative utility.

An example may illustrate the nature of the conceptual problems involved in discussing politics. If it is said that George W. Bush became president of the United States in 2001, this is a simple historical statement that does not employ any concepts. If it is said that the American president wields extensive executive powers conferred on him by the constitution, this statement employs a concept with a fairly low level of generality, namely 'executive powers'; but it does not involve any ambiguity or uncertainty as the powers in question are set out in a legal document. However, if it is said that the American president enjoys more political power than the prime minister of Britain, this statement hinges on a concept with a rather high level of generality, namely 'political power'. There are problems about defining political power and disagreements between political analysts as to how its extent should be assessed or measured. That these problems and disagreements are serious will be clear to anyone who reflects for a moment on a further proposition sometimes advanced, namely that the industrial-military complex in the United States wields more power than the president.

There are similar problems about the terms commonly used in the classification of political systems. There is fairly general agreement about which systems can be called democratic, now that the people of eastern Europe have made it clear that they were never deceived by the term 'people's democracy'. However, there is endless disagreement about whether democracy should be defined in terms of institutional arrangements or in terms of the ideals which those arrangements are claimed to promote. When it is said that the United States is a pluralist democracy, this raises questions about the exact meaning of the term 'pluralist'. If it is said that Austria or Sweden have corporatist systems of policy making, this raises questions about the definition of 'corporatist'. If it is said that the state in capitalist society is an agent of the capitalist class, this raises problems about definition together with problems about the evidence that might be adduced to establish or refute the proposition.

It is my belief that everyone concerned with the study and analysis of politics needs to give more direct consideration than is normally given to the definition and understanding of the basic concepts involved in this field of study. Many of these concepts are commonly used without definition because they are familiar to us from general usage and we think we know what they mean. But they have ambiguities that need to be cleared up and shades of meaning that need to be distinguished if they are to form the basis of significant generalizations. Conceptual clarity is desirable in all academic disciplines, but students of politics seem to stand in special need of it. To illustrate this point, let us consider, for a moment, the differences between the study of politics and the study of history, on the one hand, and economics on the other.

Students of history have little need to make a special study of concepts, for the academic discipline developed by historians makes little use of generalizations based on concepts. The concern of historians is to provide a chronological account of the more important events in the country and period they are studying, including an account of the behaviour of the more significant political, military or economic leaders. As Gottschalk has said, the historian 'is distinguished from other scholars most markedly by the emphasis he places upon the role of individual motives, actions, accomplishments, failures and contingencies in historical continuity and change' (Gottschalk 1954: 279). Historians use concepts of a fairly low level of generality when they group events together and give them a collective label, such as 'civil war' or 'the industrial revolution'. However, conventional historians (as distinct from Marxist or neo-Marxist historians) rarely use concepts as the basis of empirical generalizations, so that precision in defining them is not all that important. Conventional historians do not believe in laws of historical development and the study of history does not normally involve either the theorizing or the attempts to make empirical generalizations that political scientists constantly engage in. It is true that every now and again individual historians commit themselves to law-like propositions, such as that certain kinds of industrial development were bound to lead to the rise of the middle classes. But no sooner do some historians say this kind of thing than other historians jump in to point out that the middle classes have been rising ever since the end of the feudal period, whether or not the specified types of industrial development occurred. Historians as a class are sceptical about attempts to generalize and theorize, with the consequence that students of history can do quite well without getting involved in conceptual analysis.

The position of economists is very different. The whole science of classical economics has been built up on the basis of simplifying assumptions about human behaviour that have enabled scholars to develop models, theories and causal generalizations based on technical concepts that are peculiar to the discipline. They write of marginal cost, marginal utility, indifference curves, the law of diminishing marginal utility, marginal cost pricing, and so forth; all these terms being concepts that have precise meanings and will be learned by students in their first few weeks of studying the subject. The law of diminishing marginal utility, for example, holds that the marginal utility to the consumer of acquiring each extra unit of a commodity will at some point begin to diminish. If one is buying bread, diminishing marginal utility will set in early, after two or three loaves have been bought; if one is drinking beer it may not set in until later; but eventually all commodities are subject to the law. When the utility of an extra unit comes to be less than the marginal cost of the unit, demand will cease, so that the level of demand for each commodity by each consumer, or by aggregating preferences by the whole body of consumers in a market, can be determined by the intersection of curves on a graph.

Economic concepts such as these are precise, because they have been formulated by academic economists and derive their meaning from the whole body of theory that economists have constructed. Students of the subject have to be able to define and use these concepts, but they can hardly avoid doing so as they are the building blocks of the discipline. One cannot complete a diploma or degree in economics without acquiring conceptual precision.

Students of politics lie somewhere between the historian and the economist in their use of generalizations and concepts. Political scientists constantly seek to go beyond the description of institutions and events in order to generalize about them. They compare the institutions and political cultures of one country or region with those of another, using some kind of conceptual framework in the attempt to give rigour to their comparisons. They produce theories of political development and political change. However, only a few of the concepts they use are technical concepts comparable in precision to those used by economists. There are certainly a few technical concepts that have been evolved within the discipline, but the great majority of the generalizations made by political scientists are based upon concepts that are constantly used and misused by politicians, journalists and the general public. In these circumstances it takes a conscious effort for students of politics to be precise and consistent in their use of concepts.

As an example, consider one of the most fruitful generalizations ever made about politics. Alexis de Tocqueville, after studying the events leading up to the French Revolution of 1789, produced the generalization that revolutions are most likely to take place when autocratic regimes are partially liberalized. The theory is that partial liberalization awakens expectations of more rapid progress than the regime is willing or able to provide, while also creating greater opportunities for the expression of dissent and the organization of opposition. The validity of this generalization has gone virtually unchallenged and in the past few years it has been of direct relevance to events in the former Soviet Union and in the Republic of South Africa.

The concepts used in the generalization are, however, far from precise. There is, for instance, room for disagreement about the definition of the term 'autocratic regime'. Everyone would agree that during most of the eighteenth century French government could be categorized in this way, as could the Soviet regime between 1917 and 1989. However, there is room for disagreement about the South African regime, which has been exceptionally autocratic in regard to its black population but reasonably liberal in regard to its white citizens.

The term liberalization may also lead to arguments, and there is even more room for doubt about the precise meaning of the term 'revolution'. As John Dunn has pointed out (Dunn 1989: 337–8), before 1789 the term was applied loosely to various kinds of political disturbance, change and restoration. It was only as a consequence of the political and intellectual impact of the French Revolution that it came to be defined as a violent change of regime leading to significant social changes, and thus to be distinguished from leadership replacements known as coups d'état. In the strongest modern sense of what constitutes a revolution, there have been only a handful of revolutions in world history, such as those in France in 1789–94, in Russia in 1917, in China, Albania and Cuba (see Dunn 1972). However, the American achievement of independence in 1776 is also generally regarded as a revolution, even though it did not result in immediate social change, because it involved violent conflict with the British and set the former colonies on a new political course. There is room for difference as to whether the achievement of independence from Moscow by Ukraine and other former Soviet republics should be regarded as revolutions, attained as they were with only a minimal amount of violence but leading to extensive economic and social change. There is clearly scope for honest disagreement about when the term should be applied this way rather than that. The object of this book is first to make this kind of analysis and then to examine various normative controversies in the light of the analysis.

This conceptual vagueness does not render Tocqueville's generalization useless, for it has been shown to have predictive value. Nor am I suggesting that political scientists should try to prescribe precise meanings for terms like revolution in the way that economists have prescribed precise meanings for terms like diminishing marginal utility. Such an attempt would be doomed to failure, for there is no way of preventing politicians and political commentators from using political terms in ways other than those favoured by academics, even if academics were able to agree. Technical concepts can sometimes be very helpful, but to stipulate special meanings for terms like liberty and democracy would be a pointless exercise. These are the terms in which political discourse is carried on. The scholar has to work with these terms, and the suggestion here is simply that academic students of politics ought to make a systematic effort to analyse the ways in which these and other basic concepts involved in the explanation of political activity are used and to understand the consequences of using them in this way rather than that. It is to this kind of analysis that this book is devoted.

THE CHOICE OF CONCEPTS

There are a very large number of political concepts in general use and it is obviously impossible to deal adequately with more than a small proportion of them in a book of reasonable length. It has therefore been decided, in the first place, to limit the analysis to concepts used in the study of the process of government in the modern democratic state. This means that we shall not deal with the concepts used in the study of international relations and defence policy, nor with those used exclusively in connection with the history of political ideas, nor with those appropriate to systems of tribal government or, for that matter, the Greek city-state.

Two further criteria of exclusion have also been adopted. First, we shall not examine constitutional and institutional concepts such as federalism, the separation of powers, the sovereignty of Parliament, ministerial responsibility and so forth. Almost all books on constitutional law and on particular systems of national government explain the meaning of these concepts and there is no reason why serious students of the subject should find them ambiguous or difficult to understand.

Second, we shall omit ideological concepts such as liberalism, conservatism and social democracy. These concepts are of crucial importance to political scientists and all students of the subject should acquire an understanding of them. To help them do so, there are some excellent texts as well as a voluminous and rewarding literature on each of the ideologies. For this reason, it is not felt necessary to include specific discussions of these concepts in this book, though a partial exception has to be made for Marxism. The reason for this partial exception is that an acceptance of Marxist or neo-Marxist assumptions by political scientists affects the way they analyse political activity in a very special fashion. Whereas liberals, conservatives and social democrats may well share similar or identical understandings of what is meant by political power or democracy, and may well engage in similar or identical styles of political analysis, Marxists and neo-Marxists see matters differently and handle their material differently. In a book devoted to conceptual analysis it would be wrong to ignore this. It is not thought necessary to give a summary of Marxist ideology as such, which would in any case require more space than is readily available, but from time to time (and particularly in Chapters 12, 14 and 16) reference will be made to Marxist approaches and concepts, such as cultural hegemony and false consciousness.

If these types of political concept are omitted, there remain a fair number of basic concepts for analysis. In Part I of the book we shall examine the concepts of nationalism and the nation-state, which logically come first because the nation-state is now the predominant unit of government in the world. This will lead into a discussion of authority in the modern state, which raises various interesting problems. Part II will contain an analysis of the concept of democracy and the various concepts associated with democratic systems of government. It is true that only a minority of the world's states can clearly be categorized as democratic, but the number of democracies has recently increased and may be expected to increase further in the future. The extraordinary events that took place in eastern Europe in the winter of 1989–90 indicate the strength of democratic ideals, a strength which surprised many commentators and political scientists.

In Part III of the book we shall turn to an examination of the concept of political power and the conceptual questions associated with the study of policy making in the modern democratic state. The three most common models used in the analysis of policy making are the pluralist model, the Marxist model of class dominance, and the corporatist model. There are questions to be discussed about the definition of terms, about the evidence that has been adduced in support of each model, and about the utility of the models in political analysis.

Finally, in Part IV we shall discuss some of the more important concepts used to categorize styles of political analysis. All students of politics will know that political scientists vary in their methodologies and frequently argue about them. In such arguments, concepts like positivism, historicism, and hermeneutics tend to be employed without definition, in the assumption that readers will not only be familiar with them but also have a full understanding of them. In my experience this assumption is untrue in relation to the average undergraduate, and in the final two chapters of the book an attempt will be made to elucidate the origins, meanings and significance of these terms, as well as to say something about the styles of analysis themselves.

QUESTIONS ABOUT POLITICAL CONCEPTS

In analysing political concepts, it is helpful to ask four questions about them. One preliminary question is whether the concept is a purely political one or whether it is a concept in more general use that has a political application. The concepts of nationalism and corporatism are examples of concepts that are only used in a political context and have no non-political meanings. On the other hand, power and representation are concepts that have non-political as well as political applications. We talk of powerful motors, powerful waves and powerful personalities as well as of power in the political arena; of representative samples and representational art as well as of representation by election or lobbyist. Non-political usages are apt to colour or give overtones to the political usages and it is as well to be aware of this.

A second question, not quite the same as this, is whether the concept has one central meaning or several distinguishable meanings. Political participation has one central meaning whereas political representation, it will be argued in Chapter 6, has four distinguishable and logically independent meanings. Positivism has one central meaning whereas historicism has been used as a label for two different modes of thought. It is essential for the student to understand that historicism type A is logically different from historicism type B, even though they are occasionally lumped together under the same heading.

A third question was first raised by the philosopher W. B. Gallie, who argued that some concepts are 'essentially contested' whereas others are not (Gallie 1955–6). An essentially contested or, better, essentially contestable concept is one that is so permeated and surrounded by values that reasonable people may argue interminably without ever reaching agreement on the true meaning and implications of the concept. The utility of Gallie's distinction has been accepted by many theorists, but has been called into question by Terence Ball on the ground that the distinction is ahistorical. Ball points out that concepts which are hotly contested in one period of history may be the subject of virtual consensus in another period, so that it would be a mistake to characterize them as 'essentially' contestable or non-contestable: 'Conceptual contestation remains a permanent possibility even though it is in practice actualized only intermittently' (Ball 1988: 14).

This is a good logical point and it draws attention to the historical fact that the meanings attributed to a number of political concepts have been modified over the centuries; a fact that has also been emphasized by Farr (1989) and Skinner (1989). In this book I am concerned only with the period of the modern democratic state, namely the past two hundred years, and readers should appreciate that some of the concepts under discussion were used in slightly different ways in earlier periods of history. It is also the case, of course, that the meanings of political concepts in the western world are not necessarily the same as their meaning in other civilizations, such as those of China or Japan or Arabia. The fact that these complexities are rarely mentioned in the chapters that follow should not be taken to imply that they are unimportant, only that, to keep the discussion within bounds, the book is confined to the problems of conceptual meaning and usage in the western world in the modern period.

Not wishing to reject Gallie's suggestion entirely, I shall replace the term 'essentially contested' by the term 'currently contestable', and shall note in passing that some of the concepts are currently contestable whereas others are not. This distinction is different from the distinction between two or more agreed meanings that a concept may have. Even though representation has several meanings, reasonable scholars may be expected to agree on these once they are defined, and this does not appear to be the case with concepts like liberty or democracy.

A fourth question is whether the concept gives rise to normative issues. This fourth question overlaps the third question posed above but is not identical with it. All concepts that can be described as currently contestable involve or raise normative issues, for this is why they are contestable. But some concepts that are not contestable in meaning are nevertheless rarely used except as part of a debate about normative questions, and when this is the case I shall follow the explanation of the concept with a discussion of the normative issues. An example would be political participation, a concept that is reasonably clear in meaning but is rarely invoked except as an introduction to or a part of a debate about whether a new form or a higher degree of participation is desirable, for this reason or that.

The concepts to be examined below are too varied for it to be feasible to ask exactly the same questions about each of them and tabulate the answers.

However, it is important to be as systematic as possible and the four questions just itemized will assist the enterprise of clarifying the concepts and underlining their meanings, usages and implications.

Before turning to this enterprise, a word about my own stance may be appropriate. There are some scholars who believe that political scientists should always attempt to be value-free in their analysis, while others believe that, as this is impossible, the writer should declare his own political outlook and allegiance. My own position lies somewhere between these extremes. I think that the attempt to be completely value-free when writing about value-laden concepts and theories such as those analysed in this book could lead only to sterility. My belief is that the scholar's duty in these circumstances is not to attempt freedom from values but to be balanced and fair in his discussion of values. Scholars should express their views in such a manner that readers who disagree with these views may yet gain from the argument, and scholars should acknowledge the existence and, if space permits, indicate the nature of alternative views. My own central beliefs about politics are quite conventional, for someone living in the industrialized west in the current period of history. I place a high value on individual liberty and mutual toleration, I think that the state should provide social services for the security and welfare of its citizens, and I believe that representative democracy is the best institutional arrangement for government yet devised. Beyond this, I have various views that will emerge in the following chapters, but I doubt whether they add up to a consistent ideology. My views about many of the issues under discussion are eclectic rather than committed, and my aim has been to illuminate the issues rather than to lay down the law about them. It will be, of course, for readers to judge how far I have succeeded in this aim.

Part I

Authority in the modern state

Chapter 2

Nationalism and the national state

The entire land surface of this planet, with the single exception of Antarctica, is now divided for purposes of government into territories known as national states. This is a relatively recent development in human history. Only two hundred years ago, there were fewer than 20 states with the shape and character that we should now recognize as deserving description as national states, with the rest of the world being divided between a host of very small principalities and city-states, a few untidy empires, and large areas that were the home of tribal communities who lived without fixed territorial boundaries. By 1945 there were 51 national states and by 2000, following the virtual end of colonial empires, there were 192. Today the only relics of empire are a few miniscule territories such as Gibraltar, the Falkland Isles, Martinique and Guadeloupe. The transformation has come about largely because the doctrine of nationalism has both triumphed in Europe and been exported to the rest of the world.

Because of this transformation, in the contemporary world we all live under the political authority of the national state within whose borders we reside. Political authority is a concept which raises a host of interesting questions and problems. Of course, in the practical experience of day-to-day life, everyone knows what the authority of the state means to the citizen. In the simplest terms, it means the ability of the state to make and enforce laws binding upon its inhabitants, including the ability to take their money in taxation, to confine them in prison, and (providing they are citizens) to conscript them into the armed forces. There are, however, important questions about the character, bases and limits of this authority, and these will be discussed in Chapter 6. There are also problems about its justification that have been discussed by political philosophers over the centuries, most notably by Hobbes, Locke and Rousseau. It is beyond the scope of this book to discuss this kind of problem, and it must be emphasized now that the fairly brisk and concise account of the nature of political authority that follows in Chapter 6 can be brisk and concise only because these large normative questions have been left to the several hundred other authors who have addressed them.

The term national state is itself a conjunction of two terms that are best dealt with separately, with the definition of the first raising more difficulties than that of the second. It is true that the question of how to define the state has led political theorists and constitutional lawyers to produce a variety of alternative definitions and generalizations. The difficulty of producing a simple and agreed definition arises from the fact that in the modern world the state is an abstraction, that is deemed to exist independently of the individuals and institutions that exercise state power. This assumed independence is a fairly recent development in human history, for in pre-modern times the state was frequently identified with its ruler, but it is not now a matter of controversy. But although one cannot see a state, in any concrete sense, one can see the manifestations of the state's existence, which have to be divided into external and internal manifestations. Seen from the outside, a state is a legal entity possessing sovereign independence, having unfettered control over its own territory, defining its own citizenship rules, and equal in international law to all other states. Seen from the inside, a state manifests itself in a collection of public institutions, legislative, executive, administrative and judicial, having the power to govern the territory and all its inhabitants. There is no conflict between these exterior and interior manifestations, however; rather, they are like two sides of the same coin. As the nature of the modern state, viewed in this double way, is fairly clear, it is not intended to pursue the problem of providing a precise short definition of it.

The one controversy regarding the state that will be addressed in this book is that raised by the Marxist generalization that the actions of the state are severely circumscribed by the need to protect the interests of the dominant economic class in society, which in the modern democratic state means the capitalist class. The question will be discussed in Chapter 14.

The term nation raises more problems than the term state. It refers to a community of people rather than to a set of institutions, but the definition of who constitutes a nation involves conceptual difficulties that, in turn, lead to practical problems. Thus, the Irish are everywhere recognized as a nation, but what about the Northern Irish? Given that the English and Scots are both nations, can there also be a British nation? If the Palestinians are a nation, in spite of never having governed themselves, is this also true of the Kurds, the Sikhs, the Tamils, the Karens and the Chins? The French-Canadians living in Quebec seem to constitute a nation, but how should we describe the English-Canadians who also live in Quebec?

Because the term nation is different in character from the term state, there was some discussion in 1919 about whether the new international organization that was being created should be called the League of Nations or the League of States. The second of these alternatives would have been more logical and more precise, but the doctrine of nationalism had achieved such a hold on people's minds by 1919 that the first alternative was chosen. In

1945 the United Nations Organization was created without any debate on this point.

In this chapter we shall discuss in turn the concept of nationalism, the concept of nationhood, and the concept of national integration.

THE CONCEPT OF NATIONALISM

As suggested in Chapter 1, political concepts can be divided into three broad categories. There are age-old concepts that have both political and other usages, such as power and representation. These terms are widely used by the public at large and tend to be applied to political life in more than one way, so that differing usages have to be distinguished. There are a number of precise technical concepts that have been developed by political scientists and are used only in scholarly communications within the discipline. Somewhere between these, in terms of precision, there are concepts that have no usages outside of politics but have entered into the general currency of political debate. The concept of nationalism falls into the third category. It has been developed only in the past two centuries; it has a basic meaning that is not contestable; but it is often used loosely in public discourse and confused with related but different concepts such as national identity or patriotism.

The confusion of nationalism and national identity, for instance, is quite common in general speech. Scottish people in England or North America who celebrate St Andrew's Day, wear the kilt and eat haggis might well be described by their neighbours as 'real Scots nationalists'. However, Scottish people in Scotland would be described in that way only if they supported the eventual secession of Scotland from the United Kingdom, and this way of using the term is more correct. The Scottish people abroad are displaying symbols of national identity, which is a sentiment, whereas supporters of the Scottish National Party are invoking the principles of nationalism, which is a doctrine or ideology.

Like several other terms ending with 'ism', such as liberalism, conservatism and socialism, nationalism is a normative doctrine that embodies a particular set of assumptions and beliefs about politics. The essence of nationalism is a belief about the social basis of political authority. The prevailing assumptions of eighteenth-century Europe were that government could properly be based on force, in the conquest of empires, or on heredity or marriage, in the government of principalities and monarchies. In contrast to these assumptions, nationalists asserted the view that the only proper form of government is one in which the boundaries of the state correspond to the boundaries of a society and the rulers of the state are members of that society. It was wrong, in terms of nationalist doctrine, for the Poles to be ruled by Russians, the Greeks to be governed as part of the Ottoman Empire, the southern Italians to be ruled by Spanish or French aristocrats, the

Hungarians to be ruled by Austrians, and the Germans to be divided between scores of principalities.

The development and spread of this doctrine in Europe during the nineteenth century led to the emergence of two types of nationalist movement. On the one hand, there were movements for the national independence of peoples under imperial rule; for the independence of Greeks from Turkish rule, of Poles from Russian rule, of (later) the Irish from British rule. The generic form of the aims of this type of nationalist movement can be expressed in the proposition that 'the Ruritanian people ought to be liberated from foreign domination so that they can govern themselves'. On the other hand, there were movements to unite under a single government people who were said to belong to a single society but were actually divided for political purposes between a number of rulers. This type of movement had its intellectual origins in what is now Germany, where nationalist theories were developed in reaction to a situation in which German-speaking people were divided between over a hundred jurisdictions. (For the intellectual origins of nationalist theory, see Kedourie 1961; Birch 1989: Chapter 2.) Another obvious example is that of the Italian nationalist movement, whose aim was to unify Italy under Italian rulers. The generic form of the aims of this type of movement can be expressed in the proposition that 'the Ruritanian people ought to be united under a single Ruritanian government'.

Underlying these two types of nationalist movement is a general theory about good government that has been neatly summarized by Elie Kedourie in the three propositions 'that humanity is naturally divided into nations, that nations are known by certain characteristics which can be ascertained, and that the only legitimate type of government is national self-government' (Kedourie 1961: 9). This is the doctrine, in a nutshell, and in historical terms it has been an extremely successful doctrine. If asked to name the political doctrines that have reshaped the world, most people in the west would probably name liberalism, democracy and socialism. In practice, however, only a minority of political regimes are liberal, democratic or socialist, whereas the whole world is now politically organized on nationalist principles.

To say that the doctrine has been successful is not to say that it is free from ambiguities. On the contrary, nationalism is a doctrine marred by a central ambiguity, namely the extreme difficulty of defining the social unit that has the right to govern itself. Johann Herder and J. G. Fichte believed that a nation should be defined in terms of its language and culture, a view which led in time to the German nationalist objective of uniting all people who spoke German under the same government. Such a view, if relied on as a guide to practice, would extend German boundaries to include Austria, part of former Czechoslovakia, part of Switzerland and a small part of eastern France. Leaving aside Switzerland, this was precisely Hitler's aim, but it is not a view that commands widespread assent. Other nationalists have specified ethnicity as the proper basis of nationhood, or religion (as in the cases of Pakistan and Israel), or shared historical experiences (as in the case of Switzerland), or shared commitment to a set of political ideals (as in the United States). It is evident that there is no agreed definition of the basis of nationhood to validate the second of Kedourie's three propositions, and that without that the first of the propositions seems suspect. To elucidate the matter further, it is necessary to enquire into the concept of nationhood.

THE CONCEPT OF NATIONHOOD

The difficulty of defining this concept can best be illustrated by tabulating three groups of concepts, one sociological, one cultural and the third institutional:

Sociological concepts	Cultural concepts	Institutional concepts
Kinship group	Language	Municipality
Tribe	Literature	County
Ethnic group	Religion	Province
Community	Culture	State
Society	Civilization	Empire

The concepts in these three columns all refer to entities that can be identified by charting personal relationships or consulting documentary sources. There is sometimes room for controversy about how to categorize people of mixed ethnic origins or how to specify the boundaries of a community, but in general these concepts are clear and unlikely to lead to misunderstanding. The great difficulty about the concept of nationhood is that it seems to spread across all three columns. In ideal terms, a nation can be described as a society that has a distinctive culture and also possesses its own state. However, as a definition for social scientists, this has the crippling disadvantage that it renders the proposition that every nation ought to have its own state purely circular. One cannot say that 'every A ought to have B' if the definition of A includes B.

It would be logically acceptable to say that every society with a distinctive culture is a potential nation, but this would not in practice be true unless a further variable is added to the equation. This further variable is the existence of a territory with agreed borders that could reasonably form the geographical basis of a self-governing state. There are American political writers commonly described as black nationalists who assert that American blacks constitute a distinct community with a distinctive culture that should be protected and passed on to new generations, and a reasonable argument can be made for this point of view. However, American blacks cannot be described as a potential nation in the absence of an agreed territory that they can call their own.

If we continue to approach the concept of nationhood from the sociological end of the equation, we might define a nation as a community or society of people who share a distinctive culture, live together in an identifiable territory in which they constitute a clear majority, and either govern themselves today or have done so in the not-too-distant past or have a credible claim to do so in the not-too-distant future. The limitation on historical distance is necessary because circumstances change so much over the centuries. The people of Athens governed themselves twenty-five hundred years ago, but it would not be reasonable to use this historical fact as a reason for describing modern Athenians as a nation, because for several centuries their identity has been merged into the larger identity of the Greeks. Equally, it is fruitless to try to predict what social and political developments may take place in the next two thousand years. We can only take account of the foreseeable future, which in terms of politics is the near future.

It is also possible to approach the concept of nationhood from the other end of the equation, from the existence of statehood. The idea of a British nation followed, and was created by, the union of England, Wales and Scotland in the newly constituted British state. The idea of a French nation preceded the French Revolution, but the reality of a national identity embracing all citizens of the French state was a product of the revolution, the political changes made by the revolutionaries, and the deliberate process of socialization into nationhood that was adopted (on the wishes and orders of the government) in the French educational system. As that early nation-builder, Napoleon Bonaparte, said in 1805:

> So long as children are not taught whether they must be republicans or monarchists, Catholics or free thinkers, etc., the state will not constitute a nation but will rest on vague and shifting foundations, ever exposed to disorder and change.
>
> (quoted Herold 1955: 118)

Throughout tropical Africa, the question of nationhood is best approached from the state rather than the sociological end of the equation. The new states that emerged as a consequence of the end of colonial rule in the 1950s and 1960s had borders that had been imposed by the colonial powers with little regard to existing social geography. The loyalties of the citizens of these new states were tribal loyalties for all but a tiny minority of educated and westernized leaders, and the creation of national identities and national loyalties has been one of the tasks of the new post-colonial governments.

Political scientists call this process nation building or national integration, and there are so many modern states in which the development of a sense of nationhood has depended upon this process that Kedourie's three propositions have to be called into question. It is not that Kedourie was wrong in summarizing the essence of nationalist theory in this fashion. It is, rather, that the assumptions underlying nationalist theory are sociologically inaccurate. Humanity is naturally divided into sexes and perhaps into races, but these are the only divisions produced by nature. The divisions into societies, cultures, religions and nations have been brought about by human activities, with the divisions sometimes being accidental by-products of economic enterprise and geographical mobility, sometimes the product of deliberate action by preachers, teachers, poets, philosophers, politicians and soldiers.

Social groupings have changed remarkably over the centuries, with a general tendency for smaller groups and communities to merge together into larger societies. Thus, we now say that the British are made up of the English, the Welsh, the Scots and some of the Northern Irish, but fourteen hundred years ago the groups who combined to become the English were known as Angles, Saxons, Jutes and Frisians. It follows from all this that nationalism is an artificial and contrived theory, involving a degree of sociological mythology rather than being based squarely on sociological and historical facts. Many nationalist movements have reflected this in their propaganda. Thus, when Mazzini bolstered his arguments for Italian unity in the 1860s by writing eloquently about Italy's glorious past in the days of the Roman Empire, he conveniently overlooked the fact that the regional divisions within Italy, both then and when Mazzini was active, were so great that northern and southern Italians could barely understand each other's dialects. The process by which national societies and identities are established out of diverse social groups is known as national integration, and this needs a little elaboration.

NATIONAL INTEGRATION

With a handful of exceptions, modern nations are an amalgam of historical communities that have been brought together by various economic, social and political developments that can be bracketed under the general name of national integration. Some of these developments are unplanned whereas others are devised by political leaders and implemented as government policies.

The unplanned component of the integrative process has been given the name of social mobilization by Karl Deutsch (1953) and his colleagues. In brief outline, this is the process by which the development of a commercial and industrial economy induces agricultural workers to leave their villages to seek work in the growing centres of trade and industry, thus eroding the social communities of rural areas and mobilizing the workers for absorption into the larger national society. Kinship links become weaker, local languages and dialects give way to the dominant national language, local customs and cultures lose their hold. As smaller economic concerns are swallowed by larger ones, as means of transport improve, and as mass media of communications are established, the integrative process continues, until everyone in the country watches the same television programmes, admires the same popular heroes and supports the same political leaders.

It would be a mistake to think that the process is entirely automatic, however. It is given a large helping hand by governmental decisions about language and education. National governments ruling over a society that is accepting a commercial and industrial economy can hardly avoid the need to designate an official language for legislation, administration and commerce. As has been said, the state can be blind but it cannot be deaf; it may ignore differences of race among its citizens but it cannot ignore differences of language. The normal pattern has been to establish the language of the governing classes as the official language of the whole country.

This move is invariably followed, however, by the decline of other languages, for it is not natural for people to be bilingual and the experience of history shows that the stronger language in an area always tends to drive out the weaker one. (On this, see Laponce 1987.) If local languages decline to the point of extinction or near extinction, like Breton in France, Gaelic on the mainland of Scotland, or Cornish in England, this is a cultural loss to be set against the political, economic and social advantages of linguistic unity. Some states are forced by circumstances to recognize more than one language as official, but the recent histories of Canada and Belgium show that this can be politically expensive.

Compulsory education is also a planned move that is integrative in its effects, often intentionally. This is both because instruction is normally given in the official national language and because the teaching of history and (where it is in the curriculum) civics tend to strengthen feelings of national identity and loyalty. The importance of education in this respect is illustrated by the examples of Canada and Northern Ireland. In Canada the fact that the French schools in Quebec teach a rather different version of Canadian history from that taught in the rest of Canada is one of several factors that have weakened the process of national integration and contributed to the possibility that Quebec may secede from the federation. In Northern Ireland, with a few recent exceptions, Protestant children attend Protestant schools and Catholic children attend Catholic schools, which until the 1990s have taught different versions of Irish history and Anglo-Irish relations, so that to some extent children have been socialized into conflict.

In addition to their language and educational policies, national governments also pursue a variety of tactics designed to minimize the political effects of ethnic and religious cleavages within society and thus to strengthen the authority of the government. One obvious initiative is the creation of symbols of national identity. Flags, anthems and uniforms all serve this purpose. In recent years new states of the developing world have thought it important to establish national airlines, sometimes at great expense, to emphasize their independence. As Kenneth Minogue has pointed out, new names for towns, new palaces for rulers and even new capital cities have been thought necessary parts of what he calls 'the equipment of a proper nation' (Minogue 1967).

Another form of nation building (as the planned parts of the process of national integration are sometimes called) is the establishment of political institutions seen to represent all sections of society. In relation to class divisions, this is achieved by the adoption of universal adult suffrage. In relation to regional divisions, it is sometimes achieved by the device of giving peripheral regions more-than-proportional representation in national institutions. Scotland and Wales have more Members of Parliament than England, in proportion to their relative populations. The Senates of Australia and the United States give the smaller states more members than their populations deserve, and in Canada there are elaborate conventions to ensure that the peripheral areas are represented in the federal Cabinet and Quebec is fully represented in the Supreme Court. In relation to ethnic cleavages, minorities are often given the support of legal bans on ethnic discrimination, insistence on unsegregated schools and (in the United States and India) measures of positive discrimination in certain areas of employment.

Of course, the process of national integration does not always proceed smoothly. Occasionally, the measures adopted rebound, as when American white parents rioted in Boston to prevent their children being sent by bus to unsegregated schools, or when Mrs Gandhi was assassinated by the Sikh bodyguards she had appointed to demonstrate her confidence in the loyalty of the Sikh minority. More frequently, the cleavages in society are just too deeply rooted for integrative measures to have their desired effect. Canadian efforts at national integration have failed to prevent Quebec from demanding either full or substantial independence. French and Spanish attempts at nation building have failed to stop Breton and Basque nationalists from attacking public buildings and (in Spain) public officials with bombs. Elaborate Belgian attempts to maintain a linguistic balance between Flemish-speakers and French-speakers have failed to prevent a deterioration in relationships between the two communities since the 1960s. A widespread revival of ethnically based minority nationalist movements in the 1970s has put paid to the hopes of many that political cleavages other than those based on economic cleavages were losing their force. Much more could be said about the process of national integration, about the various theoretical justifications of it that have been put forward, and about the recent tendency for some theorists to move away from that position in order to justify policies of multiculturalism. Enough has been said, however, to define and illustrate the concept itself.

Chapter 3

Ethnic cleavages, multiculturalism and the national state

The last three decades of the twentieth century saw the growth of two very different trends in world politics that were anticipated by only a few politicians and writers before the 1970s. Although this book is concerned with political concepts and theories rather than with historical developments as such, these trends must be outlined because they have brought with them a new emphasis in political studies involving the concepts of ethnicity, multiculturalism and globalization.

ETHNICITY AND ETHNIC CONFLICT

From the 1860s to the 1960s nearly all liberal and socialist political theorists both anticipated and welcomed the growing diminution in the political significance of religious, cultural and ethnic cleavages within national societies, leaving economic and class differences as the most important issues in political debate. This was an entirely rational point of view, because conflicts deriving from religious, cultural and ethnic cleavages are usually more difficult to resolve than conflicts deriving from economic cleavages, whether the latter be between regions of the country or classes within society. One reason for this is that people are locked into their religious, cultural and ethnic groups, having no wish to change even if they could, whereas people can hope to escape from a depressed region or class by individual mobility. If they cannot themselves escape, they can hope that their children will do so. A second reason is that it is easier for governments to mitigate economic cleavages, by a process of incremental adjustment, than it is for them to mitigate religious, cultural or ethnic conflicts.

In the twentieth century the growth of industry, urbanization and prosperity in western societies has been accompanied, everywhere except in the United States, by a decline in the intensity of religious feelings. Whatever the moral consequences of this, its political benefits have been demonstrated by the marked decline of political conflicts exacerbated by religious cleavages in Europe (with the exception of the Balkans and Northern Ireland) and, in contrast, their continuance in the United States, where twenty-eight abortion clinics were bombed by religious zealots in 1986 and individual surgeons performing legal abortions were subjected to murderous attacks in the 1990s.

Similarly, the growth of political integration in most developed western societies has led to the decline of minority languages, with some of them becoming virtually extinct. As was suggested in Chapter 2, this trend is best regarded as a cultural loss but a political benefit.

In contrast, political conflicts based on ethnic cleavages have become considerably more widespread since the early 1970s. The concepts of ethnicity and ethnic identity are somewhat elastic and have led to occasional disagreement among journalists and scholars. Such disagreements are not really significant, however, as they all derive from the simple fact that ethnicity, like other forms of group identity, is a social construction that can be self-defined or defined by others in more than one possible way. Any individual's ethnic identity can be defined in terms of heredity or upbringing or culture, chosen according to which seems most salient in the circumstances of the time. The present author, for example, is English, Scottish, French and Irish in terms of heredity, wholly English by upbringing and culture, British, Canadian and European by citizenship, and has other group identities that in some circumstances are more relevant than any of these, such as being male in a dance hall or white on a visit to South Africa.

The recent growth or revival of ethnic conflicts within several national societies, leading to the emergence of minority nationalist movements, is the consequence of social, economic or political changes that have made ethnic identities seem more salient than other identities or loyalties that are national in scope. A good example is the decision of 840,000 Scottish electors to vote for the Scottish National Party in October 1974, as against only 64,000 who had done so ten years earlier. This did not mean that they had ceased to be British or socialists or liberals or conservatives, only that the discovery of a vast oil field in the Scottish part of the North Sea made their identity as Scottish seem more salient to them. The 1970s saw new or renewed claims by ethnic minorities in several other states for forms of cultural autonomy or political independence. France experienced demands for autonomy from Bretons and Corsicans, Spain more violent demands from Basques and milder claims from Catalans. Quebecois nationalists demanded independence from Canada. The people of East Bengal rebelled against the Pakistani government and secured independence as Bangladesh. In the 1980s, India had to cope with Sikh nationalists and Sri Lanka with Tamil nationalists.

In the 1990s ethnic conflicts became increasingly violent. In the Balkans, age-old conflicts between Serbs, Croats and Albanians flared into civil war. In east central Africa, conflicts between Tutsis and Hutus led to genocide in Rwanda and massacres in Burundi. Civil war in Zaire (now the Democratic Republic of Congo) brought ethnic groups into conflict and led, by 1999, to a confused situation of near-anarchy in the eastern part of the country. In March 2000 it was reported that five ethnic groups there had relapsed into a pre-colonial state of tribal warfare, raiding each other's villages with spears and bows and arrows. The same month saw brief but murderous riots in Nigeria between Muslim Hausas and Christian Ibos.

In the context of this book, the most relevant question is how far this revival of ethnic conflict has affected the state system. The answer is that its impact was modest until 1990 but has since become appreciable. Until 1990, the Irish, the Algerians and the Bengalis of Bangladesh were the only ethnic minorities within an established national state to achieve political independence from it in the twentieth century, but since 1990 the Soviet Union has split into fifteen constituent parts, Yugoslavia has disintegrated, Czechoslovakia has split in half, and altogether twenty-three successor states have been given international recognition as independent, with Kosovo on its way to becoming the next. These developments have led some writers to speculate that the world system of national states is beginning to disintegrate along ethnic lines. As early as 1979, Dov Ronen predicted that the nation-state is likely to disappear as the main unit of political organization and to be replaced by a world order composed of 'hundreds, maybe thousands, of social and political frameworks' (Ronen 1979: 179). Following the break-up of the Soviet Union and Yugoslavia, John Naisbitt put this view into the present tense, declaring that 'we are moving towards a world of a thousand countries. . . . The nation-state is dead' (Naisbitt 1995: 40).

For two quite different reasons such a view, although understandable, is very questionable. One reason is that this untidy planet contains something between 6,000 and 15,000 ethnic groups (depending on the defining criteria adopted), the great majority of which are so intertwined by migration and intermarriage and so interdependent in economic terms that it would not be feasible for them to be separated into self-governing territories. A handful of existing states may well be partitioned along lines that are more or less ethnic in character, but ethnicity in itself cannot reasonably be proposed as either a better or a more probable basis for political jurisdiction than the existing state system, imperfect though this is.

A second reason which makes the concept of the end of the nation-state unlikely is that existing states, in addition to possessing organized armies, have a variety of political tactics available to them that can be grouped under the heading of system maintenance devices. Minority areas can be given regional councils and/or representation in national institutions, as Scotland and Wales have long had fuller representation in the British Parliament than the size of their populations justifies. Belgium has invented a complex system whereby certain powers over cultural matters are given to linguistic councils that are largely, but not entirely, territorial in jurisdiction. Tito held Yugoslavia together not only by force and his control of the Communist Party but also by giving politicians from each of the main ethnic groups some fairly conspicuous positions in national authorities. By one means or another, national states have many ways of maintaining their integrity and authority.

It cannot, therefore, be concluded that the revival of ethnic politics is breaking down the state system around the world, though it may do so in particular localities. As Anthony Smith noted in 1995,

> As of now, the national state remains the only internationally recognized structure of political association. Today, only duly constituted 'national states' are admitted to the United Nations and other international bodies, though aspirant ethnic nations may be admitted as observers.
>
> (Smith 1995: 104)

It can also be observed, however, that the revival of ethnic politics is making the political process more complex in many states. The distribution of political authority has in some countries been complicated by the devolution of powers to regional authorities, such as for Scotland and Wales within the United Kingdom and for Catalonia and the Basque country within Spain. Government spokespersons in both countries have claimed that these measures have taken the wind out of the sails of minority nationalist movements wanting independence, but the fact remains that the creation of regional assemblies provides fora in which nationalist movements may thrive in the future, so that the constitutional equilibrium is potentially less stable than it was. A more widespread development has been the growth in influence of ethnic pressure groups claiming privileges of one kind or another for their groups. There has also been a tendency for a new generation of liberal writers to advocate policies of multiculturalism in place of the policies of national integration advocated by previous generations of liberals.

MULTICULTURALISM

The concept of multiculturalism was first publicly articulated by Pierre Trudeau, Prime Minister of Canada, in 1971. He did this in response to complaints about the title and report of the Royal Commission on Bilingualism and Biculturalism, which had laboured from 1963 to 1969 to propose ways of remedying certain French-Canadian grievances. Spokespersons for ethnic groups that were neither French nor British in origin, such as the large Ukrainian community in the western provinces, argued that this report ignored their own distinctive cultures. In answer, Trudeau proclaimed that Canadian society, though officially bilingual, was multicultural rather than bicultural in character, and his government quickly established an administrative agency with funds to promote multiculturalism. In its early years this agency devoted much of its resources to the provision of grants for community centres organized on ethnic lines, for ethnic festivals, and for similar activities designed to encourage the maintenance of diverse immigrant cultures. Some politicians and public servants turned these policies into a kind of ideology, arguing that cultural diversity is a positive advantage for society and should therefore be encouraged by the government. This naturally provoked controversy among social scientists.

The main argument in favour of the principle was that it differed from the American belief in promoting social unity by way of the melting pot and would therefore help to maintain Canadian distinctiveness from its large southern neighbour. One sociologist noted that 'in the absence of any consensus on the substance of Canadian identity or culture, multiculturalism fills a void' (Weinfeld 1981: 94), while another said that multiculturalism 'helps to define a distinct collective identity and thus to differentiate Canadians from Americans' (Breton 1986: 50).

As against this, Porter argued that multicultural policies encourage ethnic separation, maintain and perhaps strengthen barriers to upward social mobility, and thus perpetuate what he called the vertical mosaic and others have called the cultural division of labour (Porter 1975, 1979). Brotz alleged that the principle of multiculturalism corrupted liberal-democratic and egalitarian ideals 'by projecting the ideal of Canada as some kind of ethnic zoo where the function of the zoo keeper is to collect as many varieties as possible and exhibit them once a year in some carnival where one can go from booth to booth sampling pizzas, wonton soup and kosher pastramis' (Brotz 1980: 44). Kallen complained that 'by stressing the particularistic, expressive functions of immigrant ethnocultures, the multicultural policy shortchanges the goal of national unity and . . . the goal of ethnic equality' (Kallen 1982: 169).

While sociologists differed in their assessments of multiculturalism as an ideal and a policy, Canadian voters hardly differed at all. Overwhelmingly, they disliked it. In 1990–1 an extraordinary national survey of public opinion on this and other issues was commissioned by the federal government under the name of *The Citizens' Forum on Canada's Future*. By having open telephone lines, inviting written comments and briefs and sponsoring discussion groups the energetic committee in charge managed to secure the opinions of about 400,000 citizens. Nearly 80 per cent of the telephone calls and nearly 60 per cent of the letters and written briefs expressed hostility to the government's policy of multiculturalism, while most of the other comments were ambiguous or uncertain and only a handful expressed support for it. The final report on the survey stated that most citizens wanted better integration of immigrants through language training and 'assistance in transferring foreign degrees and qualifications to meet Canadian standards', while most members of cultural minorities wanted 'to play their full role in the country as equal members of society – no more and no less'. The conclusion of the committee was that 'federal government funding for multiculturalism activities other than those serving immigrant orientation, reduction of racial discrimination and promotion of equality should be eliminated' (Citizens' Forum 1991: 128–9).

The government had actually moved in this direction during the late 1980s and it moved further following this report. It seems fair to conclude that the belief that the promotion of cultural diversity should be a policy objective of governments in liberal societies has been pretty well discredited by the Canadian experiment. This conclusion was strongly supported by a best-selling book written by a Canadian novelist who argued that it was a mistake for the government to promote policies likely to have the effect of artificially preserving the traditional cultures of immigrants or their ancestors, often in stereotypical versions, although the values and manners of immigrants or their children normally change as they adapt to their new society (see Bissoondath 1994: Chapters 5 and 6).

By this time, Trudeau's vision of multiculturalism, which he had declared 'might become a brilliant prototype for the moulding of tomorrow's civilization' (Trudeau 1977: 179), had been written into the constitution. The Charter of Rights and Freedoms of 1982 included an article stating that: 'This Charter shall be interpreted in a manner consistent with the preservation and enhancement of the multicultural heritage of Canadians'. As the word 'heritage' can hardly apply to a controversial policy introduced only eleven years earlier, it must be taken to refer to the long-standing arrangements whereby Canadian governments have passed special laws designed to protect the interests of French-Canadians, one of the nation's two founding European peoples, and the Indians and Inuit, who had arrived from Asia thousands of years earlier. It is therefore relevant to consider how successful these arrangements have been.

Francophone Canadians were given constitutional protection for their language by the British North America Act of 1867 and have acquired additional privileges since the growth of a Quebec independence movement. Since the 1980s Quebec provincial governments have been able to insist that all migrants to the province from outside Canada must have their children educated in French, that French must be the language of business in all sizeable firms, that French must be the dominant language on public hoardings and must be at least equally prominent in shop windows and on labels on merchandise for sale. In such ways the group rights of francophone Quebecois have been given legal priority over the individual rights of other residents, though equivalent measures in any of the other nine provinces would be struck down by the courts as contrary to the Canadian Charter of Rights. In the same period Quebec has been given substantial financial advantages under the tax equalization arrangements, and some Quebec industries and firms have been given special help by federal government.

Supporters of these policies point out that Quebec has a vibrant francophone culture, and that in two provincial referendums a majority of voters have opted to stay in Canada rather than secede. Sceptics note that in spite of all these incentives the majority in the 1995 referendum amounted to less than 1 per cent of the voters and that there would have been no majority at all had it not been for what the leader of the secessionist party called 'the ethnic vote', the 'ethnics' in question being the million or so English-Canadians who had their homes in Quebec.

Regarding the Indians and Inuit, now known by the legal title of aboriginal peoples, the record is less ambiguous. The hope that they would become fully integrated into Canadian society has not been realized, and in the 1970s government policies reflecting this hope were widely criticized as having involved distinct cultural losses for inadequate social and economic benefits. Opinion moved in favour of giving these peoples more independence to protect their cultural traditions and the 1982 Charter of Rights contained an article giving constitutional protection to 'the existing aboriginal and treaty rights of the aboriginal peoples of Canada'. As nobody knew (or even claimed to know) what these rights were, this was equivalent to entrenching a blank cheque, and a further article specified that a Constitutional Conference should be held in 1984 to identify and define the rights in question. This conference failed, as did further conferences in 1985 and 1987, and the attempt to reach agreement was then abandoned. However, at the 1984 meeting the federal government produced a document stating that the aboriginal peoples have 'the right to self-governing institutions', subject to agreements to be negotiated with the federal and provincial governments, and many Indian politicians have taken this to imply that they have a right to full independence. While this ambition is understandable, the Indians are divided between so many reserves that it can never be fully achieved. At the end of the 1970s Canada had 573 Indian Bands occupying 2,287 reserves, only 13 per cent of which had populations of over 1,000 (Gibbins and Ponting 1986: 242–3), while very many of them consisted of a few blocks in urban or suburban areas. A few large reserves in sparsely populated areas of northern Canada have been given substantial political autonomy in 'land claims agreements', after years of difficult and expensive negotiation, while many bands elsewhere have acquired some degree of municipal administrative devolution. However, no general policy is geographically possible and as a general policy is what many Indian leaders think they have been promised, political debate on the matter tends to be fruitless.

One consequence is that there have been prolonged stand-offs in which militant Indians have blockaded public highways outside their reserves on the ground that proposed commercial developments there would violate territory inhibited by the spirits of their ancestors, and the police have been unable to uphold the law because of political fears that this might provoke widespread violence. Another consequence has been financial. Although total government expenditures on Indian policy have been sufficient to provide every Indian family on the reserves with an annual income equal to the average non-Indian family in Canada, so much of it has gone to public officials, Indian politicians, expert advisers, and fiscally unaccountable band councils that tens of thousands of Indians on reserves live in dire poverty with high rates of disease, substance abuse and suicide. It is a story of almost complete political failure.

In view of this record, it is impossible to take seriously the claim that Canadian policies towards ethnic minorities can be an example to the world. Some Canadian scholars have defended multiculturalism as an ideal, notably Will Kymlicka and Charles Taylor, but Canadian practice has had some success only in regard to the large francophone minority. The problem of dealing with a society of settlers with two founding peoples instead of one is unique to Canada and the Canadian technique is better put under the heading of 'asymmetrical federalism' than that of 'multiculturalism'.

Australia is the only other country to have pronounced multiculturalism to be its national policy, which it did in 1973, but in practice Australian policies with that label have been very different from Canadian policies. Instead of encouraging the maintenance of cultural diversity, they were designed to facilitate the integration of newcomers into Australian society and have been rather successful in pursuing this objective. Australia has managed to achieve more economic equality between ethnic groups than exists in Canada and also to gain greater public understanding and acceptance of its ethnic policies.

European debates

In Europe, debates about multiculturalism have developed more recently than in Canada and Australia and the term has been used to describe a bundle of practices more than a doctrine or national policy. British and Dutch practices in regard to recent immigrants from non-European countries have been more multicultural than French policies, and the comparisons are interesting. Dutch immigrants since 1945 have been overwhelmingly Muslim and come mainly from Turkey, Morocco and Suriname (formerly Dutch Guiana), with smaller numbers from Somalia and Iraq. The Netherlands has for long had a political and social policy known as 'pillarization', whereby the Protestant, Catholic and socialist groups in society have each had their own pressure groups and political parties, with an elaborate electoral system of proportional representation which ensured that every government was a coalition of several parties. Religious schools have been given state financial support and when substantial numbers of immigrants were recognized as settlers, rather than temporary guest workers, state schools offered classes in their languages of origin.

The growth of a substantial Muslim minority, numbering between 5 and 6 per cent of the population, has given Muslims the opportunity to become a fourth 'pillar', and to a limited extent this has happened. There are many Islamic primary schools and some secondary schools given government financial support. The Netherlands has a privately financed Islamic university and other post-secondary institutions with government finance that offer courses for Muslim students, including imams.

There is no problem about girls in state schools wearing headscarves in the Muslim style, and the courts have decided that Muslim women workers can be banned by their employers from doing this only if they come into direct contact with customers, as in the case of waiters and shop assistants. There has been no problem about the construction of traditional mosques, except that in the smaller towns they have not been allowed to have minarets because of town planning rules that religious buildings (of whatever denomination) cannot be higher than secular buildings. Muslims have been active in politics and have achieved proportionate membership in city councils and the lower house of the Dutch parliament, where in 2006 they had 10 out of 150 members.

Dutch policies may therefore be described as largely multicultural, but since 2000 there has been a public reaction to this based on the realization that many Muslim imams and politicians were in open opposition to the very liberal Dutch social attitudes and policies regarding sexual matters, gay rights and soft drugs. A populist party developed that favoured a revision of national policy, including changes in immigration policy that would hinder a growth in the size of the Muslim minority. However, in the 2002 national election campaign this party's leader, Pim Fortuyn, was assassinated in a parking lot. The party was quite unlike the large National Front in France and the miniscule British National Party, which are both right-wing anti-immigrant organizations. The Dutch party was centrist in orientation and its leader was an openly gay sociologist. His concern was to protect Dutch liberal policies from being undermined by socially conservative Muslim influence.

The assassin did not deny his guilt and, though not himself Muslim, stated that his motive had been to protect Dutch multiculturalism from a new party that seemed intolerant of Islamic beliefs.

In 2004 the Dutch got another shock when a well-known film director, Theo Van Gogh, was shot, stabbed and had his throat cut, in a public street with many witnesses, because he had made a documentary criticizing practices towards women in Muslim societies. The assassin was an Islamic fundamentalist of Moroccan origin who made no attempt to evade arrest and clearly wanted the murder to be well publicized as a warning to others who might be inclined to criticize Islamic practices. The immediate consequence of this event was a brief breakdown of public order, with non-Muslim gangs or mobs attacking Muslim schools and centres while Muslim gangs or mobs retaliated by attacks on Christian schools and centres. Altogether twenty public buildings on both sides were set on fire or otherwise badly damaged.

Death threats were then made against Ayaan Hirsi Ali, who had largely written the script for the documentary, herself a Somalian refugee who had been elected to the Dutch parliament and was well known as a politician. She had to go into hiding with police protection, and eventually decided to emigrate to the United States to escape the threats and stress. It emerged that the assassin had been associated with a terrorist group known as the Hofstad Group, nine of whose members were later convicted and imprisoned.

A consequence of this change in the political climate is that the Dutch government has revised some of its policies. After Van Gogh's murder, a parliamentary report declared that 'multiethnic society had been a dismal failure; huge ethnic ghettos and subcultures were tearing the country apart and the risk of polarization could only be countered by Muslims effectively becoming Dutch' (Fekete 2004: 20). In 2005 the Amsterdam Free University was given a special government grant to train imams in Dutch culture and Christianity.

In 2005 also the Dutch revised their immigration rules to insist that foreigners wanting to settle in the Netherlands have to pass a 'civic integration test' in Dutch language and culture, taken in their country of origin, as a condition of securing an entry permit. This new rule is rather clearly aimed at Muslims, both in its list of those exempt from its provisions and in some of the questions asked. The exemptions include citizens of EU member states, Switzerland, Norway, Canada, Australia, New Zealand, Japan and the United States. The exempt also include asylum seekers and people covered by the provisions for family reunion. However, all those exempt will have to take an integration test after their arrival in the Netherlands. The questions asked in the tests include some about Dutch values, including a readiness to accept gay marriage and affectionate public behaviour between gay couples, which are contrary to Islamic doctrine. The new rule specifically includes religious leaders coming to work in the Netherlands and young resident foreigners who have to go abroad to take the test when they reach the age of 17. It seems that the Netherlands is moving away from its previous commitment to multicultural policies.

British policies and practices

British experience regarding non-European immigrants since 1945 has been greatly affected by the fact that they have nearly all come from former colonies whose residents had British nationality and unrestricted rights of immigration until these were somewhat, but not greatly, curtailed by the Commonwealth Immigrants Act of 1962. By 2003 Britain had just over a million citizens of Afro-Caribbean origin, about 900,000 Hindus and Sikhs, and 1.6 million Muslims, mainly from Pakistan and Bangladesh.

As members of these ethnic minorities had British citizenship on arrival or soon afterwards, the government saw no need to develop special policies for them. It was, however, concerned to prevent racial discrimination and to that end introduced the Race Relations Act of 1965 supported by all parties and extended in 1968. This legislation is as comprehensive in scope as similar legislation in any other democracy. The 1965 Act established a national Race Relations Board and the 1968 Act added a Community Relations Commission. In 1976 these two bodies were replaced by a Commission for Racial Equality, with wider powers. There are numerous local branches of the Commission and other bodies with similar aims, so that altogether Britain has a small army of people working to improve relations between the host society and immigrant communities.

British society has long been exceptionally liberal and tolerant. There are, for instance, no identity cards, no laws to ban people calling themselves by any name they choose, no laws against trespassing on private land unless damage is caused, and no requirement for private schools and clubs to be registered or subject to government inspection.

The Commonwealth immigrants had presumably migrated to improve their living standards and official concern about them was related to this ambition rather than to cultural matters. The major concern to prevent racial discrimination in employment and housing was followed by concern about educational achievement. When cultural issues did arise, they were dealt with on a piecemeal and often local basis rather than as important issues of national policy. For instance, general laws about the slaughtering of animals had for long (since the 1920s) been subject to local exemptions to enable Jewish abattoirs to slaughter in the kosher manner, and similar exemptions were made for Islamic abattoirs in the 1960s. There have been no objections to Muslim girls wearing their traditional headscarves at school. The insistence of Sikhs on wearing turbans instead of caps or helmets caused some argument, but it was settled in favour of the Sikhs more quickly and with far fewer public protests than the same question had been settled in Canada, the other main destination for Sikh migrants. Town planning regulations, a municipal matter, have very rarely been used to hinder the construction of mosques and temples in traditional styles, as has happened to some extent in the Netherlands and to a large extent in France.

However, in 1981, there was a long week of rioting and looting, partly racial in origin, that affected twenty-seven urban areas in England. The main reason for the widespread incidence of the violence was a short-term growth of mass unemployment, which had reached its highest level since the 1930s and had particularly affected young people. However, the first riot occurred in Brixton, a south London neighbourhood largely populated by Jamaican immigrants, and this was precipitated by a cultural factor as well as by unemployment. During the late 1970s many West Indian immigrants had been converted to Rastafarianism, a millenarian creed that had emerged in Jamaica in the 1920s and is essentially a creed of underprivileged black people in a world dominated by whites. The creed holds that the blacks of Jamaica were descendants of slaves whose homeland was Ethiopia, and it takes its name from the family name of the former Emperor Haile

Selassie of Ethiopia, Ras Tafari. White society is regarded as corrupt as well as oppressive and is known to Rastafarians as 'Babylon'. The creed promises that, come the millennium, Babylon will collapse and the blacks will go back to Ethiopia, idealized as a 'promised land'. In the mean time, blacks should not work in the white economy, should have contempt for white institutions and should smoke marijuana to induce relaxation and passivity while awaiting the great day.

Knowing of this, the police in parts of south London made extensive use of their 'stop and search' powers to search West Indians for drugs. This practice led the latter to accuse the police of racial profiling to which the police response was, in effect, 'of course'. In April 1981 the police decided to descend on Brixton in force to search for drugs in what was known as Operation Swamp. This caused great resentment and led to three days of rioting, in which young black residents attacked the police with stones and fire-bombs and set fire to shops owned by whites. An official report showed that 401 police officers were injured while 204 vehicles and 145 shops and offices were destroyed or damaged. No figure was given for the number of rioters injured.

The disturbances spread to the Toxteth area of Liverpool, where they were more prolonged and worse. The riots in other areas were less serious, with looting as their main cause, but many thousands of young people, white as well as black, were involved in them. (For a report on the police and political violence, see Birch 1990: Chapter 17.)

Following a judicial report criticizing police insensitivity, tactics were changed. Street patrols in black neighbourhoods were largely replaced by closed-circuit television cameras. The worries about the possibility of crime during the three-day Notting Hill Festival, held every August with reggae bands, dancing in the street and so forth, were replaced by police cooperation with the Afro-Caribbean organizers. By the late 1990s this had become the largest ethnic festival in Europe, with over 200,000 people enjoying themselves. In 1985 there had been short local riots in districts of Birmingham and north London, but since then there have been no public disturbances involving Afro-Caribbean groups and unemployment has ceased to be a problem except briefly around 1991. By 2000 about one-third of Afro-Caribbean men were living with white partners. The general conclusion must be that the integration of Afro-Caribbean immigrants into British society should be regarded as successful.

Asian immigrants have not made headlines in the same way. In 1979 there was a large street fight in a Sikh area of west London, provoked by a gang of white skinheads and eventually won by the Sikhs, with the police trying vainly to separate the two groups and incurring injuries to eighty-one officers for their pains. However, until 2001 this was the only riotous assembly involving Asians, and widespread complacency about their situation was reinforced by the publication of statistics showing that, in areas of comparable economic status, Asians were doing rather better than whites in school examinations.

However, in 1996 a leading student of ethnic relations, John Rex, suggested that this complacency was misplaced in respect of working-class Muslim immigrants. He observed that there was 'mostly in London, a professional and business Muslim bourgeoisie' who interacted well with British elites but did not fully understand the alienation of Muslim workers in the industrial north (Rex 1996: 232). He noted that in the woollen textile city of Bradford (Yorkshire), where about one-quarter of the population are Muslim, protests about some obscure passages in a novel that were apparently blasphemous about the Islamic religion led to public bonfires of the book. The author (Salman Rushdie) was a British writer of Indian origin, and there were some protests in India and Pakistan, but the demonstrations in Bradford lasted longer although 'it is extremely unlikely that many of these young people in Bradford had read Rushdie's book' (Rex 1996: 235). The demonstrations had been organized by imams and teachers but the sizeable participation in them clearly indicated feelings of social alienation. Rex also noted that in the early 1980s twelve Pakistani youths in Bradford had been prosecuted for possessing offensive weapons in the shape of gasoline bombs, 'but were actually acquitted when they argued in court that the bombs were for self-defence' (Rex 1996: 234).

In 1991, meetings had been held in the Bradford area to protest against British participation in the first Gulf War because Iraqis were Muslims. This was logically absurd because the war was fought in defence of two other Muslim states, Kuwait and Saudi Arabia. Rex's warnings were underlined in the summer of 2001 (before 9/11) when rioting of two or three days broke out in textile industry towns. It started in Oldham (Lancashire), where a man of 62 taking a short cut through a few blocks regarded as Muslim was beaten up by youths, groups of whom then wrecked a pub said to be favoured by anti-immigrant groups, set fire to newspaper offices and fought the Greater Manchester police. It spread to Bradford, where white-owned shops were vandalized and the police felt it necessary to defend a chapel. In December 2001 a fair number of British Muslims went to Afghanistan to fight against the allied invasion and nine of them were captured by US troops and sent to Guantanamo Bay. And in 2006 it was reported that others had gone, or tried to go, to Iraq to join the insurgents. No figures could be given, but police statements indicated that scores of suspects had been stopped, many at Manchester Airport, on some such pretext as passport irregularities.

One of the 2005 London Underground suicide bombers (himself from Leeds, near Bradford) made a video before his death justifying his behaviour by saying that it was a response to British fighting in Afghanistan and Iraq that had killed numerous Muslims. This attitude reflects the traditional Islamic belief that being Muslim involves not only a religious identity but also a political one. Historically, the division of humanity into religious faiths predated its division into national states by many centuries, and Muslims tend to regard it as also logically prior, with Islam shaping a whole way of life and Muslims belonging to the worldwide community of 'Ummah'.

What of British policies towards religion and education? There is a privileged state church in England whose spiritual leader is responsible for the coronation of monarchs, but it has suffered more than most churches from religious decline in recent decades and surveys in the early 1990s showed that no more than 4 per cent of nominal members attended church on an average Sabbath.

Before 1944 many schools were owned by churches although their running expenses were largely paid by county or city councils. However, when the Education Act of 1944 was negotiated a deal was offered whereby ownership would be taken over by the local councils but the schools would have to provide two periods of religious instruction (RI) for each class every week. The Protestant churches all accepted this deal but the Roman Catholic Church refused, so that Catholic schools became wholly private. The instruction is by law non-denominational and in practice a great many schools share the responsibility around the staff, with the result that largely irreligious students get RI twice a week from largely irreligious teachers. In areas of mixed ethnicity part of the time has often been spent on creeds other than Christianity, and in 2004 this uneven move in a multicultural direction was made official by a new National Framework for Religious Education issued by the Department for Education and Skills. This called for children, as appropriate, not only to study the six main religions within British society, namely Christianity, Buddhism, Hinduism, Judaism, Islam and Sikhism, but also not to ignore less common creeds like the Baha'i faith, to give equal respect to the views of religious and non-religious pupils, and to deal with secular philosophies such as humanism (London *Independent*, 29 October 2004; see also Preece 2005: 38).

Another move in a multicultural direction had been made in 2001 when the government introduced an Education White Paper on 5 September making clear that government grants would henceforth be available for independent faith-based schools if local circumstances made this appropriate. The Secretary of State defended this change of policy on the ground that accepting grants would ensure that such schools taught the national curriculum and would be subject to government inspection. She mentioned schools from minority faiths and it was generally understood that she was thinking of the 80 or so Islamic schools that were financed by Saudi-Arabian institutions. This new policy has led to the development of a limited number of state-funded religious schools of the Christian, Muslim, Hindu and Jewish faiths, but the policy remains controversial.

In January 2005 the Chief Inspector of Schools expressed his concern that 'many young people are being educated in faith-based schools, with little appreciation of their wider responsibilities and obligations to British society'. He mentioned Islamic schools in particular, saying that a traditional Islamic education 'does not entirely fit' children for life in modern Britain, and that the government must monitor such schools to make sure that pupils are taught about 'other faiths and the wider tenets of British society' (*Manchester Evening News*, 17 January 2005). On 26 July 2005 Tony Blair gave a press conference on the issue at which he was met with a barrage of hostile questions reminding him of the experience of state-financed Protestant and Catholic schools in Northern Ireland, which had socialized generations of young people into sectarian conflict and intermittent violence. Faced with this undeniable truth, Blair completely lost his normal eloquence and could say only that 'I hadn't realized that you all felt so strongly'.

The only significant grievances of a religious kind have been those coming from Muslim spokesmen, and in respect of Muslims the British position is a little paradoxical. A comparative study by two American academics has shown that the British state has done markedly more than the state in France or Germany to look after and advance Muslim requirements for the exercise and preservation of their religion. The study concludes that on the issues of 'religious instruction in state schools, state aid to religious schools, and mosque building Britain has been remarkably accommodating to Muslims' (Fetzer and Soper 2005: 60). At the same time, another American academic has discovered in the course of interviews with moderate Muslims in leading positions in six European countries that the British are much more likely than the others to regard Islamic values as 'inherently incompatible' with the values of their host country (Klausen 2005: 87). This has more to do with the varieties of Islam prevalent in their homelands (see Chapter 5) than with policies in Britain, but it is not irrelevant.

Grievances sometimes voiced by Muslim spokesmen in Britain are not very serious. It is complained that the Race Relations Acts do not cover Muslims because the courts have decided firmly that they do not constitute a race. This is an entirely logical decision and it makes little practical difference as only a handful of converts are white, all other resident Muslims being covered as Indians, Pakistanis, Arabs, or whatever. The complaint simply reflects the wish, already mentioned, for Islam to be regarded as a form of political identity as well as religious identity. Another complaint, following the Rushdie affair, is that the British law against blasphemy covers only the Christian religion. This is true but makes little practical difference as the law is virtually obsolete. It would perhaps make sense to abolish it, but there are scores of obsolete laws on the Statute Book and the British tradition is to let them lie dormant rather than spend parliamentary time tidying them all up. In any case, it is highly unlikely that a British jury would have convicted the author of this difficult work (in which the offending passages occur in a dream or fantasy) so if the law were changed in the direction wanted by zealous Muslims, the probable consequence would be to replace a rather theoretical grievance by a series of controversies and complaints about court procedure and juries.

Exactly the same may be said about the proposal to add a law banning 'religious hatred' to the large arsenal of laws already available to bring prosecutions for expressing racial hatred, for 'offensive behaviour' for 'behaviour whereby a breach of the peace might be caused', and so on. Very few such prosecutions are ever brought, because of the deep attachment of the British people, including police, lawyers and judges, to the value of free speech. The Blair government, anxious to please Muslim organizations after the London bombings, introduced a Bill of this nature to Parliament, but a backbench revolt led to its defeat in 2006.

French policies and practices

France is a fascinating country, in this as in many other ways. As Walzer (1997) and Jennings (2000) have pointed out, it has had many waves of immigration and has a high level of ethnic diversity but still regards itself as a monocultural society (Walzer 1997: 8; Jennings 2000: 375). This belief derives from the republican tradition, starting from the original Revolution of 1789, rooted in the thought of the Enlightenment, and having survived repeated clashes with monarchs and the Roman Catholic Church. One aspect of this tradition is that all citizens should be regarded as equal, with no mention of ethnicity or class or religion in censuses and other government documents. Another aspect is that the system of state schools should consciously prepare children for citizenship and should inculcate republican virtues. Another is that the separation of church and state should be vigorously observed. There is no place in this ideal for individual citizens to have loyalties to intermediate groups or organizations between themselves and the state, nor is there any place for the idea of minority rights. In view of this, it is natural for French intellectuals to have open contempt for the novel concept of multiculturalism, which they tend to regard as a new form of tribalism, likely to cause social disintegration on Lebanese lines, and totally un-French (Jennings 2000: 587–9).

This republican (sometimes called Jacobin) tradition has lasted as an ideal for over two centuries, although during that period France has experienced regime changes, violent or peaceful, in 1815, 1830, 1848, 1852, 1870, 1940, 1944, 1946 and 1958; has been invaded three times and occupied for four years; and has been through an appalling civil war in Algeria. That the ideal has survived through all these crises indicates the tenacity with which it has been held.

Of course, the practice of government in France, though organized on more of a national plan than public administration in Britain has ever been, is not quite as uniform as the republican model suggests. A French scholar has outlined some of the complexities in an article entitled 'Multiculturalism in France' (de Wenden 2003), using the term to cover an assortment of administrative variations rather than a doctrine. She notes that in the three Rhineland *départements* that were under German rule from 1870 to 1918 religious affairs are still governed by 'an agreement between the state and the three faiths of Roman Catholic, Protestant and Jewish' as the area was not governed by France when the legal separation of church and state was enacted in 1905 (de Wenden 2003: 83). She points out that in Alsace the German language is used in local administration, that in the Perpignan region street and town names are displayed in Catalan as well as in French, and that since 1968 the teaching of regional languages has been authorized in schools and universities of Brittany and Corsica (de Wenden 2003: 83). The arrival of millions of non-European immigrants has led to the recognition of cultural mediators in industrial suburbs and municipal housing blocks built for the immigrants, and Algerian groups, being familiar with French administrative styles, have been particularly successful in getting state subsidies for cultural activities (de Wenden 2003: 85).

It is doubtful whether these marginal inconsistencies justify the author's conclusion that 'the rise of claims to be different means that the republican model of integration has no other choice but to negotiate with multiculturalism' (de Wenden 2003. 86). This whole question was thrown into relief by the 'affair of the headscarves' that began in 1989. To explain this affair some historical introduction is necessary.

From the founding of the Third Republic in 1870 until the 1960s, the most important cultural division in society was that between the church and its sympathizers on the one hand and the secular or anti-clerical groups on the other. As the influence of the church waned, this source of anxiety for republicans has gradually been replaced by anxieties about the impact of non-European immigrants, most of whom are Muslim. Although France has received many non-Muslim immigrants since 1945, mostly from the Caribbean territories and former colonies in West Africa and Indo-China, it is clear that they have been outnumbered by Muslims, mainly from North Africa. Although precise statistics are not available, it is believed that between 5 million and 6 million Muslims now live in France, between 9 and 10 per cent of the population and thus a higher proportion than in any other western country. Since the 1980s, two political crises have developed involving them, of which the affair of the headscarves was the first.

When a universal system of state education was introduced in the early years of the Third Republic, the Catholic Church encouraged faithful girls to attend school wearing conspicuous symbols of their religion. As the church had always been opposed to the republican form of government and had indeed campaigned for the choice of a monarch rather than a president as head of state when the new regime began life, the wearing of religious symbols was taken to be a form of political demonstration. As such, it was naturally resented by teachers and school administrators with republican sympathies, and in 1904 the Ministry of Education published a regulation, affecting the entire national system, that banned the wearing of religious symbols in school. The official justification for this ban was the principle of *laïcité*, meaning secularity, that was part of the theoretical basis of the French state. As all state agencies were secular institutions, there was no place in them for religious symbols.

Suddenly, in 1989, three Muslim girls from North Africa produced a great shock by arriving at school wearing the *hijab*, the Muslim headscarf. The headmaster banned them from attendance and the response of the French public to news of the challenge 'was almost unanimously hostile, not to say at times hysterical' (Jennings 2000: 584). Other girls challenged the ban and the Minister of Education, seeking calm, asked the highest administrative court, the Conseil d'Etat, for an advisory ruling. The ruling was that girls should be permitted to wear the headscarf provided that it was not ostentatious or worn in local circumstances that made it an act of provocation or propaganda, the decision to be made by the local education authority. This compromise lasted uneasily until 1994, when a teenager reacted to a local ban by announcing that she was taking the local authority to court on the ground that it was violating her human rights. This caused a crisis that was both legal and political. Unlike Anglo-Saxon countries, France does not have a common law system that can cope with novel challenges. French law is based on the Napoleonic Code, and any observant tourist will know that even a notice banning spitting or smoking bears details of the statute and clause authorizing the ban. Because the headscarf ban was based only on an administrative regulation, not a statute, French courts could not handle a case regarding it unless a law was passed. As teachers, public opinion and all political parties favoured the ban, parliament duly enacted one.

The consequence of the challenge was therefore an empathic reassertion of the French belief in *laïcité* and their rejection of the view that the growth of religious minorities in society should lead to the adoption of multicultural policies. This may not last for ever in regard to headscarves, as the new law is worded in a way that may make possible a future move to the flexible position favoured by the Conseil d'Etat in 1989, but the general principle of monoculturalism remains intact.

The other political crisis involving ethnic minorities erupted in late 2005, when tens of thousands of residents of industrial suburbs, mainly of African origin, rioted in protest over high unemployment rates (reaching 40 per cent among young men) as well as poor housing and inadequate social services. The riots lasted for three weeks, spread widely across France from their origin in the industrial suburbs around Paris, and were TV spectaculars, with about 10,000 cars and 500 public buildings set on fire. The reaction of the government was to introduce measures to moderate the exceptional rigidity of French labour laws, in ways that would make it easier for employees to hire unemployed young people without being committed to keeping them for life, but this proposal met with so many hostile demonstrations by trade unionists and students that the government abandoned the plan. The reaction of the police was to put the events into perspective by publishing figures showing that disorderly behaviour by young people after dark was not uncommon: from 1 January 2005 to mid-November, about 28,000 cars and 17,500 trash cans had been set on fire in France, with about 9,000 police cars stoned.

An academic reaction was to take comfort from the two facts that the rioters were multiethnic and, although the majority were Muslim, the degree of religiosity among the immigrant Muslim community was not high. A sociologist had reported that observance of Muslim rules of behaviour was now 'minimal among young people'. Few of them observed the ban on alcohol, the requirement of daily prayer, or the insistence on halal food. They tended to fast during the first three days of Ramadan (though not for the month), but 'this is frequently the only individual rite observed by young people' and their 'degree of theological knowledge is generally negligible' (Roy 1994a: 57). The realistic general French reaction to the riots was to regard them as a consequence of poverty and unemployment, similar in character to the British riots of 1981, and not therefore requiring any modification of policies relevant to cultural divisions.

Philosophical approaches to multiculturalism

The two most sophisticated analyses of this kind are by the British political theorists Brian Barry (2001) and Bhikhu Parekh (2000). Barry's basic position in *Culture and Equality* is the classical liberal one, a product of Enlightenment thought and therefore of the views underlying both the French and American revolutions, that a liberal state should treat all citizens as equal before the law. He accepts that a state may properly give special assistance to groups lacking certain opportunities or resources, provided that the assistance should be available to all citizens needing it for the reasons specified and that it should be temporary, ceasing to be given when the need is alleviated (Barry 2001: 12–13). He asserts that the wish of multiculturalists to give special privileges to groups defined by their ethnicity and culture, so that the help would not be generally available to citizens and not temporary in duration, amounts essentially to a rejection of Enlightenment ideals about politics (Barry 2001: 13 and 15).

Barry very carefully criticizes a whole set of arguments used by writers favouring multicultural policies, designed to give special rights and permanent help to groups defined by a culture which is not that of the majority, and his analysis is entirely consistent with his basic assumptions about the character of the liberal state.

A quite different approach is made by Parekh in *Rethinking Multiculturalism: Cultural Diversity and Political Theory*. He begins by asserting that most classical political theorists have made individualistic assumptions about the proper relationship between the citizen and the state, without paying adequate attention to the role of culture in shaping individual desires and beliefs. Although human character is not completely determined by culture, the culture in which people are raised 'shapes them in countless ways', influences their 'modes of reasoning' and leads them to assess their 'options in certain ways' (Parekh 2000: 170). Different cultures have different views about sex and gender relationships, about death, about the nature of religion, and so forth, and there is no universal criterion for evaluating the differences (Parekh 2000: Chapter 4). All cultures should therefore be treated with equal respect.

In regard to politics, Parekh accuses liberals of attaching too much importance to liberalism and of being unfair to groups within society with non-liberal beliefs. At one point, he defines the latter as including 'conservatives, socialists, communists, Marxists, religious communities, indigenous peoples, long-established ethnic communities and newly-arrived immigrants' (Parekh 2000: 112). This is much too sweeping and includes several groups defined simply by their political opinions rather than by their cultures. This distinction is vitally important to any discussion of liberal democracy, which depends upon the ability and readiness of voters to change their opinions from time to time. If voters are so bound by their cultures that they cannot or do not do this democratic institutions will fail, as they failed, sometimes tragically and bloodily, in former colonies of tropical Africa where the electorate was divided by tribal loyalties.

Parekh goes on to discuss the virtue of cultural diversity, which he says is wrongly defended by other liberal theorists on instrumental grounds, that in this way or that it produces beneficial consequences, and must be defended as simply a good in itself, essential to human freedom (Parekh 2000: 165–71). And in the second half of his book he presents a long and thoughtful discussion of ways to make cultural minorities feel fully part of their nation as a political entity. Noel O'Sullivan (2004) has offered a philosophical critique of Parekh's position, noting that it is weakened by its failure to define a cultural community, by its assumption of certain Enlightenment values that he criticizes in other liberal thinkers, and by optimistic assumptions about the existence of universal moral truths that will prevent political disagreements between cultural groups leading to conflict and even violence (O'Sullivan 2004: 48–54).

While Parekh's book is written at a high level of generality, its year of publication also saw the publication of a report entitled *The Future of Multi-Ethnic Britain* prepared by a commission of which he was chair, and frequently (though incorrectly) known as the Parekh Report. The commission was established by the Runnymede Trust, 'a think-tank devoted to the cause of promoting racial justice in Britain' (Runnymede Trust 2000: viii). This report, 399 pages long, includes a vast list of desirable changes in government policy. In the present context, its most relevant feature is the insistence that 'colour-blind and culture-blind approaches don't work' (Runnymede Trust 2000: 80–7). The problem about this, put starkly, is the belief that membership of a certain racial or cultural group in itself entitles a citizen to special rights and assistance. This may be reasonable in respect of a country that imported slaves or has indigenous peoples who were conquered by settlers, but it is hardly reasonable in respect of a country whose cultural minorities consist mainly of people who (or whose ancestors) freely migrated in search of better living conditions. Taxpayers of the host society cannot be expected to accept such a view. It conflicts with liberal principles and could be put into practice only if the British system of democratic government were replaced by a dictatorship of social workers.

Conclusions regarding multiculturalism

This is a confusing concept. In the hands of Canadian liberals, it started as a guide to the distribution of government subsidies and quite quickly changed to being a label to distinguish Canadian society from the apparently similar society south of the border. It has been thought to have the magical quality of protecting Canada against terrorism, so that when 17 Muslim Canadians were arrested on plausible charges of planning mass murder in Toronto, a leading journalist wrote a syndicated column under the heading 'Terror plot allegations hurt our multicultural dream' (CanWest News Service, 6 July 2006).

In the hands of Parekh (2000) it is a novel philosophical understanding of human nature. Its most common use is as an omnibus title for a package of government policies, but our outline of Dutch and British policies shows that they are characterized by inconsistency and are liable to change at short notice. They do not add up to a doctrine, as communism or socialism or conservatism are doctrines.

It seems fair to conclude that while 'multicultural' is quite a convenient adjective for students of politics to use, 'multiculturalism' the noun is so vague and uncertain in meaning that it is entirely unhelpful.

Chapter 4

Globalization and the national state

Globalization is a rather new concept in political discourse and in the social sciences. Malcolm Waters reports that the first sociological article to include the word in its title was published in 1985 and that by February 1994 'the catalogue of the Library of Congress contained only 34 items with that term or one of its derivatives in the title', none of them published before 1987 (Waters 1995: 2). In the late 1990s the term became fashionable, however, and by the turn of the millennium it had appeared in scores of books and hundreds of articles. There is no point in trying to itemize or categorize these very numerous references, because the concept is not in itself contentious. It is simply an omnibus term used loosely as a shorthand label for any or all or, most commonly, some combination of five rather different trends in world affairs that can easily be enumerated.

One such trend is a growing concern and international action about environmental problems of global significance, including threats to rare species, global warming and the dangers of nuclear fallout. Another is the growth of a world market as the consequence of lower transport costs and the widespread reduction of customs duties, coupled with the creation of the World Trade Organization to protect trade agreements and to reduce non-tariff barriers to trade. A third is the establishment of international courts to protect human rights, either in specific regions or more widely. A fourth is a new view that liberal governments, or coalitions thereof, should have the right, and perhaps the duty, to intervene in the internal affairs of other states if the latter are guilty of gross suppression of human rights within their territories. A fifth is the very rapid growth of worldwide means of communication, leading to the possibility of the globalization of culture.

In considering the impact of these developments on the theory and practice of modern democracy, which is the subject of this book, it is vital to distinguish speculation from fact. As the chief arena for the exercise of democratic politics is the government of the national state, the following brief review will focus on the extent to which these globalizing developments have actually diminished the authority and powers of national states and the effect of the changes on the character and extent of democracy.

ENVIRONMENTAL ISSUES

Growing concern about environmental issues in the last decades of the twentieth century led to a number of international conferences and agreements, but the impact of these on the status and powers of national states has been varied. Conference agreements depend very largely on the decisions of national governments for their implementation. A concerted effort to limit the impact of national rivalries on the extraction of minerals from the seabed led to elaborate recommendations being hammered out at the Law of the Sea Conference in the 1980s, but several powerful states, including the United States and Britain, simply refused to be bound by all of the recommendations made. The bio-diversity treaty signed in Rio in 1992 was an ambitious attempt to protect rare plants and species, but when the United States refused to sign there was nothing that other governments could do. The signatories to the Montreal Protocol of 1988 promised that between 1989 and 2000 they would halve the emission of chemicals dangerous to the ozone layer, but progress in this field depended entirely on the actions of individual state governments, most of which failed to meet the targets. The Kyoto Convention of 1997 contains enforceable provisions but it was not until 2005 that it was ratified by a sufficient number of states to activate it and it is not yet clear how effective these provisions will be. The international agreement on the non-proliferation of nuclear weapons, hailed as a very significant achievement by western politicians and mass media in 1997, did not stop India and Pakistan from conducting test explosions of nuclear bombs in 1998. However, this is not to deny that there is a move towards international action on environmental matters, because clearly there is, and clearly it is important. The point is simply that this move has not yet undermined the authority of national states.

A GLOBAL ECONOMY

On this topic, again, there are facts, speculations and controversies. It is true that since 1950 international trade has expanded much more quickly than world production (*Economist*, 27 November 1999: 21); that more than half of this trade is accounted for by the actions of multinational corporations (see Gray 1998: 62); that electronic means of communication enable billions of private dollars to be transferred between countries every day in foreign exchange speculations; and that, with one or two exceptions like Cuba and North Korea, the whole world has moved or is moving towards a market economy. It is also a fact that supranational institutions like the European Union (EU) and worldwide institutions like the World Trade Organization (WTO) now protect trading agreements and make it difficult for individual countries regulated by them to erect trade barriers unilaterally.

On this basis of fact it has been said that economic globalization has eroded the independence of national states. As John Gray has pointed out, some writers have been very emphatic about this. Keniehe Ohmae, for instance, has asserted that 'in a borderless economy, the nation-focussed maps we typically use to make sense of economic activity are woefully misleading' (Ohmae 1995: 19–21). Susan Strange has said that 'the authority of the governments of all states . . . has been weakened . . . by the single global market economy' (Strange 1996: 13–14). Manuel Castells has declared that 'bypassed by global networks of wealth, power and information, the modern nation-state has lost much of its authority' (Castells 1997: 354). This kind of assertion (and there are numerous other examples) can only be analysed by breaking down the generalizations on which it is based.

One claim that has questionable foundations is that the growth of large transnational corporations has undermined the authority of national governments. This is questionable because it has always been true that governments have had to consider the possible impact of their taxation policies and labour laws on the behaviour of international investors. There is nothing new about this. Another questionable claim is that the vast daily movements of capital by electronic means have destroyed the ability of governments to control their exchange rates. British experience between 1945 and 1979 showed rather clearly that political attempts to protect the international value of their currency, for some time by 'fixed' exchange rates under the Bretton Woods Agreement and always by tight exchange controls, could only postpone the devaluation of sterling by a year or two, not prevent it, if international trading balances made devaluation appropriate.

Bilateral treaties on customs duties necessarily limit the freedom of national governments to change the duties unilaterally so long as the treaties are respected, but this has always been true and in any case history is replete with examples of treaties being revoked or broken. The only significant new developments are, first, the role of the International Monetary Fund (IMF) and World Bank, second, the growth of the European Union, and third, the role of the WTO.

The IMF and World Bank make very large loans to developing countries, together with occasional short-term loans to industrialized countries experiencing temporary financial difficulties, such as Britain in 1976–7 and South Korea in 1998–9. The money comes mainly from the United States and other western countries and the loans are accompanied by conditions about economic policy that reflect the beliefs and policies of these countries. The loans that have been made to Russia since 1990, for instance, have been conditional upon that country moving towards a market economy. In that kind of way, the IMF and the World Bank have reduced the independence of the recipient governments, but this is simply the price of getting the loans.

The European Community (EC, the economic arm of the EU) is an unprecedented move towards the economic integration of the member states.

By joining it, these states have surrendered their powers to negotiate and control their own tariffs and have increasingly lost control over agricultural policies, fisheries, open or concealed subsidies to industry, and various aspects of labour law, in the interests of creating a 'level playing field' for internal competition. The EC has been immensely successful in its two main original aims of increasing prosperity through the creation of a large tariff-free market and increasing agricultural production through modernization. On the political level, it has made a major war between member states unthinkable and, since its enlargement into the European Union under the Maastricht Treaty of 1992, has taken steps towards the development of common policies on immigration, refugees and policing.

These developments add up to a significant surrender of national independence by the member states. However, moves towards greater integration are hampered by the fact that the EC and EU are elitist rather than democratic organizations and have failed to gain majority support among their citizens. Numerous surveys have shown that national loyalties remain much stronger than any sense of European identity (see Birch 1998: 223) and the *Economist*, a generally pro-European journal, concluded in 1997 that 'the EU's deepest problem of all is the disenchantment of its citizens' (*Economist*, 31 May 1997).

The WTO is different again. It is a young institution, having come into existence in January 1995 with the objective of enforcing the decisions made by trading nations subscribing to the General Agreement on Tariffs and Trade (GATT), that had grown in coverage and membership in successive instalments since its inception in 1948. Its enforcement procedure provides for any of its 135 member states to launch a complaint against another member state for alleged violation of an agreed rule, and for a panel of three officials to hear arguments from both sides and reach a decision that, subject to appeal to another panel of three officials, is then legally binding on the states concerned. If the state that loses the argument declines to comply with the ruling, the other state may impose tariffs on imports from the loser equivalent in total value of lost trade to the estimated loss to the winning state resulting from the continuance of the banned practices. This amounts to a loss of national independence, though the fact that the losing state cannot be forced to comply, but only forced to expose its exporting firms to financial loss, somewhat reduces the direct impact of the punishment.

WTO procedures cannot by their nature be subject to direct democratic controls, but they have offended democrats who believe in open decisions, openly arrived at, by the secrecy in which the decision-making panels work. In this respect the WTO compares very poorly with the United Nations. The UN Security Council and General Assembly are not exactly democratic bodies either, but debates in both bodies are conducted in the full light of publicity so that citizens the world over can observe what their national representatives are saying and make informed judgements on their behaviour. In contrast, the WTO panels operate behind closed doors and produce only brief justifications of their decisions.

In the first five years of its existence, the WTO produced a number of decisions that have been very controversial and have increased the scope of its authority in ways that were not generally anticipated. Because its responsibilities extend only to trade, it has not felt able to take account of widely held values other than free trade, such as the protection of the environment, the protection of threatened species, or the protection of public health by food safety regulation. Many measures adopted by governments to protect these other values can be shown to have an adverse effect on some trading interest or another, and each time a trading nation has appealed to the WTO on this basis the decision has favoured the appellant. For example, when four Asian states challenged provisions of the US Endangered Species Act that forbade the sale in the United States of shrimp caught in ways that kill sea turtles, the WTO required the United States to amend its statute. Conversely, when the United States attempted to reduce air pollution by requiring oil refineries to produce clean gasoline if it was to be sold in the American market, Venezuela successfully appealed to the WTO on the ground that this rule discriminated against Venezuelan refineries.

When the US administration appealed against an EC ban on the import of beef from hormone-injected cattle, the WTO upheld the appeal on the ground that the Europeans had no scientific proof that the beef would endanger human health. This infuriated the Europeans, well aware that no scientists had predicted that the improved feeding stuff fed to British cattle in the 1980s might produce the epidemic of 'mad cow disease' (bovine spongiform encephalitis: BSE) that has led to many human deaths so the European Community refused to comply with the ruling. As a result, the United States imposed crippling (100 per cent) tariffs on a range of European products.

These and several other decisions mean that the WTO has acquired, or (as some would say) arrogated to itself, the power to deny national govern ments the right to make their own laws and regulations to protect their citizens. It is the first, and so far the only, worldwide organization to have this kind of power, which necessarily involves a reduction in the extent of democracy. Controversy over this has been heightened by allegations that the power has been used to protect the profits of large corporations at the expense of what most liberals would regard as the public interest. In addition to the rejection of arrangements and laws designed to protect the environment or public health, the WTO decided in 1999 that the agreement whereby the EU gave a protected market for bananas to farmers in former European colonies in the Caribbean was contrary to its rules, following an appeal by the United States that this discriminated against a slightly different type of banana produced in parts of central America by a US company using industrialized farming methods. As this would probably throw tens of thousands of small farmers in the Caribbean into bankruptcy and devastate the economies of several small island nations, the decision further upset Europeans, who did not fail to note that the US administration acted not to help US farmers (who do not grow bananas) but simply to enhance the profits of a large American transnational corporation operating in foreign countries. In consequence of these developments, there was widespread concern that the world conference held in Seattle in December 1999 to launch a new round of trade negotiations might result in a process that enlarged still further the scope of WTO authority.

Happily for nationalists and democrats, this conference turned out to be a complete fiasco. The various heads of government invited to dignify the conference by their presence all declined the invitation. The steering committee that met in Geneva failed to agree on an agenda. The leader of the US delegation upset some of the other delegations by insisting on chairing the conference herself. And when the delegates arrived in Seattle they found the streets blocked by about 100,000 demonstrators carrying placards denouncing the WTO.

On the first day the delegates were unable to get to the conference hall. On the second the Mayor of Seattle declared a state of emergency that authorized the police to get tough. On the third day, with several hundred demonstrators behind bars (and denied legal representation) the conference finally got down to business. On the fourth it came to an end without reaching agreement on anything at all, even a final communiqué.

So ended the attempt to launch a millennium round of trade negotiations. The hope of critics that the fiasco might lead to a reform of the WTO in one way or another has not been realized, but more and more states have been admitted to membership. The organization now has 149 members, of which well over half are developing societies. In November 2001 a meeting at Doha (Qatar) launched a new round of conferences with the specific aim of helping poor countries by reducing barriers to their export of agricultural products and textiles. However, in September 2003 a much heralded world conference in Cancun (Mexico) resulted in complete failure. The European Union refused to make major changes to its agricultural policies; the United States refused to reduce its subsidies to the cotton industry; Japan refused to reduce its help to rice farmers. On the other side, many poor countries saw the pro-poor slogans of the Doha round 'as an excuse for making demands of the rich world while doing nothing to lower their own trade barriers' (*Economist*, 20 September 2003). They refused even to reduce barriers to trade with each other, which according to the World Bank would have brought them great economic benefits. The conference ended acrimoniously.

A slightly more positive world conference was held in Hong Kong in December 2005. It was agreed to eliminate export subsidies on agricultural exports by the end of 2013; the United States agreed to reduce help to its cotton industry; and there was general agreement that the rich countries should give a large package of aid and trading concessions to the thirty-two countries deemed to be 'least developed'. However, all this added up to only a small step towards world free trade.

In July 2006 another meeting of the world's trade ministers was held in Geneva, for 'what was billed as a final attempt to salvage the Doha round of global trade talks'. The failure of this meeting led *The Economist* to predict that bilateral and regional trade deals (of which there are more than 250) may 'replace multilateralism as the organizing principle of world trade' and that the WTO 'may eventually lose its legitimacy as an arbiter of trade disputes' (*Economist*, 8 July 2006).

HUMAN RIGHTS AND INTERNATIONAL JUSTICE

Another relevant development is the move to establish international tribunals and courts with the power to prosecute individuals for offences against human rights, even if these offences were committed within their own countries and did not violate national laws. The first example of this was the 1945 decision of the victorious powers in the Second World War to establish International Military Tribunals in Nuremburg and Tokyo to hear allegations of 'crimes against humanity' committed by German and Japanese leaders and soldiers during the war. This was an unprecedented and controversial action, because the crimes for which people were prosecuted were not known to either national laws or international law at the time that the events took place. In effect, the victorious powers were acting as legislators, prosecutors and judges in a process that contravened most liberal assumptions about the nature of justice, but was nevertheless widely accepted by liberals because the behaviour in question had been so horrific. These tribunals did not affect the authority of national governments because at the time Germany and Japan, having surrendered unconditionally, were occupied territories with no governments of their own.

In 1948 the proclamation of the Universal Declaration of Human Rights by the General Assembly of the United Nations set out some general principles that could be used as standards of reference in future cases, though it was over-ambitious in scope and for this reason was not suitable for adoption as a legal code. The provisions of the Declaration will be examined in Chapter 10; at this point it is sufficient to note that its adoption (by 48 votes to nil, with 8 abstentions) did not make it binding on national governments and that it was not accompanied by any provisions for its enforcement.

The Declaration was followed in 1950 by the publication of a shorter and more modest document entitled the European Convention for the Protection of Human Rights and Fundamental Freedoms. This was produced by the Council of Europe, a rather odd body established in 1949 by agreement of ten western European governments, of which seven had been Allies; Ireland and Sweden had been neutral; and Italy had been on both sides in the war. The Council had vague aims and was denied any real powers because some of its founding members, notably Britain, were reluctant to hand over any of their sovereign authority to it. This reluctance was justified by Ernest Bevin, the British Foreign Secretary, in the memorable phrase: 'Once you open that Pandora's Box, you'll find it full of Trojan Horses' (quoted in Nugent 1991: 16). However, in 1959 the Council, now swollen to fifteen members, created the European Court of Human Rights to adjudicate complaints brought before it by citizens, including complaints about the behaviour of their own national governments. This was a highly significant step, being the first occasion on which national governments voluntarily surrendered part of their sovereignty to an international court of justice. European states have signed on to this court's jurisdiction one by one over the years, with seven having done so by 1984 and twenty-eight by 1994. As the Court has no direct powers to implement its decisions, it can be (and has been) argued that the reduction in sovereignty is limited. The strength of this argument can be judged in the light of three examples from the 1980s involving the United Kingdom.

A 1985 decision of the Court that British immigration laws discriminated against women in one respect resulted in an immediate change in British law to comply with the judgement. Another decision held that the human rights of parents had been violated when their son was caned in school without their permission. This led to protracted debate, but in the end the British Parliament banned all forms of corporal punishment in state schools. In 1989 the Court decided that the British Prevention of Terrorism Act violated human rights because it permitted the police to detain suspected terrorists for up to four days before bringing them before a court, as against twenty-four hours for people suspected of other crimes. However, this judgement was declared to be unreasonable by the British government on the ground that it took insufficient account of the threat to British lives posed by the murderous activities of the Irish Republican Army, and no change was made to British law.

Overall, the European Convention and European Court must clearly be counted as successful and important. Most states that subscribe to it have added some or all of the articles of the Convention to their own constitutions, so that they can be implemented by national courts with the European Court needed only to hear appeals, and in 1999 Britain (which has no written constitution) followed this example by adding several of the Convention's provisions to its own laws. An immediate result of this was a decision by a Scottish court that the practice whereby some Scottish magistrates (known confusingly as sheriffs) were appointed for only annual terms of office did not give them sufficient independence of the executive to be acceptable under these new rules. As British judicial procedures are out of

step with those of most other western European countries, they may face
further legal challenges.

In 1993 and 1995, the UN Security Council established two new military
tribunals on the lines of the Nuremburg and Tokyo tribunals, one to try
persons accused of war crimes in the conflicts following the break-up of
Yugoslavia, the other to try persons accused of genocide in Rwanda. By the
spring of 2000 a little over twenty suspects had been arrested by NATO
troops in Bosnia and tried by the new tribunal in The Hague. This seems
like a form of globalization, but as Bosnia had never had an effective national government it is not clear whether these actions represent an infringement of national sovereignty. In 1999, during the conflict in Kosovo (to be
discussed below), the tribunal named several suspects to be arrested for
crimes against humanity, including President Milosevic of Yugoslavia. As
Kosovo, unlike Bosnia, was still a province within Yugoslavia, such action
was clearly a violation of Yugoslav sovereignty. In the event, NATO
military action led to the de facto separation of Kosovo from what remained
of Yugoslavia; there followed a domestic revolution in Belgrade; and the
new regime eventually yielded to EU and American pressure by handing
Slobodan Milosevic over for trial. The trial itself was hardly a success, as
Milosevic proved to be at least as good at defending himself as the prosecutors were at establishing his guilt, many of the charges had to be dismissed,
and after nearly two years he died of natural causes in March 2006 while the
trial was nowhere near conclusion.

The situation in Rwanda is very different, as in 1994 between 500,000
and 800,000 members of the Tutsi minority were slaughtered by the Hutu
majority, in the world's first case of genocide since the Holocaust. The
Tutsis were victorious in the subsequent civil war and a vast number of
Hutus were arrested. However, it has proved impossible for either the international tribunal or the Rwandan courts to try more than a small proportion
of them. The international tribunal, set up in 1995, had to be restructured in
1997 after a UN inspection revealed gross mismanagement and financial
irregularities, and by August 1999 it had still secured only seven convictions. The Rwandan courts have done better, but by 2005 about 120,000
suspects were still in makeshift prison camps awaiting trial.

A development of very much greater potential importance took place in
1998, namely the decision by a large international conference in Rome to
recommend the establishment of a world court of justice to be entitled the
International Criminal Court, with power to exercise jurisdiction over in-
fringements of human rights anywhere in the world if these were not being
prosecuted by national courts. The recommendation was approved by a
majority of 120 votes to 7, but did not come into force until 2005 because it
required ratification by at least sixty national parliaments.

Soon after this conference, in October 1998, an astonishing attempt was
made to jump the gun on this process when a Spanish high court judge

applied to British authorities to extradite General Pinochet, the former president of Chile, to stand trial in Spain for crimes against humanity that he had ordered his police and troops to commit in Chile. This application threw the British judicial authorities into confusion. A London magistrate found the extradition papers to be in order, but when this was appealed against the Lord Chief Justice allowed the appeal on the dual grounds that the Spanish courts had no jurisdiction over crimes committed in Chile by a Chilean citizen and that, in any case, a retired head of state travelling on a diplomatic passport was exempt from extradition.

When an appeal against this decision went to Britain's highest court, the House of Lords, the case had to be heard twice because the deciding vote at the first hearing was cast by a Law Lord who should have disqualified himself from the case on grounds of a conflict of interest. The second hearing eventually produced seven somewhat varied judgments, with a majority of six to one deciding that extradition was possible. On the general question of whether a retired head of state could be prosecuted internationally, the majority reached a slightly ambivalent conclusion. They upheld the traditional principle of international law that a state itself, its government and its serving head of state are absolutely immune from international prosecutions, but they yielded to the moral demand for legal action against breaches of human rights by removing this immunity from retired heads of state in respect of actions they had authorized while in office. On the particular question of whether British courts could authorize the extradition of Pinochet, they concluded that only two of the thirty-five charges were relevant, these being allegations of torture in two incidents in the final months of his presidency, after Britain had ratified the 1984 UN Convention against Torture on 8 December 1988.

In all the circumstances, the seven Law Lords 'made a strong plea to the Home Secretary to reconsider the exercise of his discretion in allowing extradition proceedings to continue' (Fox 1999: 690). However, the Home Secretary rejected this plea, the case went back to three further court hearings, and Pinochet was kept under arrest until March 2000, when he was freed because a panel of medical experts reported that the 84-year-old man was mentally unfit to stand trial.

This case can be considered both in itself and in terms of its wider implications about international justice. In itself, it is a prime example of what games theorists call a negative-sum game. Relations between Chile and Britain were damaged; the Spanish government was embarrassed; the reputation of the English judicial system was tarnished; British taxpayers had to pay the substantial costs involved; and nobody benefited directly apart from the British lawyers who made a small fortune by arguing on both sides of the case.

In terms of wider issues, the case has established a precedent for international action to enforce the Convention against Torture. After the Law

Lords had made their final decision, spokespersons for the Swiss, French and Belgian governments all indicated that Pinochet could be tried in their own courts for authorizing torture. However, in terms of procedure the Pinochet precedent is entirely unhelpful. If it were followed, then any of several thousand high court judges in 192 states would be entitled to apply for the extradition of some suspected citizen of the other 191 states from any of the remaining 190 that the suspect happened to be visiting. This would be so chaotic and absurd that national courts may be expected to use the establishment of the ICC as a reason for rejecting any such application.

The ICC now has an official prosecutor, a Canadian lawyer appointed by the UN, and early in 2006 it issued its first indictments. These are of five leaders of a particularly brutal gang called the Lord's Resistance Army, operating in the extreme north of Uganda. There is little doubt of their guilt, but considerable doubt about whether the Ugandan authorities will be able to arrest them and some doubt about whether they would hand them over to the ICC if they do. The UN Security Council has given the prosecutor the names of 51 Sudanese whom it suspects of rape and murder in the Darfur region, but this has not been followed up. The creation of the ICC is clearly a move towards the globalization of justice, but it remains to be seen how effective it will be.

TRANSNATIONAL MILITARY INCURSIONS AND THE CASE OF KOSOVO

It is generally accepted that the principles of the modern state system of international relations date from the 1648 Treaty of Westphalia. This ended the Thirty Years War, the worst and last of the religious and dynastic conflicts that had ravaged much of Europe. The main principle established was that each national state should be regarded as legally independent and equal in status, with no right to interfere in the internal affairs of another state. It has been reasonably claimed that this principle gave order to the international system and has prevented the occurrence of numerous wars that might otherwise have been fought.

It is possible to argue that the increased number of transnational incursions made in violation of this principle since 1970 is an example of the move towards globalization. In 1971, for instance, the Indian army crossed the border to help East Bengal (now Bangladesh) to secure independence from Pakistan. In 1978 Vietnam sent troops into Cambodia to get rid of the murderous Khmer Rouge regime. In 1979 Tanzania sent troops into Uganda to depose the tyrannical Idi Amin and force him into exile. In 1983 the Americans invaded Grenada, claiming that its left-wing regime threatened naval security, and in 1989 they invaded Panama, said to be acting as a pipeline for drugs destined for American cities. However, these five incursions had certain similarities that prevented them from having a lasting impact on international opinion or the world order. They were all sudden incursions by one state into the territory of an immediate neighbour; they were all justified (more or less plausibly) as being in the national interest of the invading state; they were all quickly successful; and they achieved their objectives without great loss of life or material damage.

The 1999 war over Kosovo was very different. The territory involved is a landlocked province of no strategic or economic importance, very distant from the United States, which was the chief organizer of the campaign. The conflict was justified by the aggressors not in terms of national interests but in terms of humanitarian objectives; it was embarked upon not suddenly but only after a period of negotiations and threats; it was expensive in terms of lives and material damage; and it was said by some to usher in a new period of world history, in which national sovereignty would be no protection for governments that grossly violated the human rights of their citizens. It is therefore appropriate to outline the history and character of the conflict.

Kosovo is a territory with a tortured history. It was conquered by the Turks in the fourteenth century and remained part of the Ottoman Empire until the second half of the nineteenth century. Its rulers converted the majority of its citizens to the Muslim faith, but the territory nevertheless remained of great historical and symbolic importance to its Christian neighbours in Serbia, partly because Kosovo had been the 'cradle of the medieval Serbian monarchy' (Hagen 1999: 58), partly because it had been the scene of a great historic battle between the Serbs and the Turks, partly because it contains the religious centre and main cathedral of the Serbian branch of the Christian Orthodox Church. In 1912 the Serbs conquered Kosovo, massacred many of its Muslim citizens, and incorporated the territory into Serbia. It remained as a province of Serbia (and therefore part of Yugoslavia when that state was created) until 1941, when the Germans invaded Yugoslavia and Kosovo was transferred to Albania, then an Italian colony. When Mussolini fell in 1943 the German army marched into Albania and Kosovo and 'raised an SS division among the Kosovar Muslims' which carried out murderous attacks on anti-Nazi Serbian groups (Hagen 1999: 60). It follows from this all-too-brief outline that Kosovo has for much of its history been the scene of bitter ethnic and religious conflict and that there has never been a Kosovar nation.

Ethnic conflict was largely suppressed from 1948 to 1968 under Tito's government, but in 1968 violent demonstrations by Albanian-speaking and largely Muslim groups persuaded Tito to grant the province a measure of political and cultural autonomy. This continued until 1989, when Tito's successor, Slobodan Milosevic, centralized power in Belgrade and filled most administrative positions in Kosovo with members of its ethnic Serb minority. This led in turn to demands from the Albanian-speaking majority for Kosovar independence, at first peaceful but later, by 1997, led by an armed resistance movement called the Kosovo Liberation Army (KLA). The KLA, easily acquiring arms from neighbouring Albania, waged a violent campaign to end Serbian control of Kosovo much as the IRA was fighting to end British control of Northern Ireland and the ETA (the militant wing of the Basque independence movement) was fighting to end Spanish control of the Basque region in northern Spain. The KLA was therefore classified by the CIA as a terrorist movement.

By the summer of 1998 the Yugoslav army was deployed in Kosovo to suppress the KLA and the US administration was warning the Yugoslav government to use less brutal ways of doing this. The warnings had no effect and in the coming months the Americans were joined by British and French governments in expressing growing concern about attacks on Kosovar civilians and the destruction of their homes. NATO was involved as an organization and in early February 1999 a conference convened in Rambouillet (France) gave Milosevic an ultimatum (with an early deadline) to the effect that he must withdraw his army from Kosovo or face NATO military intervention. The deadline was ignored, as were subsequent deadlines, so that the NATO leaders painted themselves into a corner, leaving themselves no choice but to carry out their threats or make NATO a laughing-stock. In late March the bombardment started, the product of western miscalculations and a clear breach of international law.

Now, many governments have employed 'gunboat diplomacy', being a small threat of violence (by naval or other forces) made to secure a modest concession. James Cable's careful analysis of 211 examples of this tactic between 1919 and 1979 showed that it can be successful if, but only if, the small threat is backed up by a larger threat (Cable 1981). A gunboat in an estuary is likely to secure the wanted concession only if the threatened government knows that a larger fleet of warships offshore will enforce much more painful concessions if the first threat is defied. In the case of Kosovo the larger threat could only be that of a land invasion, but Madeline Albright (US Secretary of State) promptly removed that by declaring that US troops would in no circumstances be used in a land war. This blunder ensured that the bombardment would have to be prolonged if it were to succeed. It also emboldened the Yugoslav army to do exactly what NATO leaders had hoped to prevent, namely to engage in a campaign of 'ethnic cleansing' that forced most ethnic Albanians to take refuge in the mountains or over the border into Macedonia or Albania. It is estimated that about 500,000 took to the mountains and 800,000 went over the border.

The concept of ethnic cleansing requires a word of explanation. It is a campaign by the ethnic majority in a given territory to drive the members of an ethnic minority from their homes and land in order to secure something approaching ethnic homogeneity in the territory. It is quite different from genocide, which is a campaign of mass murder undertaken to eliminate a minority, whether to 'purify the race', as the Nazis tried to justify the massacre of 6 million Jews and Gypsies, or to ensure tribal domination, which was the Hutu motive in murdering over half a million Tutsis in Rwanda. At one stage President Clinton attempted to justify the bombardment of Yugoslavia under international law by declaring that the Yugoslavs were guilty of genocide in Kosovo, with 100,000 ethnic Albanians already buried in mass graves, but this statement revealed conceptual misunderstanding as well as being statistically inaccurate. When UN inspectors examined the graves it was found that they contained only a handful of bodies, and by the end of 1999 it was clear that the total number of deaths in Kosovo was under 10,000, some of them caused by the KLA or NATO. This is horrific enough, but it is nothing like genocide.

A feature of the bombardment was that, to avoid the possibility of NATO casualties, the bombers flew above the level of anti-aircraft missiles, namely above 15,000 feet, from which height it was impossible for them to hit small moving targets such as Yugoslav armoured vehicles. Inevitably, many civilians were killed. As attacks on Kosovo were not helping the people they were intended to help, the bombardment increasingly concentrated on Belgrade and other Serbian cities, causing great damage. After eleven weeks concern over industrial damage, combined with diplomatic pressure from Moscow, persuaded Milosevic to accept a compromise peace whereby he agreed to withdraw the Yugoslav army from Kosovo and to offer no opposition to its replacement by NATO troops, but there was no agreement about the political future of the province. *The Economist* greeted this with the headline 'Messy war, messy peace' and concluded that the whole Kosovo campaign had 'turned into a disaster' (*Economist*, 12 June 1999: 15–16).

When NATO troops took control of Kosovo, they soon faced several problems. One was their inability to prevent some of the returning Kosovar Albanians from wreaking revenge on the Serbian minority in the province (about 10 per cent of the population) by murder and their own form of ethnic cleansing. By January 2000 three-quarters of the Kosovar Serbs had fled out of the province to escape these reprisals. Another problem was the absence of an effective civilian administrative apparatus, as most of the senior police, judges and civil servants had been Serbs. A third was a shortage of financial help to rebuild the province, and in December 1999 the new NATO Secretary-General, Lord Robertson, said that without substantial aid the allies look like 'losing the peace'.

Beyond all these problems there was a basic contradiction in NATO policy that has been well articulated by Michael Mandelbaum. As he points out, the refusal of the western allies to support independence for Kosovo means, in effect, that the alliance had 'intervened in a civil war and defeated one side, but embraced the position of the party it had defeated on the issue over which the war had been fought. This made the war, as a deliberate act of policy, a perfect failure' (Mandelbaum 1999: 5).

If the Kosovo affair was in itself misconceived and bungled, is it likely, nevertheless, to be the first of a series of forceful transnational actions by some states to protect the human rights of minorities in other states? The questions that this possibility raises have been addressed in a short but considered article by Kofi Annan. He declared that the conflict in Kosovo

> has cast in stark relief the dilemma of so-called 'humanitarian inter-vention'. On the one hand, is it legitimate for a regional organization to use force without a UN mandate? On the other, is it permissible to let gross and systematic violations of human rights . . . continue unchecked? The inability of the international community to reconcile these two com-pelling interests in the case of Kosovo can be viewed only as a tragedy.
>
> (*Economist*, 18 September 1999: 49)

Considering prospects for the twenty-first century, Annan gave a cau-tious welcome to the use of international force to prevent humanitarian disasters, but only on condition that such measures should be universal in their application, should receive the approval of the UN Security Council and should be accompanied by a commitment to preserve peace in the affected region after the end of fighting. He noted that national attitudes towards the definition of national interests would have to change if these conditions were to be met, but did not venture any prediction about when or whether such a remarkable change might come about (*Economist*, 18 September 1999: 50).

Since then, in September 2005, the UN has agreed in principle that state governments have 'a duty to protect' their citizens, and that a clear failure to carry out that duty may justify international intervention. There is one case that qualifies under this new provision, namely the gross violation of human rights in the western Sudanese region of Darfur. This has led to the dis-placement of over 3 million people from their homes to live in desperate conditions in tented refugee camps, to deaths estimated to be over 300,000, and to the flight of tens of thousands of refugees over the border into Chad. The African Union has sent about 7,000 peacekeeping troops to the region, but they are insufficient in number and lack the money, transport facilities and supplies to make much difference to the situation. Kofi Annan has called for a UN peacekeeping force of 14,000 or more to go to Darfur, but the Sudanese government has refused entry to a UN military assessment mission and there is little that the UN can do in face of opposition from the legal government of the area.

GLOBAL COMMUNICATIONS AND CULTURE

It is obvious that since the 1950s there has been a vast increase in the volume of international communications, by radio, satellite television, cheap air travel, telephone calls made inexpensive by fibre-optic cables, mobile phones, email and the Internet. There are questions about how far this development has produced a global culture and how far it has changed the conduct of politics.

One important unifying development has been a reduction in the number of languages commonly used and, beyond that, the increased spread of knowledge of English. Linguistic concentration has been a long-term process resulting from industrialization and mass migrations, and it has been greatly hastened by modern communications. Jean Laponce estimated in 1987 that only 69 of the 2,000 or so languages thought to exist were spoken by more than 4 million people (Laponce 1987: 67–8) and that many of the others were spoken by only a handful. For instance, only 3 of the 53 Indian languages listed for Canada were actually spoken by more than 5,000 people (Laponce 1987: 58), and a similar situation exists in Australia. Moreover, in many ex-colonial territories English or French is still the dominant language among political and social elites: in India and Pakistan, for instance, which have local languages spoken by many millions, English remains the dominant language at cabinet meetings and in the civil service (see Laponce 1987: 204–7). In addition to these long-term developments, the exploding use of satellite television and the Internet has further spread an understanding of English. The market for international news services carried by satellite television is dominated by CNN, Sky News and the BBC, all of them broadcasting entirely or mainly in English, while the multilingual Euronews has a much smaller audience (see Waters 1995: 149–50).

The answer to the question of whether these developments in communication and language have contributed to the emergence of a global culture depends on the perspective and timescale of the observer. Given a western perspective and a short timescale, say of the past century, these positive factors may be supplemented by a marked reduction in differences of lifestyle caused by recent economic developments. In the poorer agricultural areas of the world, the move from subsistence farming to cash crops has drawn millions into the market economy, their welfare depending somewhat upon commodity trading in London, New York and Tokyo. In newly industrializing areas the growth of branch plants of large American, Japanese and European firms has led to the development of mass production techniques in textiles and electronic goods. In developed industrial societies, rising standards of living have led to some homogenization of consumer demands and fashions. All of these developments have been said to be indications of a globalization of culture on western, and particularly American, lines.

If we turn from economics to values and beliefs, however, the picture is rather different. In the first place, the capacity of the United States to lead the world in social values has been somewhat undermined by an increasing clash of attitudes in American intellectual circles. In the 1940s, 1950s and 1960s a great many American universities offered survey courses to undergraduates on Western Civilization, which were unifying in their message. However, in the 1970s and since, these courses were challenged as Eurocentric, male-dominated and even racist in character, so that they have increasingly been replaced by courses in Black Studies and Women's Studies.

Post-modern theorists have challenged the whole idea that literary critics can identify the great works of western literature and provide criteria by which new writing can be assessed. This kind of intellectual scepticism has even spread to discussions of science and technology. J. W. Grove has said that 'postmodern scholars now feel secure enough to patronize scientists for their absurd belief in objectivity, truth and other holdovers from the Enlightenment' (Grove 1999: 384). Radical feminists have argued that science is the product of a male-dominated society. The American philosopher Sandra Harding, for example, has described modern science as 'Eurocentric, androcentric, racist and imperialist and inadequately linked to projects for advancing democracy' (quoted in Grove 1999: 387).

Another development that undermines the case for the existence of a global culture is the growth of religious sects and extremist groups since the early 1990s. Strange sects in North America and East Africa have gone in for mass suicides and mass murder. A sect in Japan has released poison gas in the Tokyo subway system. Australian and other Christian missionaries in India have been harassed and threatened by Hindu extremists. The growth of Ultra-Orthodox Jewish groups in Israel has led to rising political tension between them and the liberal majority. Riots between Muslim extremists and Christians in parts of Indonesia killed thousands of people in the winter of 1999/2000 and caused the destruction of many churches and mosques. And all this is in addition to the examples of ethnic conflict outlined in Chapter 3.

A third, and politically most important factor, is the growth of Islamic fundamentalism and the emergence of a new kind of terrorism that derives part of its motivation from this. Terrorism of all kinds has become so much the focus of world news and attention since 2001 that an entirely new chapter on the subject has been added to this edition. One of the intellectual consequences of this development is that it forces us to consider the whole question of cultural beliefs and assumptions from a global rather than a western perspective and with a timescale that encompasses a millennium rather than merely a century.

If we do this it immediately becomes obvious that the people of this planet have long been divided between four major cultures or civilizations plus others that are either less clearly defined or of less worldwide importance. The four major cultures or civilizations are the Chinese, the Indian, the Islamic and the European. The others include the Buddhist and the Japanese.

The Buddhist faith is quite distinctive and was once widespread in eastern Asia, but has declined in relative influence except in Thailand, Cambodia and Sri Lanka. Japanese culture was subject to both Chinese and Buddhist influences but has long been distinctive, though its history has been rather a mystery to the outside world until quite recently and the culture has not spread beyond the islands of Japan. The cultures of tropical Africa, though permeated by Islam in the north and by European influences in former colonies, are in themselves difficult about which to generalize or to classify. There are of course questions about the identity of the four major civilizations. Should the first be called Chinese or Confucian, to include the societies of Vietnam, Singapore and Korea and people of Chinese ethnic origin in other states? A fair case can be made for either alternative, but I prefer the former because the differing political and economic systems of the various countries have made a difference to the values and behaviour of their ethnic Chinese communities. Some aspects remain fairly constant, such as the importance of the extended family and the acceptance of a familial duty to support elderly relatives. But any migrant or visiting western business executive will find customs among the Chinese of Singapore much less of a cultural shock than customs in mainland China. Western executives doing business in China may find it particularly difficult to adjust to the customs of exchanging gifts before reaching a deal and using a paid intermediary when approaching public officials. Such customs raise questions of business ethics and possibly even legal allegations of corrupt practices in the homeland of the executive's head office.

A similar question may be asked about whether Indian culture should be called Hindu, to include the large expatriate communities in Trinidad, Britain, Fiji and elsewhere. I would again prefer the geographical term to the religious. One of the problems of westerners doing business in India is of coping with the caste system that plays such a large part in Indian society, but is not of much relevance among overseas communities of Indian ethnicity. Social values among international migrants tend to be modified over the generations, as Neil Bissoondath (cited in Chapter 3) has insisted.

Three questions may be raised about the name I have given to the fourth major culture listed above. One is whether the title should be Christian rather than European, which I would reject as outdated in view of the striking decline in the Christian faith in much of contemporary Europe. Another is whether American society is properly included under the title of European, which may seem strange to Americans because so much of their education stresses their history as a society that contrasts to the class-bound societies of Europe. But, as Lewis (1995) has suggested, to the rest of the world American civilization is seen as essentially European in character and this is undoubtedly correct. A third question is whether Latin America should be bracketed with North America in this classification. It is certainly possible to argue that Latin America is culturally distinct from the United

States, but so much of Latin American culture has been influenced by Spanish and Portuguese colonists that in a broad classification such as the current one I regard the title of European as reasonably appropriate.

That Islamic culture is distinct is quite clear. The renewed western interest in it in the past few years owes a lot to the growth of global terrorism, but this is unfortunate and potentially misleading, not only because (as will be shown in Chapter 5) terrorist activities have been carried out over the centuries by many groups from other cultures but also because it may detract from the great contributions that Muslim architects and scholars have made to the world. It was, after all, Islamic mathematicians of the tenth century (when Europe was in the Dark Ages) who developed trigonometry and algebra (an Arabic word).

For any discussion of global culture, a global perspective is needed, and this suggests that much recent speculation is too narrowly focused.

GLOBAL COMMUNICATIONS AND POLITICAL ACTION

In the arena of global communication there have been important developments, of which the most interesting are the impact of television news programmes on public attitudes to foreign policy and the impact of email and Internet usage on transnational pressure groups.

The problem about television news is that it depends on visual images, and bad news is more visually interesting than good news. An ever-increasing proportion of television news is devoted to disasters like earthquakes, floods, terrorist bombings, famine in Somalia, civil wars in Africa, or destroyed villages in the Balkans. This leads to public demands for transnational intervention, based on moral feelings rather than on assessments of national interest. This may be desirable in humanistic terms but, as Joseph Nye has pointed out, quick responses urging intervention may change to dismay if casualties among troops of the viewers' own country are subsequently depicted (see Nye 1999: 32). This was dramatically emphasized in the case of the UN mission to relieve the famine in Somalia. American public support for this evaporated overnight when US television showed the bodies of American soldiers being dragged through the streets by trucks driven by members of local gangs, and the whole mission was quickly terminated. The relatively new American practice of sending the bodies of US troops killed in action back to their homeland, where their arrival is also shown on television, has made this kind of reaction more likely. It was a reason for the decision to use only high-level bombing or guided missiles in the Kosovo campaign, and it raises the whole question of how far it is realistic for political leaders to press for a new world order in which liberal democracies will use military force to protect human rights in other countries.

The impact of email and Internet usage on the organization and tactics of pressure groups has been truly remarkable. Within national societies it has proved possible to rally more citizens for demonstrations using these cheap and rapid means of communication than was previously feasible, a notable example being the growth of demonstrations devoted to animal welfare and environmental issues in Britain. However, the impact on transnational groups has been much more dramatic, in terms of both their number and their variety. Some of them, like Médecins Sans Frontières, are concerned mainly with the delivery of aid and services and are only tangentially involved in politics, while others, like Amnesty International and the Council of Canadians, are entirely devoted to political campaigns. They are so varied in character that in the 1990s a new collective name was coined for them; they are now usually known as non-governmental organizations (NGOs). In itself, this is an absurdly imprecise term that could logically cover any private concern in the world, from a retail store to a football club. In the current literature about world affairs, whether academic or journalistic, it is just accepted as meaning citizens' organizations that are involved, directly or marginally, with campaigns about issues of public concern. Some more sensible nomenclature will doubtless emerge in due course, but for the time being we have only this ambiguous omnibus label.

The number of NGOs active across national borders has grown at a remarkable pace in the past few years. According to the *Yearbook of International Organizations*, it grew from about 6,000 in 1990 to about 21,000 in 2005. Most of them are concerned with environmental issues, consumer issues and issues that can be broadly described as humanitarian or liberal in character. They tend to be organized by well educated and fairly young people who are adept at using the Internet and talented at handling the mass media. Greenpeace, one of the earliest and most successful of them, is a good example. Its ultimate aim is de-industrialization; in the words of its Executive Director, it regards the modern economy as 'a fire-breathing vampire of petroleum which is slowly cooking our planet' (letter in *The Economist*, 11 December 1999). As this would drastically reduce living standards, it could get little public support in itself, but Greenpeace organizers have shown great skill in taking up other issues, like nuclear testing or ocean pollution, that have attracted large numbers of idealistic supporters. In 1998 Greenpeace shocked business leaders by threatening a worldwide boycott of Shell petroleum that induced that firm to abandon its plan to dispose of a North Sea oil platform by sinking it, which was both legally and scientifically permissible. Other NGOs, or coalitions thereof, have mobilized European opinion against genetically modified foodstuffs and against the export of powdered baby food (deemed less nutritious than mother's milk) to African countries. Hundreds of NGOs in many countries pushed their governments to outlaw landmines, in a successful campaign led by the

Canadian government. This was an interesting case in that the Canadian Department of External Affairs used the Internet to encourage NGOs in other countries to press their governments to act in this way.

To the question of whether the increased international activities of NGOs have undermined the power of national states, the answer must be 'not greatly, so far'. They have certainly embarrassed police forces and magistrates by staging demonstrations involving civil disobedience, but they have had little direct impact on state policies. For example, the much-publicized protests by Greenpeace against the French government for carrying out nuclear tests in the Pacific, against the British government for dumping nuclear waste into the Atlantic, and against the US Navy for carrying nuclear arms into Canadian waters, did not change official policies.

On one very important issue NGOs have successfully defended the sovereignty of national governments. This was the defeat of the proposed Multilateral Agreement on Investment (MAI). The campaign against this was led by the Council of Canadians, alarmed when they found that the proposed agreement contained a clause modelled on a little-publicized but highly significant provision of the 1987 North Atlantic Free Trade Agreement (NAFTA). Under this provision a commercial firm which finds its activities in a foreign country frustrated by government legislation or regulations passed after the signing of the Agreement can sue the government involved for compensation that is not limited to the investments made but can also include compensation for the loss of anticipated profits in future years. Under this provision a firm in California has proposed to sue the government of British Columbia for $15 billion, this sum representing the profits that the firm thinks it might have made if its tentative plan to pipe water from British Columbian reservoirs to the parched areas of southern California had not been frustrated by an Act of the British Columbian legislature forbidding the export of fresh water from the province. When the Council of Canadians publicized the equivalent clause in the MAI by sending it to the other NGOs around the world, the latter successfully put pressure on many of their own governments to turn down the whole proposal.

The future role of NGOs in world politics is hard to predict. They may have more impact on international organizations than directly on national governments. The World Bank regularly consults NGOs regarding its projects. The UN has a fair number of 'accredited' NGOs which advise UN officials on policy. There is a proposal to create a second chamber of the UN General Assembly, possibly to be called the People's Assembly, in which the views of NGOs can be articulated. This may be a pipe-dream, since it is unclear who would decide which of the thousands of NGOs would be represented in it, but some move towards regular international conferences of NGOs is quite likely. How far this should be regarded as an extension of democracy is another question.

CONCLUSIONS

It is clear that the new developments outlined in this chapter have complicated the political world and to some degree challenged the authority of national states. However, as David Held has suggested (Held 1991: 210–12), this change has to be put into historical perspective. In 1950 the world contained 54 recognized states, of which 5 in eastern Europe were so dominated by the Soviet Union that their independence was little more than nominal. By 2000 there were 192 recognized states. It follows that for three-quarters of the existing states the second half of the twentieth century was a period in which national independence dramatically increased. Cracks appeared in the state system in the last years of the century, but it would be an exaggeration to say that the state or the system is in decline.

At the UN each state has one vote. The International Court of Justice can arbitrate between states if requested to do so, but state governments frequently refuse to refer their disputes to it. The member states of the EU have surrendered some of their authority to the collectivity, but only over some fields of action. There is a European passport, but residents qualify for it only by being citizens of one of the member states, and the ways that new residents can acquire citizenship are not uniform. There has long been a commitment for EU states to work towards common policies towards the outside world, but this has not prevented Britain from differing from the majority on the question of sanctions against South Africa under apartheid, Britain and France from taking opposite sides regarding sanctions against Iraq, Germany from having a more friendly relationship with Croatia than have most other members, Italy a more friendly relationship with Libya, Greece a less friendly relationship with Turkey. Each member state has a veto over the admission of new members, and in 1994 Spain used the threat of vetoing the admission of Sweden, Finland and Austria to get fishing regulations changed to allow Spanish fishing boats access to British and Irish waters. Even within the EU, national states and governments retain considerable power.

In the economic field, if we leave aside the EC as unique and lacking global implications, the main development that has actually reduced the authority of states, as distinct from merely having an influence on government policies, is the North American Free Trade Agreement of 1987. For the first time in the modern age, this gives commercial corporations the same legal status as governments. Moreover, although at the time of writing this has yet to be established beyond doubt, the terms of the Agreement appear to give corporations an enforceable advantage over governments in cases of dispute. If provisions modelled on NAFTA were to be extended to the other countries of Central and South America, as was at one time proposed by the Clinton administration, this would involve a partial loss of sovereignty by 19 additional states.

The WTO is in principle different from this, as only national governments and the EC can be parties to disputes dealt with by the organization. The readiness of many governments to act on behalf of sizeable corporations reduces the practical significance of this distinction but does not eliminate it, as is shown by the readiness of the EC to allow some of its firms to pay the cost of defiance of WTO rulings. For this, it helps that EC policy-makers are more insulated from domestic pressures than is the average democratic government.

If the principles enshrined in NAFTA were to be included in a new version of the MAI, and this were to gather much more international support than the original version, the result would be a partial loss of national independence on a global scale. If the world were to move in this direction, it must be asked how this would affect the theory and practice of democracy. The answer can only be discouraging for democrats. As the fiasco in Seattle illustrated, the main political actors in such a world would be not elected politicians but corporation directors, international bureaucrats and the leaders of countless NGOs. In some sense the NGOs may represent the opinions of consumers and informed citizens, but NGO leaders are appointed by a variety of procedures and many of them are, in effect, self-appointed. They may or may not be accountable to their members for their actions and they are certainly not accountable to parliaments or electors. As public accountability is the essence of democracy, the transfer of authority over economic issues from national governments to international institutions appears to involve a democratic loss and no democratic theories have yet been developed to justify it.

The war over Kosovo is a precedent for international action to protect human rights. In pure logic, the arguments used by NATO leaders to justify the bombardment of Belgrade might also be used to justify the bombing of Beijing over the question of Tibet, of Moscow over Chechnya, of Rangoon over the treatment of political dissidents and ethnic minorities, and of an uncertain number of African cities. The arguments could be a prescription for wars that could destroy civilized life on this planet.

In reality political leaders are unlikely to be so negligent about their own national interests. In the summer and early autumn of 1999 no government was willing to take action against Indonesia regarding the gross abuses of human rights that its troops were committing in East Timor. This would have been legally much easier to justify than the Kosovo campaign, because Indonesian sovereignty over East Timor had never been recognized while Yugoslav sovereignty over Kosovo had never been disputed. The reasons for inaction were entirely practical. Indonesia is a large state with a large army and its stability is important to the western powers because they (especially the United States) have enormous investments there. The 'international community' therefore took no action until the Indonesian government gave permission for peacekeeping units to arrive.

It is also relevant that American opinion is divided, at all levels, about the wisdom of embarking on forcible interventions overseas for humanitarian reasons. Peter Rodman, a former State Department and White House official, has pointed out that 'ethnic conflicts are a swamp', far from easy to resolve (Rodman 1999: 51). Joseph Nye, Dean of Harvard's Kennedy School of Government, has said that the United States 'should generally avoid the use of force except in cases where our humanitarian interests are reinforced by the existence of other strong national interests' (Nye 1999: 32). E. N. Luttwak, of the Center for Strategic and International Studies, has said that international intervention to impose cease-fires in local wars is often misguided, as it is apt to give the combatants a respite to recuperate and re-arm, so that the conflict can be resumed with renewed vigour when the peace-keeping forces are withdrawn (Luttwak 1999: 36–44). American voters are apt to withdraw support for a venture that leads to numerous American casualties.

To conclude, exploring the concept of globalization in this chapter has led us into a discussion of diverse developments and a rather confusing debate. At the level of practice, it seems that the world, or at any rate the industrialized part of it, is staggering, partly as a result of economic forces and partly by the intention of politicians, towards more complex political arrangements. The process is hesitant, uncertain and controversial, and it will take decades, if not centuries, to bring about a state of affairs that could be reasonably described as a new world order. In the meantime, we have a more complex political world with an increased and increasing number of actors having meaningful roles in political dramas.

Commenting on this, Michael Keating concluded that 'the state has not faded away, or even retreated', but has lost its uniqueness as the 'arena in which policy differences are negotiated and resolved'. This has poor implications for democracy, for 'it brings into question the whole purpose of politics as a means of reconciling economic needs with social and cultural ones and the nation-state as the institutional forum which not only provides the mechanisms for this but legitimizes the outcomes' (Keating 1996: 39–40). Held posed the question: 'If the efficacy of the system of representative democracy is being strained and eroded in the face of global interconnectedness, what mechanisms could ensure accountability in the new international order?' (Held 1991: 225). He could offer no answer to the question. Ever since the 1950s, political science students have been made acquainted with the 'systems theory' approach to the study of democratic politics (outlined in Chapter 16), whereby pressure groups are said to articulate public interests and values and political parties to aggregate them, so that voters can be presented with more-or-less coherent clusters of policies between which to choose. It is a simplistic model, but not at all worthless, and it illustrates a basic problem, for democrats, of the globalizing developments here discussed. The world has an ever-increasing number of transnational pressure groups that articulate particular interests and ideals, but there is no prospect of transnational political parties to aggregate them, let alone of global elections to legitimize the decisions that emerge.

At a more theoretical level, the years around the turn of the millennium present an extraordinary paradox in the character of world politics. The growth of supranational and international institutions and the moves towards a world system of justice represent a development of the humanistic and rationalistic ideals that characterized the Enlightenment of the eighteenth century and inspired both American and French revolutionary leaders. Simultaneously, the revived incidence of ethnic and religious conflicts represents a rejection of Enlightenment ideals in favour of a much older kind of tribal and religious rivalry. The attempts to reconcile these divergent trends by liberal thinkers and politicians who favour supranational government by bureaucrats and judges for large issues combined with popular government in small ethnic or cultural communities for minor issues involve a further paradox. This is that such a development would involve the gradual destruction of liberalism's greatest achievement in the past two centuries, namely the establishment of democratic systems of government in national states that are virtually all to some extent multi-ethnic.

How, if at all, these paradoxes will be resolved in the future can only be a matter of conjecture. It is not within the capacity of political scientists to make predictions about the long-term future and in the remainder of this book we shall therefore concentrate on problems that are within our capacity, namely the conceptual and theoretical problems involved in the study of democratic politics within the modern national state.

Chapter 5

Global terrorism

Ever since the murderous attack on the World Trade Center in New York on 11 September 2001 (henceforth simply '9/11'), the mass media in western Europe and North America have featured endless reports and articles about examples and threats of world terrorism. The subsequent attacks on a nightclub in Bali, commuter trains in Madrid, a school in Russia, and the London transport system have kept the pot boiling, and the reports and debates have involved the use of concepts that, while far from new in themselves, are relatively new in western political commentary. The first of these is the concept of terrorism itself.

Journalists and politicians have professional skills that are quite different from those of academic historians or political scientists. It is therefore not surprising that some elementary blunders have been made when using the concept of terrorism, such as to imply that it is a new activity, whereas in fact it is centuries old; that it is always committed by revolutionaries, whereas it has been used as a tactic by all kinds of groups, including state agencies like the SS in Nazi Germany or the KGB in the Soviet Union; or that it is a tactic used mainly by Muslims, whereas since 1990 (to go no further back) it has also been used by IRA bombers who were Christians and by the Tamil Tigers of Sri Lanka who are overwhelmingly Hindu. The most confusing mistake, however, is to mix up the method used and the objectives of the group using it, as when it is claimed that some groups who use suicide bombers are not terrorist groups but national liberation movements or freedom fighters.

As political scientists interested in this kind of activity have long understood, it makes much better sense to keep the nature of the tactic quite distinct from the objectives of those employing it. Most civilized people regard terrorism as morally repugnant, but this is (or should be) simply because it involves the infliction of grievous harm on innocent and defenceless people, irrespective of whether the observer happens to approve or disapprove of the policy objectives of the terrorists. The key feature of terrorism as a political tactic, as distinct from political assassinations or guerrilla warfare, is that it is directed at an audience rather than at the victims themselves. It should be regarded as a form of public theatre, its nature neatly summarized by the Chinese aphorism, 'Kill one, frighten ten thousand'. It can be defined as the infliction of grievous harm on one or more members of an identifiable group or category of people with the aim of frightening other members of that group or category into changing their intended behaviour.

The form of terrorism that has attracted most public attention since 2001 is that used by al-Qaeda and related Islamic groups against western societies, and to understand this it is necessary to know a little about Islamic history and Islamic concepts, such as *jihad*. Before moving to this, however, it will be helpful to consider what can be learned from history about the various types of terrorism that have been employed over the years and the reasons why some of them have been partially or entirely successful in achieving their objectives while others have been completely unsuccessful.

An essential characteristic of terrorism, unlike other forms of political violence, is that it always involves three parties rather than just two. The parties are the terrorists, the victims and the target group among the audience. To assess the consequences of terrorist attacks, it is usually more rewarding to focus on the probable or actual behaviour of the target groups than to focus on the character of the individual terrorists or the victims. While some terrorists have remained anonymous, suicidal ones have not, and numerous studies of them have shown that the average suicide bomber is a little better educated and at least as well-off as the average member of his or her society (see Pape 2005: 199–216). There is no evidence to support the hypothesis that they are driven to their actions by ignorance or mental incapacity or extreme poverty. They simply have a cause for which they are willing to lay down their lives.

As for the victims, the fact that there is normally a degree of randomness in their selection renders a focus on them somewhat unhelpful. It is more productive to consider the extent to which members of the target group are likely to yield to the threats of the terrorists, and for this purpose a typology of terrorism is necessary.

FIVE TYPES OF TERRORISM

One of the differences between the natural sciences and the social sciences is that the categories used in the former normally resemble watertight compartments, whereas in the latter there are apt to be marginal cases and confusing examples. This is certainly true of the categories identified below. The Irish Republican movement, as a possibly extreme example, is a movement that from 1919 onwards has sometimes engaged in guerrilla warfare, sometimes contested democratic elections, and sometimes resorted to terrorist tactics; and when it has used terrorist tactics they have sometimes fallen into the second, sometimes the third, and sometimes the fourth of the following categories. While this illustrates the complexity of political activity, making generalization and prediction notoriously difficult, I nevertheless believe that the following typology can be of considerable assistance in the task of explanation and understanding.

- repressive terrorism
- small-group terrorism
- domestic revolutionary terrorism
- international terrorism
- millenarian terrorism.

Repressive terrorism

Repressive terrorism is the use of terrorist tactics by a government agency to frighten dissidents into refraining from activities likely to weaken the authority of the groups in power. It has been used from time to time by dictatorial governments throughout recorded history.

One form of repressive terrorism has been the use of spectacular types of public execution. The most obvious example has been the use of the guillotine to kill people suspected of conspiracy against the revolutionaries w ho had seized power in France in 1789. In 1793–4, and to a lesser degree up until 1797, the French ruling group had something like 20,000 people put to death in this way, and the whole period has been called 'the Terror' by historians (see Woodward 1934: 54–74). However, this was by no means the earliest example. In the Spanish Inquisition thousands of Roman Catholics suspected of heresy were burned at the stake. In Elizabethan England a number of prominent Roman Catholics known to have organized secret masses were hanged, drawn and quartered, a particularly dramatic punishment for the audience. An ongoing example in some Islamic societies is the punishment of death by stoning imposed by Sharia courts on married or divorced women found guilty of adultery.

Another form of repressive terrorism is imprisonment without trial, normally for life, used against dissidents identified by secret police. As already noted, the activities of the SS and the KGB are the most obvious examples of this. Statistics suggest that the SS was more effective than the KGB, because only a few thousand non-Jewish German dissidents (many of them Protestant clergy) were sent to concentration camps whereas between 10 million and 20 million people were sent to Siberia. However, there are several other reasons for this difference and a clearer example may be the role of the secret police in eastern European countries between 1948 and 1989 in preventing the millions of citizens who detested the communist regimes that had been imposed on them from revolting against their rulers.

While repressive repression must be recognized as such, it is of limited value to scholars because it is impossible to determine how many members of the target groups are actually persuaded to modify their intended behaviour. Who can tell how many married or divorced women in Islamic societies are dissuaded from adulterous relationships by fear of the drastic punishment that these might incur, as distinct from the number who engage in adultery in spite of the possible punishments?

Small-group terrorism

Small-group terrorism takes place when terrorist tactics are aimed at small target groups, and the reason why it is more likely to achieve its objectives than other types of terrorism is quite simple. Most people, when considering alternative forms of behaviour, make rough-and-ready estimates of the costs or benefits they can expect from pursuing one option or the other. If terrorists make actual or implied threats to members of a target group, their threats are likely to have more impact on a small group than on a large group. The smaller the group, the more likely its members are to feel that they might be the next victims.

This logic is supported by historical experience. A clear example is the success of the Mafia in maintaining a rather dominant influence on Sicilian society for over a hundred years. Sicilian towns and villages have close-knit communities in which it is difficult for behaviour to remain secret. People who know that any cooperation with the police is likely to be punished by drastic reprisals against themselves or their families are apt to keep silent when facing police questioning. Magistrates who know that sending a member of the Mafia to prison may endanger their own lives or those of their families are apt to be lenient in their judgments.

Another example is the vulnerability of international aid groups in strife-ridden areas. When the leader of Care Canada's operations in Iraq was abducted in 2004, the organization agreed to terminate its activities in that country in an attempt to save her life. Aid groups in the extreme north of Uganda curtailed their operations in 2005 in response to the murder of six of their staff by the Lord's Resistance Army, whose character has been indicated in Chapter 4.

Yet another example was the largely successful efforts of the IRA to discourage members of the Roman Catholic minority in Northern Ireland from joining the Royal Ulster Constabulary (RUC). When this police force was established in 1921 it was determined by the British Parliament that its composition should, as far as possible, mirror the composition of the population in religious terms, meaning that about 35 per cent of the police should be Catholic and the rest Protestant. The Irish Republicans, seeking to discredit the RUC as a symbol of British rule and Protestant dominance, prevented this target from ever being reached, not only by propaganda but also by threats of violence against Catholics who ignored the propaganda, backed up from time to time by assassination of Catholic police recruits. By the time of the peace settlement of 1998, less than 10 per cent of the police were Catholics (English 2003: 324). (The RUC became the Police Service of Northern Ireland (PSNI) in 2001.)

Domestic revolutionary terrorism

In contrast, domestic revolutionary terrorism has hardly ever been successful. Revolutions (as distinct from mere *coups d'état*) have been caused by defeat in war, by military takeovers, and occasionally by prolonged mass demonstrations, as in several eastern European states since 1989. But the use of terrorist tactics by revolutionary groups has normally done nothing to advance their causes. Attacks on prominent industrialists and bankers, intended to undermine the capitalist system, have failed because the target groups are too large for their numerous members to be frightened. Attacks on the government itself, such as by the murder of politicians, judges or senior administrators, have failed because the perceived cost to ruling groups of yielding to terrorist demands is very much higher than the cost of suppressing the terrorist groups.

The latter costs may be far from negligible, as they require a readiness to accept further instances of death and destruction and may also involve restrictions of civil liberties apt to alienate sections of the population and attract international criticism. Nevertheless, governing authorities normally feel that they have a public duty to uphold the system while successful politicians normally enjoy the power and privileges of office. The combination of these two factors ensures that revolutionary terrorism within an established state normally fails.

There is no need for a whole catalogue of domestic revolutionary groups that have used terrorist tactics, but it may be helpful to itemize some that have attracted world attention since the late 1960s. Four such groups have had ideological motives of a neo-Marxist kind. These have been the Red Brigades of Italy, active from 1970 to 1985; the Red Army Faction of West Germany, active from 1968 to 1976; the Tupamaros of Uruguay, active from 1963 to 1972; and the Shining Path of Peru, active from 1983 to 2004. Minority nationalist movements using terrorist tactics have included the Basque nationalists of Spain, active from 1958 to 2002; the Sikh nationalists of India, active from 1983 to 1995; and the Tamil nationalists of Sri Lanka, pursuing violent measures from 1982 to 2002. All these groups failed.

The most dramatic consequences of these campaigns were those in India. In 1984 leading Sikh nationalists sought to evade arrest by congregating in the cluster of buildings known as the Golden Temple of Amritsar, the most sacred of Sikh shrines. They underestimated the determination of Indira Gandhi, the Indian Prime Minister, who ordered the army to attack the temple, in which over 400 Sikhs perished. In revenge for this attack, Gandhi herself was assassinated by two Sikh bodyguards, whom she had appointed as a gesture of multiculturalism, while an Air India jet was destroyed by a bomb planted by Sikh nationalists in Canada, killing over 300 passengers and crew. In all, about 18,000 deaths resulted from this nationalist campaign. Even this large number has been exceeded in Sri Lanka, where the Tamil campaign for independence had led to 64,000 deaths by the end of 2005, partly by terrorism and partly by guerrilla warfare and its suppression. But neither the Indian nor the Sri Lankan government has yielded to the nationalists.

These events were clearly tragic, but in fact all terrorist campaigns by domestic revolutionaries have to be regarded as tragic, because they never achieve their objectives and their cost is thousands of deaths, injuries and wasted lives. It is not a question of weighing the costs against the benefits, because there are no benefits. Terrorism may be not only useless and costly but actually counter-productive, as was the case in Uruguay where the perceived need to crush the Tupamaros led to the replacement of South America's most democratic regime by right-wing dictatorship.

International terrorism

International terrorism, defined as terrorism with the object of changing a state's foreign policy, is another story altogether. It is much more likely to be successful, simply because modifying foreign policy is much less costly to a government than yielding to the demands of domestic revolutionaries. There are familiar ways to save face while retreating. A government faced with an awkward kind of international terrorism can get itself off the hook by announcing that it is withdrawing its troops to save lives, that it has decided to give diplomacy another chance, that it is sending a prominent politician to act as an intermediary, or that it is referring the issue to the United Nations.

There are numerous examples of success for international terrorists. In 1954 the British government decided to withdraw the 60,000 troops it had in the Suez Canal Zone, not because they were defeated in conflict but in response to a series of painful attacks by Egyptian nationalists on some of the 20,000 civilians accompanying the troops. In 1967 the British decided to abandon Aden in the face of terrorist attacks. In 1983 Hezbollah units in Lebanon launched simultaneous attacks on American and French barracks by suicide bombers, killing 241 US marines and 58 French troops who had been sent there to prevent Lebanon falling into a state of complete civil war. Very quickly, the US and French governments decided to abandon their missions there. In 2004 a well-timed attack on five commuter trains in Madrid by al-Qaeda operatives, coming near the end of an election campaign, killed over 200 passengers. This induced tens of thousands of citizens to march through the streets with their hands up, indicating that they wanted Spain to yield to the demand that Spanish troops should be withdrawn from coalition forces fighting in Iraq. The left-wing opposition party won the election and promptly announced that it would do just that.

It should not be thought that international terrorism always achieves its objectives. In Malaya the British army fought for eight years (1948–56) to defeat a campaign by Chinese communist terrorists to plunge the colony into chaos. The rubber plantations had made Malaya one of the most valuable territories in the British Empire, and although decolonization was the overall policy the British were determined that the colony would be in good shape when they handed it over to a Malay government, which they did in 1957. Equally, the British did not yield to a long campaign by Greek nationalists in Cyprus, from 1957 to 1974, who wanted to unite Cyprus with Greece, largely because of the danger that this might lead to warfare between Greece and Turkey. The difference between these two examples and that of Aden is that in these cases the costs of yielding to the terrorists would have been great whereas in Aden the cost was small, its earlier importance as a coaling station for the Royal Navy being no longer significant.

The general point is that the success or failure of terrorist tactics depends on more-or-less rational assessments by the target groups of the costs or benefits of alternative responses. Domestic revolutionary terrorism invariably fails because the costs of yielding to it are too great to be acceptable, but international terrorism may or may not bring success, depending on particular circumstances that vary from one case to another.

Millenarian terrorism

Millenarian terrorism is a strange phenomenon. In the later Middle Ages the term 'millenarian' was used to characterize the belief of certain religious groups in northern Europe that at some time in the future Jesus Christ would return to earth to make a final judgment, taking the pure and the poor to spend a millennium in paradise while leaving the corrupt and sinful to a less happy fate. In more recent times the adjective may be used to characterize terrorists willing to commit murder and risk their own lives in pursuit of a vision that is regarded as irrational and unattainable by those who do not share it. It is not always easy to distinguish this kind of behaviour from violence that is no more than a gesture of hatred and despair, best called nihilistic after the nihilists of Tsarist Russia.

A more recent case that may qualify as millenarian is the 1995 action of a Japanese religious group called Aum Shinrikyo, which claimed to have 50,000 adherents worldwide, in releasing sarin gas into Tokyo subway trains in the morning rush hour. This injured over 5,000 passengers, apparently in the hope of precipitating some kind of apocalypse. A case that was no more than nihilistic was the behaviour of the so-called Unabomber, a professional mathematician who so detested American industrialism that he posted a series of home-made letter bombs to prominent industrialists. Another example is that of a white supremacist who killed 168 people in Oklahoma City in 1994 by bombing a federal office building, for no logical reason.

The activities of al-Qaeda should probably be classified as millenarian, but to understand them requires some knowledge, however sketchy, of Islamic history and beliefs.

SOME ASPECTS OF ISLAMIC HISTORY

The Islamic religion, founded in the seventh century by Muhammad, resembles Christianity in that it is proselytizing, with no assumption that it is suitable only for a particular ethnic group or territory. However, whereas Christian churches send out missionaries with the hope of making individual conversions, Muslims have a collective duty to spread the faith, either by individual conversions or by conquest of a territory and the imposition of Islamic law on the inhabitants. Whereas Jesus was a pacifist, Muhammad was a man of action, who turned his early band of disciples into warriors and led them to the conquest of both Medina and Mecca.

From this base in the Arabian peninsulas the prophet's followers spread the message with remarkable speed, so that within a hundred years of his death in 632 CE they had established Islam as the dominant religion in much of the known world, ranging from the Atlantic coast of Portugal in the west to the borders of China in the east. They did not normally ill treat the conquered peoples physically, but they imposed Islamic rules of behaviour on their societies, enforced by Sharia courts in which the procedure is biased to favour the faithful. If there is a conflict of evidence between witnesses, as between landlord and tenant or employer and worker or husband and wife, judges in Sharia courts are bound by law to accept the word of Muslims as against that of infidels, of men against women, of Muslim men who have made the pilgrimage to Mecca as against those who have not. Governed in this way, this Islamic Empire survived for seven centuries, longer than either the Roman Empire or the British Empire, until the fateful year of 1492 when the Muslims were driven from the Emirate of Granada, their last toehold on the Iberian peninsula.

The concept that is relevant to this expansion is *jihad*, an Arabic word meaning striving or struggle, and the derivative term *jihardist*, meaning a faithful Muslim who strives to uphold or extend the faith. This is occasionally equated with the Christian concepts of crusade and crusader, but there are several differences between them. One is that the duty of pursuing *jihad* has a much wider range of practical meanings. It can mean the attempt to keep Muslims faithful to their prescribed duties, such as to pray five times a day and avoid alcohol, and/or to defend Islamic territories against invasion by infidels, and/or to participate in a campaign to extend the area of Islamic dominance. Crusades, on the other hand, have been authorized only for the second of these objectives, to recover territories that had been lost to the true religion. Another difference is that *jihad* is a permanent collective duty for Muslims, whereas the first crusade was authorized by the Pope in 1095, to recapture Jerusalem and surrounding areas, and the last to be given papal blessing was the Spanish Armada of 1588, stated to be an 'expedition of the Cross' to bring an end to the Reformation in England and reconvert the English to Roman Catholicism. Of course, the term is sometimes used loosely, as when western politicians talk of a 'crusade against AIDS' (see Cooper 2004: 111), but this confusion need not detain us.

While the average contemporary Muslim has little or no wish to be a jihadist, this concept and history mean a great deal to Muslim political and religious leaders. A very sad illustration of their significance occurred in 1947. In that year a special committee of the United Nations, after much study and consultation, proposed a partition of Palestine into Jewish and Arab territories. The proposal was accepted by Jewish leaders but opposed by Arabs. There followed a long discussion in London between David Horowitz, an official of the Jewish Agency, and Abdul Azzam Pasha, an Egyptian who was Secretary-General of the Arab League. In search of a possible compromise, Horowitz proposed a plan for security guarantees and the joint economic development of the area. In response Azzam Pasha, while conceding that the plan was rational and logical, said that

> the fate of nations [is] not decided by rational logic. . . . We shall try to defeat you. I am not sure we will succeed, but we will try. We were able to drive out the Crusaders, but on the other hand we lost Spain and Persia. It may be that we shall lose Palestine. But it is too late for peaceful solutions.
>
> (Horowitz 1953: 233)

In this way Azzam Pasha made it crystal clear that he and his colleagues were motivated not by rational calculations but by feelings of religious compulsion. As faithful Muslims, they felt bound to resist the establishment of a Jewish state in what they regarded as Islamic territory. There followed four Arab–Israeli wars (in 1948, 1956, 1967 and 1973), all largely or completely lost by the Arabs, which were tragic not only because of the thousands of casualties on both sides but also because the violent conflict has been totally dysfunctional for the overwhelming majority of Palestinian Arabs. For almost sixty years, they have been markedly worse off than they would have been if their leaders had felt able to accept the UN plan for partition.

After the four wars, both Egypt and Jordan were willing to abandon armed struggle and they gave diplomatic recognition to Israel in 1979. However, Syria did not follow suit and some Palestinian groups have resorted to terrorist tactics, particularly since the failure of the Camp David peace talks in 2000. These tactics are quite futile, since there is no chance that random suicide bombings in Israel will persuade 6 million Israelis to abandon their state, but they have caused much needless suffering.

To return to earlier history, 1492 was a turning point for the Islamic world, not only because it saw the expulsion of the Moors from Spain but also because it saw the discovery of America. This led to a decisive change in the balance of power and influence in the world (see Lewis 1995: 72–3). European migrants colonized both North and South America and made these areas predominantly Christian in their religion. Nautical explorers developed new trade routes between Europe and the Far East, so that the Mediterranean lost some of its importance and Middle Eastern traders lost quite a lot of the profits they had previously made because of their geographical situation. Arab societies missed the European scientific discoveries of the seventeenth century and the industrial developments that transformed the western world in the nineteenth century. By the turn of the millennium, in 2000, only four of the world's forty-five most prosperous countries, as measured by GDP per head, were primarily Islamic in religion, these being the small oil-rich countries of Kuwait, Bahrain, Qatar and the United Arab Emirates. The Muslim religion had spread eastwards through Malaysia and Indonesia and southwards into parts of tropical Africa, but it had become mainly a religion of the poor.

There were two important reactions to this situation. One was envy, turning into resentment about what came to be called western imperialism. This had a territorial aspect, as in the nineteenth century the British gained control of the entire Indian subcontinent, with its many millions of Muslim inhabitants. The French invaded Algeria and incorporated it as a province of France in 1842 and, a little later, the British came to be dominant in an uneasy partnership with the nominal government of Egypt. In 1919 much of the defeated Ottoman Empire was parcelled out between Britain and France.

There were also economic and cultural aspects. In the nineteenth century all the European powers, actually led by Russia, engaged in the commercial penetration of the Ottoman Empire (Lewis 1993: 21). In the twentieth century western industrial firms, mainly British and American, led the discovery and exploitation of the enormous oilfields around the Persian Gulf. And in the second half of the twentieth century the western media had a marked cultural impact on Islamic societies that was resented by traditionalists, with western fashions and lifestyles gaining favour through magazines, films and television.

ISLAMIC FUNDAMENTALISM

The other reaction was for some religious leaders to blame their own people for their weakness in the face of external threats. The problem was that they had accepted compromises to the only true faith and the remedy was 'return to the pure, authentic Islam of the Prophet and his companions' (Lewis 1993: 137). The scholars and religious leaders who had this reaction came to be known as Islamic fundamentalists, and they founded sects in several countries.

In understanding this historical development, there is the difficulty that although the Muslim religion is very strict in its behavioural requirements of members, it is very loose in its organization. There is no Islamic equivalent of the Papacy to make binding decisions on matters of doctrine, or to denounce heresy or expel heretics. A mosque is a place where the faithful regularly gather for prayers, but there is no procedure for mosques to be consecrated. An imam is a man who gains acceptance as a regular leader of prayers, but there is no procedure for imams to be either ordained or defrocked. This situation leaves ample room for individual preachers or scholars to gain disciples and establish sects.

Divisions within Islam began soon after Muhammad's death in the seventh century, when a split developed between the majority, known as Sunni Muslims, and a minority known as Shiite Muslims. The split proved to be permanent, with the Sunnis always more numerous and now having a worldwide majority of about five to one. The rivalry has sometimes led to violent conflict, as has happened in the central areas of Iraq since 2004, with Sunni extremists bombing several Shiite mosques and shrines and Shiite extremists seeking revenge. Both branches of the faith have produced fundamentalist leaders since the eighteenth century, of whom the two most famous have been Shiites.

One of these was a Sudanese called Mohammed Ahmed, who called himself the 'Mahdi' (meaning messianic figure) and declared in 1881 that 'the Prophet himself had bidden him lead a jihad against unbelievers' (Feiling 1963: 987). He turned his disciples into a formidable band of warriors who in 1883 annihilated an Egyptian army under British command and in 1885 captured Khartoum, killing General Gordon in the process. They then ruled most of Sudan until 1898, when they in turn were annihilated by a sizeable British expeditionary force, using the world's first machine guns, at the Battle of Omdurman.

The other was Ayatollah Khomeini, an Iranian spiritual leader, who in 1979 inspired a successful revolution against the western-leaning Shah of Iran that replaced his regime with a theocratic dictatorship based on fundamentalist principles. This regime imposed Sharia law on the country, required women to wear the veil and modest black gowns, and in 1989 shocked the western world by imposing a *fatwa*, a religious judgment that in this case meant a sentence of death, on a British author of Indian origin for an obscure passage in one of his novels that was said to be blasphemous according to Islamic law. Salman Rushdie had to have police protection and go into hiding for over ten years. A newly appointed President of Iran,

Mahmoud Ahmadinejad, further shocked the western world by declaring in October 2005 that the state of Israel should be 'wiped off the map' and by subsequently announcing that Iran had developed or acquired ballistic missiles capable of reaching Tel Aviv.

These developments constitute further evidence of the error of supposing that the world has moved towards acceptance of a global culture, but they do not in themselves involve terrorism. However, in 1982 the Iranian government sponsored the establishment of an organization in Lebanon that has used terrorist tactics in pursuit of its anti-Israeli objectives. The year 1982 was a disastrous one for Lebanon, finally ending the elaborate political compromise, devised mainly by the French, that had shared power between the country's Christians and Muslims from 1944 to 1975. The year 1982 saw the arrival of the leaders and many warriors of a Palestinian Liberation army, controlled by Yasser Arafat, that had been expelled from Jordan, and then the invasion of the southern and western part of Lebanon by the Israeli army in pursuit of the Palestinians. In the second half of the year the Iranian Ambassador to Syria, with the agreement of the Syrian government, brought together various Shiite groups and clerics to form an organization called Hezbollah, meaning 'party of Allah', that gained control of part of the country and declared it to constitute an autonomous Islamic republic (see Kepel 2002: 126–9).

Hezbollah engaged in educational and social activities, including a charitable campaign to help the poorest members of the Shiite community. But in 1983 it attracted the attention of the world by its suicide bombings of American and French barracks in Beirut, already mentioned as a highly successful act of international terrorism. The Italian government, which had sent a small number of peacekeeping troops, decided to join the Americans and French in their decision to abandon the mission, without waiting for its own troops to be attacked. Following this, Hezbollah suicide bombers became very active for three years, making two attacks on the US Embassy in Beirut (killing 87 people), one attack on the US Embassy in Kuwait City (killing 7), twelve attacks on the Israeli army in Lebanon (killing 194) and eighteen attacks on the South Lebanon Army, an outfit of Christian militiamen allied with and financed by Israel (killing 155) (see Pape 2005: 253–4). This burst of violent terrorist activities was partially successful. The Americans did not close their embassies, but the South Lebanon Army was weakened and eventually disbanded while the Israelis withdrew their troops to a strip across southern Lebanon, where they stayed until 2000. From 1986 to 2006 Hezbollah engaged in only a few kidnappings and bombing attacks, resulting in about 26 deaths. But then, in July 2006, it launched a direct assault on northern Israel, using rockets supplied by Iran.

Among Sunni Muslims, the most influential fundamentalist theologian was Mohammed ibn al-Wahhab of Arabia (1703–87). Whereas the Mahdi and the Ayatollah were not only religious leaders but also power-seeking politicians ready to organize violence to achieve their ends, al-Wahhab was simply a *ulama*, meaning a religious teacher. He was deeply concerned by the decline of Ottoman authority over the Balkans and the southern regions of the Russian empire that had been taking place since the late sixteenth century, and he 'reached the conclusion that Islam as practiced in cities of the Ottoman Empire and in Persia was corrupt' (Cooper 2004: 98). He argued that Islam needed a return to 'the virtue and piety of the pristine early days', strict 'reliance on the Koran' and on Sharia law, strictly pre-scribed times and postures for daily prayer, and the infliction of traditional punishments by the courts (Cooper 2004: 98–9).

Al-Wahhab acquired political influence by reaching a formal agreement in 1744 with a tribal leader called Mohammed ibn Saud by which they and their followers would support each other, with Wahhabi religious practices in political communities controlled by Saudis. Ibn Saud married al-Wahhab's daughter and the agreement has lasted ever since. The Saudi family acquired dominance over varying but increasing areas of Arabia, an arid land inhabited largely by nomadic tribes, until the country acquired international recognition as the Kingdom of Saudi Arabia in 1926. It has developed a comprehensive system of state schools in which the Wahhabi form of the Muslim religion is taught.

The Wahhabi sect has spread internationally. After the Arabian peninsula was invaded by an Egyptian army in 1818, many Wahhabi preachers and teachers migrated to north-western India and then to Afghanistan. Pakistani Muslims have been greatly influenced by Wahhabism, particularly through the establishment of religious schools, known as *madrassas*. Pakistan has always been a somewhat fragile state, with marked regional and linguistic cleavages, held together by the Muslim religion and a large army that has acted rather in the manner of a political party. Its governments have gener-ally welcomed the establishment of *madrassas*, partly because of a shortage of funds to provide an adequate number of state schools. Under the rule of General Zia-ul-Haq, from 1977 to 1988, their number increased to well over 2,000. However, *madrassas* teach mainly in Arabic, because much of the instruction consists of learning the Koran by heart and it is a feature of the Muslim religion that the Koran has to be studied in its original language. It was in *madrassas* of northern Pakistan that *talibs*, meaning religious students, from Afghanistan received much of their education. In 1996 an armed band led by these former students established the Taliban regime in Kabul that welcomed Osama bin Laden to settle in their country.

THE DEVELOPMENT AND NATURE OF AL-QAEDA

The emergence of al-Qaeda can be summarized in terms of three develop-ments. The first was the prolonged struggle between the Soviet army and Afghani resisters after the Soviet Union invaded Afghanistan in the final week of 1979. Afghanis have always been fierce and determined fighters, as they showed when they drove out Persian invaders and again when they defeated the British in the two Afghan wars of the nineteenth century. In the 1980s they were massively helped by the United States during President Reagan's period of office. Reagan wanted to make Afghanistan the Soviet Union's equivalent of Vietnam, and to this end he not only supplied the Afghanis with arms but also ordered the CIA to sponsor, through intermediaries, the recruitment, training and payment of Muslim volunteers from other countries to join the struggle. A similar operation was organized by Saudi Arabia and it has been estimated that forty-two countries in addition to Pakistan contributed volunteers, with at least 10,000 of them receiving 'some degree of military training'. After the war was over, the *Los Angeles Times* sent a team of reporters to make enquiries in four continents and their conclusion was that about 5,000 had actually fought (see Mamdani 2004: 137).

In Saudi Arabia the main recruiting officer was Osama bin Laden, a civil engineer who belonged to an immensely wealthy Saudi family. It has been reported that in 1982 he moved to Peshawar (the nearest Pakistani town to Kabul) and that in 1986 he was 'the major contractor to build a large CIA-funded project, the Khost tunnel complex . . . that housed a major arms depot, a training facility, and a medical centre' (Mamdani 2004: 132–3).

In 1988 the Soviet Union abandoned the fight and withdrew its troops. The United States naturally stopped its payments to the volunteers, widely known as 'the Afghani Arabs'. Some of them went back to their own countries but many stayed in Afghanistan. Towards the end of 1989 bin Laden and nine others held a meeting in Khost at which it was decided to create an organization to wage *jihad* beyond the borders of Afghanistan, using the Afghani Arabs as a nucleus. The organization was called al-Qaeda, meaning simply 'the Base' (Mamdani 2004: 133). This development was not widely known, but in 1991 bin Laden was so horrified by the fact that his own Saudi government had invited American, British and French troops onto Saudi soil to fight the other Muslims of Iraq that he went into exile, denounced his government, and stated that the aim of al-Qaeda would be to drive all infidels out of the entire Arabian peninsula.

In terms of the typology of terrorism developed earlier in this chapter, this aim was almost, but not quite, millenarian, being unlikely but not impossible of attainment. In late 1995 and June 1996 two suicide bombings in Saudi Arabia by al-Qaeda claimed twenty-four American victims. But the US government showed no signs of willingness to give in to this kind of threat, and its Saudi military bases were indeed used in 2003 for the invasion of Iraq.

The third development occurred at the end of July 1996, when a two-day meeting of al-Qaeda leaders and members was held in a remote tribal area of north-eastern Pakistan, which was not in practice controlled by the

Pakistani government. At this meeting it was concluded that the objective of al-Qaeda should be widened to include the provocation of a global religious conflict between the Islamic world and its enemies that would end with the destruction of the Christian/Judaic/secular civilization of the West (see Gannon 2005: xvi). This was definitely millenarian in character and will not succeed. However, we all know how much damage it has caused and it will be a problem for years to come.

Since 1996 bin Laden has issued a series of public statements, many of them shown on television. The most dramatic of these was the *fatwa* of February 1998, published by the World Islamic Front, from which the following extract has been taken:

> For over seven years the United States has been occupying the lands of Islam in the holiest of places, the Arabian Peninsula, plundering its riches, dictating to its rulers, humiliating its people, terrorizing its neighbours, and turned its bases in the Peninsula into a spearhead through which to fight the neighbouring Muslim people. . . . We issue the following fatwa to all Muslims: The ruling to kill the Americans and their allies – civilians and military – is an individual duty for every Muslim who can do it in any country in which it is possible to do it.

In terms of action, the University of Chicago's Project on Suicide Terrorism identified twenty-one attacks by al-Qaeda operatives between the widening of objectives in July 1996 and the end of 2003, of which two were in each of Afghanistan and Saudi Arabia, two in the United States, three in each of Pakistan, Indonesia, East Africa and Turkey, two in North Africa, one on a US destroyer in Aden harbour and one on a French oil tanker off the coast of Yemen (see Pape 2005: 258–9). The three most deadly attacks were those in US embassies in Nairobi and Dar-es-Salaam in 1998, which killed 225, on the World Trade Center and the Pentagon in 2001, killing 2,955, and on a nightclub in Indonesia in 2002, killing 202 victims, of whom most were Australian tourists. The targets were not all American, as they included British, French, Australians, Germans and the Jews attending three synagogues in Turkey and Tunisia. Subsequent attacks have included those on commuter trains in Madrid and on a bank in Turkey that is jointly owned by the British and Chinese. It is indeed a global campaign of violence. It has not induced western governments to yield to Islamist demands but it has had two distinct and costly consequences.

One consequence is a continuing western involvement in Afghanistan. The decision to invade that country was taken by President Bush and the British government the day after 9/11, and was not politically controversial in either country. After the attacks on US embassies in East Africa in 1998 President Clinton had ordered the bombardment of the Khost area by cruise missiles, while the UN had condemned the Taliban regime and imposed sanctions on it. The assault by US and some British forces in 2001 was well planned and executed, and Kabul was captured in weeks. In December a plausible pro-western government was established and recognized by the UN. Bin Laden himself escaped into the tribal areas of Pakistan, but his training camps were closed and his organization was weakened.

However, this initial success was followed by the continuing problem of how to control Afghanistan, a mountainous and wild country with very poor communications that has never been successfully governed. Most of its territory has always been controlled by regional warlords, deriving their income partly from informal taxes extracted from villagers and partly by the export of heroin, of which Afghanistan contributes over two-thirds of the world's supply. Allied troops have therefore been tied up in an exceptionally difficult task of state-building in an essentially lawless Islamic society. In June 2006 the Americans handed over control of this operation to a NATO force containing Americans, but the troops are faced with spasmodic guerrilla warfare and there is no predictable end to their engagement.

The other costly consequence of al-Qaeda's terrorism has been a partial restriction of traditional liberties. To guard against aircraft hijacking, passengers have had to accept security procedures at airports that have added hours to travelling time. This has led to a decline in passenger traffic that, when combined with rising petroleum costs, has forced several major airlines into bankruptcy in both Europe and the United States. The understandable American determination to protect its homeland against further infiltration by terrorists has led to border controls that have upset Canadians and led in 2006 to something of a political crisis about illegal immigration by Mexicans. In Britain new legislation to control terrorism, passed quickly after 9/11, led to the arrest and imprisonment, without access to a telephone or lawyer, of an unknown number (thought to be between 100 and 200) of alien suspects. Most were released after short periods, usually on condition that they left the country, but a few were kept in prison for over four years.

OTHER EXAMPLES OF TERRORISM

In the earlier part of this chapter numerous examples of terrorism were mentioned, carried out by neo-Marxists and minority nationalist groups whose members were agnostic or Christian or Hindu. In very recent years there have also been a variety of terrorist activities carried out by Muslims of extreme views, usually called Islamists, without connection to al-Qaeda.

Many of these have been in North Africa. In Algeria, which had gained independence from France in 1962 only after a long and deadly civil war, politics continued to be a complex and intermittently violent affair. In 1992, when a coalition of Islamist groups were ahead in a national election campaign, the military-backed government cancelled the election abruptly and imposed a dictatorial regime. The Islamist groups responded with violence and there followed six years of guerrilla warfare, massacres, political assassi-nations and horrific acts that fall under the definition of terrorism. The violence spread to France in 1994 and 1995, with attacks on the Paris Metro and the hijacking of an Air France plane, but the French police responded effectively and the Islamist movement fell apart in 1998. The death roll was in excess of 60,000. (For a good account of this period of turmoil, see Kepel 2002: 254–75.)

Another North African country that must be mentioned is Libya, ruled since 1969 by the charismatic Colonel Gaddafi. He is a devout Muslim and has regarded himself as a fundamentalist, but he has disagreed with most other fundamentalist leaders and his foreign policies have been so erratic that they cannot be explained in religious terms.

In December 1988 his agents planted a bomb on a Pan-American plane bound from Munich to New York by way of London; the plane exploded over Scotland and killed all 259 people on board plus 11 people in Lockerbie. His inconsistency led Laqueur (1987: 285) to describe him as a megalomaniac and he is not mentioned by other leading students of terrorism or Islamism. In 2005, tired of experiencing western sanctions against his country, he changed sides, agreed to pay compensation to families victimized by the Pan-American bombing, and re-established diplomatic relations with the United States and Britain.

In Asia, a group of Islamic extremists in the southern part of the Philip-pines got worldwide headlines by abducting a group of western tourists in 2004 and holding them hostage for a week in bad conditions, and unidentified extremists in Pakistan have bombed several Christian churches.

In India, there have been bomb attacks in Delhi and on commuter trains approaching Mumbai, thought to have been planted by Muslim groups based in Kashmir.

In Iraq, the great majority of the casualties since the open fighting was over have to be classified as either guerrilla warfare against an occupying army or sectarian violence between Sunni Muslims and Shiite Muslims. However, there have also been several attacks that must be classified as terrorist, such as the bombing of the first UN offices and the early recruit-ing centres for the new Iraqi police force. These attacks have had temporary success, but the UN opened more secure offices later and insurgents in some areas (such as Basra) have opted to infiltrate the police force rather than bomb it.

In Russia, there have been several terrorist attacks by Chechen nationalists, of which the most horrific occurred in 2004 when a gang of militants attacked a school on the opening day of the session, causing 373 deaths, mostly of children.

In England, four British citizens shocked the world on 7 July 2005 by exploding bombs on three London Underground trains and a London bus, killing 52 people besides themselves and injuring over 300. Three of them were born in England of families of Pakistani origin while the fourth was a Jamaican immigrant who had been converted to Islam. Two of them had spent months in Pakistani *madrassas* and the one thought to be the leader left a message, made public two months later by Arab media, saying that he had been inspired by Osama bin Laden and had acted on behalf of al-Qaeda. Two weeks later another quartet, this time migrants from Somalia, planted bombs in another four Underground trains, but these failed to explode and the Somalis said that they had merely intended their action to register a protest against British participation in the occupation of Iraq.

What do these examples tell us about theories of terrorism? The examples of Algeria in the 1990s, Russia and the Philippines in 2004 are all cases of domestic revolutionary terrorism, destined to fail against determined governments like the various other cases mentioned earlier. Gaddafi's extraordinary behaviour is of no general interest. The Pakistani bombings of churches were expressions of sectarian hatred, very unpleasant but not likely to affect the beliefs or behaviour of the several million Christians in Pakistan. It is too soon to know how Iraq will settle down, and to what extent it may prove to be a breeding ground for future terrorists. The London bombings of 2005 have no chance of frightening Londoners away from using their Tube, which handles just over 5 million passengers every day. Their main significance is to draw attention to the possible problems posed by the existence of large Muslim minorities in western Europe, a new development in world history that will be discussed below.

CONCLUSIONS

Although political terrorism is far from new, it has become more common since the middle of the twentieth century, possibly because television has multiplied its audience. Most examples of it have been indicated and categorized in an earlier section of this chapter, and there will doubtless be endless future examples of the same types of activity. However, until the 1990s, all cases of terrorism, whether repressive or revolutionary, were confined to a single political territory, be it province, state or colony, in a few cases spreading to an immediately adjacent territory. What is completely novel about al-Qaeda and associated groups is that they have no such territorial limits. This concluding section will deal with theories about the possibility of a continuing global conflict between Islamic extremists and the western world.

The first western scholar to draw public attention to the danger of this was the historian Bernard Lewis of Princeton University, who in 1990 published an article in *Atlantic Monthly* entitled 'The roots of Muslim rage'. In this he pointed to the growth of Islamic fundamentalism and the growing resentment that fundamentalists felt about what they called American imperialism. He asked why they did not direct their hatred towards the Russians, who had over 50 million Muslims in the Soviet empire, while the Americans had never controlled more than a small Muslim minority in the Philippines. His answer, in effect, was that they viewed the United States as a symbol of western power, modernism, secularism and female emancipation, all of which they saw, quite correctly, as a 'challenge to the way of life they wish to retain or restore' (Lewis 1990: 59). Lewis added that they were encouraged in this view by the emergence in the 1970s and later of radical critics among the American intellectual elite who had described their own society as imperialist.

In 1994 Lewis emphasized this warning in three public lectures he gave at the University of Wisconsin, which ended with the lament that western culture might indeed be in terminal decline. Borrowing some of the words from Yeats' famous poem 'The Second Coming', he declared that 'the lack of conviction of many of those who should be its defenders and the passionate intensity of its accusers may well join to complete its destruction' (Lewis 1995: 79).

A much more elaborate analysis of the same emerging problem was made in Samuel Huntington's 1996 book entitled *The Clash of Civilizations and the Remaking of World Order*. In this major work the author, a Harvard political scientist, asserted that 'culture almost always follows power' (Huntington 1996: 91) and he noted that the west, dominant throughout most of the world in the late nineteenth century, had lost much of its power in the second half of the twentieth century because of the dissolution of European empires and the growing economic and defensive capabilities of many developing and newly industrialized societies. He also asserted that globalization is weakening the tendency of westerners to identify themselves principally in terms of their nationality or statehood and thus making it more likely that they will identify themselves in ethnic, cultural and religious terms. He notes that in the Islamic world clan, tribe, and religion have always been more important than statehood as forms of group identification. He follows American sociologists like Donald Horowitz (1953: 68) in believing that we are seeing a 'global religious revival' and reaches the conclusion that the world, no longer divided between empires and colonies or capitalists and communists, is moving towards a global clash of what he calls 'civilizations', defined in terms of religion and culture.

In discussing Islam, Huntington emphatically rejects the view espoused by President Clinton and others, 'that the west does not have problems with Islam but only with violent Islamic extremists. "Fourteen hundred years of history," he said, "demonstrate otherwise"' (Huntington 1996: 209). He expresses pessimistic views about what he sees as the developing struggle between Islam and the west.

Despite his scholarship, Huntington's views are in parts controversial. As I have argued in Chapter 4, it is not clear that loyalties to the national state are greatly weakening in the west. Nor is it clear that there is actually a global religious revival. Survey statistics suggesting this are skewed by the fact that citizens in the former Soviet Union are now more ready to tell interviewers of their religious beliefs than they were under Communist dictatorship. The United States is the only country not to fall into the general pattern of an inverse relationship between industrialism and economic growth on the one hand and the extent of religiosity in society on the other. The decline in religious observance throughout western Europe since the 1960s has been dramatic. The growth of Christian fundamentalism in the United States has certainly brought religious issues into politics there, but this is not evidence of a global development.

Huntington's (1996) analysis of the Islamic world's reaction to the first Gulf War is interesting. He notes that when Iraqi troops invaded Kuwait the Arab League condemned Iraq by fourteen votes to two, with five abstentions, and that the governments of seven predominantly Muslim countries gave material help to the American-led coalition that went to Kuwait's defence. However, he also quotes seven reporters as saying that the general population of Arab countries – what came to be called 'the Arab street' – was 'seething with resentment against the US' (Huntington 1996: 248). There were massive anti-American demonstrations in several countries, particularly those where 'politics was more open and freedom of expression less restricted' (Huntington 1996: 248).

This is a cautionary tale, but it should be put into perspective by recalling that demonstrations against US foreign policy have not been uncommon since the United States became the world's greatest power. Those against the Gulf War, or even against the 2003 invasion of Iraq, have not been as widespread as those against the US war in Vietnam, which led to the torching of several US information offices around the world and even to a dramatic night in London where hundreds of police had to protect the US Embassy from possible attack by thousands of demonstrators.

If Clinton's view seems preferable to Huntington's, there remain the problem of how to understand and deal with al-Qaeda and the possible problem posed by the existence of large Muslim minorities in western Europe. The peculiarity of al-Qaeda terrorist groups is that it rarely has any concrete objective or policy demands. The Madrid bombing was exceptional among al-Qaeda attacks because it did have a demand, that Spain withdraw its troops from Iraq, and that demand was satisfied. It fitted my definition of terrorism exactly, in that it frightened the target group into changing its behaviour. But the attacks on US embassies in East Africa in 1998 and on New York and Washington in 2001 were not accompanied by any equivalent demands. They were just episodes in a Holy War against the United States, described by bin Laden as 'the great Satan'. The purpose of such a war, essentially, is to please Allah. As Cooper put it, 'when politics is understood foremost as a spiritual or religious quest, the only audience that counts is divine' (Cooper 2004: 56). Ruthven made a similar comment when he observed that 'religious violence differs from violence in the secular world by shifting the plane of action from what is mundane, and hence negotiable, to the arena of cosmic struggle' (Ruthven 2002: 30).

Why are Islamic terrorists willing to lay down their lives as suicide bombers? When an American sociologist interviewed one of the founders of Hamas in the Gaza Strip, the latter said that he did not approve of the term 'suicide bombers', which might suggest impulsive acts by neurotic persons, and preferred the Arabic term *istishhadi*, meaning 'self-chosen martyrdom'. Another Hamas member explained that all people have to die sooner or later, and a martyr has the advantage of being able to choose both the time and the manner of his death. He also has the advantage of knowing that a certain consequence of his action would be a future life in Paradise, welcomed by seventy (or seventy-two) virgins and promised an equal number of wives, while (if he is Palestinian) his family on earth would receive a cash payment from Saudi Arabia of at least US$12,000 (Juergensmeyer 2003: 72–9).

A practical consequence of this is that the US government cannot negotiate with al-Qaeda, because there is nothing to negotiate about. As Paul Bremmer, formerly of the US State Department, said:

> There's no point in addressing the so-called root causes of bin Laden's despair with us. . . . He doesn't like America. . . . He doesn't like what we stand for. . . . And short of the United States going out of existence, there's no way to deal with the root cause of his terrorism.
>
> (quoted in Ruthven 2002: 29–30)

All that can be done to counter al-Qaeda's future operations is to continue and extend various protective activities, which are both tiresome and expensive. However, they are not ineffective. Bin Laden's organization has been weakened and it has become difficult for him to transmit orders and money by electronic means. In the five years following 9/11 there have been only two attempts to attack the United States; both of them failed. One was by the so-called shoe bomber, a British citizen of Jamaican family background, who had been converted to Islam by a Muslim prison chaplain in London. His attempt to blow up an American airliner in mid-Atlantic failed when he was overpowered by a female steward and other passengers. The other was by an Algerian living in Canada who entered the United States in a car packed with explosives with the intention of bombing Los Angeles Airport, but was apprehended by alert customs officers at the port of entry.

There is of course a continuing danger of copycat terrorist activities against western targets by Muslim extremists who are not part of the al-Qaeda network. Chairman Mau Zedong once observed that terrorists need communities to live in just as fish need water to swim in, and recognition of this has led to concern about the sizeable Muslim communities in western

Europe. In addressing this, Francis Fukuyama of Johns Hopkins University has suggested that radical Islamism 'is a manifestation of modern identity politics' (Fukuyama 2006: 6). In this view, he follows the French sociologist Olivier Roy, who has emphasized the difference between the position of a young person growing up in a traditional Muslim society, where his religion is an essential part of the local culture, and that of a second or third generation immigrant in western Europe, where there is a dysfunction between his inherited religion and the local culture so that his feelings of group identity are to some extent a matter of choice (see Roy 1994b: Chapter 3). Roy insists on the importance of this 'delinking of religion and culture' and says that 'the "clash of civilizations" debate, by ignoring this delinking, cannot explain what is going on in the process of globalisation' (Roy 1994b: 206).

Fukuyama claims that the United States has been more successful than European countries in 'the assimilation of new immigrants into American political and social life' (Fukuyama 2006: 18) and attributes this partly to the American addiction to 'quasi-religious ceremonies and rituals' of a patriotic kind, such as saluting the flag, taking oaths of naturalization, and celebrating national holidays like the Fourth of July. Now, nobody can doubt the striking success of the United States in assimilating waves of immigrants from various backgrounds over the past two centuries. This is the great American story. But European history has been quite different, as it has been a continent from which migrants left rather than one of settlement, and there has been no need for rituals of welcome.

Regarding European Muslims, an American political scientist has spent a year in six European countries interviewing about 300 Muslims who had established positions of leadership in political or social organizations. Klausen (2005) discovered an interesting difference between Britain and the other five countries, in that British Muslim leaders are significantly more likely to regard Islamic values are 'inherently incompatible' with the values of their host society and to have what she calls 'neo-orthodox' views, meaning that they 'oppose the integration of Islamic institutions to existing European frameworks for the exercise of religion' (Klausen 2005: 87). She attributes this difference mainly to the fact that nearly all British Muslim families came originally from Pakistan, Bangladesh and India, where the Muslim religion is more fundamentalist than it is in Turkey or North Africa, the areas of origin of most Muslims in continental Europe. Related to this is the fact that Britain has about 2,000 imams, of whom only between 200 and 300 were raised and educated in Britain. The overwhelming majority of the others moved either from Saudi Arabia and therefore adhere to the Wahhabi version of Islam or from the Indian subcontinent where, as noted earlier, Wahhabi religious teaching is very common. This presumably explains why imams educated in Britain are just as likely to have neo-orthodox views as those from elsewhere.

What do these observations tell us about the danger of terrorist activities by members of the Muslim minorities in Europe? Only that it poses problems for governmental authorities. On the one hand, they cannot afford to ignore it and must feel obliged to engage in counter-terrorist activities. On the other hand, they must be careful lest these activities cause widespread resentment on the ground that they curtail traditional civil liberties. What is apt to cause resentment varies widely between societies. The British do not mind being observed by a multitude of closed-circuit television cameras, so that working Londoners may be photographed scores of times a day, but in some other societies this would be regarded as a gross invasion of privacy. The French and most other continental Europeans take it for granted that they have to carry official papers showing their names and addresses, but the British have never had to do this in peacetime and Prime Minister Tony Blair's repeated statements in favour of national identity cards have been met with bitter criticism.

Another issue in Europe, particularly since the London bombings of 2005, is concern about the constant tendency for the size of Muslim minorities to increase, largely because new immigrants arrive under the provisions for family reunion in immigration laws. The Danish government has amended its law to make this more difficult, which was the reason for the whipped-up protests in 2006 about cartoons in a Danish newspaper. The Dutch government has insisted that potential immigrants must pass examinations about Dutch language and culture in order to get a visa. The French and British governments are changing their rules so as to give priority to skilled migrants helpful to the domestic economy. In March 2006 ministers and senior officials met in Germany to discuss proposals for an 'integration contract' that would require potential migrants to respect the values of the society they wish to join. The development of global terrorism is thus leading to new forms of cooperation between national governments and to questions about national integration additional to those already discussed in Chapter 2.

Chapter 6

Political authority and legitimacy

THE DEFINITION OF POLITICAL AUTHORITY

For the ordinary citizen of a modern democratic state in times of peace, the nature of political authority is not problematical. It is embodied in a complex system of laws and administrative regulations that most citizens accept without question and that the questioning or recalcitrant minority are forced to comply with by the actions of tax inspectors, police officers and other public officials holding what are commonly called positions of authority. It has to be recognized, however, that the very notion of authority has caused difficulty to philosophers, who have argued among themselves about its meaning and nature.

In part, this difficulty flows from the fact that there are significant differences between political authority, moral authority, divine authority, parental authority and so forth, so that it is a good deal more difficult to define the single term 'authority' than it is to define each of the various types of authority. In part, the difficulty flows from the fact that philosophers commonly concern themselves with the meanings given to concepts from the time of the Greek city-states onwards, during which period the meaning of each concept has often been modified. In this book our task is simpler, as we are concerned only with the meaning, nature and basis of political authority, not with other types of authority, and only with the period of the modern democratic state, that is to say from the late eighteenth century onwards.

On the question of definition, it is perhaps best to start with a dictionary, as the word authority clearly has more than one meaning in contemporary English usage. The first, and politically most important, meaning of authority is defined in the *Oxford English Dictionary* (*OED*) as 'the right to command, or give an ultimate decision'. This is the type of authority wielded by presidents and prime ministers and parliaments, by generals in charge of armies, by judges and police officers, by managing directors of business firms, or (in a weaker form) by school principals and teachers. This meaning of the term implies a community or group with some kind of hierarchy, a widespread acceptance within the community of the right of certain persons or institutions to take decisions and issue commands, and probably some kind of sanction against individuals who might wish to ignore particular decisions or commands.

A second meaning, invoked in both political and non-political situations, relates to the possession by one person of a conferred right or title to speak or act on behalf of others. A lawyer might say that she has 'the authority of her client' to reject offers made by another party. An ambassador to the United Nations has this kind of authority when he speaks on behalf of his country's government. This is the authority enjoyed by representatives, be they politicians, lawyers, or union negotiators in wage disputes, who have been appointed to carry out certain duties.

A third meaning relates to expertise. A literary critic might be described as an authority on Shakespeare, an historian as an authority on the French Revolution, or a House of Commons clerk as an authority on parliamentary procedure. None of these persons wields power as a consequence of his expertise, but they might well exercise a good deal of influence over the opinions and in some circumstances the actions of others.

Students of politics are mainly concerned with authority in the first of these three senses, namely with the power to take decisions that are binding on others and to induce or force others to abide by these decisions. As noted, this kind of authority is exercised in non-political as well as political situations, but in modern industrial societies the state is so thoroughly enmeshed in societal relationships that the exercise of authority by some people over others nearly always depends ultimately upon the existence of state authority. It is the state that provides the legal framework within which social and economic relationships are defined, and it would now be somewhat unrealistic to draw the clear distinction between the state and civil society that was often drawn by political theorists in earlier periods. It follows that a clear understanding of the nature of political authority is helpful to all students of modern government and society.

In practice, the exercise of authority, in the first of the senses itemized above, depends upon the readiness of the people over whom it is exercised to accept the decisions and orders that are given. If players in a football match refuse to accept a referee's decision and hold up the game, or if school children take no notice of their teacher's instructions, it could properly be said that the referee or teacher in question have temporarily lost their authority. Having formal authority over a situation or a group of people does not necessarily mean that the person having the right to issue orders will always be obeyed. It may be that other qualities are necessary to ensure compliance, such as a certain amount of authority in the sense of expertise. A referee is likely to lose control of the game if he or she repeatedly misinterprets the rules. A teacher who displays ignorance of child psychology or ignorance of the subject he or she is supposed to be teaching may lose control of the class. It helps to ensure compliance if the person nominally in charge not only is *in* authority, in a formal sense, but also is *an* authority on the activity being engaged in by the group. It may help even more if they have personal qualities that inspire respect. A sociologist has listed the qualities of an authority as 'assurance, superior judgment, the ability to impose discipline, the capacity to inspire fear' (Sennett 1980: 17–18).

This kind of consideration has led R. S. Peters to suggest that there is a continuum between three senses of authority: namely, being appointed to be in authority; having special knowledge or qualities that make the person an authority; and the ability to exercise authority in practice (see Peters 1958). It is undoubtedly the case that authority relationships work most smoothly when the leader enjoys authority in both the first and second of these senses of the term; when, for instance, a minister appointed to control a department possesses an incisive understanding of the problems and work of the department that commands the respect of his or her staff. However, there are two reasons why it is important not to overemphasize the importance of expertise and related personal qualities in the exercise of authority.

The first reason is that these qualities by themselves are not all that much of an asset. Spectators or team managers at a game might possibly have a better understanding of the rules than the referee does and might indicate this in shouted comments, but they never get to take charge of the game themselves. A senior civil servant often understands departmental problems better than the minister in charge does, but this does not enable the civil servant to replace the minister. It may enable the civil servant to persuade the minister to modify his or her policies and may sometimes enable the civil servant to frustrate a minister who persists in issuing instructions that the civil servant regards as unwise, but if there is a direct clash the minister always has the power to come out on top. In the highly organized and bureaucratized societies of the advanced industrial countries, having the official right to exercise authority is four-fifths of the battle.

The other reason is that most people who are legally in charge have a weapon not available to others, namely the threat of coercion. Sergeant-majors can nearly always get their orders obeyed, even if they are ignorant people, because the expected consequences of disobedience are too serious for those under them to think disobedience is worth the candle. This raises the whole question of the relationship between coercion and authority (in the first sense of the term), on which the views of political theorists differ markedly. Robert Michels, writing in 1930, said that 'one of the principal means of exercising authority is the dispensation of rewards and punishments' (Michels 1930: 319). The acceptance of authority, he declared, 'may be due to a fear of force' and 'submission to authority may result either from a deliberate recognition of it as a good or from an acquiescence in it as inevitable, to be endured permanently or temporarily with scepticism, indifference or scorn, with fists clenched but in the pockets' (Michels 1930: 319).

On the other hand, Hannah Arendt has said that 'if authority is to be defined at all . . . it must be in contradistinction to both coercion by force and persuasion through arguments' (Arendt 1968: 93). April Carter has followed Arendt in this view, saying also that authority excludes 'appeals to self-interest through promises, incentives and bribes' (Carter 1979: 14). Authority, she says, 'entails a belief in the right of the authority figure to issue commands or judgments' and 'to recognize authority is to be persuaded in advance that whatever is advocated will be worthy of respect and compliance' (Carter 1979: 14). C. W. Cassinelli has also gone some way towards this kind of view, saying that 'fear of . . . legal sanctions is a fear normally held incompatible with the exercise of political authority' (Cassinelli 1961: 639).

Between the views of Michels on the one hand and Arendt and her followers on the other, there is clearly a large gulf. Which view is more appropriate for the student of politics in the modern democratic state? My belief is that Michels' view is the more realistic and thus more helpful. The Arendt/Carter view is appropriate for students of moral authority, but political authority differs from moral authority. When we discuss authority in modern systems of government we are not discussing the kind of authority that priests enjoy over their parishioners. Relatively few citizens in modern democratic states now believe in the laws of God, the laws of nature, the divine right of kings, or similar concepts that bolstered political authority in times past. Political authority in the modern state is seen to be wielded by identifiable and fallible human beings over their fellow citizens, and is therefore always open to question. That it is usually accepted by most citizens clearly owes something to the fact that non-compliance is likely to lead to penalties of one kind or another. It seems to me that to deny this is to be unrealistic.

Having said this, the proviso should be added that the actual use of force, as distinct from the implied threat of force, usually indicates a partial loss of authority. A government that is regarded as legitimate should not have to use force over more than a very small minority of its citizens, just as army officers should not have constantly to put their subordinates on disciplinary charges and police officers should not often have to use their batons. Ideally, authority should be exercised by word of mouth or by the pen, without any need to use force.

In the real world of politics, however, it must be accepted that the threat of coercion is always present. Thomas Hobbes likened life to a game of cards in which the player who has a trump has authority. But 'in matters of government', he added, 'when nothing else is turned up, clubs are trumps'. This is undoubtedly true, and it is not just that the breakdown of political authority can be expected to lead to violence, it is also true that most kinds of political authority are backed by the threat, open or veiled, of coercion in cases of non-compliance. When a motorist pulls over and stops in response to flashing lights and sirens on a police car just behind him, he may be doing so out of inherent respect for the authority of the police. On the other hand, he may be stopping because he knows that a refusal to stop will eventually result in his arrest and punishment. The observer cannot tell which reason is predominant, and the two reasons may be so intermingled in the mind of the motorist that responses to questions on the subject would not be very meaningful. It is best to recognize that political authority is usually backed by the possibility of coercion, even in circumstances where the actual use of coercion is rare.

In view of this, political authority is best defined as a combination of political power and legitimacy, where power is the ability to get things done and legitimacy is the quality of ascribed entitlement to exercise that power. The appropriateness of this definition can be seen most clearly in circumstances where authority breaks down. In normal circumstances, for instance, the captain of an aircraft has both the legitimate right to control the movements of the aircraft and the actual power to do so, but if the aircraft is hijacked she loses this power and therefore loses her authority. In a hijacked aircraft nobody has authority, as the hijackers possess power without legitimacy and the captain possesses legitimacy without power. It could equally be said that nobody has authority in a riot where the police lose control or a classroom where pupils pelt the teacher with chalk. Power is an essential ingredient of authority and those theorists who have denied this have simply shown a lack of realism.

The problems associated with the concept of power will be examined in Chapter 12, and it is now appropriate to discuss some of the issues surrounding the concept of political legitimacy.

THEORIES ABOUT POLITICAL LEGITIMACY

The rise of the modern state was accompanied in the seventeenth and eighteenth centuries by a good deal of speculation and theorizing about the ways in which the authority exercised by the state could be justified. Expressed in one way, this is the problem of political obligation. Why should citizens feel obliged to obey the orders of the government? Expressed in another way, it is the problem of political legitimacy. Why should the actions of the government be regarded as the legitimate exercise of political power? Some of the most impressive works in the history of political thought have been addressed to these questions. Writings of this kind deal with the moral basis of political authority. Writings of a rather different kind deal with the sociological and practical bases of authority in the modern state. The most famous example of this second kind of theorizing is the work of Max Weber in the early years of the twentieth century.

Weber was a sociologist – indeed one of the founders of that discipline – whose contributions to political analysis were limited in number and significance. His best-known contribution is directly relevant to this chapter, however, as it was a classification of the sources of political legitimacy. Weber asked what it is that makes people accept that a political regime enjoys legitimate authority and he produced three answers. Each of these, he claimed, was an 'ideal type' to which actual situations approximated, with the possibility that any particular regime might be supported by more than one type of legitimacy. In this analysis, as in his other contributions to social science, Weber was careful to avoid the claim that sociological or political categories resembled watertight compartments. He maintained that patterns of social and political behaviour are too complex to be fitted into watertight categories, but that categorization is nevertheless an essential aid to understanding so long as it is recognized that each category represents only an ideal type of behaviour or relationship.

Weber's first type of political legitimacy is that based on tradition and inheritance. Traditional legitimacy is the legitimacy enjoyed by tribal chiefs, princes and kings. In this kind of regime the essential factor that ensures compliance with the orders and laws of government is personal loyalty to the chief or king or ruling family. In such regimes public administration tends to be in the hands of a ruling class defined by birth and upbringing, while key positions such as chief of police are often given to members of the ruling family such as the king's younger brother. Among modern states, Saudi Arabia and Kuwait conform most closely, though not completely, to this ideal type.

Weber's second type of political legitimacy, described by him as 'legal-rational', is that enjoyed by the governments of most modern states. In this kind of regime loyalty is given not to a person or a ruling family but to an impersonal set of institutions, the powers of which are defined (except in the United Kingdom) by a written constitution. In one example, namely the United States, recruits to the national army pledge themselves 'to defend the United States Constitution against its enemies, internal or external'. Public administration in regimes of this type is characteristically in the hands of trained specialists, recruited by an open competition based on merit, showing substantial neutrality as between the political parties competing for power. Public compliance with the orders and laws of government is based not on loyalty to persons but on general acceptance of the procedures by which these orders and laws are produced.

It is an obvious aspect of world history that the past three centuries have been marked by a widespread transition from regimes enjoying political authority of the traditional kind to regimes enjoying political authority of the legal-rational kind. However, there is a joker in the pack in the form of a third type of political authority, appearing irregularly and unpredictably. This is what Weber called 'charismatic authority', depending on the personal qualities of a political leader who appears as a kind of hero or saint and inspires his followers to accept his rule. Napoleon was an example, as were Mussolini, Hitler, Mao Zedong and Ayatollah Khomeini. Fidel Castro and Colonel Gaddafi are contemporary examples. Public administration in this type of regime is in the hands of people who are neither members of a traditional ruling class nor neutral bureaucrats recruited on the basis of merit, but followers of the leader who have faith in his wisdom, his vision and the religious creed or ideology that he promotes and manipulates.

The concept of charismatic leadership is frequently misused to apply to popular leaders like John F. Kennedy and Pierre Trudeau, whose actual authority was essentially legal-rational in character. However, these names draw attention to a feature of political life that Weber did not discuss, since he was suggesting ideal types of authority rather than writing descriptively about it. This feature is the role that 'humanly significant leadership', to use John Schaar's phrase (see Schaar 1981: 40–3), can sometimes play in enhancing political authority. Margaret Thatcher is perhaps a more interesting example than Kennedy or Trudeau, as in the 1980s she persuaded millions of British voters to accept mass unemployment in their country without blaming the government for it. She changed people's attitudes. Winston Churchill would be a better example still, as during the Second World War he changed people's behaviour. His leadership and rhetoric inspired British citizens to do things that they would otherwise have been unlikely to do, such as continuing to work while bombs were falling around them or volunteering to spend their spare time drilling as members of the Home Guard.

The most remarkable example of humanly significant leadership in the democratic state is undoubtedly the leadership of Charles de Gaulle. His achievements were so great that he could be said to have exercised both charismatic and legal-rational authority. He exercised charismatic authority to acquire power both in 1944 and in 1958, to secure the adoption of a completely new constitution in the latter year, to change that constitution when he wanted the president (namely himself) to be directly elected, and to end the civil war in Algeria by granting independence to that country. At the same time, de Gaulle was careful to follow constitutional procedures whenever this was possible, deviating from them only to secure direct election for the presidency, which could not have been achieved by purely constitutional means.

One of the problems of the charismatic form of political authority, as noted by Weber, is that authority may die when the leader dies. It is not easy to pass this kind of authority on to heirs, as can be done in the case of traditional types of authority. It may, however, be possible to convert charismatic authority into a form of legal-rational authority, a process that Weber called 'the routinization of charisma'. The most outstanding example of this is again the career of Charles de Gaulle. During the early years of his rule commentators referred to the Fifth Republic as 'de Gaulle's Republic' and commonly predicted that it would give way to a Sixth Republic when he retired from the scene. In practice, the constitution of the Fifth Republic has proved to be durable, almost certainly the most successful France has had, and succeeding presidents have, without serious controversy, exercised powers that were previously thought to be dependent on de Gaulle's personal qualities.

THE LIMITATIONS OF WEBER

Weber's contribution to the understanding of the sources of political authority is generally accepted as useful. It is, however, only a limited contribution to a complex topic, because Weber directed his attention only to the legitimacy of regimes. This is important, but a study of the conditions in which political authority is seriously challenged in the modern state would reveal that it is only in a minority of cases that the dissenters object to the regime itself. This happened in 1989–90 in Poland, Czechoslovakia, Hungary, East Germany and Romania, where Communist Party regimes were overthrown in quick succession by popular demonstrations and revolts. However, these were exceptional events in that, first, the Communist regimes had been imposed by Soviet power rather than emerging internally, and second, these regimes had been both brutal and conspicuously inefficient.

A more common cause of challenges to political authority in recent years has been the decision by leaders of particular ethnic and cultural groups in society to query or reject the legitimacy of governments dominated by other such groups. Challenges of this kind may be called challenges to the legitimacy of the political community. Another common cause of challenges to political authority has been the rejection of specific government policies by groups who are affected by them. Challenges of this kind may be called challenges to the legitimacy of policies.

Challenges to the legitimacy of the political community arise when there is a lack of congruence between community, territory and government. In an age of self-determination it is important that the citizens of a state should believe that they are rightly ruled, even if not well ruled, by leaders drawn from their own community. Colonial regimes do not qualify, and Northern Ireland is a classic example of a political unit that is perceived as colonial, and therefore as illegitimate, by a sizeable proportion of its citizens. Since the late 1970s we have seen violent challenges to political authority mounted by Basque nationalists in Spain, Palestinians in the West Bank and the Gaza Strip, Muslims in Lebanon, Tamils in Sri Lanka, Kurds in Turkey and Iraq and Sikhs in India. The ideology involved in such cases is that of nationalism, which (as noted in Chapter 2) can in one form be the cement that holds a political community together and in another form be the explosive that tears it apart.

Challenges to political authority based on objections to specific government policies have also been widespread in recent years. The Americans who burned their draft cards during the Vietnam war were not revolutionaries who wanted to replace the American constitution with a different form of government, but simply radicals who objected passionately to conscription to fight in a war they regarded as unnecessary and unjust. The Americans who bombed twenty-eight abortion clinics during 1986 were not even radicals, but religious zealots wanting to protest about the liberality of the laws regarding abortion. Pickets from the British mineworkers' union who fought the police during the long miners' strike of 1984–5 did not want to abolish Parliament, only to make the government's policy of closing uneconomic pits unworkable. Supporters of the Welsh Language Society who bombed television relay stations did so in protest against the British government's refusal to authorize a television channel using Welsh. German feminists who placed a bomb in the West German Constitutional Court were protesting about the toughness of German abortion laws at that time. French farmers who periodically block highways with farm tractors or dumps of manure do so to protest about agricultural policies. Canadian Indians who barricaded one of Montreal's main bridges for two months in 1990 took this action to protest against a plan to build a golf course over an old Indian burial ground. Anti-nuclear demonstrators who engage in civil disobedience do so to express their outrage at the possibility that nuclear weapons might be used. Examples could be multiplied to produce an extremely long list, for political authority in the modern state is not so secure as some textbooks would lead readers to assume.

In order of generality, the reasons why people reject political authority can be therefore categorized as:

1 objections to the composition and boundaries of the political community
2 objections to the constitutional arrangements within the community
3 objections to specific policies pursued by the government.

Challenges to authority in categories 1 and 3 are much more common than challenges in category 2 because most people are not political theorists. To get involved in activities that may involve personal sacrifice, most people need to be motivated by some kind of direct interest. They have such an interest if they are subject to government by a group whom they regard as alien, or if they are outraged by specific policies of the government. They can be mobilized for political action by leaders who play on these feelings and interests. It is more difficult to mobilize people for action in support of a better constitution. The cultural or material interests of citizens are pre-judiced indirectly, rather than directly, by institutional inadequacy. Leaders of dissent on this ground cannot appeal simply to community or group interests, but must try to educate their fellow-citizens to a higher level of political awareness and sophistication.

It follows from these arguments that as Max Weber's contribution to the understanding of political authority deals only with the character of the regime, its value must be regarded as limited. It was useful in its way and in its time, but we now have more experience of popular involvement in politics on which to base our generalizations.

LEGITIMACY AND THE ECONOMIC SYSTEM

Another approach to the problem of political legitimacy has been developed by several writers of neo-Marxist inclinations, of whom the most prominent are Jurgen Habermas and Claus Offe. One of the central features of Marxist analysis is the conviction that the political and economic systems of any society are so intimately linked that one of them cannot sensibly be studied in isolation from the other. Marx and Engels believed that the capitalist economic system is fundamentally unjust and exploitative, that workers in an advanced capitalist society would realize this, and that when capitalism moved into a state of crisis (as it inevitably would) the workers would seize control of the government and use their newly acquired political power to transform the economic system from capitalism to socialism. The problem for contemporary Marxists is that this prediction has not been validated by events. The workers have seized power only in the relatively backward societies of Russia, China and Cuba, while the more advanced capitalist societies have grown more and more prosperous and less and less class divided.

An early attempt to explain this predictive failure was made in the 1930s by Antonio Gramsci, the leader of the Italian Communist Party. Gramsci's argument was that within capitalist societies the social and political values of the capitalist class enjoy what he called an 'ideological hegemony'. These values are promulgated through the educational system, the mass media, popular novels and the cinema, so that the great majority of citizens come to accept them as natural. They emphasize the virtues of hard work and thrift and suggest that the poor themselves (rather than the system), are largely to blame for their poverty. They endorse competitive individualism as a way of life and they propagate the view that conflicting interests could be accommodated through the free competition of parties and group spokesmen in the political system. In these ways workers are socialized into accepting the capitalist system, despite its manifest inequalities, and are led to believe that democratic political institutions could alleviate the problems of the working class. This bourgeois ideology, spread throughout society, prescribes the channels and limits within which political conflict is normally confined. As the French Marxist, Nicos Poulantzas, put it:

> The dominance of this ideology is shown by the fact that the dominated classes live their conditions of political existence through the forms of dominant political discourse: this means that often they live *even their revolt* against the domination of the system within the frame of reference of the dominant ideology.

> (Poulantzas 1973: 223)

Another explanation of the predictive failure of Marxism was developed in the 1970s by Habermas and Offe. Their argument had three main themes. First, it was declared that in western industrial societies the capitalist system had been largely legitimized in the eyes of the workers by the liberal-democratic state. In Offe's words, this process of legitimation can be defined as one by which 'the capitalist state manages, through a variety of institutional mechanisms, to convey the image of an organization of power that pursues common and general interests of society as a whole, allows equal access to power, and is responsive to justified demands' (Offe 1975: 127). This image disguises the dominant role of the capitalist class in society and in the formation of state policy, but it serves to keep the workers quiescent and willing to accept the authority of the state.

The second argument is that the liberal-democratic state has adopted various policies and tactics to protect both its own legitimacy and that of the social order. The most important of these policies is the development of welfare services designed to shelter disadvantaged groups from the inevitable hardships resulting from the operation of the capitalist system. In this way the groups with the most right to feel aggrieved are pacified. The hard edges of capitalism are softened by welfare spending.

Alongside this strategy, the state has protected itself by ensuring that those forms of social conflict that are most likely to upset sizeable groups take place outside the institutions of the state itself. Thus, group conflicts over taxation or import duties are resolved in Parliament or Congress but conflicts over wage levels, which upset the losers much more directly, take place in other arenas. It is true that these conflicts are resolved in a framework of rules that are to some extent determined by the state, but so long as no significant group challenges the rules themselves the state is protected from the wrath of losing groups in the bargaining process. The point is to safeguard the appearance (or illusion) of state neutrality in class conflicts. As Offe has put it, the 'capitalist welfare state bases its legitimacy on the postulate of a universal participation in consensus formation and on the unbiased opportunity for all classes to utilize the state's services and to benefit from its regulatory acts of intervention' (Offe 1972: 81).

Third, these writers claimed that in the late capitalist state this whole system of legitimation has begun to break down. Pressures within the system have led to the extension of social benefits in one form or another – student loans or grants, subsidized housing, health services, unemployment benefits, pensions, etc. – to virtually the whole population. The inevitable consequence of this, which European democracies were facing in the 1970s, would be to create a fiscal crisis by overloading the burden of public expenditure. Governments would then find themselves in a cleft stick. If they cut social expenditures they would alienate large numbers of citizens who had become dependent on them, thus reducing the ability of the state to legitimize the system. If they did not do this they would have to raise taxes or run a deficit, either of which would have deleterious effects on the economy.

The overall consequence of this kind of crisis, in Offe's view, would be the development of new kinds of group conflict in society, not so much between classes, in the old Marxist sense, as between sections. These might include conflicts between those dependent on social benefits and those who perceive themselves as paying for them, conflicts between depressed and prosperous regions, conflicts between generations, conflicts between ethnic minorities and the dominant community. Such conflicts would no longer be confined to the channels regarded as legitimate in a liberal-democratic state and the consequence of this would be that the outcomes of the conflicts would lack legitimacy in the eyes of the losers and the general public (see Offe 1980: 8–11). The general effect would be to undermine the whole process by which the democratic state legitimizes an unjust economic system, and thus to reduce the authority of the ruling classes in that society.

The belief that western societies were heading for a fiscal crisis in the 1970s was not confined to writers with Marxist sympathies. In 1978 two non-Marxist political scientists made a substantial impact on academic opinion with a book entitled *Can Government Go Bankrupt?* (Rose and Peters 1978). A central concept of this book was 'government overload', defined as a situation in which 'the national product grows more slowly than the costs of public policy and the claims of take-home pay, and there is not enough money in hand to meet both public and private claims' (Rose and Peters 1978: 29–30). This was said to be an immediate and serious problem in Italy, Sweden and the United Kingdom, while other western industrial states would be heading towards the same problem if the economic trends of the 1970s continued.

Governments facing this kind of dilemma have only three possible courses of action. One is to make policy changes to restrain the growth in public expenditure, a policy which is certain to be unpopular with bureaucrats, social workers and all those citizens who benefit from the social services that are affected. A second possibility is to maintain growing public expenditures by raising taxation, a course that would reduce the level of disposable personal incomes, be unpopular with most citizens and have a depressing effect on the economy. A third option is to dodge the issue by letting public expenditures rise without increasing taxation, which would increase the national debt and only postpone the task of getting to grips with the problem.

According to Rose and Peters, any of these options is likely to reduce public confidence in their government and to provoke a decline in political authority. Citizens could be expected to become cynical about government, unwilling to cooperate with it, and reluctant to comply with its edicts unless they are forced to do so. Governments would therefore become less effective and a cycle of declining authority would be initiated, to which the authors gave the label 'political bankruptcy'.

How much truth is there in these various theories about the relationship between the economic system and the level of political authority? To begin with Antonio Gramsci, the answer must be that his theory about the ideological hegemony of bourgeois values in capitalist society is undoubtedly correct. Since the end of the Second World War, the social values of the 'consumer society' have become dominant in all western industrial states. Capitalism has had such a beneficial effect on the living standards of the great majority of citizens in these states that alternative values have lost their attraction to all but a small minority. The revolutionary changes in eastern Europe in 1989 and 1990 have shown that forty years of brainwashing by socialist governments failed to convert their citizens to socialist values. Public ownership and central economic direction in these societies was a conspicuous failure, as it was in the Soviet Union, and people reacted accordingly. Radicals may regret that Gramsci was so penetrating, but the validity of his insight can hardly be denied.

The neo-Marxist argument that the capitalist system has been legitimized in the eyes of the workers by the liberal-democratic state is also both valid and helpful. There can be no doubt that political authority in the modern state is enhanced by democratic institutions. In past eras, when the functions of the state barely extended beyond foreign affairs, defence, customs duties and the maintenance of internal order, democracy might have been desirable but was not actually necessary. Governments could carry out their limited duties effectively so long as they had the support of the bureaucracy and the army, without needing much support from the general public. This could also be said of many developing countries today. But in modern industrial societies where the state regulates all aspects of public life, provides services for all its citizens and spends nearly half the national income, all sections of the community have to feel that they have some influences over government decisions if they are to acquiesce in government policies and cooperate willingly with government agencies. The modern state depends upon the cooperation of its citizens and this is a central fact of political life. It is beyond dispute that modern states with dictatorial systems of government have had to use stronger measures of coercion to secure public compliance with laws and policies than democratic states have needed.

The argument that welfare policies adopted by modern governments protect their legitimacy and that of the social order is also undoubtedly valid. If proof is needed, it is provided by examples of the partial breakdown of political authority among groups affected by prolonged unemployment, a tragic condition for which unemployment benefits can never be an adequate compensation. In Britain, unemployed workers engaged in riots and fights with the police during the period of mass unemployment immediately after the end of the First World War, and did so again in the depression years of the early 1930s. The large-scale unemployment of 1980–1 produced more riots, accompanied by widespread looting of shops, in twenty-seven urban areas in the summer of 1981. There was a racial element in the 1981 riots, for the first and worst of them (in Brixton and Liverpool) were fights between blacks and the police, and many of the subsequent disturbances were started by black teenagers. But most of the participants in the later riots were white and unemployment was clearly a major factor.

The final set of arguments examined in this section of the chapter, namely those relating to fiscal crisis and political overload, are particularly interesting in that they suggest that the modern state may be running into unavoidable problems as a consequence of its acceptance of responsibility for protecting its citizens against many of the hazards of life. People have higher expectations of what their government can do for them than were entertained by earlier generations. The efforts by governments to meet these expectations have put a heavy burden of costs on the national exchequer, which cannot easily be met unless the national economy is constantly growing, so that enhanced revenues are available to meet increasing costs.

The concern about fiscal overload arose during the 1970s because that was a bad decade for the industrial economies of the western world. A period of continuous economic growth since 1945 was checked by the four-fold increase in oil prices imposed by the Arab states in 1973, and western economies fell into a period of stagnation and growing unemployment accompanied by inflation. These conditions pushed several countries towards a position of fiscal overload, which might have had the serious political consequences predicted by some social scientists had the stagnation continued through the following decade. Fortunately, the last two decades of the century were years of almost continuous economic growth, so the predicted crisis did not develop. However, although the predictions made in the 1970s were unduly pessimistic, the analyses pointed to a significant potential problem. If western economies fall again into serious recession there will doubtless be renewed concern about the possibility that the problems created by fiscal overload might lead to a withdrawal of public confidence in government and a consequent decline in political authority.

Even without serious recession, there is, in Habermas's opinion, a danger that the legitimation of political authority by economic growth and welfare policies will be thought inadequate by some groups in society, either because (like the homeless or some ethnic minorities) the system has not worked for them, or because (like anti-nuclear protestors or radical environmentalists) the economic aims of the modern state are thought to be incompatible with moral principles that ought to govern the relationship between human beings and the natural world.

It may be concluded that the bearing of economic issues on political authority in the modern state is quite important. It is not as dominant as Marxists believe, but it certainly cannot be ignored as Max Weber and others seemed to assume. To understand the character and bases of political authority, we have to take both economic and non-economic factors into account, together with sociological factors like the composition of the political community. We have also, as suggested above, to consider not only the legitimacy of political, economic and social systems but also the legitimacy of particular policies, that may either elicit popular support or lead to public protests and cynicism. The maintenance of authority is central to the whole process of government, and an understanding of the factors supporting or diminishing that authority is therefore central to the understanding of how states are governed.

Part II

The democratic state and the citizen

Chapter 7

Democracy

THE WORD 'DEMOCRACY'

The word 'democracy' comes from the Greek and literally means rule by the people. It is sometimes said that democratic government originated in the city-states of ancient Greece and that democratic ideals have been handed down to us from that time. In truth, however, this is an unhelpful assertion. The Greeks gave us the word, but did not provide us with a model. The assumptions and practices of the Greeks were very different from those of modern democrats. The Greeks had little or no idea of the rights of the individual, an idea that is tied up with the modern concept of democracy. Greek practice granted the right of political participation to only a small minority of the adult inhabitants of the city. When those granted this right were able to take political decisions, they did so by a direct vote on issues, which is very different from the system of representative government that has developed in the west in the past two centuries. 'Modern men', asserts Sartori, 'want another democracy, in the sense that their ideal of democracy is not at all the same as that of the Greeks' (Sartori 1987: 279).

Greek democracy was poorly regarded by all the Greek philosophers and historians whose writings have survived, including Plato, Aristotle and Thucydides. They depicted it as government by the ignorant or government by the poor. It was subsequently held in general disrepute for over two thousand years. During the English civil war of the seventeenth century the Levellers briefly raised the banner of democracy, but they were a small group who had little or no influence on events. The founders of the American constitution shared in the generally poor view of democratic government. In *The Federalist*, James Madison, assuming that democracy involved direct rule by citizens, wrote that 'democracies have ever been found incompatible with personal security, or the rights of property; and have in general been as short in their lives as they have been violent in their deaths' (Hamilton et al. 1901: 48). The Founding Fathers talked of creating a republic, based on representative institutions, not a democracy; the leaders of the French Revolution talked of a republic also; and in Britain people described their system as one of representative and responsible government.

The term 'democracy', in its modern sense, came into use during the course of the nineteenth century to describe a system of representative government in which the representatives are chosen by free competitive elections and most male citizens are entitled to vote. In the United States this state of affairs was reached in the 1820s and 1830s, as the franchise was extended state by state. In France, there was a sudden leap to adult male suffrage in 1848, but parliamentary government was not established securely until 1871. In Britain, parliamentary government was secure from 1688 onwards, but the franchise was not extended to the majority of male citizens until 1867. Democracy is therefore a fairly new phenomenon in world history, though it is spreading.

Democratic institutions and practices have been firmly established for four decades or more in about 30 of the 192 states that now exist. In addition, there are younger but seemingly secure democratic regimes in Spain, Portugal and South Africa, an uncertain number of regimes that are best described as partially democratic, such as those of Cyprus, Mexico and Malaysia, and a very large number of regimes (mostly in eastern Europe and Latin America) that have freshly claimed the title of democratic since 1990. This last category will be discussed below under the heading of 'Democratization'.

In defining and discussing democracy in the twentieth century, there have been two sources of confusion. One source of confusion is that the term has been used not only to describe a system of government but also to describe other social relationships. Thus, Americans have said that their country not only has a democratic set of political institutions but also has or is a democratic society. Some socialists have advocated industrial democracy. Communists used to describe the Communist Party states of eastern Europe as people's democracies.

However, this kind of confusion does not pose serious problems so long as language is used with some precision. Thus, a democratic society, in the American sense, is one without hereditary class distinctions, in which there is something approaching equality of opportunity for all citizens. The term 'democratic' is used to indicate a degree of social equality, not a form of government. Industrial democracy, a term coined by Sidney and Beatrice Webb in the early years of the twentieth century, means a form of workers' control within industrial plants.

The term 'people's democracies' is an essentially misleading one that was coined in the aftermath of the Second World War. No sensible person has ever been deceived by this into thinking that these Soviet-controlled states were democratically governed in the accepted sense of the term. Clearly the citizens of the states themselves had no such illusion.

It follows that we need not be concerned about these extensions of the term 'democracy', but should focus our attention on the other source of confusion, namely the vagueness of the terms commonly used to define a democratic political system, the difficulty of clarifying these terms in a value-free way, and the array of partially incompatible justifications for democracy advanced by democratic theorists. It is because of these difficulties that the concept has to be regarded as currently contestable.

DEFINITIONS OF DEMOCRACY

If we start from the dictionary definition, that democracy means the rule of the people, we immediately run into the problem of how, in practical terms, to define the people and how to define the meaning of rule. Does 'the people' mean the whole adult population, or only those who possess enough property to give them what nineteenth-century politicians called a stake in the country? Does it matter if women are excluded from the franchise, as they were until after the Second World War in several European countries that were universally recognized as democratic, including France and Switzerland? Can one say that a system is partially democratic if the right to participate in politics is confined to one section of the population? The South African regime under apartheid, for example, rested on democratic institutions for its white citizens, but not for the majority of its people, who are black or coloured. Would the answer to this question be different if the great majority of South African citizens were white? In practice, the answers that people give to these questions depend on their political values, so it is impossible to formulate a value-free definition of 'the people'.

This is even clearer in regard to the question of what is meant by 'rule'. If ruling is taken to mean the activity of reaching authoritative decisions that result in laws and regulations binding upon society, then it is obvious that (apart from occasional referendums) only a small minority of individuals can be rulers in modern, populous societies. So for the dictionary definition to be operational, ruling must be taken in the much weaker sense of choosing the rulers and influencing their decisions. But how weak can this sense be and still remain meaningful? Is it essential to a democracy that governmental decisions, though made by only a small minority of politicians, should nevertheless reflect or embody the popular will? If so, how can the popular will be defined and how can it be identified in practice? The answers that people give to these and various similar questions clearly depend on their values and ideals.

It follows that we cannot arrive at an objective and precise definition of democracy simply by elucidating the intrinsic meaning of the term, in so far as it might be said to have an intrinsic meaning. We are therefore left with two alternatives. On the one hand, we can start with the observation of political practice and common usage, which leads to a definition in terms of institutions and processes and leaves the question of justification to a distinguishable (though not entirely separate) intellectual exercise. On the other hand, we can spell out our democratic ideals and consider what the practical implications of these are. Some theorists of democracy have taken the first approach, which can best be called the empirical approach, while others have taken the second, best called the idealist approach. Others again have tried to blend the two approaches.

In discussing theories of democracy, there is another distinction that is very relevant, namely the distinction between theories about parliamentary democracy and theories about American democracy. Because American political scientists occupy a rather dominant position in the discipline, it is sometimes forgotten that, among democracies, the United States is a unique case. All other securely democratic states have political systems based on the principle that sovereignty inheres in the national parliament or assembly. The controversies about democracy in these countries are essentially controversies about the selection and functions of representatives in this parliament.

The United States, in contrast, has a political system based on the principle that sovereignty inheres in the people. The US constitution begins with the words 'We the People of the United States . . . do ordain and establish this Constitution.' Members of Congress, Senators, the president and the judges are all regarded as deriving their authority from the people. In view of this difference, it will be convenient, in what follows, to deal with theories about American democracy separately from theories about parliamentary democracy.

AMERICAN DEMOCRACY

Simplifying somewhat, it can be said that Americans have defined their democracy in three different ways: a populist way, in terms of the rule of the people; a pluralist way, in terms of competition between sections and pressure groups; and an institutional way, in terms of a set of institutions and processes. All three versions had their origins in the thought and writings of the Founding Fathers of the American republic.

A belief in the principle of popular sovereignty was common to all the Founding Fathers, whether they were relatively conservative or relatively radical. One of the latter, James Wilson of Pennsylvania, declared in 1787 that:

> in our governments, the supreme, absolute, and uncontrollable power remains in the people. As our constitutions are superior to our legislatures, so the people are superior to our constitutions . . . In giving a definition of what I meant by a democracy . . . I termed it, that government in which the people retain the supreme power.
>
> (quoted Padover 1963: 19)

Madison and Jefferson, while sceptical of democracy because of its Greek connotation of direct rule, were quite clear that the American republic must have frequent elections so that the people could keep the politicians in check. They and their colleagues were, indeed, much more sceptical than British and French liberals have been of what could be expected of politicians. Thus, Madison declared that 'it is in vain to say that enlightened statesmen will be able to adjust . . . clashing interests. Enlightened statesmen will not always be at the helm' (Hamilton et al. 1901: 47). Jefferson believed that unless politicians and public officials were kept under the direct eye of their constituents, the result would be 'corruption, plunder and waste' (quoted Birch 1975: 227). Alexander Hamilton observed more than once that men love power. Thomas Mason said that 'From the nature of man, we may be sure that those who have power in their hands . . . will always, when they can . . . increase it' (quoted Dahl 1956: 8).

This scepticism about the motives and behaviour of politicians underlies the American belief in frequent elections. Hamilton said it was essential that representatives should 'have an immediate dependence on, and an intimate sympathy with, the people. Frequent elections are unquestionably the only policy by which this dependence and sympathy can be effectually secured' (Hamilton et al. 1901: 290). Jefferson was of the same opinion, declaring that legislators should have to submit themselves 'to approbation or rejection at short intervals' and saying that the executive (by which he meant a state governor or the president) must be 'chosen in the same way . . . by those whose agent he is to be' (quoted Padover 1969: 27). The president, be it noted, was regarded by Jefferson as an agent of the people; a view that has never been taken of a prime minister in a parliamentary system of democracy. In fact, the several state constitutions that existed between 1776 and 1787 all provided for frequent elections of legislators: in Connecticut and Rhode Island elections were held every six months; in South Carolina, every two years; and in the other ten states, every year. The decision to have biennial elections to the US House of Representatives, which is more frequently than in any other national legislative chamber in the world, followed naturally from these assumptions and practices.

This belief in popular sovereignty and frequent elections did not at first lead American theorists and leaders to identify their system of government as democratic. They preferred to call it republican, both because of the eighteenth-century tradition of republicanism among advanced thinkers and because the term was thought more appropriate to the balanced constitution that had been adopted in 1787 than the term democratic, with its connotations of lower-class dominance. (For a discussion of republican rhetoric during the early years of the republic, see Hanson 1985: Chapters 2 and 3.) It was not until the Jacksonian period that the term democratic came into widespread usage, and at first it had partisan connotations.

By the 1860s it had gained general acceptance, however, and the belief in popular sovereignty was reflected in Lincoln's famous definition of democracy as 'government of the people, by the people, for the people'. As

Sartori has pointed out, this phrase defies exact analysis. The three concepts in the phrase can be interpreted in a variety of ways; Stalin could have used it to characterize his regime without doing violence to the wording; and the phrase as a whole has rhetorical value rather than logical meaning (Sartori 1987: 34–5). It has rhetorical value because it reflects a strain in the American political tradition that all Americans can recognize; a strain that has been otherwise identified as faith in the common man. When Woodrow Wilson inspired popular enthusiasm for democracy during the First World War – which he described as a war to make the world safe for democracy – much was said about the twentieth century being the century of the common man. Padover reports that in the six years following the end of Wilson's presidency in 1921, 'there were, in the United States, no less than 120 books in print with "democracy" or its derivatives in their titles' (Padover 1963: 29).

There is another strain in American democratic thought that is also important, namely the pluralist strain. The origins of this, like the origins of the populist strain, can be found in the writings of the Founding Fathers. In *The Federalist* no. 10, Madison argued that the size and diversity of the proposed federation would safeguard the rights of minorities by making it difficult for any coherent majority to be formed.

> Extend the sphere, and you take in a greater variety of parties and interests; you make it less likely that a majority of the whole will have a common motive to invade the rights of other citizens; or if such a motive exists, it will be more difficult for all who feel it to discover their own strength, and to act in unison with each other.
>
> (Hamilton et al. 1901: 50)

In *The Federalist* no. 51, Hamilton repeated this argument.

> In the federal republic of the United States . . . the society itself will be broken into so many parts, interests, and classes of citizens that the rights of individuals or of the minority will be in little danger from interested combinations of the majority.
>
> (Hamilton et al. 1901: 287)

This suspicion of majority rule runs through a great deal of political debate in the United States. It goes along with the attachment to the separation of powers between the legislature and the executive that operates at both federal and state levels of government. It adds up to a preference for weak government that has no clear equivalent in other democratic states. In parliamentary regimes there have been some groups at some periods who have favoured laissez-faire economic policies (as in Britain in the mid-nineteenth century) or have shown suspicion of state power (as in France in the Third Republic), but the dominant strain in theories of parliamentary democracy has been a preference for government that has the capacity for firm leadership, though being responsible to elected representatives for the way this leadership is exercised.

In the post-war period these early theories about sectional pluralism were given a new emphasis by writers who argued that disciplined national parties were undesirable and probably impossible to achieve in a society as large and heterogeneous as the United States. And, following that, writers like Earl Latham (1952) and David Truman (1951) developed a new form of pluralism which hinged on the activities of organized interest groups rather than on pressures from geographical sections. American government, it was urged, is democratic because policy making is an arena for conflict between organized groups, which represent all relevant interests and ensure that the outcome would be a series of compromises which took these interests into account. All citizens were free to organize and join such groups, and the politicians responsible for reaching decisions would be influenced not only by the activities of existing groups but also by the knowledge that new groups would undoubtedly be formed to defend any interest that was presently unrepresented, if decisions were reached that were harmful to that interest.

This line of argument was in part persuasive, because one of the characteristics that stands out in American politics is the openness of the system to group pressures and the vigour of the conflicts between interest groups. However, the argument was open to the criticism of being complacent in its assumption that all interests are adequately represented, because it is evident that some groups are much more influential than others, while some categories of people, such as the homeless, have no effective group to look after their interests.

In general, it seems clear that scholars of the pluralist school are broadly correct in their insistence that conflict between group pressures is a central characteristic of American politics, but controversial when they equate this with democracy. To populists, it is not good enough to show that power is divided between competing elites and pressure groups, when democracy, properly defined, would be a system in which power belonged to the common people.

Without necessarily accepting the superiority of the populist approach, it must be conceded that there are grounds for doubting the claim that a pluralistic dispersal of political influence in a political unit can be equated with democracy. Imagine an American city divided on ethnic lines, as New York, for example, was during the 1950s. Suppose that in the government of this city representatives of the Irish community tended to have a dominant influence on issues relating to the police and the appointment of magistrates; that representatives of the Jewish community tended to have a dominant influence on policy regarding education and the social services;

and that representatives of the Italian community tended to have a large say in decisions about highways and the award of construction contracts. This would be a pluralistic system, but it would not be a fully democratic system if representatives of the black community lacked influence over any area of policy. Nor would it be fully democratic unless the representatives of the various communities were answerable to the electorate for their actions.

Some writers of the pluralist persuasion are more cautious than others in their claims. It is fair to say, however, that the pluralist view of democracy rests upon the three propositions that the United States is democratic, that the American political system is pluralistic, and that pluralism equals democracy, it being possible to start with any of these propositions and move to the other two, as if moving round a circle. And it is not unreasonable for critics to be sceptical about the third of these propositions, even while accepting the first two. One might well take the view that the American system is both pluralistic and democratic, but that its democratic character depends on more than its pluralistic dimension.

PARLIAMENTARY DEMOCRACY

The debates over the definition of democracy in countries enjoying parliamentary systems have been more limited in scope than the American debates. Very few writers in these countries have adopted populist definitions or pluralist definitions. The great majority have defined democracy in institutional and procedural terms, as parliamentary government with free competitive elections and a wide franchise. However, the normative theories by which they have justified democracy have varied considerably.

In discussing European ideas about democracy it is appropriate to begin with French ideas, because the French have influenced more countries that have remained democratic than the British have done. The British have certainly planted parliamentary institutions in nearly all their former colonies, but it is only in a few cases that these countries have remained democratic for more than a few years after the achievement of self-government. The French, in contrast, have influenced the growth of democratic institutions and practices throughout most of continental Europe.

A discussion of French democratic ideas has to begin with the theories of Jean-Jacques Rousseau. It is, of course, arguable whether Rousseau should be regarded as a democrat. He did not believe in representative government, because he did not think that people's wills could be represented by others. His ideal revolved around direct self-government in small communities, and even there he did not apparently think it important that all adults, or even a majority of adults, should be entitled to participate in political decisions. He wrote admiringly of the government of Geneva, where he had spent his youth, even though less than 10 per cent of the residents of that city had the right to participate. He is, nevertheless, important, because he developed a vision of popular self-government that has influenced the ideas of subsequent generations and affected the way they regard politics in large communities where representation is the norm.

One of the main keys to Rousseau's thinking is his commitment to the idea of civic virtue. Whereas most democratic theorists in both the United States and Britain have thought in terms of the protection and promotion of individual interests through political action, Rousseau considered that in an ideal polity individuals should put their personal interests on one side when they participated in politics, and commit themselves instead to the promotion of the communal welfare. He postulated the possibility that citizens could have two levels of consciousness, leading to two types of political will.

On the one hand, they would be conscious of their own individual or group interests, leading to a set of 'particular wills' to promote measures favourable to those interests. On the other hand, they could, in the right conditions, be led to think in terms of the interests of the community as a whole, leading to a 'real will' to promote measures that would protect these shared interests. The particular wills of citizens would be diverse and to some extent mutually incompatible; their real wills, on the other hand, would merge into a consensus that Rousseau called the 'general will'. It followed that if the laws of the state were based on the general will, they would not restrict the liberty (properly defined) of citizens, who would be forced to obey only laws that they had prescribed for themselves. It was in this way, Rousseau declared, that people could resolve the most fundamental problem of politics, that of how to achieve freedom while being bound by the laws of the community.

Rousseau was not naive enough to believe that this ideal state of affairs could easily be achieved. On the contrary, he set out some quite stringent conditions for its achievement. The community must be small enough for its active citizens to meet and cast their votes directly, rather than through representatives. Members of the community must be educated to accept what Rousseau called a civil religion – 'a purely civil profession of faith of which the sovereign should fix the articles, not exactly as religious dogmas, but as social sentiments without which a man cannot be a good citizen' (Rousseau 1913: 121). The laws to be determined by the general will must be general in their scope, not regulations on specific matters which would be bound to divide citizens according to their particular interests. The formulation of the questions to be put to the sovereign body, namely the assembly of citizens, must be left to a statesman described as the legislator.

It is obvious that when Rousseau wrote of the laws he was thinking of a small body of laws on fundamental questions of state, not of a mass of detailed legislation such as regulate the affairs of industrial societies in the twenty-first century. It is also made clear that in his ideal state the day-to-day business of government would be conducted not by the sovereign assembly, but by a body of public officials answerable to the sovereign assembly (see Rousseau 1913: Book III, Chapters 16–18).

This very brief sketch is intended only to indicate the character of Rousseau's vision of an ideal self-governing community, not to serve as a guide to his rich and rewarding philosophy of politics. Rousseau's ideas have had a profound influence on subsequent thought in many countries, including most notably the philosophies of Kant, Hegel and numerous followers of Hegel in Germany and, much later, the social ideas of the English Idealists. It is Rousseau who was the originator of what is now called the positive concept of liberty, to be discussed in Chapter 10.

Within France, Rousseau has always been a controversial figure, revered by some and reviled by others. What French attitudes to democracy have in common with Rousseau's ideas is the assumption that democracy is to be advocated in collective terms rather than in the individualistic terms common in the United States and Britain. French republicans tended to see the French revolution and the later extensions of the franchise as nation-building activities. Although French revolutionaries talked of the rights of man, they did not share the American belief in popular sovereignty. The doctrine of the revolutionaries was not that the French people were sovereign and that their views were represented in the National Assembly. The doctrine was that the French nation was sovereign and the National Assembly embodied the will of the nation. The 1789 *Declaration of the Rights of Man and of the Citizen* stated that members of the Assembly should not be 'bound by the instructions of their constituents', while the 1791 constitution said clearly that 'the representatives elected in the departments will not be representatives of a particular department but of the whole nation, and they may not be given any mandate'.

This doctrine marked a turning point in continental European ideas about political representation. Before this, the political representative had been viewed on the continent as a delegate, so that there were three parties in the representative process: the principal, the representative, and the authority to whom representations were to be made. According to the new theory promulgated by the French revolutionaries, political representatives were no longer to be thought of as intermediaries of this kind but were to contrive, in their collective capacity, to act as the voice of the nation. This theory clearly differs from both the populist view of democracy and the pluralist view of democracy; it is a European but not an American theory. It views the elected representative as an independent maker of national laws and policies, not as an agent for his constituents or for sectional interests.

This French view has been generally accepted in Europe. The French constitutional provisions that prohibited mandates and instructions were subsequently copied or followed in the constitutions of most of the countries of western Europe, including those of Belgium in 1831, Italy in 1848,

Prussia in 1850, Sweden in 1866, Austria in 1867, Germany in 1871, Switzerland in 1874, the Netherlands in 1887, and Denmark in 1915. Similar provisions are included in the 1948 constitution of Italy and the 1949 Basic Law of the German Federal Republic.

In Britain, which has no written constitution, the same attitude is embodied in the constitutional doctrine that sovereignty belongs to Parliament, there being no mention of the people, and also in the conventions that protect the privileges of Members of Parliament (MPs). In the 1950s, for instance, the Committee of Privileges of the House of Commons found that a serious breach of privilege had been committed by the editor of a national newspaper (with a circulation numbered in millions) who had published the private telephone number of an MP and advised those of his readers who disagreed with the views of the MP to telephone him and say so. The committee insisted that MPs must be free to say what they pleased in the House without the fear that it might lead to their being pestered in this way. The editor had to apologize to the House and could conceivably have been sent to prison for his offence.

It is unnecessary to follow the vicissitudes of French democratic thought since the revolution, but two general points about it should be noted. The first is that the French, unlike the British, have not had protracted arguments about the extent of the franchise. This was based on a property qualification from 1791 to 1848; was then extended to all male citizens; and was extended to women in 1946 as the result of the changed status of women brought about by the Second World War rather than as the consequence of a debate about democracy.

The other point is that French debates have been influenced by the ideological factionalism that was for long a characteristic of political life. In the Third and Fourth Republics the existence of a multi-party system meant that every government was based on a coalition, while the weakness of party discipline increased the frequency with which these coalitions fell apart. In the life of these two regimes, totalling 81 years, France had 118 different governments, with an average duration of only eight months each. Some theorists were quite happy with this situation, feeling that it had the desirable result of keeping the executive in check. Others were critical, feeling that the representatives were spending much of their time on political intrigues and factional disputes rather than advancing the interests of the nation. The Chamber of Deputies in the Fourth Republic was sometimes described as a 'house without windows' for this reason.

The situation changed with the establishment of the Fifth Republic in 1958. De Gaulle was called to power because French governments had been unable to deal effectively with the political crisis and civil war in Algeria. He then adopted the tactic of appealing directly to French electors, over the head of the National Assembly, by holding referendums on critical issues. Two of these dealt with Algeria, the result being that de Gaulle's favoured policies were endorsed and he claimed that he had a mandate from the nation to grant independence to that territory. He also claimed a popular mandate for a constitutional revision to provide for the direct election of the president, and succeeded in carrying this through, although the use of a referendum in these circumstances was not authorized by the constitution.

The present system of government in France is a hybrid system, not only in the sense that it combines some of the features of normal parliamentary democracy with a strong executive presidency that is not answerable to parliament, but also in the sense that it has broken with the traditional republican doctrine that the National Assembly (and only the National Assembly) embodies the will of the nation. De Gaulle claimed on occasion to speak for the national will himself, while on other occasions he declared that the electorate had done so. He saw himself on these latter occasions in the role of Rousseau's legislator, putting a simple question to the people and eliciting a large majority in favour of a course of action that would probably not have emerged from factional debates in the Assembly. De Gaulle is not normally regarded as a democratic theorist, but the undoubted success of his approach to democratic government has added another strand to the French political tradition.

The history of the development of democratic government in Britain differs from the French case in three significant ways. First, Britain had a liberal culture and a constitution based on the doctrine of parliamentary sovereignty for nearly two centuries before the system became democratic. Second, British politicians and theorists engaged in a debate over the extent of the franchise for the greater part of the nineteenth century. Third, British liberal theories were more individualistic in their assumptions than French theories.

From 1688 onwards the British political system was liberal in two senses. First, it was established that ultimate power rested with Parliament rather than with the king. Whereas most European states, including France, were ruled in the eighteenth century by monarchs who claimed absolute powers, the British king depended on Parliament for the passage of laws and for finance. As taxation could not be authorized for more than 12 months, Parliament had to meet at least once a year – a sharp contrast to the position in France before the revolution, when the Estates-General (the three legislative bodies meeting simultaneously) had not been summoned for 175 years.

Second, Britain had a liberal regime from 1688 onwards in the sense that there was substantial freedom of speech, freedom of the press, and freedom of political association. Along with these freedoms, British residents had the right to trial by jury and they had a judiciary whose members were appointed for life and were independent of both the legislature and the executive government. In the eighteenth century, Britain had the most liberal regime in the world.

This regime was, however, far from being democratic. Fewer than 5 per cent of adult citizens were entitled to vote, constituencies were wildly unequal in size, the electoral process was highly corrupt, and wealthy land owners controlled almost half the seats in the House of Commons. Various radical reformers objected to this system and argued in favour of franchise reform, on the ground that all citizens should have equal political rights. The French Revolution stimulated demands for reform, particularly among the working classes. Tom Paine's book, *Rights of Man*, published in 1792 and sold about 200,000 copies within 2 years (see Brown 1918: 84). From this period until the major parliamentary Reform Act of 1832, there was constant agitation for radical changes in the electoral system, based on a belief in natural rights and popular sovereignty. (For a fuller outline of these radical movements, see Birch 1964: Chapter 3.)

British legislators were to some extent influenced by these agitations and demonstrations in industrial areas, but were quite unable to accept the validity of demands that invoked the concept of natural rights. They were more willing, however, to accept the proposals for reform put forward by the Utilitarians, based, as those were, on the concept of interests. In the view of Jeremy Bentham and his collaborator, James Mill, the key to good government could be found in two propositions. The first is the principle of 'self-preference', by which it was affirmed that all men, including legislators, know what will promote their own happiness and try to maximize this. The second is the principle of 'utility' by which it was claimed that 'the right and proper end' of government is to promote 'the greatest happiness of the greatest number' of citizens (Bentham 1838–43: vol. 9, p. 8).

These propositions, if accepted, established a case for parliamentary reform which was quite independent of cloudy ideas like natural rights. The unreformed Parliament of the early years of the nineteenth century could not be expected to maximize the happiness of the general body of citizens, it was said, for its members were drawn from a very narrow section of society and would reflect the interests of only that section. If Parliament were to promote the general welfare, the franchise must be extended so that elected members were drawn from all sections of society. The logic of the argument pointed to universal suffrage, though Mill, anxious to make his ideas acceptable to a middle-class male audience, declared that it would be enough to give the vote to men over the age of 40.

This theory had philosophical limitations and, as a prescription for action, was not without ambiguities and difficulties. For one thing, it is not easy to see why a process of free election in geographical constituencies should automatically produce a House of Commons that would be a microcosm of the interests of the whole citizen body. Some interests, being those of a minority in each constituency, might never be represented at all. The assumption that women had no interests of their own, not represented by male members of their family, is clearly faulty. Beyond this, there is the problem presented by the differences in the intensity with which pains and pleasures are felt or anticipated. If such differences were ignored by legislators, as Bentham suggested, the interests of the majority would always be put first, even if the majority were only mildly in favour of a proposed policy or law while the minority felt that it threatened their wellbeing in a quite drastic way.

Despite these shortcomings, the Utilitarian theory acquired a great deal of influence in Britain in the first half of the nineteenth century. It did so largely because it met the needs of influential groups. The manufacturers of the northern industrial towns and the traders and craftsmen of London were alike in wanting fairly radical reforms in the system of parliamentary representation. The theories of the Whigs, though somewhat supportive of reform, were too moderate and too aristocratic in tone for them; the views advanced by Tom Paine and his followers were unacceptable because they insisted on the dangerous doctrine of natural rights of man. The Utilitarian theory had the advantage of being radical without seeming revolutionary; it was apparently logical and apparently hard-headed; it was admirably suited to be a vehicle for the claims of the new middle classes.

These middle-class groups were given the vote by the Reform Act of 1832. At about the same time, the principle of ministerial responsibility to Parliament was established, while the procedure by which the Reform Act was passed seemed to establish the dominance of the House of Commons over the House of Lords. The system therefore became more liberal; but was still undemocratic because the property qualification for the franchise excluded the great majority of the population.

The system was democratized in the period 1867–85, when (in two bites) the franchise was extended to include nearly all adult male citizens, the distribution of seats was reformed to provide something much nearer to equality in the size of constituencies, and effective measures were taken to stop electoral corruption. The campaign leading up to these reforms, however, was conducted in the name of liberalism rather than that of democracy. It was marked by caution and by openly expressed doubts about the political reliability of the working classes. There was precious little rhetoric about the intrinsic wisdom of the people, as had long been commonplace on the other side of the Atlantic.

Reformers placed their faith not in this but in the view expressed by John Stuart Mill (son of James Mill) that political reform would lead to the gradual education of the masses; that granting men the right to vote would develop their sense of social responsibility and would stimulate them to understand political problems and prepare themselves to take part in political life. The younger Mill's views therefore stressed the possibility of civic education rather than just the simple representation of interests. In this way he was more of an idealist than his father or Bentham had been. However, he was a rather cautious idealist, recommending that the extension of the franchise to working-class citizens (provided they paid taxes and could pass a literacy test) should be accompanied by the granting of multiple votes to citizens who had a higher education or were working in skilled or managerial occupations (J. S. Mill 1946: Chapter 8).

In 1865 William Gladstone summarized the cautious liberalism of the period by offering a definition of the attitudes of the two main parties to the franchise question. The Liberal attitude, he said, was 'trust in the people, only qualified by prudence', while the Conservative attitude was 'mistrust in the people, only qualified by fear' (quoted Bullock and Shock 1956: 143). In the event it was a Conservative government that took the plunge by introducing the Reform Act of 1867.

Universal suffrage was not established until women were granted the vote, which was done in two instalments, in 1918 and 1926. However, it was generally accepted that the reforms of 1867–85 made the British system democratic. Moreover, these reforms, having been supported by both major parties, and not leading to any serious problems, were quickly accepted by all shades of opinion as having been desirable. Lord Bryce, writing in 1920, said: 'Seventy years ago the word "democracy" awakened dislike and fear. Now it is a word of praise' (Bryce 1920: vol. 1, p. 4).

Since 1920, with the franchise issue settled, there have been three other developments in British democratic theory that deserve mention. First, the political ideas of the English Idealists influenced the attitude to democracy taken by several theorists in the inter-war period. The Idealist social philosophers, writing in the last two decades of the nineteenth century, introduced some of Rousseau's notions to British intellectual circles. They advocated what has become known as the positive concept of liberty, and their approach to this topic will be discussed in Chapter 10. They and (more particularly) their followers also developed a less individualistic and more uplifting view of the purpose of representation than had been common in the nineteenth century.

One such theorist was A. D. Lindsay of Oxford. In a book called *The Essentials of Democracy*, published in 1929, he said this:

> The purpose of representative government is to maintain and preserve different points of view, in order to make effective discussion possible . . . it is democratic in so far as it is recognized that anyone . . . has something special and distinctive to contribute . . . But this belief that everyone has something to contribute does not mean that what everyone has to say is of equal value. It assumes that if the discussion is good enough the proper value of each contribution will be brought out in the discussion.
>
> (Lindsay 1935: 40–1)

About the same time, Harold Laski wrote in similar terms: 'The underlying thesis of parliamentary government', he said, 'is that discussion forms the popular mind and that the executive utilizes the legislature to translate into statute the will arrived at by that mind' (Laski 1928: 13). Ernest Barker of Cambridge followed the same trend when he wrote that the real basis of democracy is the 'discussion of competing ideas, leading to a compromise in which all the ideas are reconciled and which can be accepted by all because it bears the imprint of all' (Barker 1942: 41).

Peter Bachrach has suggested that Lindsay and Barker, along with J. S. Mill, should be regarded as the authors of the 'classical theory of democracy' (Bachrach 1969: 4). This is quite implausible, both because there is no classical theory and because Lindsay and Barker were not particularly influential. They are quoted here only because their views indicate the width of the Atlantic Ocean in regard to democratic theory. The predominant tendency in Britain in this field has always been to favour pragmatic Utilitarian views, but those British theorists who did briefly (because their views did not survive the Second World War) develop more idealistic theories produced ideas that were far removed from the idealism of American populists.

A second line of argument in Britain has revolved around the theory of the electoral mandate, developed by Labour Party spokesmen. This theory states that each party has a duty to present the electorate at a general elec tion with a detailed manifesto setting out the policies that the party proposes to follow, and the legislative changes it proposes to introduce, if it wins the election and forms the next government. The incoming government would then be entitled to claim that it had a mandate from the electors to carry out its promises and would therefore be acting democratically in using party discipline to press these policies through Parliament.

To some extent, this theory reflects the traditions and practices of the British trade-union movement, which has always believed that leaders should not only be elected but also be mandated to pursue specific policies endorsed by the rank-and-file members. Beyond this, however, it can be and has been claimed that the theory is the most appropriate one for a country whose politics are dominated by two highly disciplined national parties. It is said that individualistic theories of representative government like those of the Utilitarians are outdated in a situation in which the role of the voters is not to get their individual interests represented but simply to decide which of the two main parties should govern the country for the next four or five years. This may be a restricted choice, but if the parties are democratically organized (as the Labour Party is), so that all who are interested in party policy can play a part in framing it, then the ordinary citizen can have a continuing role in the democratic process and the policy of a party winning a general election can reasonably be regarded as reflecting the will of the majority.

This theory has some plausibility in the context of a parliamentary system dominated by two disciplined parties. It is, however, highly controversial and much academic opinion is against it. The theory runs contrary to the accepted constitutional doctrine that the government of the country has a responsibility to protect and advance the interests of the whole nation, not just to look after its own political supporters. The theory also seems to be incompatible with the fact that the victorious party at a general election in Britain rarely gets the support of a majority of voters and virtually never gets that of a majority of electors.

In reviewing the theory of the electoral mandate in the early 1960s I reached the conclusion that it had little descriptive validity, citing as evidence the results of sample surveys of public opinion and voting behaviour. These showed that in the 1950s there was a poor match between opinions on policy issues and voting behaviour. In the 1950 general election in a London constituency, 41 per cent of Labour voters agreed with Conservative policy positions, while in the 1955 election in Birmingham 39 per cent of Labour voters had pro-Conservative policy positions as against only 34 per cent who had pro-Labour policy positions (see Birch 1964: 120–1).

It was also shown that most voters decide how to vote on the basis of factors other than their view of the rival election manifestos; the authors of a study of voting in Birmingham in the 1951 election concluded that 'the maximum proportion of voters whose vote was primarily decided by an issue or issues cannot have been more than 10 per cent, and may have been much smaller' (Milne and Mackenzie 1954: 139). These data suggested that it would be unrealistic, as well as controversial on constitutional grounds, to interpret election results as conferring a mandate for the victorious party to pursue the particular policies listed in its election manifesto.

Is there any reason to revise this verdict? The answer to this question has to be a little ambiguous. The constitutional argument against the mandate theory remains, and the argument in terms of the opinions of voters can still be put. A 1970 survey showed that only four out of sixteen policies set out in the Labour Party's manifesto had the support of a majority of Labour voters (Rose 1976: 309). In 1982 a leading student of voting behaviour reported that 'for at least the last fifteen years people have voted Labour despite its policies' (Crewe 1982: 37). A 1987 survey found that only about a third of the voters favoured four of the central proposals put forward in the manifesto of the victorious Conservative Party (Oliver 1989: 128).

In view of these rather powerful arguments against the mandate theory, why is it suggested that the evidence of recent years is slightly ambiguous? The reason is that there has been a growing tendency for politicians to place more stress than previously on the claim that they have a mandate for certain specific policies. The behaviour of the House of Lords has been one reason for this. Their Lordships have adopted the convention, quite voluntarily, that they will not mutilate or reject government Bills to which the ruling party committed itself in its last election manifesto, though they might mutilate or reject other Bills. In consequence, Conservative ministers in the 1980s were heard arguing that their government had a mandate for such policies as the compulsory sale of municipal housing or the abolition of the Greater London Council, about which the Lords had reservations.

Another relevant development is that British electors have become more volatile since the 1960s, apparently more willing to switch votes between parties in reaction to specific policies carried out or promised. This does not mean that the theory of the electoral mandate is much more convincing, because voters are not any more likely to endorse the whole platform of the party they support at the polls. However, it does mean that parties are apt to place more emphasis on specific policies they have designed to attract votes, and to claim that they have a mandate to implement such policies if they win the election.

The consequence of these developments is that, although the theory of the mandate, in its strong form, may have been undermined by empirical evidence, British politicians still talk about mandates to do this or that, and are likely to continue to do so. The theory of the mandate may be dead, but it won't lie down.

If British government is viewed in comparative perspective, it can be said that the mandate theory at least has the merit of drawing attention to one of the most democratic features of the system. One of the strengths of British democracy is the existence of a closer connection between electoral behaviour and government policies than can exist in a system fragmented by the separation of legislative and executive powers, or competition between numerous parties. British electors have the opportunity to base their vote on the plans of the rival parties, with some expectation that these plans will be carried out by the winner, and that must be regarded as a distinct advantage in democratic terms even if only a minority of electors actually decide on this basis. British general elections give the public a more meaningful influence over future government policies than congressional elections in the United States, parliamentary elections in Italy (where every government is a coalition), or federal elections in Canada (where the parties do not publish detailed manifestos). Perhaps this aspect of the British system should be called 'manifesto democracy', to avoid the awkward connotations of the term 'mandate'.

Another controversy about democracy that has occurred in Britain is a controversy about intra-party democracy. This has been essentially a controversy within the Labour Party rather than between parties, but it raises a question of theoretical interest. Up until 1981, leadership selection and policy determination in the Labour Party were effectively in the hands of the parliamentarians. In 1981, the rules were changed so as to provide that the parliamentary leader would be chosen by an electoral college in which the Labour MPs would have only 30 per cent of the votes, the rest being divided between the local party branches (30 per cent) and the affiliated trade unions (40 per cent). It was also provided that sitting MPs would no longer have an automatic right of re-nomination, but could be deselected by their constituency party branches. The object of the changes was to give the unions and the party activists in the country more power to influence party policy and the behaviour of Labour MPs.

This objective would not be thought controversial in the United States, but it provoked a storm of controversy in Britain. Within months of the changes, twenty-five Labour MPs had left the party in protest and joined the new Social Democratic Party. They believed, as did many constitutional commentators, that giving extra-parliamentary organizations the power to influence party policy in Parliament contravened the principles of parliamentary democracy. R. T. McKenzie had declared in his magisterial book on the party system that if the extra-parliamentary organizations of the Labour Party 'attempted to arrogate to themselves a determining influence with respect to policy or leadership they would be cutting across the chain of responsibility from Cabinet, to Parliament, to electorate, which is a fundamental feature of the British parliamentary system' (McKenzie 1955: 588). In a much later article he said that 'intra-party democracy, strictly interpreted, is incompatible with democratic government' (McKenzie 1982: 195).

The vigour with which this view was expressed by McKenzie, an academic supporter of the moderate wing of the Labour Party, reflected his concern that radical party activists might gain the upper hand in struggles over party policy. However, the general principle involved has the support of most theorists of parliamentary democracy, in Britain as in continental Europe. It underlay Edmund Burke's famous 1774 speech to the electors of Bristol asserting that MPs should not surrender their judgement to the views of their constituents, to be quoted in Chapter 8.

The modern justification for this principle is that party leaders, when in office, have to balance the doctrinal aims of their party with a myriad of conflicting pressures, financial problems, and international developments. It is the responsibility of these leaders to get the balance right and to answer for their decisions to Parliament, and subsequently to the electorate. It would be wrong, so the argument goes, for leaders to be subject in this difficult task to instructions or threats from party committees whose members do not have the same duty of governing the country, are not engaged full-time in this activity, do not have expert advice from the bureaucracy, and are not answerable either to Parliament or the electorate. The position of ministers in a parliamentary system is very different from that of US Members of Congress and Senators, who do not have executive responsibilities, and this is one of the reasons for the differences between European and American democratic theories. Europeans are rarely populists, in the American sense, and while in the nineteenth century this was partly because Europeans were more sceptical about the political wisdom of the people, in the late twentieth century it is mainly because of the constitutional differences between a parliamentary system and one based on the separation of powers. These transatlantic differences are so great that any attempt to generalize about democracy which ignores them must inevitably be inadequate.

DEMOCRATIZATION

The 1990s saw a dramatic increase, indeed a doubling, in the number of countries claiming to have democratic regimes, and a direct consequence of this has been a renewed interest by scholars in the process of democratization. This interest is renewed rather than new because earlier decades saw two attempts by American theorists to generalize about the matter. One of these was the theory that there is a necessary relationship between the growth of free enterprise on the one hand and the development of democratic government on the other. The more ambitious of the writers who suggested this reflected the long-standing American tendency to believe that the destiny of the world is to see a convergence of all societies towards the American way of life.

This theory was always simplistic and historical experience gives little support for it. When Germany followed the British and American examples by rapidly industrializing its economy in the period between 1871 and 1914, it did so under an autocratic system of government, not a democratic one. Despite the growth of a large and well-educated middle class, said by theorists to be the main factor that links economic progress with democracy, Germany did not become democratic (apart from the brief and messy interlude of the Weimar Republic) until pushed into doing so by the American, British and French occupying powers after 1945. Equally, Japan's industrialization and economic progress did not lead to democratic politics until General MacArthur and his colleagues imposed democratic institutions on the country after its surrender. More recently the newly industrialized societies of eastern Asia, led by Singapore, South Korea and Taiwan, have achieved very high rates of economic growth with political systems that have been somewhat undemocratic. The Asian countries with the longest experience of democracy, namely India and Sri Lanka, have remained economically backward.

The other attempt to generalize was that by behaviouralist scholars who tried to find statistical correlations between the growth of democracy and a number of other variables. As Paul Cammack has pointed out, and as four or five behaviouralists admitted in the period from 1985 to 1991, this whole effort was unsuccessful (Cammack 1994: 174–5). Having learned from those mistakes, recent scholars have simply used historical methods, producing case studies of democratization in various areas with only modest attempts to generalize about them.

History shows that it is easier to establish democratic institutions than to develop the political conventions and practices that are needed to build a stable system of democratic government. The latter requires not only a system of free elections but also free mass media, freedom to organize political parties, a non-partisan judiciary, a readiness of voters to accept electoral defeat, a readiness of governing elites to hand over power to their rivals, and a willingness of the military to refrain from using their power to intervene in the democratic process. Some examples of failure follow.

After the defeat of Tsarist Russia and the Austro-Hungarian Empire in the First World War, nine successor states in eastern and south-eastern Europe were established with democratic institutions. Of these, only Czechoslovakia remained democratic until 1939. In the other eight, democracy gave way to authoritarian government of one kind or another in the following order: Bulgaria, June 1923; Poland, May 1926; Lithuania, December 1926; Yugoslavia, January 1929; Austria, March 1933; Estonia, March 1934; Latvia, May 1934; and Romania, February 1938 (see Bermeo 2003: 23). It should be noted that none of these moves to authoritarian systems was caused by ethnic cleavages in society, economic collapse, mass revolution or civil war, all of which have led to democratic breakdowns elsewhere. In these eight states the cause was either the unwillingness of the military to keep out of politics or manoeuvres among ruling elites to keep themselves or their friends in power (Bermeo 2003: Chapter 2).

Another wave of newly independent democratic institutions came into being in consequence of the decolonization of European empires in the period 1945–65. In Africa the results have been highly discouraging for democrats. The former Belgian Congo (now Democratic Republic of the Congo) has been a political shambles since the early 1950s, with dictatorship, ethnic violence and periods of civil war. In Portuguese East Africa (now Republic of Mozambique) independence was followed by a period of civil strife, while Angola has seen a protracted civil war lasting since 1976. The former British colonies have seen their parliamentary institutions disrupted by ethnic conflict, military takeovers and personal dictatorships, while Nigeria, the most tragic case, had a civil war that cost up to one million lives. They have also been affected by widespread corruption that has held back economic development and wasted vast amounts of international aid. The former French colonies have been the most stable, partly, perhaps mainly, because the French colonial administrators stripped power from tribal leaders and developed a French-educated elite to whom they could transfer power. Another reason was that after the colonies had nominal independence they retained close economic ties with France, which also provided their new governments with military support in what was often called a neo-colonial relationship. But these states have had long periods of single-party dominance and their claims to be democratic are questionable.

A quite different set of factors has created problems in South America. In that continent, which has seen numerous moves towards democratization, institutional arrangements have been more significant than ethnic cleavages in leading to reversions to authoritarian rule. Because of the natural influence of US ideas and examples, democratic reformers have generally favoured directly elected presidents. However, the US system has several disadvantages for a newly democratized state that, unlike the United States in its early decades, needs strong central government to cope with the myriad problems of the modern world. It provides for two centres of power, the executive and the legislative, each of which enjoys democratic legitimacy but which may be far from agreement. As Linz and Valenzuela (1994) have pointed out, it is often the case that the presidents owe their majority to the support of large urban centres while legislative houses are more representative of the very different interests of rural areas and small towns. There is no democratic principle to resolve conflicts arising from this kind of difference, so that there is a recurrent temptation for the president to seize power by organizing mass demonstrations or for the military to intervene on one side or the other (Linz and Valenzuela 1994: 7–8).

If no single party has a majority in the country, which is quite common in all systems, a parliamentary system can produce a coalition cabinet, but there cannot be a coalition president. A presidential election produces a winner-take-all situation, and frequently a loser who loses all, having no other office to fall back on. Another disadvantage is that presidential systems normally provide for fixed terms of office, unlike parliamentary systems which are much more flexible. If a new development provokes a crisis, a parliamentary system can respond by a cabinet reshuffle, the replacement of the prime minister by one of his or her colleagues, or a general election focused on the issue in question (Linz and Valenzuela 1994: 8–10).

Yet another disadvantage of the US system is the principle that if a president dies in office the vice-president automatically takes over for the duration of the president's term. This worked well enough in the United States in 1945 and 1963, when exceptionally talented vice-presidents acceded to office, but it is an inherently risky system. It contributed to the downfall of democratic regimes in Brazil in 1964, Uruguay in 1973, and Argentina in 1976, after death had elevated vice-presidents who had different policies from or were thought to be less efficient than their predecessors (see Bermeo 2003: Chapters 3, 4 and 6). This is no place for a catalogue, but it seems clear that a preference for directly elected presidents has played a part in the chequered political history of South American countries, with periods of democracy, one-party government and military dictatorship following one another, not necessarily in that order.

Since 2003, a new focus of interest in democratization has followed President Bush's repeated assertion that he would like to promote democracy throughout the Middle East and sees no reason to believe that Muslim societies cannot support democratic political systems. In fact there are two reasons to be doubtful about this, one theological and the other sternly practical.

The theological reason is that a basic doctrine of the Islamic religion is that all the laws humankind needs are to be found in the Koran and a very early volume of judicial elaborations of Koranic law. The democratic view that a parliament or congress can be a sovereign law-making body therefore conflicts with a fundamental Islamic belief; all that such assemblies can properly do is to interpret the laws that already exist. The current constitution of Iran is strictly correct by Islamic standards. Iran has an elected Parliament that passes laws, but it also has a Council of Guardians, composed of unelected religious leaders, that has the power to nullify these laws if they are deemed to conflict with Koranic law. It was not really surprising that during the 2005 parliamentary election campaign the Council of Guardians was able to disqualify numerous candidates, including thirty-five sitting Members of Parliament, on the grounds that they were unfit to interpret Koranic law.

The practical reason is simply that moderate leaders of Muslim states are afraid that democratic elections and all the liberalizing moves that go with them would increase the influence of fundamentalist groups whose aim is to destabilize the system and push their countries into open opposition to the United States and the western alliance. Egypt, under American pressure, held a general election in 2005 that was more free than it has held for a generation. The main fundamentalist organization, the Muslim Brotherhood, was illegal with many of its leaders in prison. It nevertheless fielded numerous candidates as independents and they shocked the government by getting almost 20 per cent of the popular vote. The government subsequently jailed a candidate who had challenged President Mubarak for the presidency, tightened its emergency laws, and summarily postponed local elections that were due to be held in April 2006.

Of course, successful democratization in a Muslim country is only improbable, not impossible. Turkey has had a nominally secular regime since 1928 and has recently developed a largely democratic parliamentary system. It has had to cope with nationalist agitation and occasional terrorist attacks from its sizeable Kurdish minority, its record on human rights is controversial, and its secular regime is unpopular with other Muslim states. But its leaders have displayed great determination in maintaining their commitments.

In this, Turkey may be compared with India, where commitment of the governing elite to democratic principles has survived every kind of problem since the country achieved independence in 1947. India has Muslim, Sikh and Tamil minorities totalling over 210 million people. It has experienced three major wars with Pakistan, a border conflict with China, civil conflict in Kashmir, a nationalist revolt in Punjab, terrorist attacks on Delhi and Mumbai, and the assassination of two prime ministers. That its democratic parliamentary system has remained intact is a great tribute to its leaders and an encouragement to all who believe, as I do, that democracy is the best form of government yet devised. The problem for social scientists, however, is that Turkey and India have very little in common apart from human commitment. In 1994 Alistair Edwards concluded that 'general questions about democratization are unanswerable. The infinite variety of conditions, actually present or counterfactually posed, which might facilitate or impede such a process can produce only bewilderment' (Edwards 1994: 101).

The period since 1945 has certainly seen progress in a democratic direction, for nearly all European states outside the Balkans now have democratic systems that seem stable, while in the developing world democratic ideals and ambitions have become more widespread. A Freedom House report has indicated that between 1980 and 2004 22 states in the developing world embarked on a process of democratization (Karatnycky and Ackerman 2005). However, prediction is difficult and the passage of time since Edwards' (1994) conclusion was reached has revealed little to challenge it.

Chapter 8

Political representation

DISPUTES ABOUT REPRESENTATION

Representation is a concept that has given rise to more disputes at the level of practical politics than at the level of political theory or philosophy. This is not to say that there are no difficulties at the philosophical level because, as I shall argue later, there are four logically distinct types of representation that are not always distinguished. But this kind of difficulty can be resolved, whereas the practical disagreements are mostly incapable of final resolution because they hinge upon normative differences about how political life ought to be conducted.

Within the period of the modern democratic state there have been three kinds of public dispute about representation in legislative assemblies, to say nothing (for the moment) about other forms of representation within systems of government. First, there have been disputes about who should be represented. Should it be sections of the country or economic interests, such as the land-owning interest, the farming interest, the merchants and bankers, the manufacturing and mining interests? Should it be social classes, with the franchise confined to citizens who have a stake in the country, to use the term used in British debates in the nineteenth century to describe people with a certain amount of property? Should women have the vote as well as men, a question that was not settled in France and Switzerland until 1946?

A second type of dispute is about how representatives should be chosen. Should they be appointed or elected? The Canadian Senate and the German Bundesrat both have appointed members, so this question is still current. If members are elected, how should they be elected? Should it be by simple plurality, as in Britain, the United States and Canada, or by some form of proportional representation, as in all the members of the European Community apart from Britain?

A third type of dispute is about how elected representatives should behave. Should they act as if they were mandated to pursue policies favoured by their constituents or should they act independently of constituents' wishes, as trustees for the public interest? This third type of dispute has been described by Hanna Pitkin as 'the paradox of representation' (Pitkin 1968: 38). 'Can both views be right', she asks, 'when they seem to support opposite and incompatible conclusions about the duty of a representative?' (Pitkin 1968: 41).

The first of these three disputes has now been resolved by a combination of campaigns by groups who were excluded from the franchise, prudence on the part of ruling groups, and propaganda by reformers and political theorists. It is now accepted that all adult citizens should be represented through the electoral system. In states where elections are not competitive the process may not give any substantial degree of influence to the electors, but at least the proper extent of the franchise has passed out of dispute.

The other two questions are still in dispute in various countries and it does not seem likely that they can be resolved by the contributions of political theorists. The mechanics of electoral systems are likely to remain as a subject of controversy in some states, because the conflicting interests of the political parties are directly affected by the way that the system converts votes in the polling booth into seats in the assembly. The mandate/independence controversy is likely to remain alive because each represents a viable view of how an elected person should behave. The views are not easily compatible, but a reasonable case can be made for each of them. It is important to note, however, that members of Congress or Parliament do not hold that status either because they may be (to some extent) mandated or because they act largely as trustees for the public interest. These are recommendations about their behaviour; but what establishes their status as representatives is that they have been appointed by a certain process of election. This is their defining characteristic; and as there are other ways of defining a representative it will be helpful now to distinguish these by a brief exercise in linguistic analysis.

TYPES OF REPRESENTATION

The best philosophical guide to linguistic analysis is Wittgenstein, who suggested that when a word has two or more distinct usages the relationship between these usages should be regarded in the way that we regard relationships between members of a family. We recognize that family members have a common origin and that they may share a recognizable family character, but we do not concentrate all our attention on what they have in common because to do so would mean that we miss the distinctive characters of the various members. In dealing with concepts that have differing usages, the shared characteristic is sometimes very important but sometimes relatively unimportant. In the case of representation, I think it is relatively unimportant, a view that is strengthened by Pitkin's reminder that the German language has three quite different words – *vertreten, darstellen,* and *reprasentieren* – 'all of which are usually translated by the English "represent"' (Pitkin 1989: 132). The view that I wish to advance here, which I have also expressed in previous publications (see Birch 1971a, 1971b), is that there are four main usages of the term 'representative', corresponding to four main types of modes of representation, each of which is logically distinct from the other. Three of them have both political and non-political connotations, while the fourth is purely political.

The first type of representation occurs when the term 'representative' is employed to describe a person who has the acknowledged duty of defending or advancing certain interests specified by his or her principal. A sales representative is a representative in this sense of the term; so is an ambassador; and so is a lawyer appointed to defend the interests of a client in a court hearing. The representative does not necessarily act exactly as his or her principal would; in some situations the representative may drive a harder bargain than the principal would feel able to do, while in others the representative may be restrained by professional etiquette and conventions. But in all cases the function of this kind of representative is to achieve certain goals set by his or her principal, and the extent to which these goals are achieved is a criterion of successful representation. As a form of shorthand, I will henceforth describe this kind of representation as 'delegated representation'. In a modern political system the most conspicuous form of delegated representation is that by spokespersons for pressure groups.

One question which commonly arises in connection with delegated representation is the extent to which the representative is, or should be, bound by the instructions of the principal. This question has been discussed in scores of books, hundreds of articles, thousands of speeches. No agreement has been reached on the answer, for the simple reason that no meaningful answer is possible when the question is phrased in general terms. It is a question to which the answer depends almost entirely on the exact circumstances of the representative relationship under discussion. For example, a lawyer cannot be so closely bound by the client's instructions as a sales representative can be bound by the firm's instructions, because the lawyer is governed by a strict code of professional behaviour and has duties to the court as well as to his or her client. How closely the lawyer will follow instructions also depends on the nature of the case: a lawyer in a divorce case might expect to receive fairly detailed instructions about the kind of evidence to call and the kind of settlement to work for whereas a lawyer defending someone charged with murder would expect a fairly free hand in reaching decisions about the best line of defence.

Another question which often arises is the extent to which a representative of this kind can bind his or her principal. It is sometimes assumed that if a representative of this kind agrees to a proposal this can be taken to imply the consent of the principal. In fact this is only sometimes the case. The relationship between representation and consent varies, and depends upon all sorts of contingent factors. Thus, modern ambassadors hardly ever have power to commit their governments, but when international communications were slower ambassadors were sometimes given such powers. The relationship between representation and commitment or consent is therefore (like the question of instructions) a matter for historical inquiry, depending as it does on the exact circumstances of each situation.

The statement that a person is a representative in the sense of being an agent therefore conveys only a limited amount of information. It does not tell us how the person was appointed, what kind of person he or she is, whether he or she acts under close or loose instructions, or whether the representative's agreement to a proposal binds the principal. However, it tells us something about his or her functions and probable behaviour, and is therefore to be sharply distinguished from the second general usage of the term, which refers not to the functions but to the descriptive characteristics of the representative.

This second usage refers to physical similarity. It is found when representational art is distinguished from abstract art. It is well exemplified in the term 'representative sample', which indicates a sample of the relevant population chosen by statistical methods so that the main characteristics of the population will be mirrored in the sample. The term is used in the same sense, but more loosely, to denote a person who is in some respects typical of a larger class of persons to which he or she belongs. This usage occurs in such statements as 'the varied membership of the club is represented fairly well in the composition of the executive committee' or 'a parliament where fewer than 10 per cent of the members are women is hardly representative of the electorate'. Since a representative body would be ideally constituted, in this sense of the term, if it were a microcosm of the larger society, I shall describe this kind of representation as 'microcosmic representation'.

The statement that a person is a representative in this sense does not tell us anything about his or her functions, intentions or even behaviour. It simply tells us something about his or her personal characteristics. However, many writers have asserted that characteristics, particularly social and economic characteristics, have a strong influence on behaviour, so the fact that ruling groups rarely represent the population in a microcosmic sense has sometimes been adduced as an explanation for their evident failure to govern properly. As is well known, Jeremy Bentham's conversion to the cause of parliamentary reform occurred when he became convinced that a House of Commons dominated by the upper classes was unlikely to do more than advance upper-class interests. Many of the arguments of the early Utilitarians were based on the belief that the country needed a parliament which would be representative in this microcosmic sense, so that its members, while pursuing their own interests, would automatically further the interests of the whole population.

Of course, this highly influential school of thought was based upon a whole set of fallacious arguments. Quite apart from the philosophical limitations of Utilitarianism, their political programme was beset by practical difficulties. One cannot get a representative sample by calling for volunteers, particularly when the job in question requires special talents and rewards them with a high degree of insecurity. The world has never seen a representative assembly which is fully representative in a microcosmic sense, but party managers are well aware of the criticisms that may be levelled against their party if no serious attempt is made to at least reflect the main social divisions of the electorate in their choice of candidates. It is for this reason that American parties frequently nominate a 'balanced ticket' for election in urban areas, ensuring that the party's list of candidates contains a suitable proportion of persons drawn from each of the main ethnic groups in the community. With less success, parties in most democratic states are currently making an effort to see that more women are nominated for office.

The criticism of unrepresentativeness, in this microcosmic usage of the term, has been levelled against various institutions besides legislative assemblies. It used to be said that the US Supreme Court was unrepresentative of the American population when all its members were white, a situation that has been corrected since 1967 by the practice of always including one black judge. It used to be said that the Canadian Supreme Court was unrepresentative of the population when all its members were male. It has often been said that recruitment to the policy-making grades of the British civil service is socially biased, with preference given to candidates from private schools and the older universities. Attempts to meet this criticism have been somewhat half hearted, as is evidenced by the fact that in 1987 a candidate who had graduated from Oxford or Cambridge 'was nine times as likely to be appointed as a candidate from another university' (Birch 1990: 141). In the United States a more determined effort has been made to eliminate the more obvious forms of social bias in recruitment to bureaucratic posts, so as to make the bureaucracy 'more representative' (on the American situation, see Krislov 1974).

The third main usage is found when an object or emblem is described as representing a larger or more abstract entity in a symbolic way. As examples, the scales of justice represent the essential character of the law, the Christian cross is a symbol of the crucifixion, the stars and stripes on the American flag symbolize the growth of the United States from 13 states to 50. Persons can be symbolic representatives also, as Queen Elizabeth is sometimes said to be a symbol of the British nation and the Governor-General of Canada or Australia is a symbolic representative of the crown and the historic connection between Britain and those countries. In one of Marx's early writings the industrial protelariat was depicted as the symbolic representative of all humanity, having 'a universal character because its sufferings are universal' and not claiming 'a particular redress because the wrong which is done to it is not a particular wrong but wrong in general' (Marx 1964: 58).

This usage is neither so common nor so important as the first and second usages, but it should not be ignored because symbolic representation plays a significant part in political activity. It is often the case that the appointment of a member of a minority group to a position of prestige is valued not so much for any real difference in policy that he or she may bring about as for the fact that the appointment symbolizes the acceptance of the group as full members of the community.

These three usages of the term representation are non-political in origin, though often applied to political situations. None of them adequately covers the position of elected members of a legislative assembly in a modern democratic state. Members of Parliament or Congress are not actually delegates of their constituents. There is no machinery whereby constituents may formulate instructions and communicate them to members, and in any case the normal situation is for the constituents to be divided among themselves in terms of their interests, values and opinions about policy. Nor can the members be said to be microcosmic representatives, either of their constituents or of the population as a whole. In all western democracies, the elected representatives of the people are disproportionately white, male and middle-class. At the same time, they are more than purely symbolic representatives.

In these circumstances the best course is to recognize that elected assembly members are representatives in a fourth sense of the term that cannot be reduced to any of, or any combination of, the other three usages. They are representatives because they have been appointed by a particular process of election to occupy that role. It was Hobbes who first maintained that representation is essentially a process of authorization, and although this is not true of microcosmic representation or symbolic representation I believe that it is true of elective representation. Members of Parliament or Congress are people who have been authorized by the process of election to exercise certain powers. This is their defining characteristic, and they remain legal representatives until they step down, die or are defeated, no matter how they behave in the assembly.

To say this is not to play down the importance of the mandate/independence controversy, only to say that it involves a separate level of debate that cannot be settled by arguing about the nature of elective representation. In practice, most elected representatives pay at least some attention to the interests and values of their constituents, but also feel free to exercise their independent judgement about what is best for their party or their country. How far they lean one way or the other depends upon the nature of the governmental system within which they work. American legislators customarily lean more towards the promotion of local interests than British or

French or Canadian legislators do, though they are elected in the same way, and this is partly because the separation of powers in the United States means that they are not committed to supporting or criticizing the executive, partly because of the relative weakness of American party discipline, and partly because their ideological commitments tend to be less rigid.

It is also important to notice that the behaviour of elected representations may vary from one period to another within the same polity. In medieval and early modern times, Members of Parliament in England leaned more towards the defence of local interests than they do in contemporary England. In those days their main representative functions were to express the grievances of propertied classes in their county or borough and to indicate how willing the latter would be to contribute their taxes for use by the king and his ministers. Attitudes and behaviour changed during the eighteenth century under the influence of the Whigs, who believed that Parliament should be the centre of political power rather than merely acting as a forum for grievances and a check on the executive. If Parliament were to be a deliberative and decision-making body, it was clearly necessary that the MP should be free to do what he thought best in the national interest rather than act as a spokesperson for the interests of his constituents. It was this that led Edmund Burke to make his famous speech to the electors of Bristol in 1774, though he was only the most eloquent, not the first, of the Whigs to do so. Parliament, Burke told his constituents, was:

> not a *congress* of ambassadors from different hostile interests; which interests each must maintain, as an agent and advocate, against other agents and advocates; but Parliament is a *deliberative* assembly of *one* nation, with *one* interest, that of the whole; where not local purposes, not local prejudices ought to guide, but the general good, resulting from the general reason of the whole.

Certainly a representative should keep in close touch with his constituents and should even:

> prefer their interests to his own. But his unbiased opinion, his mature judgement, his enlightened conscience, he ought not to sacrifice to you. . . . Your representative owes you, not his industry only, but his judgement; and he betrays, instead of serving, you if he sacrifices it to your opinion.
>
> (Burke 1921: 63–4, italics in the original)

A similar position was adopted by the Abbé-Sieyès and his fellow revolutionaries in France, who included in the first revolutionary constitution of that country the clear statement that members of the National Assembly could not be given any mandate by their voters. As was noted in Chapter 7, during the nineteenth century this doctrine, with its associated prohibition of instructions, was adopted in most countries of western Europe.

European legislators are not less certainly representatives because they lean rather more (though in practice not entirely) towards the independence side of the mandate/independence controversy than American legislators; they simply operate in a different constitutional setting.

The upshot of this analysis is to throw serious doubt on the value of searching for any true or essential meaning of representation. It is better simply to accept that there are four different types of representation, each of which has its own character.

THE FUNCTIONS OF REPRESENTATION

In most books and articles on the subject of representative government, the main focus is on the popular election of assembly members and their role and behaviour in the legislature. This is natural, for these are the activities that enable the system as a whole to be characterized as representative and democratic. However, there is some advantage to be gained from elaborating the precise functions that are involved in this process and it will also be helpful to indicate certain other functions that representative institutions can perform, on the output side of the governmental process as well as on the input side. I believe that a comprehensive inventory of the functions of political representation has to include at least six entries.

It is fair to begin with political recruitment. The existence of a variety of elective posts, at both local and national levels, provides a mechanism for the recruitment of politicians that is considerably more free of nepotism and favouritism than the mechanisms commonly in place in dictatorial regimes. It is not difficult for would-be politicians to get themselves nominated for the more modest of these positions and to gain office if they can win support from enough local voters.

A second and closely related function is to provide a series of public competitions for office during which personalities can be assessed, issues can be aired, records criticized, and policy options debated. Public elections also provide an opportunity for voluntary participation by large numbers of supporters who can thus play a larger part in the political process than simply by voting.

A third function is that of providing for both responsiveness and responsibility in the conduct of government. When we talk of responsibility in government one of the features we expect is that those in charge of policy making shall be responsive to the wishes and interests of the general public. The representative system obviously provides a strong incentive for political leaders to satisfy the majority of the electorate by their policies. However, there is another side to the ideal of responsibility in politics that also has to be taken into account. This is that a government will be regarded as irresponsible if its policies, however popular at the time they are formulated, prove to be imprudent or inconsistent in the longer run.

The usage of responsibility to mean consistency and prudence is well illustrated by a speech made on the budget by a leading British minister some years ago:

> When a government has to choose between a run on the pound and its own popularity, it has only one choice it can make. It makes it unwillingly. It must face unpopularity, loss of by-elections and even, if need be, defeat at a later general election. This is the price of responsible government.
>
> (quoted Birch 1964: 19)

This kind of dilemma is often faced by governments. In 1991, for instance, the US president and the Canadian prime minister were both caught in the dilemma of a recession that needed a large injection of public money to reduce unemployment, at a time when it was highly desirable to minimize the budgetary deficit because of the excessive burden of public debt that had been accumulated over previous years. They both decided, rightly or wrongly, that the most responsible course of action was to contain the deficit.

If political responsibility in this sense of the term is a virtue, then it can be said that one of the functions of representation – and one of its advantages over direct democracy – is that it gives political leaders the distance from immediate public pressures that is needed if they are to act in a consistent and prudent fashion, after weighing all the consequences of action in the balance. They will have to account for their decisions to the electorate in due course, but they have time that may allow them to recover from the unpopularity that their decisions may have caused. To do so they need to educate the public about the relative costs of alternative policies, so that this distance and time may contribute to political education.

The fourth function of political representation is indicated by the above paragraph. It is to ensure that political leaders are held accountable to the electorate for their actions in elections that are spaced in time, but not too widely spaced.

These four functions of representation can all be grouped under the general heading of popular control of government. However, representative institutions and processes are also constantly used by governments to help their administration and maintain the system. Their first advantage of this kind is that they help to legitimize the system and the powers of those who direct the government. The importance of legitimacy, as an essential ingredient of political authority, has been stressed in Chapter 6. In the modern democratic state the most important of all the sources of legitimacy is the fact that the power to make laws rests with elected representatives, while the leaders of the executive either depend on the support of the elected assembly, as in parliamentary systems, or are directly elected themselves, as in the United States.

The legitimizing function of representation can also be seen where representatives are appointed rather than elected. A commission of inquiry into race relations would lack legitimacy in the eyes of ethnic minorities unless it included members from the minorities. A commission on industrial relations would lack legitimacy in the eyes of workers unless it included one or two prominent trade unionists among its members.

A related function of representation is the mobilization of consent. This was the chief original purpose of the older European Parliaments, and it has been well described by historians. The English king's motives in summoning the first English Parliament have been described in the following way:

> In 1275 Edward I summoned knights to his first parliament, not to take an active part in drawing up the Great Statute of Westminster, but rather to hear and understand the reforms in local government which it contained and to carry back ... the explanations of the new provisions for restraining the corruptions of sheriffs. In 1283 and again in 1295 and 1307 Edward I was ... making use of the representative system for propaganda purposes; demonstrating to the communities of shire and borough, on whose material assistance he was bound to rely, the justice of his own cause against the villainy of his enemy.
>
> (Cam 1963: 226–7)

Things have not changed a great deal over the past seven centuries. Parliament is constantly used to publicize the government's plans and its justifications for them. The general rule is that all channels of political communication tend to become two-way channels, and this can also be seen rather clearly in the operation of advisory and consultative committees established with the ostensible purpose of representing the consumers of the service or state industry in question. The function that such committees serve is that of creating opportunities for grievances to be ventilated, so that critics are able to let off steam instead of building up their frustrations. However, it does not follow that the critics will bring about changes. Some years ago public criticisms of the quality of British radio and television services led to the suggestion that a new Broadcasting council should be established to oversee all the broadcasting media and to deal with complaints from aggrieved members of the public. The London *Daily Telegraph* made the following comment:

> Alas, this suggestion will not begin to solve the problem. It is our experience generally that boards which are set up to regulate and supervise some activity ... are soon captured by the industry in question and fashioned into its apologists.
>
> (*Daily Telegraph*, 4 January 1971)

It is highly unlikely that this tendency is confined to Britain. The generalization that all channels of political communication become two-way channels can be supplemented by the generalization that, unless political passions are aroused, the party with most expert knowledge will tend to get the better of the argument. All representative institutions, if skilfully handled, can serve to mobilize consent to the policies of those actually running the industry, agency, or government department involved. It follows from this that, when we discuss the role of political representation in the modern democratic state, we should consider the part that representative arrangements play in maintaining the system as well as the part they play in securing a degree of popular control over government.

Chapter 9

Political participation

DEFINITION OF THE TERM

Republican and democratic theorists from Rousseau onwards have either urged or assumed that a proper system of government must provide opportunities for political participation by the ordinary citizen. The opportunity to vote in periodic competitive elections is the minimum condition that a governmental system must satisfy to qualify as democratic, and most liberal theorists, indeed most political scientists, have believed that further opportunities and forms of political participation are highly desirable. The concept of political participation is not nearly as complex as the concept of representation, is not currently contestable, and can be easily illustrated by example, in the form of a list of the main forms of participation open to citizens in the modern democratic state. Before giving this list, however, a word about definition will be helpful.

Participation is an activity, that of taking part with others in some social process, game, sport or joint endeavour. The social dimension is essential to the term; Robinson Crusoe did not participate in anything, because he was alone. Political participation is participation in the process of government, and the case for political participation is essentially a case for substantial numbers of private citizens (as distinct from public officials or elected politicians) to play a part in the process by which political leaders are chosen and/or government policies are shaped and implemented.

It must be emphasized that participation is an activity, as distinct from an attitude. In their celebrated study of *The Civic Culture* Almond and Verba characterized the American political culture as a 'participant civic culture', largely on the basis that Americans had a stronger belief than the citizens of the four other countries studied in the importance of citizen participation in political life and in their competence to play a meaningful role (Almond and Verba 1965: 313–15). This is exactly what could be expected in view of the long-standing American belief in popular sovereignty, already discussed in Chapter 7. However, belief in the virtue and probable effectiveness of political participation is not the same as participation itself, as is shown by the fact that turnout figures for voting in American national elections are much lower than the equivalent figures in most other democracies. The figures are 30–35 per cent in mid-term congressional elections, compared with 75–85 per cent in most parliamentary elections in Europe.

The main forms of political participation can easily be listed, and are as follows:

1 voting in local or national elections
2 voting in referendums
3 canvassing or otherwise campaigning in elections
4 active membership of a political party
5 active membership of a pressure group
6 taking part in political demonstrations, industrial strikes with political objectives, rent strikes in public housing, and similar activities aimed at changing public policy
7 various forms of civil disobedience, such as refusing to pay taxes or obey a conscription order
8 membership of government advisory committees
9 membership of consumers' councils for publicly owned industries
10 client involvement in the implementation of social policies
11 various forms of community action, such as those concerned with housing or environmental issues in the locality.

JUSTIFYING POLITICAL PARTICIPATION

Although participation is a behavioural concept, it is one with strong normative overtones. Very few people think political participation is a bad thing. Many commend it as one of the factors in the success of western democratic systems, and, being broadly content with the systems, are broadly content with the level and character of public participation in them. Many others believe that democracy would be enhanced in quality and perhaps improved in efficiency if the level of participation were increased, either through existing channels or through additional ones that ought to be established.

To some extent participation can be justified in terms of the functional requirements of any system of government, whether democratic or not. Those who wield political power, whether this be at local or national level, will be likely to do so more effectively if they are well informed about the problems, needs and attitudes of the citizens and community they govern. Dictatorships are apt to rely for this kind of information on government agents of one kind or another, from municipal clerks to secret police, but this inevitably involves the danger that the agents will tell the rulers what they think the latter want to hear, or what the agents think will benefit their own career prospects. It is better, in the sense of more efficient, if there are open channels of communication through which private citizens or freely elected representatives can pass relevant information to decision makers.

Another general point is that the existence of channels for public participation in the political process is likely to increase the propensity for citizens to comply voluntarily with governmental rules and orders. If people have had the opportunity to play some part in the selection of public officials, to communicate their views on public issues, and to exert pressure on decision makers, they are more likely to accept that governmental decisions are legitimate, even if disliked, than would be the case if citizens did not have such opportunities. It was this kind of argument that led European monarchs to establish parliamentary bodies in the first place, way back in the thirteenth century in the English case, in the hope of increasing the probability that taxes levied by the national government would actually be collected. In some modern dictatorships, such as Hitler's Germany or the Soviet Union, mass membership in the ruling party was encouraged as a way of mobilizing support for government policies. To socialize young people into accepting the legitimacy of the regime, mass movements for children and teenagers were also created, such as the Hitler Youth movement in Germany and the Little Octobrists in the Soviet Union. A belief in the advantages of widespread political participation is not confined to democratic regimes.

A commitment to democratic principles supplements these basic arguments with others. It is part of the definition of democracy, and fundamental to all democratic theories, that private citizens should have the opportunity to vote in elections, to organize political parties and pressure groups, and to give public expression to their views on political issues without fear of reprisals if their views happen to be unpopular with the government of the day. Beyond this basic normative commitment, there are several arguments by democratic theorists about mass participation in the political process, some in favour of increased participation and some against it. These are rather varied in character and have been divided by scholars into the two categories of instrumental arguments, in terms of the benefits or dangers to the system that mass participation can bring, and developmental arguments, in terms of the benefits or costs to individual citizens (see Parry 1972: Chapter 1). In what follows I shall outline the main arguments in these two categories, though without using the terms 'instrumental' and 'developmental', which can create problems.

ARGUMENTS IN TERMS OF THE POLITICAL SYSTEM

The majority of empirical political scientists who have studied political participation in democratic states in the post-war period have been broadly content with the level of participation as sufficient to meet the requirements of the system, though some of them have noted that the level achieved falls short of that assumed by a good deal of democratic theory. In 1954 this point was made rather forcibly by three American political sociologists who had conducted an elaborate survey of public opinion and voting behaviour in the 1948 presidential election. They reported that the voters had not shown a great deal of interest in or knowledge of the political issues involved in the election, that there had been little meaningful discussion or debate of these issues, and that it seemed to be true of many voters that their political preferences were akin to cultural tastes rather than being the outcome of rational calculations (Berelson et al. 1954: 307–11).

These scholars observed that in these respects the electors failed to behave in the way that much popular democratic theory then took for granted. However, they thought that this implied a fault in the theory, which focused too much on the supposed virtues of the individual citizen and not enough on the requirements of the democratic system as a whole. They asserted that American democracy was working, 'perhaps even more vigorously and effectively than ever' (Berelson et al. 1954: 312). One of the conditions for its success was the existence of cross-cutting cleavages in society, so that there was a partial but not a complete correlation between social characteristics and political preferences; a situation that provided for more stability and consensus than would exist if there were a complete correlation (Berelson et al. 1954: 318–20). Another condition was the existence of a certain amount of political apathy. 'Extreme interest goes with extreme partisanship and might culminate in rigid fanaticism that could destroy democratic processes if generalized throughout the community', whereas 'low interest provides maneuvring room for political shifts' and compromises (Berelson et al. 1954: 314). A somewhat similar line of argument was developed by a British scholar in an article entitled 'In defence of apathy' (Morris-Jones 1954). The overall thrust of the argument was that populist theories of democracy involved unnecessary and unrealistic assumptions about the political interest, knowledge and rationality of the average citizen; and that they should be replaced by more pragmatic theories based on empirical evidence about the requirements of democratic systems.

The snag about this argument, in the view of critics, is that it ignores the existence of a strong social bias in the practice of political participation. Repeated surveys have shown a clear correlation between education, income and social status on the one hand and the tendency to vote and join pressure groups on the other. The poor and the badly educated, who might be thought to have most to gain from political reforms, are generally the most apathetic and the least active in politics. (For a comprehensive summary of evidence on this, see Milbrath 1965.) This bias means, it is said, that the system cannot be regarded as fully democratic.

What could be done to minimize this bias? One tactic, clearly, would be to make voting compulsory, as it has been for many years in Australia, Belgium and Italy. This provision is not the subject of much controversy in these countries, where the sanctions are so minimal as to be insignificant, but the existence of the rule pushes turnout in national elections to over 90 per cent of the electorate. In view of the exceptionally low turnout figures for national elections in the United States, one might expect American critics of a radical disposition to recommend the adoption of compulsory voting, but my search of the literature has not revealed any examples of this.

Another recommendation that Americans in favour of higher political participation might be expected to make, but have not made, is that the political parties should follow the example of many European parties in developing mass memberships, with branches in every town and intensive programmes of local meetings and social activities. The British Conservative Party and the German Social Democratic Party have both had memberships of over a million, and all have intensive activities that make the American (and Canadian) parties seem, in comparison, like empty shells. In many electoral districts in Britain, for instance, the Conservative Party has local branches that organize regular meetings and a programme of social activities. In some industrial areas Conservative Clubs have bars, billiards tables, darts teams and the like, whereas suburban constituency associations may hold whist drives, sherry parties and similar fund-raising events. Both parties are heavily into the publishing business, producing a stream of booklets, pamphlets and discussion papers on policy issues. The parties have discussion groups, ideological pressure groups and youth movements. One consequence of all this activity is the communication of opinions between rank-and-file members and parliamentary leaders; another is to reduce the dependence of the parties on corporate or union donations; yet another is that during election campaigns each party can call on an army of voluntary workers, making paid helpers unnecessary.

Having been a participant/observer in elections in four English-speaking countries, my judgement is that the level of public discussion of political issues is appreciably higher in Australia, which has compulsory voting, and Britain, which has parties with mass memberships, than it is in the United States or Canada, which have neither. However, this is only one observer's judgement and other factors are also relevant, such as the greater ideological gap between the Australian and British parties than between the North American parties and the sharper character of television interviews in the former countries.

As noted, the critics (mainly American) who are not content with current levels of political participation have not advocated either of these developments. Instead, they have favoured changing the system in other ways. Thus, Bachrach has argued in favour of industrial democracy. He accepts that 'participation in key political decisions on the national level must remain extremely limited' (Bachrach 1969: 95), and believes that the way to make the United States a more democratic society is to make the managers of large corporations accountable to the workers by law. Bachrach is surprisingly sceptical about the political abilities of the average citizen, saying that 'the illiberal and anti-democratic propensity of the common man is an undesirable fact that must be faced' (Bachrach 1969: 105). His proposal is to educate the factory worker by involving him in 'the solution of concrete problems affecting himself and his immediate community', which in modern America is 'the factory community' (Bachrach 1969: 103). He has no proposals to improve the participation of the majority of adult Americans, who do not work in factories.

A similar line has been taken by Carole Pateman, who argues that 'for a democratic polity to exist it is necessary for a participatory society to exist' (Pateman 1970: 43), and claims that if industrial workers were given some share in decision making at their place of work this would improve their sense of political efficacy and make it more likely that they would also participate, and participate well, in the process by which the country is governed. 'The existence of a participatory society', she says, 'would mean that [the ordinary man] was better able to assess the performance of representatives at the national level, better equipped to take decisions of national scope when the opportunity arose to do so' (Pateman 1970: 110).

A balanced discussion of participatory democracy is provided in a book with that title by Cook and Morgan (1971). They draw a useful distinction between co-determination, in which amateurs join with professionals in decision-making bodies, and self-determination, in which groups of amateurs take decisions themselves. Examples of co-determination include student-faculty committees in universities and government advisory committees of all kinds. Examples of self-determination include Israeli kibbutzim and 'some of the community-action programmes in the War on Poverty' (Cook and Morgan 1971: 5). They suggest that the best way to break the 'iron law of oligarchy' (to be discussed in Chapter 14) is:

> to shift towards non-elitist decision-making units. Hence workers should participate directly in making and applying rules on working conditions, wages and similar matters; . . . and racial or ethnic minorities should be maximally involved in decisions regarding their housing, schools, welfare payments and the like.
>
> (Cook and Morgan 1971: 14)

The implication of their discussion is that co-determination is preferable to self-determination, in that it ensures that specialized information and expertise are available to decision makers.

There are also arguments against participatory democracy. One is that groups of amateur politicians may lend themselves to manipulation by demagogues or by ideological factions. It has frequently been observed that this was the case among student groups at the time of student revolts in the late

1960s and early 1970s, when New Left activists effectively dominated the scene although they were often in a minority among the student bodies as a whole. Open participation may mean domination by those with strong ideological motivations who are willing to give their time to it, but who would not necessarily be able to win a competitive election. Moreover, normal representative institutions have rules of order that protect all parties to the debate, but this is not always the case when decisions are taken at mass meetings (see Cook and Morgan 1971: 30–1).

Another possible argument is that elected representatives and appointed officials can probably bargain and compromise over issues more easily than citizen groups can (Cook and Morgan 1971: 34). Being full-time professionals in the game of politics teaches people to accept the realities of political life, which frequently involve compromise and partial defeat. Amateurs may not be so flexible.

Another possible argument is that mass participation may mean that a spontaneous group can effectively nullify a decision by the elected body responsible for decision making. When Columbia University decided in 1968 to build a gymnasium on the edge of Harlem, this decision was ratified more than once by the elected representatives of the citizens of Harlem. However, a sizeable group of non-elected black students at Columbia decided that it would not be good for Harlem and created a crisis ending in violence. Henry Kissinger's comment on this was that it was 'government by a process of private nullification, which has never been especially good news for democracy'.

While the arguments against wider citizen participation in politics are mostly rather conservative, there is also a radical argument to the effect that many forms of participation tend to co-opt people into the system and thus blunt the edge of protest. Writing about community problems, John Dearlove has said this:

> [Participation] can force, or educate, the participants to gain an awareness of governmental problems and policies and this will not only inhibit the public from pressing for solutions to their own problems, but will also enable the authorities to legitimize their decisions with the stamp of public approval.
>
> (quoted Richardson 1983: 59)

The East London Claimants' Union, a group representing people on welfare, has declared that:

> any of this 'participation' would be a sell-out to the system and an attempt on the part of the establishment to absorb our militancy. To the establishment, participation merely means that a few of us will help 'them' to make decisions about us.
>
> (quoted Richardson 1983: 59)

There is a good deal of force in this argument. K. C. Wheare (1955), writing about the vast number of advisory committees established by British government departments, observed that there was a risk that 'all those who might influence and guide public opinion may be captured by the departments, placed on their committees, and so won over to the official side from the start' (Wheare 1955: 66). My own study of the role of the regional consumer councils attached to the British gas and electricity boards (then under public ownership) revealed that 'they are more effective in bringing the excuses of the authorities to the attention of the public than in bringing the complaints of the public to the attention of the authorities' (Birch 1959: 162). The general point (as suggested in Chapter 8) is that all channels of communication between the public and the government are or quickly become two-way channels, which can be used by both sides.

One of the conceptual lessons that may be learned from this very brief sketch of some of the arguments that have been made about political participation in recent years is the need for clarity about the forms of participation. While the general definition of the term is not problematic, it has to be accepted that it is an omnibus term. There is a world of practical difference between enhanced participation through the existing processes of representative government, participation in new institutions to be added to the existing system, participation in spontaneous demonstrations, boycotts and other forms of direct action, and participation in social and industrial institutions that may influence political behaviour but is not directly political in itself. There are also significant distinctions to be drawn between co-determination and self-determination, as already mentioned, and between participation in policy-making processes and participation in the implementation of policy. It follows that a general commitment to more widespread citizen participation in politics, while being an entirely reasonable commitment for democrats to have, does not in itself constitute a programme for reform. It is essential for critics of the existing pattern of institutions and behaviour to be specific about the changes they would like to see.

ARGUMENTS IN TERMS OF THE INDIVIDUAL

There is a basic difference of opinion here between theorists who regard political participation as a cost that the individual participant has to incur in order to secure benefits, and those who regard participation as a beneficial activity in itself. Theorists of the former type can be regarded as descendants of Jeremy Bentham and James Mill, the British Utilitarians who viewed the political arena as a kind of market-place in which individuals constantly attempted to maximize the benefits and minimize the losses they could secure from the political process. The assumptions of the theory included individual selfishness, in the sense that each participant would be motivated by the desire to protect or enhance his own personal interests, and individual rationality, in the sense that each participant could be expected to make a rational calculation of probable gains and losses before acting.

Academic economists have adopted these assumptions regarding economic behaviour in a free-market economy and have built up an impressive body of theory based upon axioms about behaviour and models indicating the reactions that could be expected to follow various stipulated changes, such as variations in the rate of interest or the overall level of purchasing power or the distribution of incomes. Since the late 1950s, a number of political scientists or political economists have tried to apply the same kind of logic to political behaviour.

The leader in this enterprise was Anthony Downs, whose book *An Economic Theory of Democracy* was published in 1957, and one of his most influential successors was Mancur Olson, whose book on *The Logic of Collective Action* appeared in 1965. Downs raised a basic question about the reasons why people participate in politics by voting. Given that the act of voting requires some expenditure of time and energy, the decision to vote could be justified only by some calculation of the probable benefit to the individual voter. It must therefore depend on the perceived difference between the policies of the competing parties, in so far as they might affect the voter, the perceived expectation that the choice of an individual candidate would determine which party emerged victorious in the overall result, and the perceived expectation that the vote of the individual voter would determine the result of the election in that district. As Brian Barry has pointed out, the chances of a single vote determining the result in any sizeable electoral district are so small that the logical decision for the great majority of electors would be not to bother to vote. This kind of analysis therefore points to a puzzle about voting behaviour in democracies (Barry 1970: 14–15).

There are various possible answers to the paradox of why most people in most democracies do actually turn out to vote in national elections. One, suggested by Riker and Ordeshook, is that people get rewards from voting other than an expected material benefit from the result. They get emotional satisfaction from such considerations as performing their civic duty, 'affirming allegiance to the political system', 'affirming a partisan preference', and so forth (Riker and Ordeshook 1968: 28). This is undoubtedly true, but it seems to undermine the value of the economic approach to the problem. These are psychological or emotional satisfactions, not calculated prospects of personal gain. Barry's comment on this is pertinent: 'It may well be that both the costs and the . . . benefits of voting are so low that it is simply not worth being rational about it. Thus habit, self-expression, duty and other things have plenty of room to make themselves felt' (Barry 1970: 23).

Olson's book deals with activities that involve a higher cost, in so far as participation can be regarded as a cost. He discusses membership of trade unions and other pressure groups, where the member has to pay subscriptions and, if he is active, to give much more time to the organization than is involved in casting a vote on election day. In so far as these organizations provide benefits to a whole category of people, whether or not they are members, it follows (according to Olson's argument) that there is no direct incentive for potential beneficiaries to incur the costs of joining and working for the group. They will benefit anyway, and it is not likely, in any sizeable group, that one extra member will make a significant difference to the outcome. The economic logic of the situation encourages people to become 'free riders' rather than participants (see Olson 1965).

This is undoubtedly true, and it explains why trade unions are so keen to impose a closed shop, or a union shop, in industrial plants. They want to force workers to join their union, or at any rate a union, because they understand that the costs of membership would otherwise keep some potential members out. It also explains why many unions emphasize the selective benefits that they provide to members, but not to other workers, such as information, representation in case of grievances, pay while on strike, and in some cases pension plans or health and accident insurance schemes (see Barry 1970: 27). This argument applies not only to unions but also to other pressure groups. Motorists' organizations would not be nearly so large and well financed if they appealed only on the grounds of their activities as pressure groups, without offering selective services in the form of emergency towing and repairs in the case of breakdowns. The British National Trust would not be so large and successful if it appealed only as an environmental pressure group, without offering selective benefits to members in the form of free admission to stately homes and gardens. Olson's theory about free riders has more explanatory value than Downs's theory about voting, because the costs of group membership are significantly higher than the cost of voting.

Olson's theory does not, however, explain everything about participation in organized groups. As Barry has pointed out, it does not explain why union membership is much higher in some periods than in others (Barry 1970: 29) or in some countries than in others. The proportion of workers belonging to a union is, for instance, over twice as high in Britain, Australia and Germany as it is in the United States or France. These variations cannot be explained in individualistic terms of selective benefits offered to union members, but only in more collective, sociological terms like feelings of class solidarity, a belief in collective action, and so forth. The very marked recent growth in environmental groups in most advanced industrial societies, or of groups for and against abortion in North America, cannot be explained in terms of individual calculations of costs and potential benefits, but only in terms of ideological and moral commitments and an altruistic readiness to spend time in pursuit of general causes believed to be worthy and important. Then again, others would say that participation in such organizations does not involve a cost at all, except in very narrow financial terms, for the activity is enjoyable and rewarding for members.

This brings us to the other point of view about the effects of political participation for the individual, namely that it is likely to be beneficial. Theorists who take this view point out that it alleviates, or would alleviate, the sense of isolation or even alienation that many people feel in modern industrial society, a sense that the growth of automation in industry and the growing use of computers in office work can only increase. It has been said that:

> the complexity of modern society's division of labour tends to isolate men from a sense of moral responsibility for the ultimate consequences of their actions ... Participatory democracy may be able to contribute to meeting the psychological and ethical problem of relating personal conduct to social consequences.
>
> (Cook and Morgan 1971: 15)

A similar line of argument is that increased participation is likely to increase the feelings of political efficacy that ordinary citizens have, so that increased confidence that their actions can have an effect on public policy will lead them to a greater sense of control over their communal lives and will have a knock-on effect, greater participation in one sphere of activity leading to greater participation in other spheres. This was Carole Pateman's main argument for the introduction of workers' control in industry, as developed in her 1970 book. However, in an article published in 1980 she reports in a very dissillusioned way about the experience of workers' control in Yugoslavia. Studies published since her book had revealed that the social bias so conspicuous in political participation in capitalist America was found also in socialist Yugoslavia. Skilled and better-educated workers were more likely to become members of workers' councils than unskilled workers, and participation in these councils was seen 'as a technocratic activity, based on skills and expertise, rather than as a matter for political commitment' (Pateman 1980: 91).

Pateman believes rather passionately that this is wrong. In this article she draws attention thirty times, in the space of forty-six pages, to the correlation between social and economic status and political participation, which she believes should be unacceptable to democratic theorists. Now, a writer as talented as Pateman does not say the same thing thirty times in a single article by accident; she wrote in this way to ram the point home, because she believes that its significance is too often overlooked. In taking the view that she does, Pateman seems to be following the example of the logical positivists (to be discussed in Chapter 16), who argued strongly that experience and empirical evidence could not in themselves lead to value judgements.

This was expressed in a phrase that became famous in the immediate post-war years: 'an "is" cannot produce an "ought"'. In Pateman's view, the argument of political sociologists that our democratic values should be modified to bring them into line with the empirical evidence about political behaviour is an argument that can only lead to the defence of the status quo. If democratic values demand mass participation in decision making plus social equality in that participation, then those values should be re-affirmed despite all evidence that in the contemporary world most citizens do not want to participate actively (that is, beyond voting) and that those who do tend to be drawn from the ranks of the more skilled, the better educated and the more affluent. It is a tenable viewpoint, even though it may lead those who hold such values into a certain state of frustration when considering the empirical evidence.

Robert Dahl is also a believer in workers' control in industry. In 1970 he claimed that American democracy would be more complete if all employees in business enterprises were given the power to control those enterprises, employing expert managers to conduct day-to-day management where this seemed appropriate. He argues that representative government in a sizeable community suffers from the remoteness of decision makers from the ordinary citizen (Dahl 1970: 142) and that self-management at work would compensate for that. It would be desirable, he says, even if it were to result in a slight loss of productive efficiency in the enterprise, for this would be balanced by the value of 'democratic participation and control, as good both intrinsically and in their consequences for self-development and human satisfaction' (Dahl 1970: 132).

In 1985 Dahl reaffirmed this view, claiming not only that employee control of business enterprises would reduce feelings of alienation in the workplace but also that it would contribute 'to the values of justice and democracy' in society and 'improve the quality of democracy in the government of the state by transforming us into better citizens' (Dahl 1985: 93, 94). He went so far as to say that citizens of the modern state had not only a right to participate in democratic forms of government but also a right to participate in the management of the firms in which they worked (see Dahl 1985: 111–35).

In reviewing reports on the results of various American experiments with workers' participation in management, Dahl had to admit that the evidence was mixed. In some firms the experiment had led to increased feelings of satisfaction and political efficacy while in others it had led to increased alienation from work and disenchantment with the idea of participation (Dahl 1985: 96–8). The evidence from Yugoslavia was discouraging, and he quoted a Yugoslav scholar's conclusion that for participants in workers' councils 'the direct experience with self-management has been so frustrating that their sense of alienation has become even greater' (Dahl 1985: 97). Nevertheless, Dahl remained optimistic, saying that American and Yugoslav experiments were still young and that a hundred years of experience with self-management might bring about a truly beneficial modification of attitudes (Dahl 1985: 98).

SOME DEVELOPMENTS IN PRACTICE

In the late 1960s there was much talk on both sides of the Atlantic of the desirability of wider participation in the governmental process, and in Britain the government sponsored a nationwide survey of public attitudes to this question. This survey did not reveal a sizeable public demand for change, however. When people were asked to say what they would like to see done to improve things in their region, only 3 per cent spontaneously said that they would like more say for people in the area as against central government, compared with 21 per cent who wanted better roads, 20 per cent who wanted better leisure facilities and 20 per cent who wanted more economic development. Of the fourteen types of improvement mentioned, more local democracy was in fact the least popular (see Birch 1977: 153–6).

However, in practice there have been developments in Britain and elsewhere that have involved wider participation in the political process, and it seems appropriate to conclude this chapter by mentioning them.

In Britain there has been a significant growth in the participation of clients (or, as some would say, consumers) in the implementation of social policies. The last decades of the century saw the establishment of local community health councils all over the country and 'patients' participation groups' in a number of areas, and of associations of tenants in municipal housing who have to be consulted under the provisions of the Housing Act of 1980 (see Richardson 1983: Chapter 3). Parents are now commonly members of school governing bodies and many schools have pupils on their governing bodies also. The Education Reform Act of 1988 made it possible for schools to opt out of municipal or county control and become self-managing if a majority of parents approve of this move. Under the legislation on race relations, every sizeable community with ethnic minorities now has a community relations forum containing representatives of the minorities. A major survey showed that in 1997 'some 85 per cent of English local authorities had undertaken public meetings or issued consultative documents', that '88 per cent of authorities had undertaken service satisfaction surveys', that '47 per cent had used focus groups', and that about a third had interactive websites (Wilson 1999: 250).

A very different type of growth in political participation has been seen in the increased prevalence of various types of direct action by groups protesting against some aspect of government policy. Trade unions boycotted the Industrial Relations Court established in 1971. Anti-nuclear groups have blockaded nuclear bases. Environmentalists and local property owners have held up plans for highway construction by obstructing public inquiries. In

1990 tens of thousands of citizens refused to pay the new poll tax (replacing municipal property taxes), the revolts against which contributed to the downfall of Margaret Thatcher as prime minister. In the 1990s, members of animal welfare groups blockaded ports to prevent the export of live calves to the continent, and several road improvements were blocked by radical environmentalists (see Doherty 1999). Like them or not, these are all forms of political participation by ordinary citizens.

In the United States in the same period the parties, and particularly the Democratic Party, became weaker, electoral turnout declined, but there was an increase in the number and vitality of single-issue pressure groups. It is a matter of dispute whether this is healthy or unhealthy in terms of the democratic process as a whole, but the development lends support to the arguments advanced by pluralists like Truman (1951) and Dahl (1985) about the significance of latent political groups that might become actual groups when new issues get on to the agenda.

Another development has been the marked increase in the use of the initiative and referendum to change state laws in the twenty-three states, mainly in the west, that allow for these procedures. The campaign for the initiative and referendum began in the Populist Movement of the 1880s and 1890s, was successful in many western states in the first two decades of the twentieth century, but did not lead to extensive changes in state laws until the 1970s. The most dramatic change was the adoption in 1978 of Proposition 13 in California, a proposal to cut property taxes by more than half. This was passed by a two-to-one majority and more Californians voted on the question than voted in 'any of the candidate contests on the same ballot' (Schmidt 1989: 132). The tendency was widespread and between 1970 and 1986 there were 158 statewide initiatives passed by voters in 22 states and the District of Columbia (Schmidt 1989: 287–94). This is clearly a move towards participatory democracy, though not one that has been universally applauded by academics who favour wider participation in politics.

In Europe also there has been an increasing use of referendums. Swiss voters have decided that their country should join the IMF and the World Bank but should stay out of the UN and the European Union, as well as reaching many decisions on domestic matters. Italy and the Irish Republic have both held referendums that authorized the enactment of divorce laws. In 1992 Denmark and France held referendums on whether their governments should ratify the Maastricht Treaty, and in 1997 the British government conducted referendums on its proposal to create a Scottish Parliament and a Welsh Assembly. In 1999 voters in Northern Ireland and the Irish Republic were invited to endorse the agreement that had been reached to end terrorist violence about the government of Northern Ireland.

In 2005 voters in France and the Netherlands decided to reject the draft constitution for the European Union that had been advocated as essential for the enlarged EU.

It seems fair to say that there has been a secular trend towards greater political participation in modern democracies. However, it also seems fair to say that the forms of increased participation have been very varied, have not always been predicted by political scientists, and have not always been welcomed by liberals. Although political participation is fairly easy to define, the arguments about it are complex and somewhat contradictory.

Chapter 10

Liberty and freedom

There is an initial question, that can be dealt with quickly, as to whether or not these two terms are synonymous. One reason for thinking that they are is that most dictionaries define each of them in terms of the other. The *Concise Oxford Dictionary* defines 'freedom' as personal liberty, civil liberty and liberty of action, while it defines 'liberty' as freedom from control. *Chambers Dictionary* defines 'freedom' as liberty and 'liberty' as freedom to do as one pleases. A second reason for regarding the terms as synonymous is that, as Hanna Pitkin has pointed out, it is only in the English language that one has a choice, as in other European languages there is simply one word (Pitkin 1988: 523). As 'liberty' comes from a Latin root whereas 'freedom' comes from a Germanic root, it would seem that the existence of the two alternative words is simply an accident of the historical fact that (as J. G. Fichte put it) English is a bastard language.

On the other hand, it has been observed by Hannah Arendt that in a political context the terms are commonly used in slightly different ways, with liberty more likely to be used when the writer means the absence of restraint and freedom more likely to be used when the writer means the opportunity to engage in some activity, such as political participation. In his famous lecture on 'Two concepts of liberty' Isaiah Berlin declared that he was using these terms interchangeably but, as Pitkin has observed, in what followed he more commonly used liberty when referring to what he called the negative concept of liberty, and freedom when he gave examples of what he called the positive concept of liberty (Pitkin 1988: 544–7). In so far as a distinction of this kind is commonly made by those who comment on political issues, the fact underlines the significance of the difference between (to use Berlin's phraseology) the negative and positive concepts. As Berlin's terminology is more descriptive and less liable to cause confusion than prescribing different meanings for the two words, in this chapter I shall follow his example (and that of the dictionaries) by treating 'liberty' and 'freedom' as if they are synonymous.

Two further preliminary points must be made. One is that the concept of liberty or freedom is essentially political when applied to human beings, as distinct from animals. The other is that it is currently contestable, for people in the most varied political situations and systems have claimed that their mode of political activity promotes liberty or freedom, so long as this is properly defined.

The inherent importance of liberty to human beings arises from the fact that they are essentially choosing creatures, constantly taking decisions about how they want to act. The limitations on liberty arise from the fact that human beings are also social creatures, constrained in their choices by all kinds of social pressures. Throughout most of history, these restraints have arisen from pressures to conform with group or tribal customs, from pressures to conform with the dictates of religion, and from the power of landowners over tenants or serfs. In the recent history of the western world, people have partially escaped from these traditional constraints, but have become increasingly subject to the power of the state. It is therefore not surprising that the political theorists of ancient and medieval times paid little attention to the concept of liberty, whereas western political theorists since the seventeenth century have made it one of their central concerns.

Berlin has made a good case for saying that the various ways in which the concept of liberty has been interpreted can be reduced to two categories. On the one hand, liberty has been defined as freedom for the individual to do whatever he or she wants to do; in short, that liberty is the absence of restraint. This is the negative concept of liberty. On the other hand, liberty has been asserted to be freedom to do things that are worth doing, to engage in self-development, to have a share in the government of one's society. In Berlin's terminology, this is the positive concept of liberty. As will be seen, the views grouped under the latter heading are somewhat diverse, and it is open to question whether they should be given the same heading. However, there can be no doubt that the negative/positive dichotomy is an aid to understanding, and the issues will be discussed under those headings in what follows.

THE NEGATIVE CONCEPT OF LIBERTY

This concept found its first clear expression by a political theorist in the writings of Thomas Hobbes, who said in his *Leviathan* that 'Liberty, or freedom, signifieth, properly, the absence of opposition; by opposition, I mean external impediments of motion' (Hobbes 1985: 261). To underline this definition, he added: 'A freeman is he, that in those things, which by his strength and wit he is able to do, is not hindered to do what he has a will to do' (Hobbes 1985: 261). This straightforward view has been repeated, or taken for granted, by a whole series of political theorists and politicians who have accepted liberal individualistic assumptions about political life, among whom, most notably, were the British Utilitarians from Jeremy Bentham to John Stuart Mill.

The most eloquent of these writers was Mill, whose essay *On Liberty* has become a classic. The main contribution of this book was to propose criteria for determining the proper limits of state action. The political implication of the negative view of liberty, in the context of the modern state that regulates all our lives, is that citizens are free in so far as they are not constrained by laws and regulations. As Bentham said, liberty is the silence of the law. However, none of these writers was an anarchist. They all regarded freedom as the most important political value, but they realized that boundaries to individual liberty had to be established in order to protect other values such as security. In an argument about these boundaries, the onus of proof was on those who wanted to restrict liberty, but there was clearly a need for theorists of a liberal persuasion to indicate what kinds of argument would be compatible with liberal principles.

Despite his massive contributions to liberal theory, Bentham did not really do this. His overriding principle for deciding whether a proposed law or regulation was acceptable or not was the so-called 'felicific calculus'. The test for all legislation, in Bentham's view, was whether it was likely to increase or diminish the sum total of human happiness. If the legislation could be expected to increase this total, it was beneficial; but if it was likely to cause more pain than pleasure, it was harmful. This theory had the virtue of simplicity, and the further virtue (in Bentham's time) of giving a logical ground on which to challenge the age-old assumption of the land-owning classes that they knew what was best for the rest of society as a result of their upbringing, education and traditions. However, it was not always a satisfactory theory for those concerned above all with the protection of human liberty. There were (and are) many possible policies and laws that would pass Bentham's test, but yet inflict grievous limitations on the freedom of minorities whose values and/or interests differed from those of the majority. Promoting the interests of the majority is clearly better than promoting those of a ruling minority, but it is not necessarily a guarantee of what contemporary liberals would call individual rights.

To understand J. S. Mill's contribution, it is helpful to know a little about his personal history and intellectual development. He was educated by his father, James Mill, who was Bentham's assistant and a significant polit-ical theorist in his own right. The aim of the elder Mill was to train his son in the principles of Utilitarianism and to launch him on a career as a politi-cian and political theorist who would propagate Utilitarian ideas. This was remarkably successful in that the younger Mill became in turn secretary of the Utilitarian Society (a reforming pressure group), an influential civil ser-vant, a Member of Parliament and a brilliant writer. However, he revealed in his memoirs that when he was in his early twenties he went through an intellectual crisis. His attachment to music, poetry and the arts led him to believe that the pleasures of life could be divided into higher pleasures and more mundane pleasures, in contradistinction to the strict Utilitarian doctrine that all pleasures were of equal value in so far as they made people happy and that, in Bentham's famous words, 'pushpin is as good as poetry'. And, following this, he came to think that the pursuit of happiness should not be regarded as the end of life, as happiness tends to be a by-product of the pursuit of other objectives. As Mill put the matter:

> Those only are happy (I thought) who have their minds fixed on some object other than their own happiness; on the happiness of others, on the improvement of mankind, even on some art or pursuit, followed not as a means, but as itself an ideal end. Aiming thus at something else, they find happiness by the way.
>
> (Mill 1924: 120)

These beliefs took Mill quite a way from the pure spirit of Utilitarianism, even though he continued to work in public for Utilitarian causes, and he took another mental step away from it when he began to have doubts about democracy. After reading Tocqueville's *Democracy in America*, published when he was 29, Mill started to worry about the possible tyranny of the majority in a democratic polity. While all citizens were in some sense equal, he did not think them equal in sensibility, culture or political wisdom. Democratic institutions, he felt, would not in themselves prevent the possibility that a government, while seeking to maximize the welfare and happiness of the majority, might harm the minority in ways crucial to their wellbeing, for instance by curtailing their personal freedom. Considerations of this kind convinced Mill of the need to formulate some guiding principle that could be invoked to protect that most precious of all political values, the liberty of the individual citizen.

The principle that Mill formulated was in essence very simple; it was that the state would only be justified in curtailing the freedom of individuals if the purpose of that curtailment was to prevent harm to others. Mill put it thus:

> As soon as any part of a person's conduct affects prejudicially the interests of others, society has jurisdiction over it, and the question whether the general welfare will or will not be promoted by interfering with it becomes open to discussion. But there is no room for entertaining any such question when a person's conduct affects the interests of no person besides himself, or needs not affect them unless they like. . . . In all such cases there should be perfect freedom, legal and social, to do the action and stand the consequences.
>
> (Mill 1946: 67)

This principle is fairly clear, but a certain amount of argument has developed about it. One line of argument challenges the validity of the distinction between actions that affect only the actor (self-regarding actions) and actions that affect other citizens (other-regarding actions). It has been said that in modern society we live such intertwined and interdependent lives that all our actions affect others. The logical implication of this argument is that the category of self-regarding actions is an empty category, like that of glass mountains or carnivorous cattle.

This criticism of Mill has been met by the comments of John Rees, who has pointed out forcibly that Mill regarded an action as other-regarding only if it affected the interests of others, not if it was merely distasteful or inconvenient to others (see Rees 1960). Indeed, Mill had himself anticipated and largely answered this criticism, saying that:

> with regard to the merely contingent . . . injury which neither violates any specific duty to the public nor occasions perceptible hurt to any assignable individual except himself; the inconvenience is one which society can afford to bear, for the sake of the greater good of human freedom.
>
> (Mill 1946: 73)

Another line of criticism focuses on Mill's famous example of the man about to cross an unsafe bridge. If there were no time to warn the man of this imminent danger, it would be appropriate to seize him and stop him, 'without any real infringement of his liberty; for liberty consists in doing what one desires, and he does not desire to fall into the river' (Mill 1946: 86). It has been said by several critics that this sentence is inconsistent with Mill's general principle, that self-regarding actions should be inviolate. However, this criticism does not survive a careful examination of the text, for Mill went on to say that if there was only a danger, as distinct from a certainty, of an accident, the man should be allowed to take the chance if he decided to do so after he had been warned about it. The case for warning people about a dangerous bridge, but not prohibiting them from taking a chance with it, is on a par with the case (also discussed by Mill) for labelling poisonous chemicals as poisonous but not prohibiting people from buying them. It is very different from the position of the paternalist who would ban the sale of poisonous substances, or alcohol or cigarettes, on the ground that people ought not to be permitted to take a chance with their health (on this topic, see Lively 1983).

Criticisms of Mill's logic and consistency are certainly possible, for he wrote with passion rather than in the manner of an academic philosopher, but in my judgement they do not seriously weaken the force of his argument. What about the utility of his theory as a practical guide to political action?

In these terms also the theory stands up rather well. Western liberal governments have indeed acted in a Millian way by labelling poisons but permitting their sale, in some circumstances (also recommended by Mill) requiring a register of sales to be kept. In the same spirit, western governments have required cigarette manufacturers to label their products as dangerous to health and the United States government decided in 1990 to take the same action in respect of wine and spirits. In most western jurisdictions one may invoke the law to prevent one's next-door neighbours building in such a way as to cut off one's daylight or create a fire hazard for one's property, but not to prevent them from painting their house in distasteful colours. In the United Kingdom people can be arrested for being drunk and disorderly, but not for simply being drunk. In most western states a woman is free to engage in prostitution, but not to organize a brothel. In all these examples, the distinction between self-regarding and other-regarding actions is observed.

The British police seem to be particularly observant of this distinction. They are much more tolerant of speeding on the open road than North American police are, but much less tolerant of driving without courtesy to other road users. On one occasion I had to stand in line for a train that was crowded with people travelling from London to Newmarket to go to a race meeting. After the journey had been in progress for a few minutes each compartment was visited by a plain-clothes police officer who warned passengers that several professional card-sharps had been seen boarding the train, so 'if you play cards with strangers, we advise you to keep the stakes low'. John Stuart Mill would have applauded with enthusiasm.

Of course, there are borderline cases, of which the control of mood-altering drugs is the most obvious contemporary example. The sale of such drugs is forbidden in all modern states, on the grounds that they are a certain danger to health, that they are so addictive as to deprive the drug taker of the capacity to make subsequent free choices, and that they are likely to increase the crime rate. However, some liberals would say that soft drugs like marijuana ought to be exempt from the ban, as they are no more dangerous than alcohol or tobacco, while others would argue that most of the crime results from the fact that such drugs are illegal, so legalization would be socially desirable. One cannot expect Mill's essay to provide a clear answer to a dilemma as difficult as this. What one can say is that, with certain limitations, the essay is a pretty good guide to political practice in a liberal state. To say this, however, is not to say that the negative concept of liberty which Mill's essay enshrines is the only valid concept of liberty, for many reasonable people think otherwise.

OBJECTIONS TO THE NEGATIVE CONCEPT

Without distorting the facts (though admittedly with some simplification), it may be said that three different kinds of objection have been levelled at the negative concept of liberty, and that these may be given the labels of practical, theological and philosophical objections.

One practical objection takes the line that an abstract freedom to do something is meaningless to a person who lacks the capacity to do it. In its classic form, the argument is that it is meaningless, if not insulting, to tell unemployed workers that they are free to eat at the Ritz. The negative concept of liberty, it is claimed, is tied up with a belief in laissez-faire and a willingness to accept gross inequalities in society that leave the poorer sections without the ability to take advantage of opportunities that are said to be open to them. Freedom, to be meaningful, must involve real opportunities, not just theoretical ones.

The trouble with this line of argument is that it involves a confusion between liberty and ability. There is a world of difference between being unable to afford the price of a meal at the Ritz and being refused admission because your skin is black. In the former situation one could save up for a meal, if one had a special occasion in mind, or could look forward to eating there when one's income improved. In the latter situation one would be outraged by the discrimination. The two situations are not on a par and it is quite reasonable to say that the former involves a lack of means, the latter a restriction of liberty. Another example would be the difference between the position of Robinson Crusoe, who cannot leave his island because he cannot swim far enough and has not yet built a boat, and that of a prisoner on Devil's Island who would be shot if he tried to escape.

Another practical objection is that the negative concept of liberty takes no account of what many regard as the most important political freedom, namely freedom to choose one's government. Individualists would say that the franchise is a legal entitlement rather than a form of freedom, and at the level of the individual this distinction makes a good deal of sense. When I had the status of a landed immigrant in Canada I did not feel that my liberty was restricted by the fact that I could not vote in national elections, though I would have felt it was restricted had I not been able to criticize the government without fear of imprisonment or deportation. The ground for making this distinction is that the ability to vote depends on an entitlement – some would say a privilege – conferred on citizens by law, whereas the ability to express one's opinions exists naturally unless it is restricted by government action. But taking this view of the matter involves pre-suppositions that not everybody would share.

At the level of collective action the idea of freedom to choose the government is less controversial. When the countries of eastern Europe rejected their communist systems of government in 1989, it was quite appropriate to say that their citizens acquired a new form of freedom, namely the freedom to vote for non-communist candidates in the ensuing elections. This way of using the term retains the assumption that freedom involves choice, and is therefore a less radical departure from the negative concept than is implied by the theological and philosophical versions of the positive concept to be outlined below. However, freedom to choose political leaders is clearly 'freedom to', as distinct from 'freedom from', and the fact that the term is commonly used in this way indicates one of the limitations of the negative concept of liberty.

Theological objections to the negative concept have a quite different basis. When Pope John Paul II addressed a vast audience in Philadelphia in 1979, he made the following declaration:

> Freedom can never be construed without relation to the truth revealed by Jesus Christ and proposed by his church, nor can it be seen as a pretext for moral anarchy. This is especially relevant when one considers the domain of human sexuality. Here, as in any other field, there can be no true freedom without respect for the truth regarding the nature of human sexuality and marriage. Moral norms do not militate against the freedom of the person or the couple; on the contrary, they exist precisely for that freedom, since they are given to ensure the right use of freedom.

The belief expressed here is that freedom, properly defined, is not freedom for individuals to do what they choose, but freedom to do what is morally right. It is an enduring belief of the Roman Catholic Church and is shared by theologians in some other Christian Churches and in most branches of Islam. It is a matter of faith and is therefore not a belief that can be discussed as if it rested on rational or pragmatic arguments. Believers accept it and non-believers reject it, but true believers are logically bound to reject the negative concept of liberty as inadequate and misleading.

The third kind of argument against the negative concept is philosophical. Critics hold that the Utilitarians and other classical liberals, such as most American thinkers, are mistaken in their assumptions about human nature and human history. The primary truth about humans, they say, is that they are social animals. The history of humankind is not a history of isolated individuals coming together to form a civil society, as social contract theorists like Hobbes and Locke assumed. On the contrary, humans have always lived in communities that were held together by social norms. The essence of humankind is not, therefore, that they are autonomous, choosing creatures who must be free from external restraint in order to set their own values and course in life. On the contrary, their most important values are socially determined, and social laws to uphold those values should not be regarded as a restriction on some pre-existing liberty but as an appropriate part of the conditions of a satisfactory life.

This philosophical outlook had its origins in the writings of some of the Greeks, most notably Aristotle, but the theorist who erected a theory of positive freedom on this kind of basis was Jean-Jacques Rousseau, writing in France in the 1760s. However, Rousseau had little impact on British or American thought until towards the end of the nineteenth century. As John Plamenatz has said, the trouble with Rousseau, in British eyes, was that he was held responsible for inspiring the French Revolution. 'The English therefore condemned his doctrines, discovered a great deal of nonsense in them and took no notice of the rest' (Plamenatz 1949: 46). It was partly for this reason that Utilitarian ideas held a dominant position in British thought for most of the nineteenth century, until they were challenged in the 1880s by the work of T. H. Green, professor of moral philosophy at the University of Oxford. The writings of Green and those who thought like him, known collectively as the English Idealists, afford a convenient introduction to the philosophical basis of the positive concept of liberty because they were writing for an audience who mostly took the negative concept virtually for granted.

THE POSITIVE CONCEPT OF LIBERTY

The contributions of the English Idealists to this topic can most easily be summarized by listing the main points at which they parted company from the theories of the Utilitarians. These comprise a denial of the psychological assumptions of the Utilitarians, a rejection of individualism, a rejection of the Utilitarian view of the state, and the formulation of a different definition of freedom.

The Utilitarian view of human nature was that men are essentially pleasure-loving and pain-avoiding creatures. This is, it was said, the one clear generalization that can be made about human motives that appears to have universal validity. Human beings' reasoning powers present them with a great variety of tactics for the pursuance of these objectives, but (as David Hume had said) their reason is the servant of their passions.

To Green and the others, this is a sadly inadequate understanding of the human situation. Animals are motivated in this simple way but men and women are more complex. What they desire in life is not just prompted by their appetites. They desire what they think is good; they wish not only to be satisfied in various immediate ways, but also to be moral. They seek to improve themselves, to make themselves capable of appreciating better things, to live in a better way.

Second, the Idealists rejected the individualistic assumptions that the Utilitarians had made, in common with earlier liberal theorists like Hobbes and Locke. Individuals live in society, the Idealists maintained, and society is much more than a collection of independent human beings who happen to live in the same territory. According to F. H. Bradley, the individual of individualist theories is an abstraction who does not actually exist: the real individual 'is what he is because of and by virtue of community . . . a born and educated social being' (quoted Milne 1962: 62). The aspirations of real people are shaped by the assumptions, traditions and ideals of their society. They wish to behave in a moral way, and moral codes differ from one society to another. It is true that some individuals sometimes harbour ambitions that conflict with social and moral norms, but the pursuit of such ambitions will not, in the long run, benefit the personalities of the people involved. Any realistic theory of society and politics must accept that, to a large extent, human ambitions and behaviour are socially determined.

Third, the Idealists had a view of the state that differed from the view taken for granted by the Utilitarians. To the latter, following Hobbes and Locke, the state is a mechanism, a set of institutions created to safeguard the security of its citizens and to make arrangements (such as the laws regulating marriage or trade) for their convenience. Because the state restricts individual liberty and relies on coercion, it must be regarded with suspicion, but it should be looked on as a kind of necessary evil.

To the Idealist, this view ignores the social basis of the state. In Green's words, 'it is a mistake then to think of the state as an aggregation of individuals under a sovereign . . . a state presupposes other forms of community, with the rights that arise out of them, and only exists as sustaining, securing and completing them' (Green 1941: 139). Ideally, the state should not have to depend on coercion except at the margin, for 'will, not force, is the basis of the state'. If society were indeed as atomistic as most liberals of the nineteenth century assumed, coercion would be needed constantly, but these liberal theories were misleading as description and wrong in their ideals. Ideally, there should be a common will in society which the state should embody and express, recognition of which would lead the great majority of citizens to conform voluntarily with the law.

Finally, the Idealist view led to a different understanding of the nature of liberty. This emerged most clearly in the writings of Bernard Bosanquet, Green's successor at Oxford. Bosanquet claimed that the term liberty has both a lower sense and a higher sense. In the lower, more literal, sense liberty is taken to mean simply the absence of restraint. In the higher sense, which is metaphorical but yet deeply meaningful, liberty means acceptance by individuals of their real will, as rational beings, to make the best of themselves. In an ideal state, the conditions of self-realization would be established through political institutions, so that citizens would be free, in this higher sense, when they conformed to the requirements of society expressed through these institutions. 'Any system of institutions which represents to us, on the whole, the conditions essential to affirming such a will . . . has an imperative claim upon our loyalty and obedience as the embodiment of our liberty' (Bosanquet 1899: 149).

In this book Bosanquet was attempting to reformulate Rousseau's ideas in terms that would be acceptable to British opinion at the turn of the century. The relevant parts of Rousseau's theory are those relating to the distinction between three different types of will, respectively the 'general will' of society, the 'real will' of citizens, and 'the actual wills' of citizens.

The general will, in Rousseau's theory, consists in agreement on a set of policies to be adopted by the citizens of an ideal republic regarding basic issues which do not divide the population into sections whose interests differ. The process of eliciting the general will requires a civic leader, known as the legislator, who will formulate the questions on which a public verdict is required, together with an institutional arrangement, such as a public meeting if the republic is small enough, that will enable an expression of public opinion to be secured. Even in an ideal republic, many issues would be divisive in terms of sectional interests and on these issues no general will could be expected. But on basic issues, given the right kind of civic education, the people should be united and a general consensus should emerge. When the general will is elicited it would, in an ideal polity, be embodied in laws and the obligation to obey those laws could not be regarded as a restriction of liberty, for citizens would have had the opportunity to participate in the process by which the laws were formulated. As Rousseau declared 'obedience to a law which we prescribe to ourselves is liberty' (Rousseau 1913: 19).

In this ideal republic, citizens would consider their common interests when they voted, so that their real wills would be consistent with the general will as it emerged. It had to be admitted, however, that on some issues a minority of citizens would persist in opinions running contrary to those embodied in the general will. They would have particular or actual wills that reflected their personal preferences rather than the interests they had in common with their fellow citizens. They might consider their preferences unrepresented on that issue and consider ignoring the law. In such cases the state would have to threaten or use coercive measures against the minority so as to ensure that the laws were obeyed. This could be done without any restriction of freedom, properly defined, for the general will embodied the best interests of all citizens and it would be for their own good that the minority were coerced. In Rousseau's famous phrase, they would be 'forced to be free'.

This phrase stuck in the gullet of most British liberals in the nineteenth century, and it was to persuade them of the validity of Rousseau's theory that Bosanquet produced a reasoned account of the difference between men's actual wills and their real will that is worth quoting at some length:

> In order to obtain a full statement of what we will, what we want at any moment must at least be corrected and amended by what we want at all other moments; and this cannot be done without also correcting and amending it so as to harmonize it with what others want. . . . But when any considerable degree of such correction and amendment had been gone through, our own will would return to us in a shape in which we should not know it again, although every detail would be a necessary inference from the whole of wishes and resolutions which we actually cherish. And if it were to be supplemented and readjusted so as to stand not merely for the life which on the whole we manage to live, but for a life ideally without contradiction, it would appear to us quite remote from anything we know. . . . In the plainest language, what we really

want is something more and other than at any given moment we are aware that we will, although the wants which we are aware of lead up to it at every point.

(Bosanquet 1899: 119)

This passage gives a clear indication of the character of the ideal that inspired Rousseau in the eighteenth century and the English Idealists at the end of the nineteenth century: a belief in the possibility of human self-improvement and self-realization in the context of a harmonious community organized for self-government. It may perhaps be counted as a nobler ideal than that of the maximization of happiness and the minimization of pain, though the latter is certainly not to be despised. It lies at the base of the philosophical case for believing that the negative concept of liberty is inadequate and should be supplemented by a positive concept of true freedom as a social phenomenon, to be found in societies dedicated to an improvement in the human condition.

TWO TYPES OF LIBERTY

The work of the English Idealists was responsible for a marked change in the thinking of British liberals. It came to public attention at a time when social conditions in working-class urban areas called out for positive intervention by public authorities, which liberal leaders felt was necessary but were chary of advocating because their party had always been committed to the view that increasing the powers of government would diminish liberty. The possibility of redefining liberty enabled them to escape from this dilemma, and the change can be seen in the following quotations from prominent supporters of the Liberal Party.

J. S. Mill: *Principles of Political Economy* (1848):

> It is no less important in a democratic than in any other government, that all tendency on the part of public authorities to stretch their interference, and assume a power of any sort which can easily be dispensed with, should be regarded with unremitting jealousy.

J. S. Mill: *On Liberty* (1859):

> The only purpose for which power can be rightfully exercised over any member of a civilized community, against his will, is to prevent harm to others. His own good, either physical or moral, is not a sufficient warrant.

T. H. Green: *Liberal Legislation and Freedom of Contract* (1881):

> When we speak of freedom as something to be so highly prized, we mean a positive power or capacity of doing or enjoying something worth doing or enjoying, and that, too, something that we do or enjoy in common

with others. We mean by it a power which each man exercises through the help or security given him by his fellow-man, and which he in turn helps to secure for them. When we measure the progress of a society by its growth in freedom, we measure it by the increasing development and exercise on the whole of those powers of contributing to social good with which we believe the members of the society to be endowed; in short, by the greater power on the part of the citizens as a body to make the most and best of themselves. Thus, though of course there can be no freedom among men who act not willingly but under compulsion, the mere enabling a man to do as he likes, is in itself no contribution to true freedom.

H. H. Asquith: *Election Address* (1892):

I am one of those who believe that the collective action of the community may and ought to be employed positively as well as negatively; to raise as well as to level; to equalise opportunities no less than to curtail privileges; to make the freedom of the individual a reality and not a pretence.

Herbert Samuel: *Liberalism* (1902):

To support a policy of state regulation in industry is quite consistent with a belief in liberty, and not merely consistent with it but rather to be regarded as its necessary consequence.

L. T. Hobhouse: *Liberalism* (1911):

There is no true opposition between liberty as such and control as such, for every liberty rests on a corresponding act of control. The true opposition is between the control that cramps the personal life and the spiritual order, and the control that is aimed at securing the external and material conditions of their free and unimpeded development.

Members of the infant Labour Party also embraced the positive concept of liberty with enthusiasm, while Conservatives found that it suited their rather paternalistic attitudes towards politics. From the turn of the century until the Second World War the positive concept of liberty was more fashionable than the negative concept in Britain, though this was not true of the United States. However, the 1940s and 1950s saw a change of opinion in Britain on this question, for two quite unrelated reasons.

On the one hand, revulsion at what had been done by the state in Stalin's Russia and Hitler's Germany led people to turn away from a theory of politics that could be used to glorify the powers of the state and minimize the threat that state controls posed to human liberty, in the simple negative sense of that term. Rousseau's theories seemed somewhat dangerous and the phrase 'forced to be free' seemed positively sinister. In 1947 Ernest Barker, in an introduction to a new edition of *The Social Contract*, declared that 'in effect, and in the last resort, Rousseau is a totalitarian' (Barker 1947: xxxviii). In 1955 J. L. Talmon said the same thing at much greater length in *The Origins of Totalitarian Democracy* (Talmon 1955).

On the other hand, the academic popularity of logical positivism (to be discussed in Chapter 16) led philosophers and political scientists to eschew metaphysics and to develop a preference for the plain, descriptive, behavioural use of language without concealed meanings. To logical positivists and those influenced by them, it seemed natural for freedom to mean the ability to do as one likes, not self-realization or self-improvement or a raised social consciousness or conformity to the general will.

Isaiah Berlin's famous 1958 lecture on 'Two concepts of liberty' faithfully reflected this new climate of opinion, for the heart of the lecture was a passionate attack on the positive concept. At the level of practical politics, the concept was dangerous, for it could be and had been used by tyrants. Once a ruler embraced the view that individuals had a real self or spirit, 'of which the poor empirical self in space and time may know nothing or little; and that this inner spirit is the only self that deserves to have its wishes taken into account', then that ruler would be

> in a position to ignore the actual wishes of men or societies, to bully, oppress, torture them in the name, and on behalf, of their 'real' selves, in the secure knowledge that whatever is the true goal of man . . . must be identical with his freedom.
>
> (Berlin 1969: 133)

At a more academic level, the positive concept involved a confusion of linguistic usage that led to a confusion of values. Berlin insisted that we must use language plainly if we are to keep our arguments clear:

> Everything is what it is: liberty is liberty, not equality or fairness or justice or culture, or human happiness or a quiet conscience. . . . If I curtail or lose my freedom . . . this may be compensated for by a gain in justice or in happiness or in peace, but the loss remains, and it is a confusion of values to say that although my 'liberal' individual freedom may go by the board, some other kind of freedom . . . is increased.
>
> (Berlin 1969: 125)

These disputes over the true meaning of freedom are never likely to be resolved. In part, this is because freedom is so universally regarded as a desirable state of affairs that people will go to almost any length to show that their own political theories and agendas are compatible with the preservation or expansion of freedom. In part, it is because thinking about the nature of freedom raises philosophical issues on which basic disagreements are certain to continue. Thus, there is a fundamental difference of view between theorists who, like Berlin, believe that 'the essence of human beings is that they are autonomous beings – authors of values, of ends in themselves' (Berlin 1969: 136), and those who believe that the essence of human beings is that they are social animals, deriving their values and ends in life from the communities in which they have their being. The ordinary individual might observe that humans are both social animals and to some extent autonomous, so that what is involved in this disagreement is no more than a quibble about the meaning of 'essence'. But to political philosophers this is much more than a quibble.

Again, there is an unresolvable difference of belief between moralists who distinguish between liberty and licence and secular thinkers who regard this as no more than an attempt to confine the stamp of approval to behaviour which the moralist happens to find satisfactory. It is deeply meaningful to some, but virtual nonsense to others, to say that 'man is not free but enslaved when he seeks merely the satisfaction of his own unrestrained desires. He becomes free when and in so far as he endeavours to act as a moral being' (Bassett 1935: 10).

The tendency in several more recent writings by political theorists has been to suggest that liberty and freedom have a range of meanings, so that it may be unhelpful to draw a stark contrast between the negative and positive concepts. In 1976 Benjamin Gibbs asserted that: 'freedom means different things in different contexts; not because the term is incorrigibly ill-defined or because we are all incorrigibly vague about its meaning, but because it has a number of meanings' (Gibbs 1976: 9). By the end of his book Gibbs had come down in favour of a collectivist version of the positive concept, stressing the desirability of a revolution to bring real freedom to the under-privileged, but this ideological preference did not destroy the validity of his more general point about the coexistence of several shades of meaning for the concept of freedom.

In 1979 Charles Taylor asserted that there are not so much as two con-cepts of liberty as two 'families of conceptions of political freedom', and within each family 'there is quite a gamut of views' (Taylor 1979: 175). Writers who favoured one concept or family of concepts tended to attack the most extreme version of the other concept, sometimes reducing the other concept to a caricature. As an example, Taylor said that the negative view of freedom should be thought of as embracing freedom from all re-straints to self-fulfilment, not just external restraints. If people have been manipulated into false consciousness of the possibilities open to them this is a restraint on their freedom, just as it would be if someone were 'paralysed by the fear of breaking with some norm which he has internalized but which does not authentically reflect him' (Taylor 1979: 177). If the negative concept of liberty or freedom is portrayed as simply the physical opportun-ity to do as one likes, without reference to internal restraints of this kind, as it frequently is even by its proponents, then it becomes too simplistic to be a good guide to the richness of meaning that the terms have. You cannot really be free, even in the negative sense, if you have been indoctrinated.

Now, not everyone would go along with Taylor in this line of argument and his examples. In the contemporary world, those who have observed the rise of Islamic fundamentalism in the Middle East and the rejection of communism in eastern Europe may find it easier to accept that a person's negative freedom may be said to be restricted if they are in the grip of a dogmatic religious code than that it may be said to be restricted by false consciousness about the desirability of free enterprise. In philosophical terms, however, there is not much difference between the two examples.

Another line of criticism would be that, by trying to extend the meaning of negative liberty in this fashion, Taylor is really trying to undermine the validity of the whole concept of negative liberty, as the title of his article suggests; and this would be unreasonable as there clearly is a well-established usage by which liberty simply means the absence of external restraints. This criticism has considerable force, but it may still perhaps be accepted that Taylor has succeeded in blurring the sharp distinction between the two concepts of liberty that Berlin and others have drawn.

In 1983 Quentin Skinner added to the debate by drawing attention to a very long-standing belief by thinkers in the tradition of classical republicanism that, to be secure in their enjoyment of negative liberty, citizens must live in a polity that embraces the republican virtue of government that is in some degree representative of its citizens' interests. This strain of thought had its roots in the traditions of classical Rome but was articulated for the modern world by Machiavelli in his *Discourses.* When Machiavelli wrote of liberty he meant just what is now meant by the negative concept of liberty, namely the absence of 'limitations imposed by other social agents on one's capacity to act independently in pursuit of one's chosen goals' (Skinner 1983: 206). As he valued liberty, he was concerned to ask what kind of state would be most likely to maximize the liberty of its citizens. His answer was a self-governing state with a republican system of government. His thesis was that 'it is only those who live under republican forms of government who can hope to retain any element of personal liberty to pursue their chosen ends' (Skinner 1983: 207).

This thesis was rejected by Hobbes, who believed that freedom was freedom, whatever the form of government, and it has not always been put forward, or at any rate not stressed, by modern exponents of the virtues of the negative concept of liberty. It was accepted by the Utilitarians, of course, but some of Machiavelli's further beliefs were echoed more faithfully by Rousseau than by any other modern thinkers. Machiavelli, like Rousseau two centuries later, believed that there could be a common will of society that was reflected in governmental decision. He also believed in the virtues of political participation. Citizens would not maintain their liberty, he maintained, unless they were willing to perform voluntary services, to participate in political debate, and to serve in public office (Skinner 1983: 214). Machiavelli was therefore suggesting that liberty, though defined in what we now call negative terms, requires positive commitment and positive action by citizens if it is to be maintained. Though he did not embrace what we now call the positive conception of liberty, he went some steps towards it by urging the case for popular participation in forming the common will.

In the light of these modern debates, it seems fair to conclude that we should be mistaken if we were to commit ourselves to one concept of liberty, to the exclusion of the other. It would certainly be wrong to exclude the negative concept, for this is exactly how the terms liberty and freedom are used, and will undoubtedly continue to be used, in everyday speech. The case against the negative concept cannot be that it is wrong, or that it is ambiguous, or that it portrays a kind of liberty that is inherently undesirable. The only fair argument against it is that it is inadequate as a guide to the varied meanings that liberty and freedom have acquired in political debate.

The positive concept of liberty is more ambiguous, more slippery perhaps, because its usage raises complex problems about the nature of an ideal political community. It may be thought difficult to reject the vision of such a community as one in which citizens will check their immediate wishes and interests as individuals against their longer-term and wider interests as members of the community. Why else could citizens be expected to support wage restraints or measures to protect the environment or expensive schemes to help the unemployed? One might, if thinking on those lines, be willing to support the distinction between the 'actual wills' and 'real will' of citizens, but yet jib at Rousseau's claim that dissenters who had to be coerced to obey the laws were being 'forced to be free'. The phrase is not only a superb piece of rhetoric but also an essential key to Rousseau's theory, so that much would be lost if it were replaced by some anodyne phrase such as 'forced to be good citizens'. However, there can be no doubt that its use, outside the strict context of that theory, has caused a good deal of intellectual and political confusion.

It is clear that different concepts of liberty, like different concepts of democracy, are used as weapons in political debate. Students of politics cannot stop this, but they have to recognize what is being done. One conclusion that the uncommitted student might reach is that some of the protagonists in this argument about the meaning of liberty are misleading in the impression of exclusivity that they give. The advocates of negative liberty would be more realistic if they acknowledged that democratic self-government is a kind of collective freedom. They might also acknowledge that extending the capacities and abilities of human beings tends to extend the value of freedom to them. Thus, Robinson Crusoe was undoubtedly a free man whereas the prisoners on Devil's Island were not, but his freedom would have been more valuable – and, one might say, would actually have been extended – if he had had a serviceable boat at his disposal.

The advocates of positive liberty should acknowledge that a large measure of liberty in the negative sense of the term is an essential prerequisite to the process of finding a consensus, for it could not be a genuine, freedom-enhancing consensus if it were simply imposed from the top. The negative and positive concepts draw attention to different kinds of liberty, but in the real world of political practice most citizens want some of each kind. If both sides always made these concessions the debate between them would be less stimulating, but their arguments would be more realistic in terms of understanding the meaning and significance of political freedom.

Chapter 11

Rights

We live in an age in which it has become common for people in democratic societies to invoke the concept of rights in political discourse. We talk of the rights of individual citizens, the rights of categories of citizens like children or women or pensioners, and the rights of groups within society like ethnic and cultural minorities. Outside the United States, this kind of talk was not very common in the first half of the twentieth century. Lawyers talked about rights and so did people involved in legal cases, but people engaged in political debate found it more natural to talk in terms of interests, needs and welfare. Americans have always tended to place more emphasis on rights, partly because their society is more individualistic than that of other democracies, but mainly because of the great importance in American political life of the Bill of Rights, added to the constitution in 1791 and invoked and redefined endlessly since that date.

The language of rights has become more general since 1945, for two quite different reasons. On the one hand, 1948 saw the promulgation of the Universal Declaration of Human Rights, which has brought the new idea of human rights into general currency in the western world. This was followed in 1949 by the inclusion of some guarantees of rights in the Basic Law of the German Federal Republic, which made it clear that entrenched rights were not necessarily incompatible with a parliamentary system of government, and in 1950 by the promulgation of the European Convention on Human Rights. On the other hand, the emergence of a new kind of radicalism in the late 1960s in the west led many persons and movements on the left of the political spectrum to change their emphasis from the advocacy of policies designed to extend state powers, by economic planning, public ownership and extended social security arrangements, to the advocacy of policies stressing the rights of the individual against the state. There was a change of fashion in political debate that has continued to this day, with radical reformers concerned less with economic issues and more with such issues as students' rights, women's rights, gay rights, prisoners' rights and animal rights. For better or worse, talk about rights is more common now than ever before, and all students of politics need to come to grips with this concept.

THE NATURE OF RIGHTS

There is some disagreement among philosophers as to whether the best synonym for 'a right' is 'a claim' or 'an entitlement'. (For references, see Feinberg 1980: xi, 154.) Although the majority preference seems to be in favour of 'a claim', I believe that, if a choice has to be made, it makes much more sense to opt for 'an entitlement'. To say that someone has a right to X is to say something much stronger than that he or she has a claim to X. We all have claims to this, that and the other; they are the very stuff of politics. We can turn our claim into a right only if we win the argument or struggle, which not everyone can do. Another difference is that the term 'claim' implies activity, for a claim has to be made. A right, however, may exist without any activity at all on the part of the person holding the right. More than this, one can have a right without even knowing that one has it, as babies have rights. The term 'entitlement' allows for this much more naturally than the term 'claim'. In the field of politics, it would seem silly to speak of a Universal Declaration of Human Claims, but only clumsy, not silly, to speak of a Universal Declaration of Human Entitlements.

The concept of rights is essentially a concept about human relationships in society. If one person has a right to something, other members of his society have an obligation to respect this right. If it is a right of action, such as a right to engage in political dissent, fellow citizens and the government have an obligation to tolerate expressions of dissent. If it is a right of recipience, such as a right to a pension, the appropriate agency or corporation has an obligation to provide the pension. If it is a right to be left alone, such as a right to privacy in sexual relationships, fellow-citizens and government agencies have an obligation not to intrude on those relationships.

The social character of rights is an essential aspect of the concept. The existence of rights always implies obligations on the part of other citizens and frequently implies obligations on the part of the person or group holding the right. Persons engaged in political dissent have an obligation not to block the public highway with their demonstrations, for this would interfere with the right of others to use the highway. Persons acting as union pickets during a strike have a right to inform potential workers about the strike, but they also have an obligation to let the workers cross the picket line if that is their wish. Persons claiming privacy for their sexual relationships have an obligation to conduct sexual activities in private, so as not to intrude on the feelings of others. It is this social aspect of rights that makes it meaningless to talk of animal rights. It is cruel, and may be illegal, for human beings to inflict unnecessary pain on other living creatures, but animals do not belong to human societies and cannot be said to possess rights in those societies.

There are two important questions to ask about a right, or a potential right, in addition to the question of whether it is a right of action, a right of recipience, or a right to be left alone. One question is whether, and if so how far, the right is limited in time and space. The great majority of rights are so limited, because they have reality only in the context of a particular human society that did not always exist in the past, may not always exist in the future, and has territorial boundaries in the present. The rights possessed by Americans in the twentieth and twenty-first centuries did not exist in the fifteenth century, may not have much meaning in five hundred years' time, and in any case do not extend to Asia or Africa. It is convenient to describe these limitations as the contextual limits of the rights in question. Some rights are said to be of universal applicability, but this is a difficult claim to make and will be discussed below in the section on natural and human rights.

A further question is the basis of the right in question. Some rights derive from law, some from moral codes, some from tradition. It is essential to distinguish rights according to their basis, and this will be the subject of the following section.

THE BASES OF RIGHTS

The most obvious basis of a right is the existence of a legally binding contract. It is in the nature of contracts that they confer rights upon one of the signatories and impose obligations on the other. They are binding in so far as they are not in conflict with the laws of the jurisdiction in which they are made, a proviso which excludes contracts to commit a crime. There may be a grey area on the margins of criminality, but apart from that there are no conceptual problems about contractual rights.

A second category consists of positive rights, which are created by decisions of the legislative body within a jurisdiction. In modern democratic states citizens have positive rights to participate in public education, to be paid state pensions when they reach retirement age, and to receive various other benefits as provided by law. In addition to such rights of recipience, they may also have positive rights of action, such as a guaranteed right of free speech or, in the United States, a right to bear arms. Positive rights are always contextual, as by definition the rights are conferred only upon residents of the territory covered by the jurisdiction, and they exist only for such time as the relevant law is not rescinded by the legislature or rendered nugatory by judicial interpretation.

A third category consists of moral rights, which derive their authority from a code of morality shared by members of the community within which the rights can be said to exist. Such rights are enforced by the conscience of individuals, by the custom of the community, or by the pressure of public opinion. They may also be enforced by law, for moral codes underlie many laws, but in that case the moral laws become converted into positive rights, which are more secure because they are enforced by the state.

Moral rights are normally contextual rather than universal, for they are limited to people who share a common code of morality. It has been argued that all known codes of morality have certain basic beliefs in common, but this is disputable and certainly difficult to establish. The contextual nature of most (if not all) moral rights has been made evident by recent international migrations. Thus, Muslims living in Britain or France come (or have ancestors who came) from societies in which they were permitted to have four wives, but this custom is unacceptable to the majority of British and French citizens and cannot be followed. British people living in Saudi Arabia cannot celebrate weddings with champagne, as they would do in Britain.

A fourth category consists of political rights. Many political rights have been embodied into law and have thus become positive political rights. In western democracies these include the rights to vote, to organize political parties and pressure groups, and to compete for political office. Like all positive rights, these are clearly contextual in nature and they do not present conceptual problems.

Interesting questions arise, however, when it is claimed that people have political rights that are not recognized by law. What is meant by saying that Afghanistani women have a right to vote, that Chinese students have a right to demonstrate in favour of democracy, that Kurds have a right to political autonomy within Iraq? What bases can be claimed for such notional rights?

In essence, there are two possible bases, namely custom and tradition on the one hand and human reason on the other. The distinction was first made clearly by Edmund Burke, the founder of British conservatism, who called the first type customary rights and the second type speculative rights. He argued strongly in favour of the superiority of customary rights over speculative rights, on the ground that the wisdom of past generations is embodied in the customs of a society whereas human reason is fallible, and therefore an unreliable guide. This position led Burke into practical attitudes that many of his contemporaries regarded as contradictory, as when, alone among British Members of Parliament, he defended the revolution in the American colonies but attacked the revolution in France. He did so because he regarded the American colonists as defending the traditional rights of British citizens, in particular their right not to be taxed without representation, whereas he regarded the French revolutionaries as led by a false belief in speculative rights into overthrowing existing institutions and customs in favour of political experiments of which the outcome was unpredictable. The fact that the American revolution was a triumphant success whereas the French revolution led to dictatorship, state terrorism and the eventual restoration of the monarchy has naturally been held by Burke's later supporters to be a vindication of his views.

As Alfred Cobban pointed out, Burke's philosophical conservatism led him to support at least five separate rebellions against authority; not only the American War of Independence but the English Revolution of 1688, the nationalistic struggles of the Corsicans and Poles, and the various Indian revolts against corrupt administrators of the British East India Company. What was common to these rebellions was 'the rising of practically a whole community . . . in defence of what were claimed to be ancient liberties' (Cobban 1960: 100).

If Burke's criteria were to be applied to the contemporary examples mentioned above, the argument would support the rights of Kurds to enjoy, if not complete autonomy, respect for their culture and freedom. It would not support the rights asserted by Chinese students and Afghanistani women, on the ground that, since the rights run contrary to local custom and experience, their assertion may lead to political instability. It is not a negligible argument, even though most modern democrats would probably regard it as excessively cautious. If it is rejected in favour of a belief in speculative political rights based upon reason, this raises the question of how universality can be claimed for arguments that seem entirely rational in some societies but are rejected by other societies. It is a difficult question to answer, and it leads us straight into a consideration of natural rights and human rights.

NATURAL RIGHTS AND HUMAN RIGHTS

Natural rights and human rights are rights claimed in respect of all human beings. They are said to be of universal rather than contextual applicability and are therefore very different from positive rights, which are limited to particular jurisdictions, and moral rights which are based on a particular moral code. To justify the large claims that are made about them they must be morally compelling, as distinct from merely desirable, and possible of achievement, as distinct from utopian dreams. They inhere in individual human beings rather than in societies or states, and the actual rights that have been nominated as human rights are in large measure rights against the state, that is, rights which it is said every state ought to respect. The promoters of human rights have not pretended that ordinary human interactions can be regulated by sweeping generalizations of this kind; their concern has been to establish criteria by which the actions of governmental authorities can be judged.

Now, the assertion that human beings may have rights against their governments has been made from time to time since the days of the Greek city-states by theorists of natural law and natural rights. The Stoic philosophers of classical Greece maintained that slavery was contrary to natural law. It was a somewhat radical proposition in its day, as slavery was not then contrary to either positive law or custom or the prevailing religion. In medieval Europe various Catholic theorists equated natural law with divine law, as laid down by the Roman Catholic Church. The authority for it was said to be God's will, as interpreted by his vicars on earth. The powers of secular rulers were said to be limited, for in all spiritual matters natural law was supreme.

By the beginning of the seventeenth century the unity of Christendom had been shattered and natural law theorists turned to human reason rather than divine revelation as the source of law that had greater authority than the dictates of governments. Grotius declared that 'the law of nature is a dictate of right reason, which points out that an act, according as it is or is not in conformity with rational nature, has in it a quality of moral baseness or moral necessity' (quoted Sabine 1937: 424).

Later in the century Hobbes and Locke made certain deductions from their logical construct, an imaginary state of nature said to have preceded the establishment of political authority. Hobbes's state of nature was essentially a condition of anarchy, marked by the struggle of all against all for the necessities of life, in which men and women had no rights other than that of self-defence – which was not a right at all in the sense used in this chapter because it was not accompanied by any corresponding obligations. Civil society was then formed for mutual security, and in this condition citizens gave up their so-called right of self-defence in exchange for the protection of their lives by the authority of the government. They then had one right against the government, namely the right to life. Locke's version of the mythical state of nature was more civilized, and in his theory men took into civil society their natural rights to life, liberty, and the property with which they had mixed their labour. In both cases the theories were rational constructs and the rights enumerated were in this sense based on reason.

Locke's theories had a direct influence on the thought of the founders of the American Republic. The Declaration of Rights issued by the Philadelphia Congress of 1771 appealed to 'the immutable laws of nature' and claimed the right 'to life, liberty, and property'. The first clause of the Virginia Bill of Rights, adopted in June 1776, proclaimed:

> That all men are by nature equally free and independent, and have certain inherent rights, of which, when they enter into a state of society they cannot, by any compact, deprive or divest their posterity: namely, the enjoyment of life and liberty, with the means of acquiring and possessing property and pursuing and obtaining happiness.

In the following month the Declaration of Independence left out property but inserted a reference to God: 'We hold these truths to be self-evident: that all men are created equal; that they are endowed by their Creator with certain inalienable rights; that among these are life, liberty, and the pursuit of happiness'. Thirteen years later the French Declaration of the Rights of Man and the Citizen asserted 'the purpose of all political association is the conservation of the natural and inalienable rights of man: these rights are liberty, property, security, and resistance to oppression'. And in 1791 the first ten amendments to the American constitution entrenched the Bill of Rights as binding on all American legislatures, so turning the rights specified into positive political rights.

It seems a little paradoxical that, after this burst of inspired enthusiasm, the whole doctrine of inalienable rights should have fallen into disrepute among political philosophers. It was so, however, for all the main theorists of the following century repudiated the doctrine. Edmund Burke attacked the whole idea of speculative rights in his book *Reflections on the Revolution in France*, written and published very speedily in 1790. The attempt to make the cold light of human reason the only guide to political action was, in Burke's view, a calamitous mistake, destructive of the customs and sentiments that bind citizens together. The science of government, he declared, is a practical science, that can only be built upon experience and has no place for a priori principles. It is a view that European conservatives have held from that day to this.

Six years later, Jeremy Bentham attacked the idea of natural rights from a liberal perspective when he wrote *Anarchical Fallacies*, written in 1796 although not published until 1816 in French and 1843 in English. Bentham, who had much more influence on British liberalism than Locke, rejected the whole idea of rights prior to and against the state. Rights were conferred by law, in his view. 'Before the existence of laws there may be reasons for wishing that there were laws . . . but a reason for wishing that we possessed a right does not constitute a right'. To talk of universal rights as if they existed would be equivalent to saying 'everybody is subject to hunger, therefore everyone has something to eat' (quoted Manning 1968: 43). He observed that 'the language of natural rights . . . is from beginning to end so much flat assertion' (quoted Waldron 1987: 74). Instead of making assertions about rights, politicians should make a careful investigation of the circumstances and the expected consequences of governmental actions. His conclusion was sweeping: 'Natural rights is simple nonsense: natural and imprescriptable rights, rhetorical nonsense – nonsense upon stilts' (quoted Waldron 1987: 53).

From Bentham onwards, Utilitarian theorists insisted that the test of good government was the extent to which legislation and government policy pursued a progressive goal, namely the maximization of happiness among citizens, rather than protecting what was deemed to exist already, namely a package of individual rights. J. S. Mill varied from this a little in his essay *On Liberty*, where he attached a very special value, beyond mere happiness, to the protection of individual liberty, but he remained faithful to the idea of the felicific calculus in his book on *Utilitarianism*.

In the last years of the nineteenth century British Liberals moved from the hedonistic assumptions of the earlier Utilitarians and the attachment to a purely negative concept of liberty towards the more uplifting views of the English Idealists and the positive view of liberty that accompanied them, as has already been explained in Chapter 10. British liberals had mostly abandoned Utilitarian views by the turn of the century, but they moved to Idealism without at any time accepting the widespread American belief in inalienable rights. Nor was this latter idea taken up by British conservatives or socialists.

This is also true of thinkers and political leaders in continental Europe, once the heady years of the French revolution had given way to the restoration of Bourbon rule. From 1815 until the Second World War, the rival heroes of European political theorists were Hegel on the one hand and Marx on the other. Hegel and his followers rejected any idea of inalienable rights because they glorified the authority of the national state and could not conceive of citizens having rights against the state. Marx and Engels rejected the idea of inalienable rights because they regarded it as a bourgeois notion, based upon individualistic assumptions rather than upon any conception of social needs. In his essay *On the Jewish Question*, published in 1843, Marx attacked the French *Declaration of the Rights of Man and the Citizen*:

> None of the supposed rights of man, therefore, go beyond the egoistic man . . . that is, an individual separated from the community, withdrawn into himself, wholly preoccupied with his private interest and acting in accordance with his private caprice.
>
> (Tucker 1978: 43)

From this time onwards, European socialists of all varieties, be they Marxists or social democrats, have been concerned to promote the interests of the working class, and beyond that the interests of the whole community, but have not focused on the rights of the individual. Almost by definition, socialists are collectivists, not individualists.

The introduction of the idea of human rights immediately after the Second World War therefore marked a sharp change of outlook. It was the direct consequence of revulsion against the genocidal policies followed by Hitler's regime. This revulsion led the victorious nations to put a number of German leaders on trial for an offence that had no place in any statute book, but was created by decision of the international court. This offence was called 'crimes against humanity', and, as a standard for the future, a special committee of the United Nations Organization then drafted, and in 1948 the General Assembly proclaimed, a *Universal Declaration of Human Rights*.

The Declaration was said to set 'a common standard of achievement for all peoples and all nations'. No philosophical or religious basis for it was claimed; the basis was said to be the pledge given by member states of the United Nations to promote 'universal respect for and observation of human rights and fundamental freedoms'. The argument, it will be noted, was circular; the rights were proclaimed because the victorious nations all believed in them; the Universal Declaration embodied a consensus of western values at the time it was formulated. The rights itemized in the Declaration were: first, individual rights of action, namely rights to life, liberty, property, privacy, emigration, freedom of speech and association, and freedom of religion; second, rights to protection under the law, namely rights to equal treatment by the law, freedom from arbitrary arrest, trial by an impartial tribunal, and freedom from cruel or degrading punishment; third, political rights, namely to participate in periodic free elections based on universal suffrage; and fourth, economic and social rights, namely to employment, an adequate standard of living, equal pay for equal work, holidays with pay, social security benefits, and free education.

Maurice Cranston has argued forcibly that it was a mistake to include the economic and social rights, on the ground that they are no more than utopian ideals for the poorer (and hence the majority) of the member states, and their inclusion may lead sceptics to regard the other enumerated rights as no more than utopian ideals also (see Cranston 1962: 38–44). It would have been more sensible, he maintains, to have restricted the list of rights to those that are both morally compelling and capable of achievement through-out the world.

Brian Barry has another criticism of the inclusion of these social rights when he points out that they involve relativities about which argument is always possible: 'An analogy to "an adequate standard of living" would be "a moderate amount of free speech", but the latter is not what is called for in a declaration of rights' (Barry 1965: 150). Quite so, but the right to free speech is not generally thought to include the right to publish libellous statements about a rival. There is always a problem about whether rights are absolute rights, such as to publish whatever you please about anything, or whether they can properly be limited in this way or that while preserving their essence.

It is reasonable to raise queries about both the philosophical basis of the Declaration and its practical utility. The assertion that human rights inhere in all human beings, irrespective of their religious beliefs or their social customs, is clearly a very sweeping assertion. It cannot be based on faith, not only because faiths differ so much, but also because the advanced indus-trial societies that actually attach most importance to the idea of human rights are societies in which religious faith is (except perhaps in North America) in sharp decline. It was stated to be based on a political commit-ment by the founding states of the United Nations Organization, but that raises questions about why the governments of those states at that moment of history should have the power to commit successor governments, despite numerous changes of regime. It must presumably be based on reason, or an appeal to common understandings about the human situation, but that raises the familiar philosophical dilemma about how values, particularly values said to be binding, can be extracted from facts. All governments might agree that human beings seem to enjoy freedom of action in this field or that without agreeing that it is good for them to be given such freedom. (For a full discussion of the philosophical questions surrounding the concept of human rights, see Paul et al. 1984; Nickel 1987.)

Despite these various doubts about the value of the Universal Declaration, it has clearly introduced the concept of human rights into the language of political debate. When this innovation was supplemented by the new type of liberal radicalism that emerged in the 1960s, the result was a search by political theorists for a formula that would establish individual rights, rather than Utilitarianism or philosophical Idealism, as the foundation of a liberal theory of the state.

Ronald Dworkin is the best known, and perhaps the most determined, of the theorists who have engaged in this enterprise. In his book on *Taking Rights Seriously* he declares that 'the language of rights now dominates political debate in the United States' (Dworkin 1978: 184), and he sets out to build a new theory of politics based on the primacy of moral rights. His theory identifies only two moral rights as inalienable – as being, in fact, natural rights – namely the right of citizens to be treated equally and their right to have their human dignity respected. This claim is not based on any general philosophy of politics and it is clearly not rooted in historical experience and tradition. It has to be regarded, therefore, as a speculative claim based upon reason.

It is a somewhat surprising claim or assertion in that its author places little or no value on the traditional American belief that citizens have inalienable rights to life, liberty, property and the pursuit of happiness. Dworkin emphasizes more than once that there can be no general right to liberty. 'The idea of a right to liberty', he says, 'is a mis-conceived concept that does a dis-service to political thought' (Dworkin 1978: 271). Some specific liberties should certainly be regarded as important, but only because they are based on the right to equality. 'Individual rights to distinct liberties must be recognized only when the fundamental right to treatment as an equal can be shown to require these rights' (Dworkin 1978: 273–4). He goes on to say that citizens 'have distinct rights to certain liberties like the liberty of free expression and of free choice in personal and sexual relations', but do not have a right to the free use of property (Dworkin 1978: 277–8).

Substituting equality for liberty as a fundamental right serves Dworkin's purpose, as an acknowledged subscriber to liberal-left views, of enabling him to defend the rights of homosexuals without defending the rights of property owners. But, as H. L. A. Hart has pointed out, the argument about equal treatment in regard to sexual behaviour would not be a sound basis for objecting to a law banning all forms of sexual intercourse, homosexual and heterosexual. Equally, it would (if generally accepted) secure minority religions against discrimination, but would not afford a basis for objecting to a law that banned all forms of public religious observance (see Hart 1979: 97). That equal treatment should be one right among several would be agreed by most democrats, but making it the only fundamental right apart from the preservation of dignity (which is too vague to count for much) places more weight on it than it can bear.

Another aspect of Dworkin's theory is its extreme individualism. When he writes about the right to express political dissent, he argues that it is wrong for the law to ban speakers at demonstrations from incitement to violence, on the ground that arguments based on considerations of general utility or public interest should not be used to restrict the individual rights of demonstrators and speakers. In answer to the point that violence would violate the individual rights of neighbouring property owners, to say nothing of the rights of citizens wishing to use the public highway, he maintains that speculative violations of rights like these should not be accorded priority over the certain rights of demonstrators (see Dworkin 1978: 192–5). In taking this stand, he is by implication condemning the state of the law in all democratic states, because incitement to violence (under whatever name) is a legal offence in all polities. It is hard to see how this stand can be derived from the basic rights of equal treatment and respect for human dignity.

In his book, Dworkin devotes a chapter to the question of affirmative action and positive discrimination, focusing on the question, hotly disputed in recent years in the United States, of whether a university is violating the rights of white applicants for places in a law school or medical school if it rejects them while accepting applications from black students with inferior qualifications. Dworkin's position is that there is no violation of rights in such a situation. Now, it is quite possible to make a case for this kind of affirmative action on the ground that it is in the public interest to have more black lawyers and doctors, or even, perhaps, on the Utilitarian ground that the expected gain to the black student outweighs the expected loss to the white applicant. However, according to Dworkin's principles both these kinds of argument must be rejected if they run counter to the individual right of equal treatment, and it is absolutely clear that in a situation of this kind the white applicant with good qualifications who is rejected is receiving less than equal treatment. Dworkin's treatment of this issue (see Dworkin 1978: 223–39) therefore contradicts his main argument.

In view of these weaknesses and inconsistencies, it has to be said that Dworkin has failed to establish a theory of liberalism based on the enumeration of fundamental rights. I would go further than this and argue that it seems unlikely that a coherent theory can be formulated on such a basis. In their different ways, Utilitarianism and philosophical Idealism are both coherent and viable theories of politics; each of them includes a view of human nature, a view of society and a view of the functions of the state. No theory that gives priority to rights has yet been advanced that can match these two theories in terms of completion and coherence; and it is not easy to envisage this happening. When Peter Jones examined the various attempts that have been made, his conclusion was that:

> there are still fundamental disagreements amongst philosophers over the conceptual question of what it is to have a right. If there has been progress

in recent years it has been the progress of an unfolding diversity rather than progress towards a single truth.

(Jones 1989: 96)

There is clearly no coherent philosophy of rights that can take the place of existing theories as the theoretical foundation of liberalism, and it seems to be putting the cart before the horse to imagine that proposing a list of preferred rights could form the foundation of a philosophy. It is difficult to see how the enumeration of such a list, based simply on the reason or intuition of the theorist, could escape a repetition of Bentham's criticism that such lists are 'so much flat assertion'.

MINORITY RIGHTS

The 1970s and 1980s saw not only an enhanced concern about individual rights but also an enhanced concern about the rights of groups and communities within national societies. This poses more difficult theoretical problems than the issue of individual rights does, because membership of groups is only sometimes fixed and certain. As was pointed out in Chapter 3, we all have various group identities, and which of them is most salient to us at any one time depends partly on the social and political circumstances of that time and partly on a subjective process of self-identification. As John Dunn has pointed out, this process is commonly influenced by theories about what ought to be done, so that it is difficult, if not impossible, to assess the issue in terms of independent and dependent variables:

> What constitutes a right-claiming human grouping in the course of social and political conflict is not an externally specifiable social location. Rather, it is precisely the espousal of a moral and political theory about its own identity and social extension.

(Dunn 1990: 53)

The problem can be made more manageable by distinguishing legally identifiable categories of people, such as women, mothers, widows or senior citizens, from groups which do not have precise legal boundaries, like cultural minorities. The rights that are commonly granted to legally identifiable categories are essentially individual rights. Members of such categories get positive rights to pensions, child allowances and so forth in most democratic states. They are also entitled to speculative political rights such as equal pay for equal work and non-discriminatory treatment by employers and institutions, these rights being included in the Universal Declaration of Human Rights and granted in principle by most modern democracies, though notoriously difficult to protect and enforce. There are no conceptual problems about rights of this kind, though there may be practical problems, as when women, for example, are refused mortgages that would probably have been granted to men in similar situations.

In passing, it is as well to acknowledge that for radical feminists the guarantee of these individual rights for women, even if they were extended by affirmative action, would not be enough to remedy the disadvantages from which women living in patriarchal societies (i.e. all contemporary societies) are said to suffer. Radical feminists want to change the whole structure of patriarchal society. In its rather extreme way, this is an understandable objective, but radical feminists do not constitute a legally identifiable category and in any case it could not reasonably be claimed that they have a right to change the structure of society. They have a right to work for this aim, as others have a right to work against it, but they do not have an inherent right to achieve the aim. Radical feminism is a social movement of our time and its adherents constitute pressure groups in several countries, but they do not have rights beyond those enjoyed by other women.

The question of what rights are, or should be, enjoyed by cultural minorities is more difficult to answer and therefore more interesting. I cannot follow Vernon Van Dyke in his view that such minorities can be said to have human rights (see Van Dyke 1985). The whole point about human rights is that they inhere in all human beings, irrespective of ethnicity or culture. Individual members of cultural minorities can certainly be said to have human rights, but this has nothing to do with the fact that they are members of a minority group. Nor is it helpful to say that minorities have collective moral rights, because these are based on a common code of morality and one of the problems in multi-cultural societies is that the minorities may not share the same moral code as the majority. It follows that the rights claimed for cultural minorities, in so far as they are not positive rights, must be political rights.

The political rights frequently claimed for minorities amount to special help for members of the minority or special protection for their language and their culture. The former claim sometimes raises problems if it seems to conflict with the principle of equal treatment for all citizens. The latter claim raises problems because languages and cultures are not right-bearing entities. It may be culturally desirable for a minority language to be kept alive, but it is not clear why taxpayers who have no knowledge of or interest in the language should be expected to pay for it. This question becomes particularly difficult to answer if it is the case, as it often is, that most members of the minority are more concerned that their children should acquire a thorough knowledge of the majority language than that they should speak the minority language. To deal with puzzles like this, it is helpful to divide the rights claimed by members of cultural minorities into four distinct categories, which can be labelled the right to be in, the right to be out, the right to stay out and the right to get out.

The right to be in is the right to enjoy full and equal opportunities in society. The absence of discrimination may not be sufficient to ensure this in the case of cultural minorities. Immigrants admitted for permanent residence can reasonably be regarded as having a right to receive education and training in the official language of the country. In Australia, an official report stated that 'to a great degree, occupational mobility in Australia depends on skill in the English language', while 'a poor knowledge of English approximately doubles the likelihood that a migrant will be unemployed' (Lo Bianco Report 1987: 56, 58). In England, the exceptionally high unemployment rate among women of Bangladeshi origin is partly explained by the fact that most of them have a very poor or even no command of English (see Brown 1984: 138). This creates a need for language instruction for immigrants of all ages, with some need for the initial instruction to be given in the language of the immigrants.

So far, this is not controversial. The controversial question about the right to equal opportunity is whether members of ethnic minorities should be entitled to affirmative action or positive discrimination if the relevant statistics reveal them to suffer from practical disadvantages in the economic or educational sphere despite legal bans on negative discrimination. Although the terms are sometimes used interchangeably, it is helpful to reserve the term 'affirmative action' for voluntary behaviour by employers and other organizations and to use 'positive discrimination' for behaviour mandated by legal regulations. The theoretical problem is the same in both cases, however. It is that measures of this kind are directly costly to members of the majority who may be passed over in spite of having better qualifications for the post (or the university place) than some members of the minority who are appointed or accepted. In such cases there is a conflict between the desire to help the minority and the individual rights of all citizens to equal opportunity without discrimination on ethnic or cultural grounds. In practice this may not be perceived as a problem when the level of competition for the appointment and the personal advantages conferred by it are not great. The fact that blacks can get a job in the New York police with lower qualifications than whites has not caused significant difficulties, for instance. But when the issue is admission to medical school or law school, affirmative action may cause resentment, and it has led to court cases brought by white students in California, Texas and the state of Washington.

Because of this problem of equity, there can be no such thing as an absolute right to positive discrimination or affirmative action. These are policies of which the appropriateness depends to a large extent on local circumstances, including not only the nature of the appointments but also the nature and history of the minorities in question. Thus, descendants of black slaves in America might be thought to have a stronger claim to special assistance than recent immigrants, while the position of the lower castes in India is different again. There is also a question of timing. Affirmative action to help immigrant groups to become integrated should presumably be a temporary measure, becoming unnecessary after a time, but cancelling it might well cause more controversy than starting it.

The right to be out is the right of a minority to preserve its cultural identity and traditions within a larger society. The General Conference of UNESCO has asserted 'the right of all . . . peoples to preserve their culture' (Van Dyke 1982: 27). In most respects this can be done without any action by governments being required. Families can preserve their cultural traditions through their attitudes to love, sex and marriage, their child-rearing practices, their celebration of anniversaries and religious holidays, their eating, drinking and recreational habits, their choice of reading material, their funeral rites and so forth. Just occasionally, minority habits and customs conflict with the interests or norms of the majority and cause controversy. Recent examples include the question of whether Sikhs should be exempt from the law requiring motor cyclists to wear crash helmets (an issue in Britain and North America); whether Sikhs should be permitted to wear ceremonial but sharp daggers when being prosecuted in court or when in prison (an issue in Canada); and whether westerners should be permitted to kiss in public in countries influenced by Islamic fundamentalism. I believe that the only general principle that can reasonably be endorsed in such cases is that the majority has a social obligation to be tolerant. It should be noted, however, that an obligation to be tolerant does not necessarily confer a right on the minority. Rights always create obligations but the reverse does not hold. If I see a child drowning in the surf I have a moral obligation to rescue him or her if I can, but the child does not have a right to be rescued. I have to weigh my obligation to help against my swimming abilities and my obligation to stay alive for the sake of my family.

Occasionally, issues arise in which public authorities have to weigh their obligations to be tolerant of minority customs against their duty to protect the rights of individuals. In England there have been several cases of teenage girls of Pakistani origin applying to the High Court to become wards of court, so as to escape from their parents' pressures or orders to enter into arranged marriages with men whom the girls disliked or had not even met. Given a favourable report from a social worker, the English courts have acceded to these requests. In the United States there have been cases of hospitals asking the courts to authorize medical treatment to save the lives of children whose parents, being members of certain religious sects, refused to permit such treatment. Some judges have acceded to these requests.

The minority right to be out, as I have called it, most commonly causes difficulties when the issue involved is the maintenance of a minority language. It is clear that bilingualism is not a natural state of affairs and that if two languages are spoken in a given area the stronger of them will normally drive out the weaker (on this, see Laponce 1987). A weaker language cannot be expected to survive over a long period unless it receives government help in the form of language teaching in schools, perhaps supplemented by media communications in the weaker language.

The problem about establishing this kind of educational policy as a right is that it may involve what scholars have called an 'ethnic trap' (see Wiley 1967; Kringas 1984). This refers to the hypothesis that there is an inevitable trade-off between ethnic or cultural identity and social mobility. The more strongly minorities retain their ethnic identities and cultural values, it is said, the less likely they are to be economically successful. The evidence for this hypothesis is scattered but apparently significant. In his authoritative study of social mobility in Canada, John Porter showed that the French-Canadians, although the first to colonize Canada, consistently held an inferior economic position there, being poorer not only than British-Canadians but also than some ethnic minorities who arrived much later than the French but have overtaken them. Porter attributed this to their education, saying that 'the more *French* and *Catholic* education has been, the less has it been adequate for the French to improve their position in the modern economy' (Porter 1965: 98, italics in the original). The problem about the religious element was not the faith itself, of course, but that, at least until the 1960s, French Catholic teachers were so keen to ensure the survival of their culture in North America that their emphasis on theology, Latin and the inculcation of spiritual and cultural values cut down the time available for instruction in subjects of greater utility in the North American economy.

Similarly, comparable tests taken by Irish and British teenagers in the 1950s shows that the Irish, on average, had poorer educational attainments, apparently because they had spent so much of their time at school learning the Irish form of Gaelic. In response to this and other evidence that Gaelic teaching was somewhat dysfunctional, the time devoted to it was reduced. In Wales, one of the reasons for the hostility of most voters to the Welsh Nationalist Party is that they do not want to have their children made to learn Welsh, which many voters regard as a waste of time in an English-speaking society. During the period of the Khrushchev reforms in the Soviet Union, there was opposition to the proposal that Russian should be replaced by local languages as the medium of instruction in some universities, on the ground that students were more likely to have successful careers if they were trained in the dominant language of the country. In the 1980s there was opposition in parts of India to the proposal that English should be replaced by Hindi as the medium of instruction in universities, for the same reason.

It is clear from these examples that the question of language training is inherently apt to cause controversy. There may well be a clash between cultural arguments and economic arguments when choices have to be made, perhaps resulting in a clash between sentimental parents and ambitious parents. In these circumstances the language of rights seems inappropriate, because too categorical in its implications.

The right to stay out is the right to maintain the culture and lifestyles of aboriginal peoples who have been numerically overwhelmed by settlers from different cultures. It deserves a separate heading because the original inhabitants of an area may well be thought to have stronger claims to the preservation of what has become a minority culture than immigrants who freely chose to move to another country have to maintain the culture of the society they left in this new environment. It is difficult not to feel sympathy with the native Indians of North America or the Aborigines of Australia, whose lifestyles have been transformed by an alien invasion over which they have had no control. It would seem that they have quite a strong claim, perhaps amounting to a right, to maintain what remains of their traditional culture and way of life.

There are, however, two serious problems about the assertion of this kind of right for aboriginal peoples. One is the great variety of ambitions that they harbour, which is not surprising in view of the fact that their integration into white society ranges from almost nil to almost complete. A few years ago spokespersons for the Indian tribes of British Columbia had the opportunity to make a case for the needs of their peoples. Their answers varied enormously, from some who wanted better secondary schools so that their children could compete more effectively for jobs in the Canadian economy, to others who wanted a greater degree of municipal self-government or greater control over the issue of fishing licences, to others again who wanted independence from Canada and representation at the United Nations. In this situation it is very difficult to frame any broad generalization about Indian rights. In the 1980s the Canadian federal government met what seemed to be a dominant mood among Indian leaders by saying that it hoped to move towards a greater measure of Indian self-government, but social, economic and geographical circumstances among the Indian peoples vary so much that it is difficult to make this move except on the basis of piecemeal local agreements. In any case it is not clear that self-management (as it is better called) will always lead to the preservation of traditional cultures; some Indian bands use their new powers to give Indian entrepreneurs exemption from government regulations in this area or that, so that they can compete more successfully in the western economy.

A second problem is the poverty of the resources available to aboriginal peoples wishing to preserve a traditional lifestyle. They can no longer hunt buffalo across the plains of North America, nor can they eke out a living from Australian land that has long been enclosed for cattle and sheep stations. They are bound to be economically dependent on government aid, whether this is given on an individual basis in the form of welfare payments or on a collective basis in the form of grants to aboriginal bands. It may be argued that they deserve specially generous treatment in compensation for the destruction of the traditional bases of their lifestyles, but I believe that the extent of this generosity is better assessed in terms of current needs than in terms of an attempt to measure such an immeasurable loss or to balance it against gains in health and housing.

In view of these two problems, it seems far from clear that the language of rights is the most appropriate language for the conduct of negotiations over future relationships between aboriginal peoples and governments. Aboriginal peoples have needs, interests and claims; they may be given positive rights to wield certain powers or enjoy certain benefits; but so much depends on local circumstances that generalizations about abstract rights are probably best avoided.

The right to get out is a shorthand label for the right of ethnic or cultural minorities concentrated in viable territorial areas to secede from their existing state and become completely self-governing. In international law and practice no such right exists, for the units of the international system are states and a unilateral declaration of independence from an existing state will not normally be recognized by other states. Rhodesia's unilateral declaration in 1965 got no recognition whatever and the country became subject to UN sanctions, on the request of the United Kingdom, until it came back under direct British rule in 1979 and was then granted independence on British terms. Lithuania's declaration in 1990 got much more international sympathy, but no official recognition until the authorities in Moscow accepted it. If we talk of the right to secede we are therefore talking in rather abstract terms about the factors that might lead theorists of a liberal disposition to feel that secession would be justifiable.

The view that I have advanced elsewhere is that, given majority support in the territory for secession, there are four conditions that should be regarded as justifying it (see Birch 1984; 1989: Chapter 6). In very brief outline, the four conditions are as follows:

1 That the region had been included in the state by force and there had been a continuing refusal by its people to give full consent to the union.
2 That the national government had failed, in a serious way, to protect the basic rights and security of the citizens of the region.
3 That the political system of the state had failed to safeguard the legitimate political and economic interests of the region, resulting in a serious form of relative deprivation for the region.
4 That the national government had ignored or rejected an explicit or implicit bargain between regions that had been entered into as a way of preserving the essential interests of a region that might find itself outvoted by a national majority.

The first of these points would cover the cases of Ireland before 1921 and Lithuania, Latvia and Estonia in 1990. The second would cover the Ibo people of eastern Nigeria, who attempted to secede under the name of Biafra in 1966, and the Kurds of Iraq. The third would cover the Bengalis of East Pakistan, who managed – after an armed struggle – to form the independent state of Bangladesh in 1971. The fourth would appear (though this is much more controversial) to cover the southern states of the United States in 1860.

Allan Buchanan has addressed this topic in much greater detail than was possible in my rather brief treatment, and his stated aim has been to provide a 'moral framework' for the assessment of cases rather than to provide a list of conditions. In the course of discussing this framework he does, however, suggest a list which includes my first three conditions, though with a variation on my third. He points out that relative deprivation need not be a part of the condition, as relatively wealthy regions such as the Basque country might suffer from 'discriminatory redistribution' of their resources. Buchanan omits my fourth condition, but he adds a fourth condition of his own in the form of a case for 'cultural preservation', which could be said to justify a claim for secession if it could be shown that membership of the cultural community is an important ingredient in the good life of its members, that the culture is imperilled, that it is a reasonably liberal culture, and that it cannot be preserved by measures that are less disruptive than secession (see Buchanan 1991: 54–61). This is an important argument, subtly presented.

The attraction of nationalism as an ideology is so great that territorially concentrated ethnic groups are now always likely to consider secession as a possible strategy, and in a democratic state a secessionist movement in one of its regions is likely at least to produce compromises or bribes. When Western Australia mounted such a movement in 1933, the result was a new plan for federal grants to the states which benefited western Australia. Spain has decentralized its system of government to please the people of Catalonia and at least some of the Basques. Canada has made constitutional concessions to Quebec and given the province much favourable treatment in regard to government contracts and grants.

It may perhaps be concluded that the question of secession is surrounded by so many contingencies and complications that the question of abstract right has only a minor role to play.

A FINAL WORD ON MINORITY RIGHTS

In view of the fact that each of the four types of right claimed for cultural minorities involves the problems that have been mentioned, it is clearly difficult to make sweeping statements about the inherent rights of cultural or ethnic minorities in the way that liberals can make sweeping statements about the inherent rights of individuals. Some minorities both should and do enjoy group rights to protect aspects of their culture that are important to them. Certain linguistic minorities in Canada, Switzerland, Belgium and elsewhere enjoy the right to communicate with government agencies in the language of their choice and to have their language preserved by being taught in schools. Native Indians living on reservations in the United States and Canada have collective property rights and in some cases have other collective rights deemed necessary to protect their cultures, such as participation in the administration of justice. Such rights are important and should be defended by liberals. At the same time, it is fair to observe that these and similar rights depend upon such a variety of local and historical circumstances that it is difficult to generalize from them. The language of rights has to be used with great care when it is applied to groups rather than to individuals, and there are occasions when political arguments about minorities would be more easily resolved if the participants would forgo the language of rights and talk instead about specific needs and interests.

Part III

Political power and policy making

Chapter 12

Political power

PROBLEMS OF DEFINITION

The *OED* defines power as 'the ability to do or act' and 'control, influence, ascendancy', while *Webster's Dictionary* defines it as the 'possession of control, authority, or influence over others'. Power can be possessed and exercised in all kinds of social contexts, from an office or factory to national or international society. Political power is power within a political system and in this book we are concerned not with the international system or the tribes of the Amazon rainforest but with the political system of the modern state.

Unfortunately, it is not feasible to begin with an operational definition of political power, even when the context is limited to the modern state, because different scholars operate with different definitions and there is no agreement between them. This raises the question of whether political power is an inevitably contestable concept in the modern world, and on this question too, more than one view is possible. At first sight, it would seem that it ought not to be contestable, because, except perhaps to anarchists, power appears to be a value-neutral concept. Power can be exercised in good or bad ways but it is not a capacity that all groups wish to claim they possess, varying the definition to make their claims more plausible. It is not, that is, an obviously contestable concept like freedom or democracy. However, in practice, the meaning of the concept is contested, and the literature is full of controversies about it. It therefore seems wise to leave open the question of whether this contestability is unavoidable, and to proceed instead to examine the difficulties of handling the concept.

One difficulty arises from the complexity of the political system in the modern state. Political power is wielded through numerous channels, by a great variety of political actors, in a large number of direct or indirect ways. Some forms of power can be readily identified, as when the police carry out an arrest or a judge pronounces sentence. However, the most interesting form of political power, which is the main concern of this chapter, is the power to influence decisions taken by government agencies, and this is often more difficult to identify.

Another problem is that of identifying political actors. Voters are political actors when they go to the polls, but are non-voters to be regarded as actors? Since their abstention may determine the result of the election, presumably they are. In between elections, political leaders will frequently be influenced by their expectations about the likely effects of proposed policy decisions on voting behaviour at the next election. Does that mean that electors are exerting influence, and therefore a degree of power, all the time? Are we to say that electors who are completely passive and uninterested in politics are nevertheless political actors because their possession of the right to vote may influence decision makers? Should we say that school children are political actors because, while lacking the right to vote, they have the ability to disrupt classes or boycott the schools if they object to certain decisions on educational policy? Should we say that financial institutions exercise political power because governments moderate their economic policies for fear of a flight of capital out of the country, even if the institutions in question make no political move? Would this be the case even if the fear of a flight of capital were quite unfounded? If we answer all these questions in the affirmative, and some do, this means that political power can be a very tricky thing to identify, let alone measure.

A further problem about the concept of political power is that of assigning causality in a chain of political events and responsibility for political outcomes. Let us suppose that a convict with a record of violent crimes is released on parole, buys a gun, and kills his former wife. There is more than one way of assigning responsibility for this death, beyond the simple answer that the murderer is responsible. Some would say that the members of the parole board are responsible, for they took the decision to release the convict. Others would say that the psychiatrist who advised the board is responsible, for the precedents and conventions that govern the behaviour of parole boards make it very difficult for a board to reject a psychiatrist's recommendation. Others again would criticize the whole system of parole and parole boards, saying that a sentence of ten years' imprisonment should mean just that. Yet another group would argue that the real trouble is the absence of effective controls on the sale of guns. None of these ways of assigning responsibility for the death can be dismissed as wrong. They differ because each of them reflects the perspective of the person or group making the judgement.

This simple example illustrates the problem of multi-causality, which affects the analysis of most political decisions in the government of modern states. It is only in relatively rare circumstances that one can say: 'X exercised power; he or she had a free choice and decided that Y should be done'. In the real world of politics X rarely has a free choice, but is constrained by many pressures and considerations. Nor can a decision normally be taken without consulting others or working through committees. There is always a procedure to be followed, and the final decision depends on the nature of the procedure, the behaviour of all the political actors who can exercise direct or indirect influence through it, the values prevalent in the society, and the external constraints that in practice limit the freedom of choice. This means that assessing the distribution of political power is an inherently difficult operation, liable to be affected by the preconceptions, perspectives and values of the analyst. However, the operation can be made somewhat easier if it is preceded by a process of conceptual clarification.

FOUR TYPES OF POLITICAL POWER

If we start with the most obvious manifestations of political power and move to the least obvious, it is possible to outline a four-fold typology.

First, there is political coercion, defined as the control of citizens by agents of the government using force or the immediate threat of force, leaving the citizens with no real choice about their behaviour. Examples include the power of a riot squad breaking up a demonstration, of the police carrying out an arrest, of prison guards controlling convicts, of a municipality using bulldozers on a gypsy encampment, of an army enforcing a curfew. This type of power rarely raises conceptual problems. Its exercise often raises legal or moral problems, but there is no real difficulty about defining coercion or recognizing it when it is used.

Second, there is political authority, defined as the exercise by certain designated persons and institutions of the right, generally regarded as legitimate, to make and implement decisions that are binding within a prescribed area of jurisdiction. Examples include the power of legislative assemblies to pass laws, of judges to interpret the laws, of ministers to take executive decisions, of civil servants to implement these decisions, of municipalities to make zoning regulations, of regulatory agencies to control pollution or license new medications, of the police to direct traffic or investigate breaches of the law. This type of political power involves a number of interesting conceptual and practical problems, which have been discussed in Chapter 6, and will not be raised again in the present chapter.

Third, there is political influence, defined as the exercise of indirect or direct influence over the personnel or decisions of governmental institutions and agencies. This sounds clear and simple, but it has to be added that there is a wide spectrum of political influence ranging from the most diffuse influence over political opinions to the most specific influence over appointments to political office or the decisions of political agencies. It is not easy to draw a hard and fast line between diffuse and specific forms of influence as if they were watertight categories, but an example may illustrate the difference.

If I persuade a group of friends or acquaintances that the government ought to spend more money on preventive medicine I am exercising a degree of political influence as an opinion leader, but the probable impact of this influence on future governmental actions is so small that it can hardly be counted as an example of political power. On the other hand, it would certainly be an example of power if I were to persuade the members of a decision-making committee on health service expenditure that their priorities should be changed in the way I preferred. In between these extremes of diffuse and specific influence, there is an example of a person who might use argumentative skills to persuade delegates at a party conference that a certain policy should be added to the party's list of long-term objectives. To cut through this maze, it might be sensible to stipulate that persuading other people about the merits of a proposed policy should be regarded as a form of political power if, but only if, the people persuaded have the ability and desire to take decisions binding on a wider category of people who have no say in the matter.

The definition and identification of political influence raises a number of conceptual and empirical problems that will be discussed below. Much of the controversy about political power in the recent literature of political science has in fact been about whether political influence has one, two, or three dimensions, and how these should be defined, recognized and measured.

The fourth and least tangible type of political power is political manipulation, defined as the activity of shaping the political opinions, values and behaviour of others without the latter realizing that this is happening. Examples include teachers teaching history or civics in a biased way, journalists disseminating partial or slanted information about a political event or issue, opinion leaders acting and speaking as if a certain set of preferred values are the only ones open to reasonable people, the mass media presenting a political or social situation as inevitable when it is actually open to change.

This type of power is inherently controversial, since it can rarely be identified, let alone measured, in a way that will be accepted by other scholars as objective. The writing or teaching of history provides an obvious example. In history the truth is everything that happened, so that every book, article or lecture on a historical topic contains a small sample of the truth chosen to form a coherent pattern. Some presentations are more partial and biased than others, but since every account is selective there is no clear way of establishing what would be truly objective. A similar comment could be made about journalistic summaries of current (meaning very recent) events, or about presentations of belief systems and social values. In these circumstances the identification of political manipulation is an inevitably tricky business that is difficult to separate from the political values of the identifier.

If we consider the work that has been done by political scientists on the distribution and exercise of political power, it is immediately apparent that scholars have nearly always concentrated on one or the other of these types of power, choosing one that fits their preferred research methods, without much effort to put their studies into perspective by discussing the relationship of their findings to work on the other types of power. Up until the 1950s, political scientists writing about the government of the modern state were concerned with political authority rather than with political coercion, political influence, or political manipulation. They wrote about constitutions and institutions; about the sovereignty of Parliament, the rule of law, the separation of powers, the structure of the administration, and the authority granted to the president, prime minister, legislative assemblies, government departments and courts. The only important exception to this generalization was research done in the United States, but not elsewhere, into the influence exerted on the legislative process by certain national pressure groups chosen for case studies.

In the 1950s two different kinds of study were made as a result of the development of new research techniques, coupled with a new emphasis on the desirability of turning the study of politics into a truly scientific activity. The object was to supplement (and in the ambitions of some to replace) the delineation of legal powers and institutional structures by the production of causal generalizations about political behaviour. One consequence was that scholars turned their attention to the attempt to assess the distribution of political influence within systems of government.

THE ASSESSMENT OF POLITICAL INFLUENCE

The first wave of this new type of research focused on opinion formation and electoral behaviour among the general body of citizens. Sample surveys of electors yielded generalizations about the relationship between demographic variables like age, sex and class, political attitudes, and political participation. They also yielded, though not so clearly, some suggestive evidence about the impact of election campaigns, the mass media and opinion leaders on the attitudes and behaviour of the ordinary citizen, which constituted political influence of a rather diffuse kind.

A second wave of behavioural research focused on the distribution of political influence on municipal government within particular communities selected for study. Several studies by sociologists reached the conclusion that political influence, which they called by the generic term political power, was concentrated in the hands of a social and economic elite. The most influential of these was a book by Floyd Hunter entitled *Community Power Structure*, which analysed the distribution of power in Atlanta, Georgia. This book can easily be criticized. In it, Hunter seemed to assume from the beginning what he claimed to have proved, namely that power in Atlanta was concentrated in the hands of a business elite. In his opening pages he stated it as a 'self-evident proposition' that 'power is a relatively constant factor in social relationships with policies as variables' (Hunter 1953: 6), thus excluding the possibility that power might vary from one issue-area to another. His method of inquiry was to ask a panel of people whom he selected to say whom they thought had most power in the city, permitting them to choose forty, but only forty, persons. The fact that most of the forty chosen were members of the business elite was taken to be evidence that this elite dominated the local political system, without it being thought necessary to investigate particular areas of policy or particular decisions.

The influence of electors was discounted on the ground that relatively few of them were politically active, while the inactivity of the majority was taken as evidence that the power structure prevented them from participating. No consideration was given to the possibility that they might not have participated because they were reasonably content with the system, or because they preferred to spend their time working in the garden or playing baseball. It was simply assumed that they would have liked to participate but were somehow prevented from doing so. In short, the analysis presented was unconvincing. It may conceivably have been true that Atlanta was dominated by a business elite – the city certainly had one very large and wealthy industrial concern in the shape of the Coca-Cola Company – but Hunter's book fell a long way short of demonstrating this to be the case. It is instructive to note that, despite its obvious shortcomings, Hunter's book received favourable reviews in the *American Political Science Review* (vol. 48, 1954, pp. 235–7), the *Journal of Politics* (vol. 16, 1954, pp. 146–50), and the *American Journal of Sociology* (vol. 60, 1955, pp. 522–3). It was in this climate of opinion that Robert Dahl and his colleagues at Yale launched their elaborate inquiry into the structure of power in New Haven, Connecticut, which was subsequently to play a central role in academic controversies about the forms or dimensions of political influence.

Dahl defined political power as a relationship in which A (being an individual or group) induces B to behave in a way that B would not have chosen without A's pressure. This was a fairly conventional definition, very similar to those that had previously been adopted in books by Harold Lasswell and Abraham Kaplan (see Lasswell and Kaplan 1950: 75) and Herbert Simon (see Simon 1957: 65–6). As Terence Ball has pointed out, in its origins this definition was three centuries old, having been first advanced by Hobbes and copied by Locke (see Ball 1988: 83–7). The assumption is that power, properly defined, is exercised only in situations where there is an overt disagreement or conflict between parties about what should be done and one side comes out on top. Dahl acknowledged that in the modern state, at either the national or local level, only a small minority of citizens actually participate in power struggles about the policies to be followed. His approach in the New Haven study was to choose three key issue areas and to discover who actually took part in the struggles in these areas.

The research carried out by Dahl and his team revealed that the active minority differed from one issue area to another and that the citizens classified as 'economic and social notables' did not play a leading role, or anything approaching a leading role, in any of the three areas. It was therefore concluded that in New Haven there was no 'power elite' (to use the term popularized by C. Wright Mills) but a distribution of political influence that Dahl described as pluralist. There were undoubtedly inequalities between citizens in the degree of power they exercised in the system, but these inequalities were dispersed rather than cumulative. The 1,066 positions identified as influential in the three issue areas were occupied by 1,029 persons, so that fewer than 40 persons had exercised influence in more than one area. The government of New Haven was said to be an example of pluralist democracy (see Dahl 1961: Chapters 6, 7, 19–24).

There was much more to Dahl's study than this bare sketch suggests and some of its conclusions and implications will be examined in Chapter 13. In this chapter what is important is the operational definition of power that was adopted, which has been criticized and has led to a prolonged debate among scholars. In a seminal article, Bachrach and Baratz (1962) disputed Dahl's assumption that political power is exercised only when an overt disagreement over an issue is argued about and subsequently resolved by the victory of one side or the other. They pointed out that power may also be exercised by preventing an issue from being brought up for decision:

> Of course power is exercised when A participates in the making of decisions that affect B. But power is also exercised when A devotes his energies to creating or reinforcing social and political values and institutional practices that limit the scope of the political process to public consideration of only those issues which are comparatively innocuous to A.
> (Bachrach and Baratz 1962: 149)

They described this second face of power as 'non-decision-making' and described the process by which issues are kept off the agenda as 'the mobilization of bias', using a term that had first been coined by Schattschneider (see Schattschneider 1960: 71; Bachrach and Baratz 1962: 150).

There can be no doubt that these writers drew attention to a significant aspect, or more precisely two significant aspects, of the process by which communities are governed. A minority wishing to get an issue considered by decision-making bodies may indeed find itself frustrated in this aim, either by the strength of prevailing opinion in favour of the status quo or by procedural rules and conventions. However, there can be practical problems about identifying the political actors in such situations. A prevailing consensus of political values may make things difficult for reformers, but it is rarely easy to say who created the consensus. A consensus is apt to be the product of many factors, operating over a period. The problem of multi-causality always arises. Institutional practices may also hinder reformers, but these practices may have been developed over the years for the convenient conduct of business, without any reference to the issue that reformers now wish to get on the agenda and possibly without any intention of hindering reformers in general. In an important article, Nelson Polsby has argued forcibly that it is difficult to make empirical investigations of the mobilization of bias (Polsby 1979).

Notwithstanding these difficulties, it is certainly true that political scientists studying decision making should take note of the prevailing social and political values in that community or society relevant to the issue and of the institutional channels through which would-be reformers have to work. If individuals can be identified as overtly reinforcing the values and procedures that favour the status quo, as is suggested by the passage quoted from Bachrach and Baratz's (1962) article, then they are exercising political influence that is rather different from the influence exerted by the people who actually participate in controversies over particular issues of policy. It is an open question whether this more general kind of influence on the political system is more significant than the specific influence exerted by those who argue about education, housing or defence policies. It is inherently difficult to compare different kinds of influence and it is best to leave this question unanswered and simply acknowledge that Bachrach and Baratz made a valuable contribution by indicating that political power takes more than one form, or has more than one dimension.

A THIRD POSSIBLE DIMENSION

Other scholars have suggested that there is also a third dimension of political influence, whose exercise prevents potential issues from even emerging as actual issues. The lead in this was taken by Steven Lukes (1974), arguing from a Marxist or neo-Marxist perspective. Lukes observed that in many capitalist societies workers accept the system even though their real interests should lead them to favour radical change. They do this because they have been socialized into acceptance by dominant groups who control the processes of socialization, such as the educational system and the mass media. The ability to influence the way people think, to induce them to accept false values, and/or to make them feel powerless should be regarded as a highly important form of political power (see Lukes 1974). While Lukes agrees that both the first and second dimensions of political influence are significant, he believes that this third dimension, by means of which the whole economic and social system is protected, may be the most significant of the three.

The great problem about this view, of course, is that it assumes people have 'real interests' that can be identified by the observer even though the people themselves are unaware of them or would reject them. How can an observer claim to know better than the people where their real interests lie? To Marxists this is not a serious problem, because Marxists believe that their understanding of the economic and social system and the way it is developing enables them to recognize that in capitalist societies the workers are inevitably exploited, and would serve their interests best by working to replace the capitalist system by a socialist system. Workers who do not realize this are suffering from 'false consciousness' and need to be re-educated. If they accept the ideas of Antonio Gramsci, Marxists will accept that western capitalist societies in the twentieth century suffer from a hegemony of bourgeois values, so that the re-education of the masses can only be a long and difficult process. But the fact that bourgeois values are generally dominant might be said only to emphasize the power of those groups who have promoted these values and inculcated them into the minds of their contemporaries.

Empiricists such as Dahl and Polsby reject this whole line of argument as impossible to verify by empirical methods and therefore worthless. Whether the masses suffer from false consciousness can only be a matter of faith or ideology, not a proposition that social scientists can establish or refute. That the proposition cannot be proved empirically is accepted by Lukes, who says, very honestly, that only scholars with a Marxist perspective can be expected to agree with his contention about the significance of what he calls 'the third dimension of power'.

However, if his contention cannot be proved, it can be illustrated, and Lukes encouraged one of his research students to make a study of a community in the Appalachian hills where the workers acquiesced in a situation of obvious exploitation and poverty. The resulting book provided an interesting case study of a coal-mining community dominated by a single foreign (actually British) company, with workers enduring low wages, poor housing and a miserable environment (Gaventa 1980). The workers did not protest or struggle to improve their conditions, as workers in other mining communities had done, and their union was remarkably passive. It was concluded by the author that the workers had been socialized into feelings of powerlessness, which led them to acquiesce in their poverty. However, it was not possible to produce evidence of the socialization process or to show that the company had controlled it, so in the end the study, though suggestive, was inconclusive in its attempt to reveal an example of what Lukes called the third dimension of political power and I prefer to call political manipulation.

At this point I should like to introduce a helpful suggestion bearing on the second and third dimensions of political influence made by Bob Jessop. He says that analysts should distinguish between the structural elements in a situation and what he calls the 'conjunctural' elements and I prefer to call the modifiable elements. The structural elements are 'those elements in a social function that cannot be altered by a given agent (or set of agents) during a given time period' (Jessop 1982: 253), while the modifiable elements are those that can be altered. The structural elements constitute a restraint on potential reformers. In some situations 'the same element can function as a "structural restraint" for one agent (or set of agents) at the same time as it appears as a modifiable element to other agents' (Jessop 1982: 253).

In the light of this, I would argue that it is helpful to distinguish four situations, rather than three, in which the exercise of power, in the form

of political influence, may possibly be identified. If we assume the existence of a potential political actor called Smith, the four situations can be
summarized as follows:

1 Smith takes the opportunity to intervene in a debate or vote so as to
   influence the policy adopted by a group, party or authority regarding
   a given issue. This is an example of the first dimension of political
   influence, the dimension studied by Dahl.
2 Smith would like to influence policy regarding a given issue, but cannot
   do so because she/he cannot get the issue on the agenda, either because
   (a) another actor called Jones is able to keep the issue off the agenda or
   (b) the procedural rules and conventions operate as a structural constraint
   preventing Smith from raising the issue. In case (a) this would be an
   example of the second dimension of influence being exercised by Jones.
   Case (b) might be regarded as an example of the second dimension of
   influence exercised by those who, in an earlier time period, framed the
   rules or helped to form the conventions. If there are people or groups in
   society who have the capacity to modify the rules or conventions, then it
   could be said that the rules and conventions operate as a structural constraint on Smith but afford an opportunity for the exercise of power by
   these other people or groups.
3 Smith would like to change the system, whether this be the system of
   industrial relations, the system of government, or (the favourite example)
   the capitalist system. However, she/he does not think it is feasible to do
   this, does not think it is worthwhile to try, decides instead to work for
   small improvements within the system, and after a time comes to accept
   the system and take it for granted. The complexity and entrenched nature
   of the system would in this case be a structural constraint for Smith.
   If his/her perception of the near-impossibility of changing the system
   had been developed by a conscious campaign of socialization by teachers,
   journalists and groups who had an interest in maintaining the system,
   then the behaviour of the latter could probably be regarded as an example
   of the exercise of the third dimension of influence.
4 Smith is quite content with the system, even though, in the opinion of a
   radical critic called Robertson, the system is oppressive and has provided
   Smith with a poorer lifestyle than he deserves, and could probably secure
   under a different system. Steven Lukes's position is that Smith's complacency can be regarded as the result of the exercise of the third dimension
   of influence by all those groups in society who manipulate the minds of
   citizens like Smith so as to make the latter content with a system that is
   oppressive and unfair, the contentment being a form of 'false consciousness'
   in the heart of Smith and others. However, most social scientists, including
   me, reject this position on the ground that the characterization of the
   system as oppressive is a value judgement by Robertson, who has no

right to say that Smith is mistaken in having reached a different value judgement. The concept of false consciousness seems, to almost everyone except Marxists, to involve a degree of certainty about highly controversial questions that is inappropriate.

FOUR ADDITIONAL CONCEPTS

At this stage in the argument it will be helpful to add a word about four additional concepts that are relevant to the study of political power. One of these is the 'raising of consciousness'; another is 'real interest' (as distinct from apparent interest); a third is 'cultural and ideological hegemony'; and the fourth is 'political socialization'.

The term 'raising of consciousness' did not come into popular usage until the 1970s, although the process has existed for centuries and was known earlier as (according to taste) enlightenment, education or agitation. It is very relevant to situations 3 and 4, as outlined in the previous paragraphs. In situation 3, radical reformers might be able to persuade Smith that, although he or she could not hope to change the system alone, Smith might be able to do so if he or she joined with others and took part in a long-term campaign of propaganda and political activity. If radicals were successful in changing Smith's mind, they would have raised Smith's consciousness about the possibilities of collective political action. In situation 4, radicals might be able to change Smith's evaluation of the system, so as to lead him or her to regard it as oppressive rather than benign. This also could be described as the raising of consciousness.

This concept has become relevant in recent years to the feminist movement, whose leaders have been able in most advanced industrial countries to raise the consciousness of women in situation 3, who were discontented with the opportunities open to women but did not previously think much could be done about the matter. In North America, and to a smaller extent in Europe and Australasia, feminists have also raised the consciousness of women in situation 4, who were previously content with the position of women in society but have now changed their minds about this.

The concept is also relevant to campaigns by homosexual and lesbian groups to increase public tolerance of differing forms of sexual preference and behaviour. When municipal authorities in Greater London established lesbian workshops in the 1980s, the object was not only to provide meeting places but also to raise the consciousness of lesbians about their position, the need to educate the general public about it, and the desirability of changes in law and custom that would make it possible for lesbian couples to adopt children.

The concept of 'real interests' is commonly used in connection with the assertion that the real interest of workers in a capitalist system is to bring about the transformation of that system to socialism or communism. However, it may be a mistake to identify the concept solely with this assertion, on which the gap between the two sides is unbridgeable, for there are other issue areas in which the idea of real interests, though hardly scientific, may spark off useful pieces of research.

As an example, British social scientists visiting the United States often come away with the belief that the real interest of Americans would be served by the creation of a national health insurance scheme, though only a minority of Americans have seemed to want this and it has only recently got on to the political agenda. This issue is one that can fruitfully be studied by scholars interested in political power. When the question of national health insurance was put on the agenda in the late 1940s under Truman's presidency, a lively debate was won by the American Medical Association, which scored a brilliant propaganda victory by the tactic of dubbing national health insurance with the name of 'socialized medicine' and thus mobilizing the strong bias that Americans have against socialism. This controversy can be studied by empirical methods as an example of pressure-group politics. Since that debate, it could be argued that all the publicists who use the term 'socialized medicine' are continuing to mobilize bias against the idea, with the aim of keeping the issue off the agenda. While the debate in 1948 was an example of the first dimension of political power, with the Medical Association coming out on top, the intermittent propaganda on the question since that time can be regarded as an example of the second dimension of power.

It would be quite a different matter to investigate why the American people have not embraced socialism. Numerous scholars have attempted an explanation, in terms of such factors as the opportunities offered to immigrants, the expanding frontier, the rapid growth of the American economy, the degree of social mobility, and the existence of ethnic divisions that led to conflict between ethnic groups rather than between social classes. However, it is doubtful whether it would be useful to employ the concept of political power when making an inquiry into this question. People were not prevented from adopting socialist ideas by censorship or controls over political association or institutional hurdles. Socialist ideas were floated, but they did not catch on.

As noted in Chapter 6, the concept of cultural and ideological hegemony (which will come up again in Chapter 14) was developed by Gramsci in the 1930s. It seems to me to be clearly true that in most advanced capitalist societies there exists a dominant set of values that is compatible with capitalism and supports the operation of the capitalist system. It is not the only set of values present, for there is also a quite widely held set of trade-union values that are rather different, though they are not normally incompatible with capitalism, together with a set of revolutionary values held by a small minority of citizens. It is fair to say that the dominant values are generally upheld by schools, churches, the mass media and other opinion-formers as well as by politicians. The process of upholding social values and passing them on to the next generation is commonly known as socialization, and in the opinion of Marxists and neo-Marxists the result of the socialization process in western societies has been the development and maintenance of an ideological and cultural hegemony of bourgeois values.

If the development and maintenance of this hegemony is to be regarded as the exercise of political power, in the third dimension of power suggested by Lukes (1974), it is important to ask how this can be studied empirically. The concept of power involves the idea of a political actor with certain intentions, who communicates a message and is able to make some difference to the political behaviour of others. If it can be shown that people who control the dissemination of ideas, be they teachers, journalists or newspaper proprietors, have deliberately presented slanted information that has had a measurable impact on the attitudes and values of their audience, then this should be regarded as a form of political power, of the type that I have called political manipulation. The audience may not have the resources of time and knowledge required to check the validity of the messages presented to them, and in the long run beliefs instilled in this way are likely to affect political behaviour. However the problems of analysing this hypothetical power to shape ideas are very great indeed. Much political communication takes the form of private conversation or classroom dialogue that is simply not on record. When communications are on record their content can be analysed, but one can rarely do more than infer the intentions of the author and it is not easy to assess the impact of the message.

A good deal of research has been carried out, but the results of it have been highly inconclusive. People are socialized throughout life, the main sources of influence being parents, schools, peer groups, colleagues at work, life experiences and the mass media. Of these, the only sources amenable to empirical research are school curricula with a political content and the mass media. However, it has been reported that 'most of the survey type research . . . on the impact of various types of political education curricula seems to confirm that their influence on children is minimal' (Dowse 1978: 408). The results of research on the influence of the mass media have also been largely negative. The public seem to take what they want from the mass media rather than be educated by the messages presented, with the consequence that 'on the whole, the mass media serve to reinforce existing orientations rather than to alter old ones or create new ones' (Dawson and Prewitt 1969: 198).

People certainly acquire and develop political attitudes as they go through life, and it may be appropriate to call this a process of political socialization, but in modern industrial societies citizens are exposed to such a multitude of communications and experiences from which they may acquire a political message that it is almost impossible to assess the impact of any one of them.

After surveying the literature, Dowse and Hughes report that 'in recent years the interest political sociologists have shown in the process of socialization has waned, due in no small part to the inconclusiveness of much of the research' (Dowse and Hughes 1986: 217).

Even in closed societies the evidence suggests that people are markedly resistant to indoctrination by political propaganda. The citizens of the Communist Party states of eastern Europe were supposedly brain-washed for forty years after the Second World War about the advantages of a socialist economic system and a single-party state. The dramatic events of 1989–90 showed that most people did not believe the propaganda. In view of these revelations, it behoves political scientists to think very carefully before using phrases like 'the power of the capitalist press'. The evidence suggests that life experiences have much more influence on people's attitudes than the mass media can exert, even when the media are substantially in unison.

SOME CONCLUDING REFLECTIONS

It sometimes happens that the discussion of a political concept comes to be dominated by the terminology used in a particular dispute, even though that dispute focuses on only one aspect of the process or activity or pattern of behaviour covered by the concept. This has happened to the concept of political power. The article by Bachrach and Baratz (1962) discussed above referred to a 'second face of power', while the book by Lukes (1974) referred to the 'three dimensions of power'. In fact these contributions dealt only with forms of political influence, or in Lukes' case with two forms of influence and one form of what I prefer to call political manipulation. They said nothing whatever about political coercion or political authority. In consequence there is some danger that the lively and useful controversy about whether 'power' has one, two, or three dimensions will divert attention from the fact that political coercion and political authority are just as important as political influence and logically distinct from it.

It is important to recognize that these types of political power are logically distinct, just as it is important (as emphasized in Chapter 8) to recognize that there are four logically distinct types of representation. This recognition promotes clarity of analysis and enables the scholar to put particular empirical or historical studies into proper perspective. Let us therefore conclude with some thoughts on each of the four types of power.

In the literature of political science, *political coercion* features mainly in case studies of particular examples of political violence. In recent years terrorism has been extensively studied and an excellent literature on that topic now exists, including a specialized journal. The literature on the coercion exerted by the police and allied security agencies, such as the US National Guard, is more patchy. Since the late 1970s half a dozen good books on the British police have appeared, but other countries have not been so well served. Since the police constitute the sharp end of the power of the modern state, it could be expected that every textbook on a national system of government would include a chapter on the powers, organization and behaviour of the police. These matters are important, both because contacts (even if usually only visual contacts) with the police are the most frequent contacts that the average citizen has with agencies wielding state power and because the police have enormous discretion in deciding on the priority they will give to different types of law enforcement and on the methods they will use. It therefore seems unfortunate that only a small minority of textbooks include a chapter on the police.

The exercise of *political authority* in the modern state has been much more thoroughly covered by the literature. Accounts of the structure, powers and work of the executive, legislative and judicial organs of government have always been at the heart of the discipline and it can be expected that this will be so for the foreseeable future.

The study of *political influence* has, as already suggested, tended to follow fashions. An emphasis on the legislative influence of economic pressure groups was followed and accompanied in the 1950s by an emphasis on the nature and influence of public opinion, through elections, political parties and promotional groups for various good causes. This emphasis was followed in the 1960s by an enthusiasm for analysing the patterns of influence within municipal government. That decade saw the completion of over thirty substantial studies of community power structure in American cities and about eight studies in British cities.

In the 1970s and 1980s the emphasis shifted again. On the one hand, as noted in Chapter 3, a revival in support for minority nationalist movements within several democratic states led to a new focus on the political significance of non-economic cleavages within society. On the other hand, a new generation of Marxist or neo-Marxist scholars stressed the influence, amounting to dominance, that Marxists believe the capitalist class to exercise over government policy in all societies where the economic system is one of capitalism.

In the three chapters that follow we shall examine some of the concepts that have been developed by scholars studying the structure of influence over policy making in democratic states. Chapter 12 will be devoted to pluralism, a label for the view that political influence in democratic (and some pre-democratic) systems is divided between a plurality of groups and sections that compete freely with one another. Chapter 14 will deal with elitism, a name for the view that democracy is always largely a sham. It is obvious that in any country government policies are actually formulated and implemented by only a small minority of the population, and the elitist argument is 'that the dominant minority cannot be controlled by the majority, whatever democratic mechanisms are used' (Parry 1969: 31). The most elaborate and sophisticated form of the elitist argument is the Marxist theory of class dominance, which holds, in a nutshell, that the interests of the most powerful economic class in society always tend to be dominant in the policy-making process. Chapter 15 will deal with corporatism, a label for a view that falls somewhere between the extremes of pluralism and elitism. According to theorists of corporatism, the main characteristic of economic policy making in many modern democratic states is that groups representing business and labour have come to work in partnership with the executive branch of government and thus to enjoy much more political influence than other groups.

Political manipulation is inherently more difficult to study by empirical methods. The enthusiasm for studying political socialization that was evident in the 1960s has largely faded away in recent years, because the many studies yielded results that were, on the whole, disappointing. Since the early 1980s, thought about political manipulation has been dominated not by empirical research but by the theoretical suggestions of Michel Foucault, the French social philosopher and, through his writings, by reflections about the ways in which we are all manipulated in our daily lives. Foucault's explorations of power relationships focused not on the power of people at the top of the political system, the decision makers and the groups that influence decision makers, but on the power relationships in the system itself, as seen in the numerous forms of local power applied to citizens so as to induce conformity in their behaviour. Some of these forms are explicit and brutal, such as the powers exercised by police officers and magistrates, while others are subtle and exercised without the subject being conscious of the fact, so that they can be regarded as manipulative power. In any area of human activity there is a multiplicity of customs and pressures that collectively limit freedom of action, pushing people to do what is thought proper and appropriate, and in the second half of the twentieth century it has been evident that one of the instruments of this kind of power is the accumulation and dissemination of various types of specialized knowledge; particularly knowledge of the human sciences. This line of reasoning led Foucault to his assertion that in modern society knowledge is itself an important form of power, giving experts a way of shaping the behaviour of others.

Foucault, himself a radical, maintained that the cumulative impact of the power of experts is conservative in its nature. Psychiatrists, by defining what is normal or abnormal, have the long-term effect of inducing conformity in behaviour. It could be added that sociologists give us generalizations about the normal family, sexologists tell us how to conduct our sex lives, and dieticians tell us what to eat. University professors, by defining what research methods are appropriate or inappropriate, may limit the new knowledge that becomes available. Art and dramatic critics may influence what kinds of painting or drama are produced. It is not difficult to find examples of the kind of power that Foucault had in mind, though it is not necessary to follow him in his apparent assumption that expert knowledge is always conservative in its impact on society. Some forms of knowledge have this kind of impact whereas other forms have a liberating or reforming impact. Anyone familiar with the outlines of history in the past two centuries knows that intellectuals have often taken the lead in promoting social and political change. A clear contemporary example of the reforming impact of intellectuals is the impact of educational theorists on school education in Britain and North America since the 1960s. However, Foucault, though in some sense a political theorist, was not interested in broad movements leading to change at the top. His concern was with the local mechanisms of social control found everywhere in modern society. The kind of power that interested him is only indirectly political, and is not state-centred but diffuse; as Ball puts it, this knowledge/power consists of 'a highly decentralised array of . . . practices operating in unsuspected and subtle ways in everyday life to produce "normal" subjects' (Ball 1988: 101). Moreover, it is central to Foucault's thinking that people may themselves assist in the process that leads to what he calls their subjugation, as in the case, presumably, of people who willingly provide data for computerized data-banks that may subsequently be used to their disadvantage.

Another general point, however, is that this kind of power is far from being absolute. Human beings are constantly influenced by it, but they can escape from it if they have the mind to do so. There are 'points of insubordination which, by definition, are means of escape' (Foucault 1983: 225). One task of the theorist, Foucault maintained, is to clarify the nature of this kind of power, 'thereby disclosing points of possible intervention and resistance and thus helping to empower others to take advantage of them' (Ball 1988: 103). When there is resistance 'the relationship of power may become a confrontation between two adversaries' (Foucault 1983: 226) which may modify the structure of dominance.

One source of resistance to the power of organized knowledge, that is, to knowledge as science which commands respect and conformity, lies in the local and 'minor knowledges' that also exist in society. An example is the knowledge of psychiatric patients and nurses, as contrasted to the knowledge embodied and formalized in medical science (see Foucault 1980: 82). Foucault explained that his research into the history of sexuality, the history of psychiatric illness and the emergence of the prison system had been intended to rediscover the 'historical knowledge of struggles' that had been 'confined to the margins of knowledge' (Foucault 1980: 83). He called these rediscoveries 'genealogies'; he described them as 'anti-sciences'; and he did not claim that in any objective way they were more correct than normal scientific knowledge. What he claimed is that knowing them would be a weapon opposed not to the contents or methods of science but to 'the effects of the centralizing powers which are linked to the institution and functioning of an organized scientific discourse within a society such as ours' (Foucault 1980: 84).

Foucault's dislike of the society in which he lived was not explained or justified in an explicit manner, but it seems to have been quite intense. He said, for instance, that 'what is at stake in all these genealogies is the nature of this power that has surged into view in all its violence, aggression and absurdity in the course of the last forty years' (Foucault 1980: 87). The overall impression left by his writings is not that of a scholar who had a coherent theory about political power to put alongside other theories, but rather that of an individualistic scholar who distrusted coherent theories, disliked the organization and discipline of contemporary society, and linked this to the dominance of orthodoxies in the human sciences. His objects in acting as an intellectual archaeologist, digging out examples of past social thought and practice for current inspection, were to open windows for speculation, to shock people out of complacency, to liberate thought from its conventional limits, and to encourage society's rebels and critics. In one of his several revealing interviews, he said that all his books were 'if you like, little tool-boxes. If people want to open them, use a sentence, an idea, an analysis as a screwdriver or a spanner in order to short-circuit, disqualify and break systems of power . . . well, so much the better' (quoted O'Farrell 1989: 110). Taken as a whole, Foucault's writings have the bracing effect of leading readers to regard familiar situations and relationships in an entirely fresh light.

Chapter 13

Pluralism

Pluralism is an American theory about the impact of sectional and group conflict on policy making. It occupied a central place in political debate in the 1950s and 1960s, but it is an enduring concept in American political thought, having been formulated in one form by the founders of the republic and still current in a modified form. As a theory, pluralism has been defined and redefined, supported by empirical studies, criticized and attacked as misleading. It no longer has such a central place in debate as it had a few years ago, but it has featured in so much of the writing about American politics that it clearly deserves a chapter in this book. Moreover, its use has spread from the United States to other countries, some writers having said that all democratic systems are pluralist in character. To some extent, the concept of pluralism is an American intellectual export.

SECTIONAL PLURALISM IN AMERICAN THOUGHT

As already noted in Chapter 7, the first pluralist thinkers in the United States were Madison and Hamilton. They were writing to advocate the proposed transition from a loose confederation of states to a federal union. Their arguments were a combination of empirical hypotheses and normative assertions. They have been subjected to an elaborate logical analysis by Robert Dahl (see Dahl 1956: Chapters 1 and 2) and I am indebted to Dahl for this analysis. In so far as Madison and Hamilton's writings were relevant to pluralism, however, I think their points can be summarized without injustice in the form of four empirical hypotheses, one normative assertion and a conclusion. The empirical hypotheses were as follows:

1 That politicians are not normally motivated by altruism or a concern for the public interest. On the contrary, they enjoy the exercise of power and can be expected to maximize it if given the opportunity to do so.
2 That a conflict of interests in society is inevitable and will necessarily lead to the development of factional disputes. As Madison put it:

> A landed interest, a manufacturing interest, a mercantile interest, a moneyed interest, with many lesser interests, grow up of necessity in civilised nations. . . . The regulation of these various and interfering interests forms the principal task of modern legislation, and involves the spirit of party and faction in the necessary and ordinary operations of the government.
>
> (Hamilton et al. 1901: 46)

3 That factions within society will, if not checked by others, seek to maximize their own interests at the expense of others.
4 That factions will be led or represented by politicians who can be expected to use their power to promote factional interests.

The normative assertion was that Americans ought to organize their system of government so as to minimize the possibility that leaders of any one faction could dominate the others, which Madison said would lead to a deprivation of rights.

The conclusion was that joining the thirteen states into a federal union would be desirable on the ground that, by multiplying and diversifying the factions, the danger of any one faction gaining a position of dominance would be greatly reduced. Hamilton's assertion to this effect in paper 51 of *The Federalist* bears repetition because it was so clear; it was that 'society itself will be broken into so many parts, interests, and classes of citizens that the rights of individuals or of the minority will be in little danger from interested combinations of the majority' (Hamilton et al. 1901: 287).

This line of argument was given a new emphasis in the 1850s by John C. Calhoun, the influential southern politician who was concerned that northern politicians, if they gained control of Congress, might use their majority to abolish slavery. Calhoun took the view that representative government could only safeguard the interests of geographical minorities if it were based on the principle of the 'concurrent majority' (see Calhoun 1943: 28). He asserted that this view was to some extent recognized in the US Constitution, by the equal representation of each state in the Senate and by the clause requiring the agreement of three-quarters of the states before any constitutional amendment could be passed. The essence of his message was that this principle should be extended by convention so that a numerical majority in Congress would never use its power to pass measures which deprived some of the states of rights that they considered essential to their wellbeing. If northern politicians refused to accept such a convention in regard to slavery, Calhoun warned, the result would be to upset the delicate equilibrium of American politics and probably to lead the southern states to secede from the union.

It is possible to argue either that the American civil war justified Calhoun's view, for the war was an undeniably tragic event, or that it rendered his extreme version of geographical pluralism obsolete by demonstrating the powcr that a national majority could exert. After the civil war somewhat less was heard about this type of pluralism, and the improvement of communications and the trend towards the nationwide organization of industry made American society more homogeneous. Nevertheless, the ideas of sectional pluralism did not die out, and were reaffirmed in 1950 by Herbert Agar, who wrote as follows:

> Successful federal policies will tend to follow Calhoun's rule of concurrent majorities. Every interest which is strong enough to make trouble must usually be satisfied before anything can be done. This means great caution in attempting new policies, so that a whole ungainly continent may keep in step.
>
> (Agar 1950: 690)

A. N. Holcombe held a similar viewpoint, arguing that disciplined national parties (as then being advocated by many political scientists) were undesirable and probably unworkable in a large and heterogeneous society like the United States. The price of union, it was said, was the acceptance of the right of minorities to veto policies that they found intolerable (Holcombe 1950). This was a fairly straightforward application of the doctrine first advanced by Madison and Hamilton. Dahl came close to this position when he suggested that the distinction between dictatorship and democracy could be described as one 'between government by a minority and government by minorities' (Dahl 1956: 133).

Not everyone in the post-war period shares the values implied by this quotation, for some critics have wanted firmer national leadership than has normally been given. However, it is true as a matter of fact that political power in the United States is more decentralized than in any other modern democratic state, with the exceptions of Canada and Switzerland. Sectional interests with a geographic base have more influence on national policy than is normal elsewhere, and the extent of congressional log rolling for regional and local interests in regard to the budget, appropriations and defence contracts would be thought shocking in most other democracies.

PRESSURE-GROUP PLURALISM

After 1950, an emphasis on the sectional and geographical basis of American pluralism was replaced by an emphasis on the role of organized pressure groups, however based, on governmental decision making. In 1952, Latham's book on *The Group Basis of Politics* asserted that the pressure group is 'the basic political form' (Latham 1965: 10) and that the political process is essentially a struggle between such groups:

> The legislature referees the group struggle, ratifies the victories of the successful coalitions, and records the terms of the surrenders, compromises,

and conquests in the form of statutes . . . The legislative vote on any issue tends to represent the composition of strength, i.e. the balance of power, among the contending groups at the moment of voting. What may be called public policy is the equilibrium reached in this struggle at any given moment.

(Latham 1965: 35–6)

The 1950s saw the publication of many books and articles with a similar emphasis, some of which have already been quoted in Chapter 7. The most influential of them was Truman's book, *The Governmental Process*, which sought to synthesize the results of numerous specialized studies so as to provide a 'systematic conception of the role of interest groups in the political process' (Truman 1951: VIII–IX). It will be noted that Truman preferred the term 'interest group' to the term 'pressure group'. He did this because he thought that the latter term had become part of 'the language of political abuse' (Truman 1951: 38) whereas the former term was more neutral. However this may have been in 1951, it would be a great pity to follow him in this usage today. The terms are equally capable of being used in a neutral way, as they usually are by political scientists, and it is much more helpful to use 'pressure group' as a generic term, to describe all organized groups that try to exert pressure on the process by which policies are made and implemented, while distinguishing between the two sub-categories of interest groups and promotional groups.

An interest group, in this usage, is a group that has the function of defending or advancing the material interests of its members, while a promotional group is one that exists to promote a particular value or cause. Thus, in regard to defence policy there is a useful distinction to be drawn between groups defending the interests of firms (and their employees) working on defence contracts and other groups, like those opposed to nuclear arms, whose members share an attitude or moral conviction about the proper nature of the policy. In regard to the law on abortion, there is a similar distinction between groups representing the interests of doctors, nurses and the owners of abortion clinics and other groups whose members simply have convictions about the rights and wrongs of abortion. The distinction is reflected in the financial and other resources available to the groups and, frequently, in the tactics of pressure they employ. Interest groups are more likely to be consulted by government agencies and thus to have an inside track in the decision-making process, while promotional groups are more likely to rely on public campaigns and demonstrations. 'Pressure group' is clearly the most appropriate generic term and it will be used in what follows.

The main thrust behind the pressure-group pluralists of the 1950s was methodological. They believed that there was an unhelpful tendency among political scientists to depict the role of pressure groups as being in some sense outside the basic process of government, or at any rate on the periphery of it. In contrast, the pluralists' view was that such groups were at the heart of the policy-making process. 'The institutions of government', Truman declared, 'are centres of interest-based power' (Truman 1951: 506). Is this true of the presidency, the Supreme Court, the State Department? Truman's answer is in the affirmative: 'The political structure of the United States . . . has adopted characteristic legislative, executive, and judicial forms through the efforts of organized interest groups' (Truman 1951: 513).

This statement seems like an exaggeration, an attempt to redress the methodological balance that goes too far the other way. Pressure groups are important, but they are not all-important. There was, moreover, an element of complacency in the suggestion that the American democratic system automatically registers a state of approximate equilibrium between conflicting pressure groups. In Truman's version the concept of a 'potential interest group' was introduced to serve a function analogous to that of 'the invisible hand' in Adam Smith's writings, namely to guarantee that the clash of private interests would not produce consequences that would upset the system. Another balancing factor was said to be the existence or likelihood of overlapping memberships between interest groups, widely defined so as to include potentially overlapping memberships in both actual and potential groups. One of Truman's conclusions was as follows: 'It is thus multiple memberships in potential groups based on widely held and accepted interests that serve as a balance wheel in a political system like that of the United States' (Truman 1951: 514).

This position went beyond the empirical evidence to produce what could be (and was) construed as a theory of American democracy in terms of an automatic balance of group pressures. The theory could be (and was) attacked by critics on the ground that it was smug, perhaps to the point of being Panglossian, and this line of criticism is understandable. In the 1950s the American system was rather obviously one in which some groups, such as those representing farmers or doctors or business interests, had more influence than others, such as those representing slum-dwellers or racial minorities or the consumers of medical or legal services. It is not clear that pluralist writers would actually have disagreed with this generalization, but their comments about equilibrium, balance, countervailing powers, potential interest groups and the like tended, by implication at least, to minimize its significance.

The fact is that the 1950s were years characterized by a good deal of political and other self-satisfaction in the United States. There was a fair amount of Panglossian writing in that decade, and a prize for pluralist complacency in this period might perhaps be awarded to Max Lerner for the following sentences in a book entitled *America as a Civilization*:

[Power in the United States] is plural and fluid. It is many-faceted rather than uniform, it is dispersed among a number of groups. . . . The pluralist, pragmatist and federalist character of American politics has compelled it to develop the arts of compromise and to achieve an equilibrium of conflicting powers in motion. . . . The American system of power has become like a system of nebulae held together by reciprocal tensions in the intergalactic space.

(Lerner 1957: 398, 405, 406)

Despite this kind of rhetorical exaggeration, writers in the pluralist tradition have pointed to an important dimension of American democracy. Thus, Truman said that 'the outstanding characteristic of American politics . . . is that it involves a multiplicity of co-ordinate or nearly-co-ordinate points of access to governmental decisions' (Truman 1951: 519). Robert Dahl said much the same thing in his textbook on American government:

> When one looks at American political institutions in their entirety and compares them with institutions in other democracies, what stands out as a salient feature is the extraordinary variety of opportunities these institutions provide for an organized minority to block, modify, or delay a policy which the minority opposes.
>
> (Dahl 1967: 326)

These two generalizations are undoubtedly valid, though it is open to question whether this feature of the American system is entirely desirable. Should democrats be pleased, for instance, that the National Rifle Association has been able to hold up effective gun control for many years, against the apparent wish of the majority of citizens to see such control? Dahl's defence of pluralism is that it provides opportunities for groups of citizens to mobilize slack political resources for whatever interests and values they wish to press, and that it also limits the power of governing bodies. As he puts it, when 'one centre of power is set against another, power itself will be tamed, civilized, controlled and limited to decent human purposes' (Dahl 1967: 24). Charles Lindblom has gone rather further than this, arguing that pluralism is not only democratic, but also likely to produce more desirable policy outcomes than any more centralized system of policy making. It involves 'muddling through' rather than political planning, but the complexity of problems in modern industrial societies is so great that it is unlikely that planners can master them all and it is better to leave the outcome to what he calls 'partisan mutual adjustment' (Lindblom 1959, 1965).

In the 1960s the emphasis changed again, as the publication of Dahl's *Who Governs?* turned attention from the role of pressure groups in Congress to the distribution of influence in municipal politics. The background to this study was the publication of seven or eight surveys of community power structure by sociologists, all of which had reached the conclusion that power within American cities was dominated by an established elite of upper-class citizens. The upper class (variously defined) was said to have a ruling position in local society, the elected politicians and officials were said to follow the orders of the upper class, and each community, it was concluded, was therefore controlled by a power elite. Dahl and his junior colleague, Nelson Polsby, took the view that the methodology used in these studies was faulty and the conclusions were mistaken. Polsby produced a detailed and searching analysis of the studies which cast great doubt on their validity (Polsby 1963), while Dahl organized the study of power in New Haven that has already been discussed in Chapter 12 (see Dahl 1961).

As indicated in that chapter, I believe that the methodology employed by Dahl and his colleagues was superior, by normal scientific criteria, to the methodology of their sociological predecessors. However, it is important to be precise about what was and what was not demonstrated by the New Haven study. It was demonstrated that the government of New Haven was an arena of conflict between small groups and factions, with different factions coming out on top in different areas of policy. It was also shown that the members of the city's social elite were not very active or powerful in the decision areas studied, so that it would be implausible to characterize the social elite as being also a political elite.

It was not shown, and not claimed, that all classes and groups in the city had equal power or equal access to the levers of power. It was not shown that the decision makers were not dominated by what may loosely be called middle-class values. It was not shown that there were no other potentially important areas of conflict in the city that had not reached the political agenda, either because (as Dahl would say) the would-be reformers in these areas had failed to mobilize enough resources to get the issues on to the agenda or because (as Bachrach and Baratz would say) the opponents of change had been able to keep the issues off the agenda. It was not shown, and not claimed, that New Haven was typical of all American cities or that its political structure should be regarded as a microcosm of the whole structure of American politics.

The New Haven study and the accompanying methodological analysis by Polsby (1963) exposed the weaknesses of the earlier studies of community power by stratification theorists and opened up an instructive debate (summarized in Chapter 12) about the nature of political power and the problems of assessing it. However, Dahl and Polsby did not exhibit the complacency of some earlier pluralist writers, as Dahl was at pains to point out in a much later book. In this he said, among other things, that organizational pluralism is apt to contribute to the maintenance of political inequalities (Dahl 1982: 40–1).

PLURALISM AND DEMOCRACY

Under this heading it is pertinent to ask whether pluralist systems of government are necessarily democratic and, conversely, whether democratic systems of government are necessarily pluralist. The answer to the first question has to be negative. Pluralism is clearly compatible with democracy but incompatible with totalitarianism, for governments cannot exercise total control over society if autonomous organizations are permitted to exercise any substantial degree of social and political influence. However, most systems of government are neither democratic nor totalitarian. It is not difficult to imagine a system of government that is characterized by competition between organized groups for influence and power, but is nevertheless undemocratic, either because only a minority of citizens are permitted to participate in political life or because the dominant groups use the power of the state to exclude other relevant groups from the competition.

History provides numerous examples of just such a system, including Britain between 1688 and 1867, Germany under Bismarck, and France during the Second Empire. Looking further back, it can be argued that many pre-modern systems of government were pluralist without being democratic, characterized by political struggles between churches, land owners, farmers and merchants while excluding most citizens from political influence.

The answer to the question of whether democratic systems are necessarily pluralist depends upon how pluralism is defined. It is clearly not the case that all democracies are characterized by sectional pluralism with a geographical base, as envisaged by Madison and Hamilton and as exemplified by the American situation. Most European democracies are not only much smaller but also more homogeneous. They also (apart from Switzerland) have more centralized systems of government with, in consequence, fewer points of access for sectional pressure groups than exist in the United States. However, it would not be sensible to say that for these reasons countries like Britain, France, Denmark and Sweden are less democratic than the United States.

If pluralism is defined as Truman (1951) and Latham (1965) defined it, in terms of a political system in which pressure groups (however based) compete for influence on the decisions of the national government, then all modern democracies have a pluralist dimension. Pressure groups are more conspicuous in some democratic systems than in others and they exhibit a great deal of variety in terms of their organization, their resources and their political tactics, but in systems characterized by freedom of organization and political communication some pressure groups are bound to exist. There are important practical questions about how far the activities of pressure groups advance or detract from the public interest, but these are best regarded as local and particular questions to which general answers cannot be given. It has, for example, been plausibly said that the power exerted by trade unions was harmful to the British economy in the 1960s and 1970s, that the influence of industrial organizations has prevented Italy from establishing adequate environmental controls, and that the influence of agricultural groups kept food prices in the European Community unnecessarily high in the 1980s. Many similar generalizations could be cited, some apparently reasonable, others evidently biased, all of them involving some kind of value judgement. However, questions of this kind are essentially questions for specific applications of political judgement, not questions that can be resolved by conceptual or theoretical analysis.

This said, it can be added that some democratic systems are more obviously pluralist than others. The United States is the extreme case, not only because of its geographic sectionalism and its decentralized system of government, but also because, within Washington, the executive branch of the national government is weaker than its equivalent in other democracies. The separation of powers, combined with the weakness of party discipline in Congress, make it very difficult for the executive to get draft legislation translated into law if influential groups are opposed to it. The executive cannot even be sure of getting approval for the annual budget, which could be taken for granted in most parliamentary democracies. One of Dahl's many accurate comments on the federal government was that, to a large extent, 'the numerical majority is incapable of undertaking any co-ordinated action. It is the various components of the numerical majority that have the means for action' (Dahl 1956: 146).

This is a comment that would not be made about the national governments of Britain, France, Germany, Sweden, or Australia. Pressure groups are very influential in these countries, and often have direct access to the administration. In this area of policy or that, some groups might have more influence than their American equivalents can muster. But the results of their pressure can rarely be counted in parliamentary votes, and they can rarely prevent a government with a parliamentary majority from pursuing and implementing a policy once the government has made up its collective mind. It is partly these institutional differences, as well as the differences in their theoretical concerns, that have led American political scientists to place much more stress on the concept of pluralism than their colleagues elsewhere have done. However, the concept can be used in the analysis of almost any system of government.

Chapter 14

Elitism and class dominance

An elite is defined by the *OED* as a 'select group or class' and elitism, as a rather loose political concept, is the theory or view that modern industrial societies are always governed by elites. The significance of the theory in the contemporary world is that it runs contrary to almost all versions of democratic theory. If the elitists are correct, all systems of government are actually oligarchic and democracy is 'either a will-o'-the-wisp or a sham' (Runciman 1963: 74). The theory therefore challenges most western liberal assumptions about politics and the organization of government.

Before discussing the work of the main theorists who are normally classified as elitists, it will be helpful to specify, at least in outline, what would have to be shown to substantiate this challenge. The first point to note is that it would not be sufficient to show that political authority is concentrated in the hands of a small group of people who take the day-to-day decisions of government. This is true of virtually all organized societies in the modern world. Even so small a society as a golf club normally has an executive committee with power to appoint, dismiss or raise the wages of staff and take a variety of decisions about the club's affairs. Golf clubs govern themselves in this way partly because it is efficient and expeditious to have a small committee do the work, partly because most members want to spend their time at the club playing golf. Authority in the modern democratic state is exercised by a president or prime minister, a cabinet, a legislature and a set of courts – a few hundred people out of a population of millions. Gaetano Mosca, arguing for the inevitability of oligarchy, said that it would be difficult to conceive of 'a real world otherwise organised – a world in which all men would be directly subject to a single person . . . or in which all men would share equally in the direction of political affairs' (Mosca 1939: 50). This is true, but not significant, because statements about the size of the office-holding group tell us nothing about who they are, how they are appointed, or the relationship of the decisions they take to the views and interests of the rest of the community.

To substantiate a theory of elite domination, it would be necessary to supplement the truism that the rulers in a political system are few in number compared with the ruled with evidence supporting one or other of the following three propositions.

Proposition A is that access to political office is strictly limited to members of a relatively small and cohesive social group whose members have a commonality of interests or values that have policy implications, and that do not reflect the interests and values of the majority of citizens. It would not be sufficient to show that most members of the US Congress have law degrees, because American lawyers constitute a rather heterogeneous group of people with varied values and interests – except perhaps on those rare occasions when Congress might discuss the regulation of the legal profession. It would be sufficient, however, to show that all members of the Cabinet and most legislators were large land owners, for they constitute a small and rather homogeneous group with many common interests of political relevance that are not shared by the majority of citizens.

Proposition B is that the office-holders are rarely responsive to the views and interests of the general public, being in the habit of substituting their own views and interests for those of the masses and being able to avoid the consequences that accountability to the masses might be expected to bring, either because the machinery of accountability is inadequate or because the office-holding elite is able to use coercion, threats or indoctrination to induce public compliance with their rule.

Proposition C is that the office-holders, while not necessarily looking after their own interests, regularly take decisions on behalf of the interests of a relatively small group or class of citizens, such as the capitalist class in capitalist societies, who possess some non-political kind of power base and have interests which differ from those of the majority of citizens.

With these three propositions in mind, I shall now turn to the work of the four writers who are normally classified as elitists. In order of date of birth, they are: Vilfredo Pareto, an Italian sociologist in the very early days of that discipline; Gaetano Mosca, a constitutional lawyer who is commonly described as the father of Italian political science and published his treatise on *Elementi di Scienze Politica* (later translated as *The Ruling Class*) in 1896; Robert Michels, a German sociologist whose main work was published in 1911; and C. Wright Mills, an American sociologist who wrote a best-selling study of *The Power Elite* in 1956.

Karl Marx and his followers are also elitists in that they believe liberal democracy to be essentially a facade which disguises the power of a minority, but they differ from the writers just mentioned in that they locate real power not in the hands of a political elite but in those of an economic class, for whom politicians act, directly or indirectly, as agents. Because of this difference, Marxist theories will be discussed in a later section of the chapter under the heading of 'class dominance'.

PARETO AND THE CIRCULATION OF ELITES

Pareto was a contemporary of Weber and Durkheim and, like them, he conceived his role to be that of laying the foundations of sociology as an academic discipline. He developed a highly ambitious and complicated framework for social analysis, with its own specialized terminology. In the event, however, he largely failed where they entirely succeeded. Few modern sociologists look up to him as a founder of the discipline and his terminology now seems outdated and irrelevant. Accordingly, and because his contribution to elitist theory is inconclusive, I feel able to give his work only cursory attention in this chapter.

Pareto held that every field of endeavour has its own elite, consisting of those persons who happen to be best at the activity in question. The condition of entry into an elite is skill, not virtue; in every field some participants are bound to be more talented than others and thus to rise to the top. There is an elite of lawyers, of scientists, of poets, of thieves (see Parry 1969: 45). Among these various elites there will be a governing elite, composed of the people who have proved themselves most talented in the art of politics. In discussing the skills involved in this field of activity, Pareto made use of the Machiavellian categories of cunning (used by 'foxes') and coercion (used by 'lions'), and suggested that the most successful governors are those able to deploy a mixture of these talents and tactics.

History shows, according to Pareto, that there is a recurrent circulation of elites, by which he meant (rather confusingly) both a circulation of individuals between the upper and lower strata in the same field of activity and a circulation between governing and non-governing elites, with different groups of men moving into positions of political power in turn. Pareto rejected both the Marxist view that political power is determined by the economic class structure and the common liberal view of his time that the history of civilization illustrated the march of progress. On the contrary, political power fell to people who exercised political skills and there was no clear strand of progress. Some governing elites were progressive, others were conservative, and overall judgements about the direction that history was taking were unscientific.

There is much more, for Pareto wrote extensively about these matters, his main treatise occupying four volumes. However, I shall not discuss his contribution at any length because he did not show that the governing elite, in Italy or more generally, dominated the general public in accordance with either of propositions A, B or C, as itemized above. There is a clear implication of proposition B, that the governors rule with their own ends in view, but no systematic evidence is presented. There are numerous illustrations, drawn mainly from ancient history, but illustrating an argument by disconnected illustrations from an almost infinite pool of possible examples does not establish the validity of the argument. A writer who claims to be offering a science of society has to do better than that to establish general laws. As T. B. Bottomore has noted, 'there are historical examples which appear at once to invalidate Pareto's generalization' (Bottomore 1966: 53). What Pareto presented is best regarded as an elaborate conceptual framework for other scholars to use when analysing particular cases.

The value of this contribution to the understanding of politics does not seem to be very great, but it has to be appreciated that Pareto was attacking some of the most fashionable ideas of his period. In self-image and mode of presentation he was a ruthless iconoclast, anxious to puncture high-flown liberal beliefs about morality, humanitarianism and the inevitability of progress, 'always talking about masks being torn away or people being led by the nose' (Runciman 1963: 71). His intention was to make his readers reject what he saw as the illusion of liberalism, that the people could rule through democratic institutions, as well as the illusion of Marxism, that human equality and freedom could be achieved by a workers' revolution. His basic political attitude was that of a cynic, but his attack on prevailing ideas had some originality and his work earns him a place in the history of thought. However, he did not go far towards establishing elitism as a viable theory of politics with general relevance.

MOSCA AND THE IDEA OF THE RULING CLASS

Mosca was an Italian contemporary of Pareto who also believed that the Aristotelian division of regimes into monarchic, oligarchic and democratic disguised the reality that all regimes are characterized by the rule of the few over the many. These points of similarity have caused the two writers to be bracketed together and to be viewed with suspicion by democratic theorists. Meisel tells us that when translations of their main works were published in America in the 1930s 'both Mosca and Pareto were believed to be at least the intellectual parents if not the open partisans of fascism' (Meisel 1965: 17).

This was an unfortunate judgement, based on ignorance, as the two authors were very different in their careers, their theories and their political preferences. Pareto was a youthful enthusiast for Italian unification and liberalism who was soundly defeated when he contested a parliamentary election in his early thirties. This experience so embittered him that he turned against liberalism and democracy for the rest of his life. He was not an 'intellectual parent' of fascism, as that doctrine, in so far as it was not invented by Mussolini, was derived from a twisted interpretation of Hegelian philosophy, not from Paretian sociology. However, he supported Mussolini's regime when it was established and accepted an honour from it.

Mosca, in contrast, was part of the political establishment in Italy's liberal regime, even though critical of some features of it. He worked for eight years as editor of the journal of the Chamber of Deputies, then served for ten years as a liberal-conservative member of that chamber, and was subsequently appointed to the Senate. He criticized the idea of participatory democracy but he admired the parliamentary system and greatly disliked the fascist regime that took over in 1923.

The success of Mosca's career is doubtless one reason why his writings are much more agreeable in manner than those of the other three writers considered in this section. Unlike Pareto and Michels, he had not been embittered by personal experiences; and unlike Mills, he did not feel alienated from the society in which he lived. He was a university professor as well as a politician and his books are characterized by thoughtful reflections on European history and politics.

Mosca's starting point in *The Ruling Class* was his observation that all societies known to historians have been divided into a minority who controlled the reins of government and the majority who were ruled by the minority. It must always be so, he maintained, for two reasons. One is that a minority can organize itself in a fashion that is beyond the reach of a large multitude: 'A hundred men acting uniformly in concert, with a common understanding, will triumph over a thousand men who are not in accord and can therefore be dealt with one by one' (Mosca 1939: 53). The second reason is that 'members of a ruling minority regularly have some attribute, real or apparent, which is highly esteemed and very influential in the society in which they live' (Mosca 1939: 53).

When he wrote of the ruling class, Mosca meant not only the holders of high office (the people Mills later described as members of the 'power elite') but also the wider class of people from whom the office-holders were drawn. This class was not to be defined simply in economic terms, as Marxists defined class, for Mosca's study of history led him to identify various groups or classes that had dominated their societies. There had been, or were still, societies dominated by an hereditary aristocracy, others dominated by a priesthood, others by a class of warriors, others by large land owners, others by financiers, others again by a ruling group to which entry was gained by education and talent.

Each ruling class develops a 'political formula' by which it justifies its rule to the rest of the population. The Chinese mandarins claimed to be 'interpreters of the will of the Son of Heaven' (Mosca 1939: 70); Muslim rulers talked of the will of Allah; French aristocrats of the divine right of kings; English politicians of the sovereignty of Parliament; American rulers of the will of the people. The use of propaganda to propagate and sustain this legitimizing formula is one of the main weapons at the disposal of the ruling class in any period (see Mosca 1939: 190–2).

Ruling classes are in a strong position to hand on their dominant role to their children and grandchildren, but history shows that from time to time political power passes from one class to another. A causal factor in such a transfer is usually a decline in general acceptance of the political formula. A priestly ruling class is in trouble when people start to question the rightness of the will of God. The French ruling class lost its grip when people ceased to believe in the divine right of kings. This shrewd observation seems obvious enough, once stated, but it was novel when Mosca made it and was one of his most illuminating ideas.

Unlike Pareto, Mosca believed in human progress. His study of history led him to the conclusion that, over the centuries, there had been, at least in Europe, a general improvement in the level of civilization. He did not think that progress was constant or inevitable, for there were instances where the erosion or collapse of a regime had led to retrogression. This had been true of Europe after the collapse of the Roman Empire and true of the Middle East after the collapse of Islamic Empires. Nevertheless, the general trend was one of progress and improvement, and this was continuing.

In the late nineteenth century, when Mosca was writing, the most advanced countries had developed systems of representative government, and he approved of these with certain reservations. He contrasted the principle of representative government with that of democracy, which he took to mean participatory democracy of the style recommended (or at least, widely thought to have been recommended) by Rousseau, which Mosca did not think would be feasible. Now, most people would agree that participatory democracy, in a full sense of that term, seems unsuitable for industrial societies of any size, and might perhaps be unworkable in them. Contemporary western societies are not without advocates of participatory democracy, but they generally recommend that it be tried in small units of government, or within economic enterprises, rather than at the level of the national state. This question has been discussed in Chapter 9. However, the term 'democracy', without a qualifying adjective, is not generally thought to have that meaning today. It is generally understood to denote representative government with a wide franchise. To ascertain Mosca's views about democracy, as generally understood, it is therefore necessary to consider his views about representative government and the franchise.

In terms of principle, Mosca was an admirer of Montesquieu, whose theories, he said, 'cannot be regarded as mistaken in any substantial respect' (Mosca 1939: 254). He accepted Montesquieu's belief that liberty was best safeguarded by a separation of powers between the legislative, executive and judicial arms of government. He also accepted that representative government and the parliamentary system were the most promising forms of government yet devised. In terms of practice, however, Mosca's experience was of an employee and then a member of the Italian Parliament, which had various limitations.

The Italian parliamentary system was created in 1871, when Italy was unified. It was a liberal system of representative and responsible government on paper, but was far from being a shining example of this style of government. The franchise was limited by a property qualification, which admitted only 2 per cent of the adult population at first. This proportion rose gradually to 7 per cent in 1912, when a reform took it to 25 per cent, so when Mosca was writing in the 1890s it was in the region of 5 per cent. The Roman Catholic Church advised its members to boycott elections, because at that time the Church disapproved of liberalism, with the result that voting turnout never exceeded 50 per cent of the qualified electors. Many of the parliamentarians engaged in dubious activities, and corrupt practices were common in elections, with the result that no Italian government was defeated in a general election during the whole life of the liberal regime from 1871 to 1923. The element of governmental responsibility to the people was there in the constitution but was not very apparent in practice.

Although, in view of his official position, Mosca did not direct his criticisms at his own Parliament in so many words, it is clear both that this is what he was thinking of when he made them and that his Italian readers would have understood this. His criticisms can be summarized as follows. First, nominations for election are controlled by small minorities in each area (Mosca 1939: 154); second, parliamentary majorities tend to become irresponsible; third, individual Members of Parliament tend to interfere excessively in public administration, in the administration of justice, and in the control of banking and public charities. He cited these forms of behaviour, along with the imperfections of the electoral system, as reasons for public disappointment with their experience of parliamentary government (Mosca 1939: 157, 255, 325). However, it must be stressed that Mosca did not allow these problems to undermine his own support for the parliamentary system. The problems of representative systems, he said, 'are merest trifles as compared with the harm that would inevitably result from abolishing them or stripping them of their influence' (Mosca 1939: 256).

On the franchise, Mosca was very much a man of his time. He wanted the electorate to be moderately large, so that only a small fraction of electors would aspire to political office and the majority of voters could act as impartial judges between rival candidates (Mosca 1939: 413). At the same time, he thought that universal suffrage would lead party leaders to engage in demagogic appeals to the electorate; to 'flatter the masses, play to their crudest instincts and exploit and foment all their prejudices and greeds' (Mosca 1939: 412). His conclusion was that a limited electorate was most likely to satisfy the requirements of liberalism, 'that those who represent shall be responsible to the represented' (Mosca 1939: 413).

The question we have to answer is whether Mosca can appropriately be described as an elitist, defined as a theorist who denies the possibility of democratic government. In considering this, it would be wrong to place much weight on his cautious views regarding the extent of the franchise. His position on that question was not unlike that of many European liberals in the nineteenth century, who favoured representative government but were afraid that enfranchising the masses would lower the tone of political debate and competition. Tocqueville had worried about the tyranny of the majority.

John Stuart Mill had wanted educated electors to have extra votes. The assumption of these middle-class theorists was not that democracy would make no difference, because the bourgeoisie would continue to rule. On the contrary, their assumption was that democracy would make an important difference, because it would put the working classes into the majority and force public policy to take account of their crude demands for the erosion of bourgeois privileges. Such writers might be described as elitist in their sentiments, but that was perhaps natural for middle-class intellectuals writing at a time when many or most of the workers were illiterate. What is important for the present argument is that they were not elitist in their theories.

The broader question is whether Mosca's views about the inevitability of a ruling class meant that he subscribed to propositions A or B, as outlined at the beginning of this chapter. Since he drew most of his examples from European and Asian history and he was writing in the early days of democracy in Europe, and before any sign of democracy in Asia, it was inevitable that his examples should suggest an affirmative answer. Feudal Europe was obviously a period of government by land owners in the interests of land owners. There had been examples of priestly rule in Asia, with the privileges of the priesthood and the maintenance of religious conformity as the main aims of government. Iran has been a contemporary example that fits the same pattern. There were examples of aristocratic rule, where power was confined to a small group of ruling families, and this is still true in Saudi Arabia and Kuwait. There were examples of rule by the military, and Pakistan has been a modern example for much of the period since 1947. These were all self-serving ruling groups who adjusted their policies to pressures from the wider society they governed only when prudence dictated it.

The essential question, however, is whether Mosca believed that democratic regimes, as they developed, would also be subject to political domination by a small ruling class acting in its own interest. He certainly believed that the activity of government would be concentrated in the hands of a small minority of the population, but this is a truism that does not amount to a significant theory. He did not try to formulate a specific answer to the more interesting question of how far the ruling minority constitutes a definite class with interests of its own, so we have to rely on scattered remarks. At one point he said that in a representative system 'the door has been left open to all elements in the governed classes to make their way into ruling classes' (Mosca 1939: 389). At another point he said that in a representative system with a universal or nearly universal franchise 'the chief task of the party organizations into which the ruling class is divided is to win the votes of the more numerous classes' (Mosca 1939: 411).

By these two comments, Mosca acknowledges that in a democratic system the ruling class will be open to penetration by 'the governed classes', which must mean all the other citizens, and that the ruling class is not politically united but is divided into competing parties. Now this is what most political scientists mean by democracy, if we add components (which Mosca did not question) such as free speech, freedom of organization and an independent judiciary. The assumption of democrats is that competition for votes will force governing parties to take account of the views and interests of the majority of voters, not only during election campaigns but also in between elections, because of what is commonly called the rule of anticipated reactions. Now, Mosca was writing in the infancy of political science as an academic discipline, one that in Europe was practically confined to the universities of Oxford, London and Paris, and he could not be expected to use modern terminology. But he indicated his understanding of this rule when he declared that in a representative system with a wide franchise 'wariness about giving offence will be much greater when every single representative, whose vote may be useful or necessary to the executive branch of government, knows that the discontent of the masses may at almost any moment bring about the triumph of a rival' (Mosca 1939: 156).

I therefore conclude that Mosca's book, though full of interesting and useful observations, does not add up to a theory of elitism which can be set against modern theories of democracy. He shows that government had in the past been often in the hands of self-serving elites, but he did not show, and did not even claim, that this must always be the case. To say that the reins of government must always be in the hands of a minority is a truism, and to call this minority a ruling class is a tautology. Political organizers and politicians in a modern democracy are a mixed bag of people, and giving them this label does not turn Mosca's ideas into a viable theory that is anti-democratic. As Bottomore has observed, 'in Mosca's theory an elite does not simply rule by force and fraud, but represents, in some sense, the interests and purposes of important and influential groups in the society'. My reading of Mosca leads me to the same conclusion that Bottomore reached, namely that Mosca 'is prepared to recognize, and in a qualified way to approve, the distinctive features of modern democracy' (Bottomore 1966: 10–11). In his old age, in a book that was not published until 1949 (after the author's death). Mosca made this pretty clear. Writing about representative government, he said this:

> Of all types of government it is the one in which the rulers on the whole will be affected by the sentiments of the majority, the one which furnishes the best means of judging and debating governmental acts. In other words, it is a rule of freedom.
>
> (quoted Meisel 1962: 324)

MICHELS AND THE IRON LAW OF OLIGARCHY

Michels was a radical socialist who was disappointed and understandably aggrieved because his political views prevented him from securing posts in

German universities for which he was otherwise well qualified. However, when he wrote his book on *Political Parties* he turned his anger not against the German government or universities (which were controlled by the government) but against the leadership of the German Social Democratic Party (SPD) and against what he took to be the oligarchic tendencies of parties in general.

His book is somewhat rhetorical and repetitive in style, so it is important to summarize his argument carefully. The first section of the book maintains that, for technical and administrative reasons, bureaucracy and oligarchy are inevitable in political parties of any size. A party has to have professional organizers and it has to have leaders. To compete successfully in a system of representative government, its leaders must have freedom of manoeuvre: 'a fighting party needs a hierarchical structure' (Michels 1962: 79). In the middle of this section he introduces a much more general comment that does not fit there logically, but gives advance notice of arguments to come in a later section. 'For democracy', he says, 'the first appearance of professional leadership marks the beginning of the end' (Michels 1962: 73).

The second section of the book is on the 'psychological causes of leadership', and consists mainly of a parade of deeply cynical remarks about the political capacity of the masses, including rank-and-file party members. They are, he maintains, inexperienced, poorly educated, apathetic, intellectually inferior to their leaders, and deferential (Michels 1962: 85–108). 'The incompetence of the masses', he concludes, 'is almost universal throughout the domains of political life, and this constitutes the most solid foundation of the power of the leaders' (p. 111). Despite all this, however, the masses are in some sense democratic, a term that Michels uses frequently but never defines. 'The democratic masses', we are told 'are compelled to submit to a restriction of their own wills when they are forced to give their leaders an authority which is in the long run destructive to the very principle of democracy' (p. 111). This usage of 'democratic' is clearly incorrect, for the term refers to a process or system of decision making and cannot sensibly be used to describe a body of people. Its inclusion in the sentence quoted serves the purpose of showing that the author's sympathies lie with the masses in spite of his expressed contempt for their intelligence and political skills. It is a rhetorical flourish to indicate to socialist readers that his heart is in the right place, but it does not advance his argument.

Michels maintains not only that party leaders set themselves above their followers, but also that elected representatives do the same. Members of Parliament become arrogant, make deals with other parties, and take it on themselves to depart from the ideological principles of their party in their search for support from broader sections of the electorate. It does not occur to Michels that appealing to the electorate is of the essence of democracy, for he was concerned with democracy within the party rather than with democracy within the political system as a whole.

Apart from one brief reference to the power of the caucus in the US Congress, all of Michels' numerous examples were taken from the socialist parties and trade unions of western Europe, and most of them from the German SPD. At the time that he was writing, the SPD was formally committed to a set of Marxist objectives but its leaders actually 'accepted the established order, social and political, and confined themselves to getting greater benefits inside it for their supporters' (Plamenatz 1973: 50). It was this apparent discrepancy between principle and practice that Michels regarded as undemocratic. A similar line of argument has been advanced by left-wingers in many European social democratic parties that started life with Marxist-sounding statements of objectives. They did so because this was the rhetoric of socialism in the early years of the twentieth century, but they moved towards advocacy of a mixed economy as the years wore on. In the British Labour Party arguments of this kind were heard as recently as the 1970s. One knows what Michels was saying and one can understand his sentiments.

In terms of the logic set out in the early paragraphs of this chapter, Michels is suggesting that this tendency in the SPD (and by implication in other socialist parties) is an example of proposition B, that members of the party elite substitute their own values and strategies for those that would be preferred by the mass membership. However, to show that the leadership departed from the ideological principles of the party is not the same thing. To demonstrate that this was elitist and undemocratic, it has to be shown that the rank-and-file members of the party would have preferred to keep to the principles. Michels makes no attempt to show this in regard to the SPD, and it is reported that most historians of the period depict the bulk of German workers as caring 'even less than their leaders did for the Marxist principles of the party they voted for' (Plamenatz 1973: 65). It must therefore be said that Michels failed to establish a case for elitism in this part of his argument.

In the last section of the book, Michels returns to this theme of the betrayal of revolutionary principles. We are told that 'organization leads to power, but power is always conservative'; that 'as the organization increases in size, the struggle for great principles becomes impossible'; and that this conservative, compromising tendency 'is reinforced by the parliamentary character of the political party' (Michels 1962: 333, 334). He was clearly writing here not as a supporter of democratic procedures concerned about the impact of bureaucratic organization on them, but as a supporter of radical socialism concerned to point out that participation in the parliamentary process is likely to lead socialist leaders to moderate their policy commitments.

In the final eight pages of the book Michels attempts to cast his conclusions in the form of general propositions. He claims that these conclusions have the status of a 'scientific law' based upon 'analytic explanation' (Michels 1962: 364). The so-called law has two parts. The first part states that every sizeable political party develops organization, and 'who says organization, says oligarchy'. The second part states that oligarchy means leadership and 'every system of leadership is incompatible with the most essential postulates of democracy' (Michels 1962: 364, 365).

What meaning and validity can be attached to these sweeping assertions? It may be allowed that every sizeable political party has a form of organization, a party bureaucracy, and a group of leaders. This most obvious of facts about parties would make them undemocratic, however, only if it could be shown that the leaders fail to reflect the views of the membership and cannot be held answerable to the members for this failure. Michels makes no attempt whatever to show this, not even in the case of his favourite example, the SPD, let alone for a sufficient number of parties to form a reasonable basis for a generalization for which he seems to be claiming universal validity.

Even if some political parties had leaders who failed to reflect the views of their members, this would not in itself make the system of government in which the parties operate undemocratic. Democracy is a system in which rival parties compete for the support of the electorate. If the parties themselves are only partially democratic in their internal organization, that may be a pity, but the system as a whole remains democratic so long as the choice between parties rests with the majority of adult citizens. It must be concluded that this book tells us very little about democratic government and suggests that the author did not really understand the democratic principle that governments are answerable to the electorate for their actions. This failure of understanding may, of course, have been the consequence of his limited experience. His choice of examples makes him appear highly ethnocentric, and Germany did not acquire a system of responsible democratic government until eight years after the book was published. Under the German system before 1919 there was party competition in elections for Parliament, but the government was not responsible to Parliament. It is a pity that Michels did not study the practice of representative and responsible government as it had developed in Britain, the Scandinavian countries, Australia and New Zealand.

The book has been overrated by many political scientists, some of whom seem to have quoted the conclusions without studying the text. In so far as it has relevance beyond the historical and ideological context in which it was written, its contribution is to point towards one of the features of democratic systems of government that is widely regarded as a virtue. This is that, because parties have to appeal to a wide section of the electorate if they are to secure power, they tend to converge in their policies. The democratic process tends to discourage political extremism, because extremists are always in a minority.

What does this book tell us about the concept of elitism? It points out that political parties need leaders, that the leaders acquire more knowledge and experience of politics than their followers, and that they may acquire the ability to reshape the party's policy objectives in the course of their struggle for support among the electorate. It says nothing about conservative or liberal parties but asserts that the leaders of socialist parties are apt to moderate the radical policy objectives to which these parties were originally committed. It claims, but without adducing any evidence for the claim, that this process is undemocratic.

The famous 'iron law of oligarchy' that Michels produced is therefore much less significant than most of his admirers have claimed. It is of course true that every sizeable political (or non-political) organization chooses leaders, such as an executive committee and a president, to direct its affairs. It is often the case that these leaders, through experience, acquire a deeper understanding of the organization's problems than most rank-and-file members possess, and that this understanding enables them to guide and perhaps for a time to dominate the mass of members. However, it is also often the case that the people in leading positions respond to pressures from the mass membership and modify their policies in anticipation of challenges to their leadership if they fail to modify their policies. How often, and in what circumstances, the leaders of political parties acquire such power over their organizations that they may fairly be described as oligarchs is a matter for empirical investigation with a fairly large number of cases. Michel's generalization from one case, even if his conclusions were correct in that case, can only have the status of a hypothesis to be tested in other cases, not the status of a law.

It has to be concluded that his book does very little to establish elitism as a viable and helpful concept in political analysis.

C. WRIGHT MILLS AND THE POWER ELITE

Mills was concerned with the government of the United States as a whole rather than with the management of parties or groups within the country. His central thesis was both institutional and historical in emphasis. It was institutional in that he assumed power to be the ability to take decisions and give orders within the three 'domains' of industry, government and the military. It was historical in that he repeatedly asserted that the organization of these three domains had become increasingly concentrated and increasingly interrelated, so that, first, power within each domain was wielded by a much smaller number of people than had been the case in the nineteenth century and, second, there had been an increasing tendency for the powerful few to communicate with each other and to exchange roles by moving between domains.

'As the institutional means of power and the means of communications that tie them together have become steadily more efficient', he declared, 'those now in command of them have come into command of instruments of rule quite unsurpassed in the history of mankind' (Mills 1956: 23). He regarded the United States of the 1950s as so dominated by this 'power elite' of powerful individuals that it did not deserve to be described as democratic, but he did not take the view that democracy was always and necessarily a sham or facade. On the contrary, he believed that the United States had been a democratic society in the nineteenth century, but had ceased to be so as a consequence of the increased scale and centralization of its main institutions.

Mills differed from Marxists in that he refused to accept that history is the product of social forces and insisted repeatedly that it is made by individual human beings holding positions of power. He asserted that in the United States these individuals are drawn mainly from the ranks of the upper classes, and he devoted about 40 per cent of the book to a rather journalistic account of the lifestyles of the rich and famous. His object in doing this was to illustrate the 'psychological and social unity' (Mills 1956: 19) that characterized members of the decision-making elite. This elite, he made clear, did not include members of Congress, apart from a few committee chairs who might in some situations acquire a good deal of influence. Members of Congress represent local interests, but are, in Mills's view, poorly informed and poorly organized when national issues are at stake. 'In pursuing their several parochial interests, accordingly, the Congressmen often coincide in ways that are of national relevance', but they occupy 'the middle levels of power', with the high levels being filled by the top members of the administration (Mills 1956: 255–6). It also emerges that the power elite is not thought to include members of the Supreme Court, who are not mentioned in the book.

By power, then, Mills means executive power, and his choice of examples indicates that he was thinking mainly of executive power in the fields of foreign policy and defence policy. Mills (1956: 267) insists that power is located within the state machine, and it is said more than once (and particularly on p. 277) that he does not believe in the Marxist conception that political decision making is dominated by an economic class. The 'corporate rich' have a place in his triumvirate of elitists only in so far as wealthy business people move into top government jobs. His treatment of this topic is unsystematic, however; he gives numerous scattered examples, but does not attempt to produce any statistics apart from a figure showing the proportion of ambassadors drawn from outside the ranks of the diplomatic service, which is only of marginal relevance since ambassadors do not normally take executive decisions.

His emphasis on the psychological unity of the very rich suggests that Mills rests his case for elitism in the American political system on what I have called proposition A, that entry to top positions of power is restricted to members of a small and cohesive social class. However, on pp. 280–6 he draws back from this position, saying only that the very successful in different walks of life come to know each other and to share certain values and attitudes. It is just as well that he was cautious about this, because the evidence would not seem to support a case for proposition A in American circumstances. The central and commanding figure in Mills's definition of the power elite is clearly the president, but only three of the eleven post-war presidents, Kennedy, George Bush and George W. Bush, have been drawn from the ranks of the United States' upper class. The other eight – Truman, Eisenhower, Johnson, Nixon, Ford, Carter, Reagan and Clinton – have all reached the top from ordinary lower-middle or middle-class backgrounds.

As Mills explicitly disavows the Marxist approach, formulated as proposition C in the opening paragraphs of this chapter, it is evident that his case must rest on proposition B, that the top decision makers formulate policy according to their own values and interests, without taking account of the values and interests of the general public. This is indeed his position, as he asserts in several places that the members of the power elite are apt to become cut off from public opinion and that from time to time they take decisions of momentous importance on which there has been no, or very little, public debate.

To substantiate this claim, Mills clearly needs to produce a fair range of examples and to show that in most of the cases cited the decisions taken were decisions with which the public might well have disagreed. It is therefore very unfortunate, for the sake of his argument, that he does no such thing. At various points he mentions Roosevelt's decision to enter the Second World War, Truman's decision to use the atomic bomb on Japan, the decision not to commit the United States to defend two tiny offshore islands near the Chinese coast against a possible Chinese invasion, and the decision not to use nuclear weapons in 1954 to save the French army that was surrounded by insurgents in Vietnam. These were all rather exceptional decisions, involving the president in his capacity as commander-in-chief of American military and naval forces. Roosevelt had no real choice but to enter the war, since Japan attacked the American fleet at Pearl Harbor and Germany then declared war against the United States. The other three decisions had, by their nature, to be taken in virtual secrecy, without public discussion. All four decisions would undoubtedly have been supported by the majority of the public if there had been a public debate. The examples therefore fail to provide evidence for proposition B, and in the absence of such evidence it must be concluded that Mills failed to establish a convincing argument for the elitist view that democracy is a sham.

THE ELITISTS REVIEWED

The foregoing summary of the four writers customarily grouped together as the theorists of elitism suggests both that they are a somewhat heterogeneous quartet and that none of them contributed a theory that offers a serious intellectual challenge to democratic theory. Pareto offered a conceptual framework rather than a theory. Mosca was a nineteenth-century liberal who would probably have endorsed democratic ideas had he lived in a later age. Michels was writing about the ideological dilemmas of European social democratic parties rather than about democratic procedures, except very indirectly. Mills was writing only about the United States and did so as a man who was 'wholly alienated' from American society, hostile to its values, its policies, its economic system, and to 'the American condition as a whole' (Miliband 1964: 78). He is said by his friends to have been a non-voter and non-joiner with the temperament of an anarchist (Miliband 1964: 82–3), and his book reveals his own attitudes very clearly without providing a considered general argument against democracy as a system of government. To find such an argument we must turn to Marxist writings, which provide a much more substantial general theory than any of the works so far considered in this chapter.

THE THEORY OF CLASS DOMINANCE

Marxist theory is elitist in the sense that it depicts the holders of governmental offices not as guardians of the public interest or responsive to public opinion but as agents of the class that is economically dominant in society. This class was described as the ruling class in Part I of *The German Ideology* (written in 1847 but published later), where it was said that 'the state is the form in which the individuals of a ruling class assert their common interests' and added that in capitalist societies the state is 'the form of organization which the bourgeois necessarily adopt both for internal and external purposes, for the mutual guarantee of their property and interests' (Marx and Engels 1970: 80). In the *Communist Manifesto* of 1848 it was stated that 'political power, properly so called, is merely the organized power of one class for oppressing another' and 'the executive of the modern state is but a committee for managing the common affairs of the whole bourgeoisie' (Tucker 1978: 490, 475).

These sweeping assertions were confirmed in Marx's 1851 article on 'the class struggles in France, 1848–1850', where it was said that the Paris insurrection of 1848 had compelled the bourgeois republic 'to come out forthwith in its pure form as the state whose admitted object is to perpetuate the rule of capital, the slavery of labour' (Tucker 1978: 590). However, they were apparently modified in the following year, when Marx's pamphlet on *The Eighteenth Brumaire of Louis Bonaparte* included the following passage:

> Under the Restoration, under Louis Philippe and under the parliamentary republic [the bureaucracy] was the instrument of the ruling class, however much it strove for power of its own.
>
> Only under the second Bonaparte does the state seem to have made itself completely independent. As against bourgeois society, the state machine

has consolidated its position so thoroughly that [Bonaparte] suffices for its head, an adventurer blown in from abroad, elevated on its shield by a drunken soldiery, which he has bought with liquor and sausages . . .

And yet the state power is not suspended in mid-air. Bonaparte represents a class, and the most numerous class of French society at that, the small peasants.

(Tucker 1978: 607)

Much later, in his 1871 pamphlet in *The Civil War in France*, Marx emphasized the point that the power of the state in capitalist society was not necessarily and always just an instrument of the capitalist class. In France, he said, the 'internal dissentions' of that class had 'allowed the adventurer Louis Bonaparte to take possession of all the commanding points – army, police, administrative machinery – and . . . to explode the last stronghold of the bourgeoisie, the National Assembly' (Tucker 1978: 621). However, Marx went on to note that in the end the policies of the new government encouraged industrial activity and actually enriched the bourgeoisie.

The transition in these quotations from a dogmatic assertion to a more circumscribed analysis is entirely typical of Marx and Engels, who were always willing to learn from history and whose theories became more refined as the years went by. It was not only from French history that lessons were learned, as Michael Evans has observed:

As the century wore on Marx found it difficult to find a bourgeoisie acting as a genuine ruling class. The Whig oligarchy in England, the Second Empire in France, the Wilhelmine Empire in Germany; all these appeared to be examples of political rule on behalf of or even independent of the bourgeoisie.

(Evans 1972: 138)

These regimes kept the workers in their place and helped the development of an industrial economy by such measures as the laws establishing limited liability and eliminating the duties on imported foodstuffs, to name two conspicuous examples from British history in the middle decades of the nineteenth century. However, the cabinets in these countries could not easily be described just as agents of the capitalist class; in Britain and Germany many, often most, ministers were themselves members of the land-owning class, who showed sensitivity to the interests of the aristocracy on one hand and the workers on the other, as well as to those of industrialists, financiers and merchants.

A good deal of Marxist theory was an extrapolation from the broad trends of European history in the period before and during Marx's lifetime. It was clearly true both that in pre-industrial society government policy had been dominated by the interests of land owners and that, with the growth of industrial capitalism, the interests of the rising middle classes were having a greater and greater influence on policy. However, the transition from aristocratic to bourgeois dominance over government turned out to be a long and intricate process, so prolonged that the interests and demands of the workers were having a significant political impact before the process was completed. Most historians would also say that, as the activities of the state increased and the institutions of government became democratized, the politicians and bureaucrats came increasingly to wield power in their own right, having a good deal of room for manoeuvre and not obviously and directly acting as agents of any economic group or class.

Democrats would of course add that the politicians in a democracy are responsible, in a meaningful and important sense, to the electorate and that they therefore act in what they conceive to be the interests of the whole national society. Marxists and neo-Marxists do not accept this, as they regard liberal democracy as something of a sham, which gives the masses the impression of governmental responsibility to and for the whole society while actually masking the dominance of the interests of financiers, industrialists and their allies. However, modern neo-Marxists have moved quite a distance from the rigid economic determinism implied by statements in the *Communist Manifesto*, and this move was started by Marx and Engels themselves.

Shortly after Marx's death, Engels wrote a long letter to Joseph Bloch in which he was at pains to play down the element of economic determinism present in their early writings and seized upon by many of their supporters. Some sentences from this letter are worth quoting:

> We make our history ourselves, but . . . under very definite assumptions and conditions. Among these the economic ones are ultimately decisive. But the political ones, etc., and indeed even the traditions which haunt human minds also play a part. . . .
>
> History is made in such a way that the final result always arises from conflicts between many individual wills, of which each again has been made what it is by a host of particular conditions of life. . . .
>
> Marx and I are ourselves partly to blame for the fact that the younger people sometimes lay more stress on the economic side than is due to it. We had to emphasize the main principle *vis-a-vis* our adversaries, who denied it, and we had not always the time, the place or the opportunity to allow the other elements involved in the interaction to come into their rights.
>
> (Tucker 1978: 761–2)

It is obviously impossible to know exactly what position Marx and Engels would have adopted if they had lived long enough to observe governments in capitalist societies that fall under the control of social democratic parties, as has happened in Britain, France, Denmark, Sweden, Australia and New Zealand. However, contemporary Marxists have formulated a body of theory that goes by the name of 'the relative autonomy of the state' to cover this and allied questions. The main proponents of the theory have been Ralph Miliband in Britain and Nicos Poulantzas in France, but contributions have also been made by Claus Offe in Germany and several other writers.

THE RELATIVE AUTONOMY OF THE STATE

As the state comprises a whole set of sometimes conflicting institutions it is linguistically awkward to make it sound like a single political actor, as this term does. However, Marxists like to speak of the relative autonomy of the state rather than that of the government, because the latter term is most frequently used to refer just to the executive, and Marxists contend that the legislative and judicial branches of the state apparatus are just as affected as the executive branch is by a concern to protect the capitalist system. They believe that what can be said about the way that the executive leaders exercise political power can also be said about the way that parliamentarians, senior bureaucrats, local councillors, police officers and judges carry out their functions. And what can be said, it has to be emphasized, is not so much that these people are relatively autonomous with regard to the capitalist class in their work, with which most non-Marxists would immediately agree, but that their autonomy is only relative, meaning that it is only partial.

Of the modern writers mentioned, Miliband is the clearest and Poulantzas the most sectarian. In the third of the latter's three books on the subject, he declares that the state 'represents and organizes the long-term political interests of a power bloc, which is composed of several bourgeois class fractions' and that 'the state maintains its relative autonomy of particular fractions of the power bloc . . . so that it may ensure the organization of the general interest of the bourgeoisie' (Poulantzas 1980: 127, 128).

The implication of these sentences is that Poulantzas does not regard political leaders and public officials as partially independent of bourgeois class interests, as the label given to the theory might lead readers to suppose. On the contrary, he regards them as consciously committed to the promotion of these interests, with their relative autonomy with respect to parts of the bloc serving only tactical purposes. This seems to be a more extreme position than the one suggested by the later writings of Marx and Engels, which was that in the last resort economic interests would usually prevail. Poulantzas' position in most of his writings is that state institutions are essentially instruments of the capitalist class. This view, held by a number of European Marxist writers, has been labelled the instrumentalist theory by Cox, Furlong and Page, to whose work I am indebted in this section (see Cox et al. 1985: Chapter 3).

An alternative and more sophisticated interpretation of Marxism holds that the government has a real degree of day-to-day independence from the capitalist class, but is never likely to transform the capitalist system because the latter is protected by an ideological and cultural hegemony. The concept of ideological hegemony derives, in the first place, from *The German Ideology*, where Marx and Engels asserted that:

> The ideas of the ruling class are in every epoch the ruling ideas, i.e. the class which is the ruling *material* force of society is at the same time its ruling *intellectual* force. The class which has the means of material production at its disposal has control at the same time over the means of mental production ... The ruling ideas are nothing more than the ideal expression of the dominant material relationships ... relationships grasped as ideas.

> (Marx and Engels 1970: 64)

This basic idea was developed in the 1930s by Antonio Gramsci, who coined the term 'cultural hegemony' and suggested that the consent of non-bourgeois classes to the capitalist system is mobilized by 'distorting beliefs, values, common-sense assumptions and popular culture' (Cox et al. 1985: 67). This persuasive and indoctrinating function is carried on not so much by the government as by the political parties, schools and mass media. The indoctrination, it is said, leads to the widespread acceptance of bourgeois values within society, in consequence of which the successful parties of the left are apt to be moderate in outlook, anxious to reform the system but not to transform it into a socialist system. They may indeed be able to use state power to pursue policies hostile to the interests of the capitalist class, but such reforming policies would be limited in scope.

In the twentieth century a number of capitalist societies have experienced government by social democratic parties that have introduced comprehensive schemes of social welfare, which are to some extent an economic burden on industry, and have also embarked on policies of state intervention in industrial affairs. Modern Marxists and neo-Marxists deal with the first of these matters by saying that social welfare policies have the effect not of challenging the capitalist system but of strengthening it, by increasing the legitimacy of the state and the whole social order in the eyes of those who have done poorly and suffered insecurity within the economic system. This view has been discussed in Chapter 6, along with the associated view that in the long run the burden of public expenditure on social services may, particularly in times of recession, create a fiscal crisis for the state.

The questions posed by policies of state intervention in industry have been discussed by Miliband. He argues that 'the *limits* of intervention, at best in relation to business, and particularly *against* it, are everywhere much more narrow and specific than insistence on the formal powers of government would tend to suggest' (Miliband 1969: 148). Business has the ability to withhold cooperation with government policies in ways that can be awkward. This ability

> is not such as to prevent *any* kind of economic policy of which business disapproves. The veto power of business, in other words, is not absolute. But it is very large, and certainly larger than that of any other interest in capitalist society.

> (Miliband 1969: 149)

In the face of these difficulties, social democratic governments have tended to forgo radical policies, and to reduce 'their own ambitions to the point where these have ceased to hold any kind of threat to conservative forces' (Miliband 1969: 101).

It should now be clear that the concept of the relative autonomy of the state is a fairly elastic concept that covers several distinguishable views about the precise relationship between the capitalist class and the institutions of government. The point has been made by Eric Nordlinger (1981) and it will now be helpful to summarize three different approaches that have been adopted by Marxist writers. The first of these is the instrumentalist view that the capitalist class not only has a collective interest but also behaves as a political actor in the sense that it is able to instruct or induce politicians, bureaucrats, judges and the like to act as servants of this interest and therefore as agents of the class. This is, of course, a somewhat simplistic way of expressing the matter, and Poulantzas has produced three volumes of tangled prose to express it in ways more challenging to the intellectual reader. However, I believe that I have summarized the essence of the argument, and I will say no more about it except that I think it is too crude to be a useful guide to the complexities of modern politics.

A view that is slightly more flexible, in that it allows more independence of action to politicians and officials, is the view that the governments of capitalist societies will invariably protect the interests of the capitalist system because leading politicians and public officials are themselves drawn invariably from bourgeois families and have invariably had bourgeois upbringings. However, empirical evidence provides only shaky support for this theory. In most capitalist societies, for instance, police officers are drawn mainly from the ranks of the working class, or the lower income groups in North America, but this does not make them noticeably more reluctant to uphold bourgeois values or the laws of private property than senior civil servants, who are usually drawn from middle-class families. At the same time, many radical socialists in western societies have been drawn from the ranks of middle-class families, as were Marx and Engels themselves, while some leaders of conservative parties have come from relatively humble origins, obvious examples being Reagan in the United States and Heath, Thatcher and Major in Britain. The correlation between class origins and subsequent political views is far from complete.

Defenders of this version of relative autonomy theory are apt to say that the police are socialized into bourgeois values by their training and successful politicians socialized in the same way by their experiences in climbing the political ladder. This may be true, but it turns the theory into a mere tautology. If all people who acquire influential positions in the government machine are said, by definition, to have been socialized into bourgeois values, it follows that there is no way of testing the proposition that the class origins of such people determine their behaviour when in positions of authority.

A third and more flexible view still is that politicians and senior officials are independent actors rather than agents of a class or prisoners of their own upbringing, but are constrained in their choice of policies by the hegemony of bourgeois values in society and the perceived need to maintain the economy, which is a capitalist economy, in a healthy and productive condition. In defending himself in 1970 against one of Poulantzas' criticisms, Miliband said this:

> I repeatedly note how government and bureaucracy, irrespective of social origin, class situation and even ideological dispositions, are subject to the structural constraints of the system. Even so, I should perhaps have stressed this aspect of the matter more.
>
> (Miliband 1983: 31)

Miliband goes on to note that recognition of the importance of these structural constraints on governmental decision making should not lead the analyst into the mistake of 'structural super-determinism', in which the determinist view that government leaders are necessarily agents of the capitalist class is simply replaced by the determinist view that they are compelled to protect bourgeois interests by the requirements of the economic system. To adopt this kind of determinism, he argues, would lead the critic to underestimate, or even to deny, the differences between conservative, social democratic and fascist governments (Miliband 1983: 32–3).

This third version of the relative autonomy theory, most clearly expressed in Miliband's various books, is directly descended from Gramsci's ideas. In his *Prison Notebooks*, Gramsci described the life of the state as 'a continuous process of formation and superseding of unstable equilibria . . . between the interests of the fundamental group and those of the subordinate groups – equilibria in which the interests of the dominant group prevail, but only up to a certain point' (quoted Simon 1982: 31). It is in line with this that Miliband makes the following assertion in the opening paragraphs of his book on British democracy:

> Democratic institutions and practices provide means of expression and representation to the working class, organized labour, political parties and groups, and other such forms of pressure and challenge from below; but the context provided by capitalism requires that the effect they may have should as far as possible be weakened.
>
> (Miliband 1984: 1)

The left-wing Labour politician Tony Benn takes a somewhat similar position, from his different perspective as a former Member of Parliament (and for some years a Cabinet minister) rather than an academic political theorist. His assessment of British politics between 1945 and 1987 includes the following statement:

> The history of the last forty years has been the story of one long attempt, by all parties, to save British capitalism, by the use of different policies each of which carried at the time a wide measure of public support. Of course the 'monetarist consensus' has been much the harshest, but when it emerged the crisis of British capitalism had become much more serious, and, if it was to survive, such measures were necessary.
>
> (Benn 1987: 304)

To a non-Marxist (like me), these assertions by Miliband and Benn seem to be perfectly reasonable and helpful comments on the situation that has obtained in Britain since 1945. The question that they raise, however, is whether it would make any real difference if the words 'British capitalism' in the Benn quotation were replaced by the words 'the British economy'. With one or two small textual changes, would the message of this third version of the relative autonomy thesis be the same if references to the perceived need to keep business interests reasonably happy, or to protect the capitalist system, were replaced by references to the perceived need to protect the competitive position of the country in the world economy or to ensure a continuation of economic growth? If, as I suggest, these changes would make no real difference except to make the message more explicit, the conclusion may be drawn that modern neo-Marxist writers like Miliband have provided a very helpful insight into the economic constraints that policy makers of any party would face if in charge of the government of an advanced industrial society dependent on the export trade to maintain its standard of living.

Who benefits from a healthy economy is of course another question. It may not be a decisive question, because the fact of benefiting from a policy or situation is logically distinct from the fact of causing that policy or situation. As Nelson Polsby noted, the fact that taxi drivers benefit from rainstorms does not mean that they cause the rainstorms. However, the question of who benefits is clearly relevant, even if not decisive.

Marxists would say that the capitalist class benefits much more than anyone else, while liberals would say that almost everyone in society benefits. Marxists would say that economic growth keeps the capitalist system and therefore the capitalist class in business, so that the constant pressure for growth can be regarded as an example of class dominance. Liberals would say that economic growth is wanted by most electors, is needed to alleviate various social problems and is in the general interest, so that the promotion of growth (and even more certainly the prevention of economic decline) is a national objective that has little or nothing to do with the alleged dominance of a class. This is a matter of evaluation that is beyond the scope of the present book, but it seems clear that the Marxist discussions mentioned in this section have raised questions about the scope of the power enjoyed by government leaders that should be considered by all political scientists, however great or small their sympathies may be with Marxist objectives.

Having said this, it should also be said that recognizing the importance of practical constraints on governmental decision making does not necessarily involve acceptance of the Marxist claim that democracy is a sham. This would be the case only if it could be shown that the majority of voters within a democratic system wanted radical changes of policy that were frustrated by the constraints of the economic system. There is no evidence that this has been true of any established democratic system in a western industrial society. To be sure, a majority of voters have sometimes demonstrated support for trade-union values, featuring job security rather than market competition, but in these situations trade-union values have usually been embodied in new legislation or changes in the way the existing laws are administered.

When the British Labour Party won power in 1945, for instance, its leaders proceeded to pass the Catering Wages Act and the legislation establishing the National Dock Labour Scheme. The Catering Wages Act reduced profit margins in the hotel and restaurant industry, and has not been repealed by subsequent Conservative governments. The Dock Labour Scheme ensured that all registered dockers who turned up for work would be paid a wage equal to the national average wage for industrial workers, whether or not there was any work for them to do. This scheme made British ports more expensive to operate than other European ports and contributed to the running down of the two largest ports of London and Liverpool. It involved some economic loss to the country for the sake of security for the dockers, and was not wound down until 1989.

British Labour governments also passed laws providing workers with the right to appeal against unfair dismissal and forcing employers to make redundancy payments, related to length of service, to workers who are laid off. These and similar examples suggest that it would be wrong to describe British democracy as a sham. Labour election victories have clearly resulted in legislative changes helpful to workers but harmful to the interests of business. It is true that these victories have not resulted in radical socialist policies, but opinion polls have repeatedly shown that there would have been no majority for such policies, and democracy is about following the wishes of the majority.

IN CONCLUSION

The Marxist and neo-Marxist challenge to democratic theory is much more substantial than the challenge offered by the four writers reviewed in the earlier sections of this chapter. It is certainly true that there is no example of the democratic process producing a government which seriously attempts to transform the capitalist system into a socialist system. The question is how to interpret this. If it is said that the state machine is inevitably a tool of the capitalist class this would be an anti-democratic argument, but one that goes beyond the evidence. If it is merely said that the perceived need to maintain economic growth places serious constraints on government policy this would be true, but not an anti-democratic argument unless it could be shown that the majority of electors are not interested in economic growth. Since all available evidence indicates that most electors give economic growth a rather high priority, Marxists have to fall back on the proposition that this preference is a form of 'false consciousness', contrary to the real interests of the workers and only held because people living in capitalist societies are brainwashed into accepting bourgeois values. Unfortunately, this proposition cannot be established by empirical evidence; it is a matter of faith for committed Marxists but is viewed with deep scepticism by everyone else. Because of this, Marxists and liberals cannot be expected to reach agreement on the issues raised in this chapter; the gap between them can be narrowed, as it has been by Miliband's work, but in the last resort a gap is bound to remain.

Chapter 15

Corporatism

DEFINITION AND HISTORY

Corporatism (not mentioned in the *OED*) may be loosely defined as a system in which national organizations representing industry and labour work in cooperation with government representatives to constitute an intermediate layer of interest aggregation and decision making between the state and civil society; and as a doctrine advocating this kind of system. The advocacy and practice of corporatism have gone through three distinct phases. The doctrine emerged in nineteenth-century Europe, largely as a branch of Catholic social doctrine; it was adapted and modified in the authoritarian regimes of Mussolini's Italy (1922–43) and Salazar's Portugal (1933–74); and in a somewhat different form it has re-emerged in the institutions of several European democracies in the post-war period under the ascribed title of neo-corporatism.

In the first half of the nineteenth century several European theorists reacted to the growth of industrial society by advocating some form of functional representation to take the place of, or to be alongside, representation by geographical area and social status (see Landauer 1983: 9–18). Nothing came of these ideas, but in the last three decades of the century the Roman Catholic Church and several Catholic writers took them up. The Catholic position in that period was that the Church approved of private property and the capitalist system, but disapproved of competitive individualism on the one hand and the Marxist idea of class conflict on the other. In a well-ordered society, it was thought, individual greed should be curbed, the authorities should ensure a fair distribution of income, and the various occupational groups should feel themselves to be part of an organic whole, linked by feelings of social responsibility, rather than divided into warring classes.

In 1891 Pope Leo XIII issued an encyclical making clear that corporatism would be 'a Christian system and a possible solution for the agitation caused by the struggle between capital and labour' (Azpiazu 1951: 77). In 1931 Pope Pius XI issued an encyclical which followed the same line.

In 1951 Azpiazu, a Jesuit scholar, declared that 'individualistic liberalism is bankrupt', because it 'ignores entirely the social character of human works and acts', considering only personal profit (Azpiazu 1951: 45). Socialism is no better, because it promotes class warfare and has as its object 'the proletarianation of all'. The answer to both these doctrines is Christian solidarity (see Azpiazu 1951: 46–7), and this kind of solidarity would best be promoted by what the author called 'the corporative state'.

There is no space to mention several other theorists who took a similar line, but it should be noted that in France the Syndicalist movement (flourishing from about 1900 to 1914) and in Britain the guild socialist movement (flourishing from about 1912 to 1922) advocated functional representation of industry from a socialist viewpoint. In addition to the Catholic theorists, there were people on both the right and the left of the political spectrum who felt that the problems of regulating industry were too difficult to be left to a non-specialized Parliament that was also dealing with foreign policy, defence and a host of other problems.

The second phase of corporatism began in 1925, when Mussolini introduced the institutions of 'the corporate state' in Italy. Corporations were established for each major industry representing employers and (in theory) employees, and they were given substantial powers to run their industries, with guidance from the government and the fascist party. However, free trade unions were abolished and strikes were made illegal. In 1933 the Portuguese dictator, Dr Salazar (a professional economist) established institutions that were substantially similar, and this takeover of the idea of corporatism by right-wing dictators gave the doctrine a very bad name, so much so that political theorists ceased to advocate it. What has happened in the post-war period has been the growth of neo-corporatist arrangements promoted in a pragmatic way by politicians, administrators, business directors and trade unionists, without much input from political theorists.

NEO-CORPORATISM

The re-emergence of theoretical interest in corporatism and the adoption of the term neo-corporatism owes a great deal to the work of Philippe Schmitter and Gerhard Lehmbruch, two students of comparative government. In influential articles from 1974 onwards, they have drawn attention to the fact that corporatist arrangements by no means died with the end of the Italian and Portuguese dictatorships, but are alive and well in a number of liberal democracies, including Sweden, Norway, Denmark, the Netherlands, Austria and Switzerland.

The essential elements of a modern neo-corporatist system are the existence of 'peak associations' of trade unions and organizations representing business, which have effective influence over the behaviour of their member associations and work in conjunction with representatives of the national government. The three constituent elements then work together to produce strategies for industrial investment and incomes policy which both sides of industry agree to implement. In exchange for this kind of influence over economic policy, trade unions are expected to curb the demands that individual members and branches may make for wage increases in excess of the agreed norm for the period of the plan.

The actual details vary slightly between countries. The government may or may not offer subsidies to the peak associations or their members. It will generally discriminate between trade associations and unions in the degree of consultation it makes available, obviously offering more consultation to those associations and unions that agree to be bound by the tripartite planning system than to others. It may license associations and unions that conform to certain conditions. It will expect leaders of trade associations and unions involved in tripartite agreements to refrain from public criticism of the government's economic and industrial policies. In turn it will exercise party discipline to ensure that the tripartite plans are supported by Parliament and by parliamentary committees.

It is important to note that these arrangements do not always work with perfect smoothness. Indidivual trade unions and business firms may not always conform to the plans reached. Leo Panitch has pointed out that in Sweden, which has had a tripartite system of this kind since the late 1940s, individual union branches have staged unofficial strikes (Panitch 1979: 141). In 1980 the system broke down altogether for a time, as the unions organized a general strike.

It is also important to note that some countries have arrangements that have similarities to the model but do not conform to it completely. Germany, for instance, has a long-established system whereby industrial planning of the type mentioned is carried out by consultation and agreement between the peak associations representing industry and labour and the national banks (which in Germany control a great deal of industrial investment). There are only seventeen trade unions in Germany, each representing all the workers in an industry rather than being divided by trades; they are well disciplined so that unofficial strikes are rare; and the federation to which sixteen of them belong has a great deal of power to control their behaviour. Partly because of this, western Germany achieved high growth rates between the 1950s and the 1990s with relatively low rates of inflation. However, the system is not fully one of neo-corporatism because the government does not play a direct and open role in the system. It is also not immune from breakdown, as on one occasion when the large metal-workers' union, not content with the wage increases proposed, staged a prolonged strike for better terms. In a free society, occasional breakdowns are almost inevitable.

France is another country where two of the parties have cooperated but the third has got only marginal consultations. In the French case the government's planning commissariat has prepared five-year plans for the

country's economic development, after full consultation with representatives of industry but only a little consultation with the union movement.
This is partly because the union movement has been divided between six
federations and partly because the largest of them was for many years dominated by the Communist Party, so that is could not easily be co-opted into a
consensual system of planning. The result has been a high rate of economic
growth, but accompanied by more strikes and a higher rate of inflation than
in Germany. The French system worked smoothly from the late 1940s until
the middle 1970s, when the problems caused by a four-fold increase in the
price of oil led the French government and Parliament to make repeated
revisions to the five-year plans.

Italy is the other country in Europe that has had a divided union movement with the largest association being in communist hands, and there too
the unions have been left out of the consultations that have taken place (in a
rather informal way) between the employers' associations (of which there
are three) and the government. In the first ten years after the war it looked
as if Italy was moving towards a loose kind of neo-corporatism (Spotts and
Wieser 1986: 209), but since then divisions in the business community have
led to a system that is essentially pluralist. Italy has achieved high, though
rather uneven, growth rates, accompanied by a high rate of inflation and the
highest rate of industrial disputes of any advanced industrial society.

Britain is an interesting case of a country that tried to adopt a neo-
corporatist strategy but failed. In 1962 the government established the
National Economic Development Council (NEDC) with representatives of
the Treasury, the Trades Union Congress (TUC) and the Confederation of
British Industry (CBI). However, this body was an almost complete failure.
The TUC could not control its member unions, the CBI had no power over
its member associations, and the Treasury officials were not as knowledge-
able about industry or as confident about planning as their counterparts in
many other European democracies have shown themselves to be. Moreover,
the relationship between unions and management in Britain has always been
essentially adversarial, with little sense of a common interest. With little of
substance achieved, the NEDC was wound down in the 1980s.

In 1974 the Labour government tried a different approach, entering into a
'social contract' with the TUC whereby the unions would get a good deal
of influence over economic and social policy in return for accepting government guidelines on incomes policy. At first there was a period of very high
inflation, reaching 25 per cent a year in 1975; then it seemed as if the social
contract was having some success; but in the last months of 1978 several
large unions revolted and led prolonged strikes against the government's
policy on wages. The business associations were not involved in this process, and the whole story seemed to demonstrate that Britain is essentially
wedded to the pluralist model of political and economic bargaining, and
unsuited to a neo-corporatist strategy.

It should be noted that some writers with social democratic sympathies, notably Andrew Shonfield, Colin Crouch and Peter Self, have argued that a move in the direction of neo-corporatism is a desirable strategy for all advanced industrial societies, and indeed that societies that appear to be pluralist are apt to have corporatist elements somewhere in their systems (see Shonfield 1965; Crouch 1979: 186–96; Self 1985: Chapter 5). Self points out that British governments do not treat all interest groups as equal, but regularly consult some while giving the cold shoulder to others (Self 1985: Chapter 5). In some cases the government established producer groups, such as the Milk Marketing Board and the Potato Marketing Board, while in the cotton industry all firms were required by law for many years to subscribe to the Cotton Board, which the government treated as the sole channel of communication between itself and the industry (see Birch 1964: 203–7). All this is true, and it demonstrates the complexity of modern government, but it would be weakening the utility of the model to regard all these ad hoc arrangements as steps towards neo-corporatism. It is essential to the neo-corporatist model that the peak associations should play leading roles.

ASSESSING MERITS

Schmitter indicates at one point that he and most of his colleagues who study neo-corporatism actually disapprove of it, but he does not explain why (Schmitter and Lehmbruch 1979: 3). As the concept is evidently one around which normative controversies occur, it is relevant to outline what seem to be its merits and disadvantages.

Its chief merit is clearly that it seems conducive to high rates of economic growth. In his elaborate and exhaustive study of the factors that account for differential rates of growth in industrial societies, Mancur Olson found only one common factor that was generally significant. This is that societies with 'encompassing organizations' (i.e. peak organizations) for business and labour interest groups have been more likely to achieve high growth rates than societies without them (Olson 1982). The countries with neo-corporatist systems in Europe mostly achieved higher growth rates in the post-war period than societies with pluralist systems of interest representation. The Scandinavian countries, Switzerland and Germany all achieved high growth rates with controlled inflation. Italy and France had more uneven growth rates with higher inflation. The pluralist societies of Britain, the United States, Canada, Australia and New Zealand all had lower growth rates in the period studied, roughly 1950–80.

The second advantage of neo-corporatist arrangements is that they generally reduce the incidence of strikes. Now, strikes are sometimes discussed as if they were zero-sum games between workers and management. This is too simple a view, for in a wider perspective a strike is a game in which almost everyone loses. Society loses production; the firm loses revenue; its suppliers and customers suffer inconvenience; the workers lose wages; their families suffer hardship; and one result is usually bad feeling or bitterness between people who have to work together. In neo-corporatist systems the unions do not lose the bargaining power that comes from the threat of being able to call a strike, but the actual incidence of strikes is lower. It is noteworthy that the three societies with the highest proportion of working days lost by strike action in the post-war years are the pluralist democracies of Italy, Canada and Britain.

Those who dislike neo-corporatism approach the question from two very different perspectives, one Marxist and the other individualist. To Marxists, it serves as a way of co-opting trade unions into the capitalist system, of holding down wages in the short run, of protecting capitalism from its contradictions in the long run.

To individualists, it seems a rather bureaucratic system that largely by-passes Parliament. It is alleged to favour large trade unions and business associations over small ones. It is thought that neo-corporatist arrangements may work to the disadvantage of small entrepreneurs, of highly specialized and perhaps new enterprises, professions or unions, of breakaway unions, of non-unionized workers, and of non-conformists in general.

There are clearly valid points to be made on both sides of the argument and any assessment of the merits of neo-corporatist arrangements must depend partly on the political values of the commentator, partly on the way that particular national arrangements work in practice.

THE SIGNIFICANCE OF THE CONCEPT

Looked at one way, corporatism is a rather unsatisfactory concept. No political theorists have made it their task to produce a convincing set of arguments for corporatism which might become the basis of a corporatist ideology. There are no corporate parties or corporatist movements. It seems to be little more than a label. Even as a label, it has a rather fuzzy outline rather than a clear definition. There have been corporatist states that were authoritarian and are now universally regarded with contempt. There have been some unstable authoritarian regimes in South America with arrangements that might qualify as corporatist. There are neo-corporatist institutions in several western European democracies, but they vary in detail. There is also a case of semi-neo-corporatism in Germany and one of temporary unsuccessful neo-corporatism in Britain. It all seems unsatisfactory to anyone with a tidy mind.

However, looked at another way, neo-corporatism is a significant and helpful concept, because it draws attention to the fact that there are a number of democratic states in which the distribution of political influence cannot fairly be described as either elitist or pluralist.

Part IV
Styles of political analysis

Chapter 16

Towards a science of politics: positivism, behaviouralism and economic models

MAINSTREAM POLITICAL SCIENCE

Learned discussions about politics have been a part of the intellectual tradition of the western world from the time of Greek city-states until the present day. Until the 1870s, most of these discussions were speculative and philosophical, but there were also some intermittent attempts to do what we now call comparative government, most notably in Aristotle's *Politics*, Machiavelli's *Discourses* and Montesquieu's *The Spirit of the Laws*. There were also some thoughtful attempts to bring general reflections about politics to bear upon pressing practical problems, most notably in the writings and speeches of the people who conceived and founded the American republic. However, political science did not emerge as a distinct academic discipline until the 1870s.

In that decade, courses in political science were introduced, more or less simultaneously, in the three universities of Oxford, Paris and Columbia. Significant contributions to scholarship were then made on both sides of the Atlantic, but the United States far outstripped Britain and France in making the subject a standard discipline throughout the country. By the 1920s it was on the syllabus in over a hundred American universities, but still largely confined in Britain to Oxford, London and Cambridge and in France to Paris. The American discipline acquired its professional association at the beginning of the century and the *American Political Science Review* began publication in 1906, whereas the equivalent developments in Britain and France did not take place until 1951.

In terms of scope and method, the discipline did not change very much between the late 1870s and the early 1950s. As W. J. M. Mackenzie pointed out in his UNESCO report, it revolved almost entirely around the affairs of the state, defined as the institution (or set of institutions) which 'claimed juridical and political supremacy' (Mackenzie 1971: 16). It dealt hardly at all with the politics of private associations. The discipline in this whole long period fell naturally into three sub-disciplines. The first of these (first because it had been studied by historians and philosophers before political scientists took it up) may be called the theory of the state, consisting of the study of the philosophical justifications of state authority and the related problems of defining the nature and role of liberty, justice, political equality and political participation within the state. The texts run from Plato to the English Idealists of the 1880s, with little of equivalent scope and value being published since the 1880s to modify the character of this branch of study.

The second sub-discipline is the study of the government of modern states, being primarily studies of particular state systems but also including attempts to generalize about the similarities and differences between states. The third sub-discipline is the study of relations between states, beginning as diplomatic history in the immediate aftermath of the First World War and developing into a more systematic and generalized study of the international state system. Study in these three fields, which may be said to constitute mainstream political science (and will be described in that way in what follows), has continued with improvements but without essential changes and may be expected to continue into the indefinite future. It has a focus that is primarily on institutions rather than on individuals; its method of study is largely historical; and normative judgements form an inseparable part of the subject. That governments should be consistent, efficient, responsible, representative and respectful of citizens' liberties are values that are built in to most mainstream analyses.

Some idea of the degree of continuity in mainstream political science may be conveyed by considering the longevity of textbooks. Take, for instance, the work of two brilliant scholars who happened to be friends, namely James Bryce of Oxford and A. L. Lowell of Harvard. In 1888 Bryce produced his very substantial text on American government under the title of *The American Commonwealth*. In 1933 an abridged edition of this great work was published for use in American colleges and schools, while in 1939 a new edition of the complete book was published to celebrate the fiftieth anniversary of the original publication. In 1908 Lowell reciprocated by producing *The Government of England*, which remained in print through the 1920s.

In the field of comparative government Lowell led the way in 1896 with *Governments and Parties in Continental Europe*, while Bryce responded in 1921 with *Modern Democracies*. This vast work, published in two volumes, contained fifteen introductory chapters on democratic principles followed by long sections on the political systems of France, Switzerland, Canada, the United States, Australia and New Zealand, followed by twenty-three chapters, comparative in nature, which summed up the conclusions that could be drawn from the study. In the post-war period a notable example of longevity is Merle Fainsod's *How Russia is Ruled*, first published in 1953, reissued in 1979 under the revised title *How the Soviet Union is Governed*, and remaining an invaluable text until the dramatic events of 1989–91 rendered it out of date.

Over a period of slightly more than a century, mainstream political science has accumulated more data, become more refined in its forms of analysis, but maintained its essential character. This character is of a discipline based upon historical study with an institutional focus, side-by-side comparative analyses, and built-in normative judgements, with no attempt to emulate the natural sciences. However, the 1950s saw the introduction of new methods intended to produce a genuinely scientific study of politics, and it is to this development that the remainder of this chapter is devoted. The development was anticipated in the writings of the scholars at the University of Chicago in the late 1930s, notably Charles Merriam and E. M. Sait, who argued persuasively that the discipline ought to become scientific. In Sait's words, the aim should be 'to turn the study of politics into a branch of positive science'. The use of the term 'positive' had the function of indicating that the author had in mind not the loose interpretation of science whereby any systematic accumulation of knowledge can be described as a scientific activity, but the more specialized interpretation whereby a subject can be termed scientific only if it is based upon methods similar to those of the natural sciences. The concept of 'positivism' has this meaning, and its history and character deserve a word of explanation before we turn to the political science research that has, to some degree, emulated natural science methods.

THE CONCEPT OF POSITIVISM

While the term 'positivism' was introduced and popularized by the French philosopher Auguste Comte in the late 1830s and explained in his *Course of Positive Philosophy*, published in 1840–2, the positivist attitude towards human understanding was a product of the European Enlightenment of the eighteenth century. It may be described as a combination of French rationalism and British empiricism. The spirit of positivism is essentially the spirit of the Enlightenment, and can be summarized as rational, secular, scientific, optimistic, progressive, liberal and associated with the belief in the inevitability of progress that developed in the eighteenth century and characterized much European thought until it was shattered by the events of 1914.

The writer who probably has the best claim to be described as the father of positivism is the Scottish philosopher, David Hume, writing between 1739 and the 1760s, an agnostic who has been described as a philosopher of common sense and experience. Things are what they are, according to Hume, that is what they seem to be by direct experience, not a manifestation of something that cannot be observed or experienced. Thunder is a noise in the sky, not a sign of the displeasure of the gods. Law is what the courts enforce, not an expression of natural law or natural rights. Human beings have appetites, passions and desires, but not souls. They have minds also, but their reason 'is the slave of the passions and can never pretend to any other office than to serve and obey them'. Historical events are events, not the unfolding of divine will or what Hegel was later to call 'the world-historical spirit'. Hume's was a basic kind of philosophy, designed to puncture a good deal of metaphysical speculation.

The next fifty years saw the foundation of economic science by Hume's fellow-Scot, Adam Smith, and the development of Utilitarianism in France by Helvetius and Condorcet, in England by Bentham. In his *Principles of Morals and Legislation*, published in 1789, Bentham stated that 'observation and experiment' are 'the sources of all real knowledge' and that the way to advance understanding was to 'take a number of . . . particular propositions; find some points in which they agree, and from the observation of these points form a more extensive one, a general one, in which they are all included' (quoted Manning 1968: 11).

It follows that Comte was not being particularly original when he announced in 1840 that this method should be the basis of all knowledge, but it was he who called it positivism and as he was also the first advocate of a discipline to be called 'sociology' he has his place in intellectual history as the first theorist to propose that the proper method for the study of society and politics was the method that we normally associate with the natural sciences. There are, declared Comte, three stages in the development of the human understanding. The first is theological; the second, almost equally useless, is metaphysical; the third and final is the positive stage. In the positive stage:

> the mind has given over the vain search after Absolute notions, the origin and destination of the universe, and the causes of phenomena, and applies itself to the study of their laws – that is, their invariable relations of succession and resemblance. . . . What is now understood when we speak of an explanation of facts is simply the establishment of a connection between single phenomena and some general facts, the number of which continually diminishes with the progress of science.
>
> (extract printed in Aiken 1956: 125)

In saying this, and in going on to say that social investigation must follow in the methodological footsteps of astronomy, physics, chemistry and physiology, Comte was the first to suggest that the language of variance (to use Mackenzie's term) was the most appropriate for the study of sociological phenomena, including politics. Events should be observed, compared, correlated, and reduced to examples of a limited number of law-like generalizations, presumably of universal validity. Moreover, as he indicates in the last few words quoted, the progress of understanding would reduce the number of generalizations needed for explanation, as simpler laws of wider applicability were constantly formulated. In saying this, Comte pointed to one of the basic differences between scientific explanation and modern concepts of historical explanation, as articulated most clearly by Michael Oakeshott; that progress in science is towards simpler and simpler generalizations whereas progress in historical understanding involves the uncovering and reconstruction of more and more complexities and details. Comte did not say this himself, of course, because he believed that human history could be subsumed under the umbrella of social studies and explained scientifically. There are a few modern philosophers of history who go along with Comte in this, for example Carl Hempel, but they are in a distinct minority and have had little influence on the actual conduct of historical scholarship. The methods of most historians conform to Oakeshott's account of them (see Oakeshott 1933).

While the positivist ideal has had little impact on the academic discipline of history, it has had a very considerable impact on both sociology and political science. In sociology it has been a dominant influence; an inspection of university calendars will reveal that courses in sociology departments are mostly based on the assumption of general regularities and laws. There are courses on the sociology of the family, the sociology of religion, the structure of industrial society, and so forth, rather than courses on religion in the United States, the family in modern Britain, and the like. In political science the influence has been more restricted. There are many mainstream courses on the American political system, British political parties, western European governments and so forth, while alongside them there are a smaller number of courses that Comte would have approved of, such as political propaganda, the psychology of political leadership, and bureaucracy in the modern state.

If we ask how far the study of politics has been turned into a scientific activity, gathering data to form general laws with predictive value, we are faced with three different answers. At the level of grand theory, there has been only one attempt to form an over-arching theory of political development, namely the work of Marx and Engels in the period of what may be called their early maturity, when they elaborated the theory known as dialectical materialism. At the ground level, there has been the use of quantitative methods of political research, beginning in the 1950s and continuing to this day, yielding low-level generalizations such as those about voting behaviour in particular countries. At the intermediate level, several models and partial theories have been formulated, notably those based upon the assumption that political actors are rational beings attempting to maximize their interests while minimizing their costs. Beyond these, there has been an ambitious attempt to construct a conceptual framework known as systems theory, intended to replace institutional analysis in the study of government. Each of these theories and developments will be outlined briefly in what follows, together with the philosophical movement known as logical positivism that flourished in the middle decades of the twentieth century.

DIALECTICAL MATERIALISM AS THE FIRST SCIENCE OF POLITICS

Dialectical materialism is a label, coined by Soviet scholars and copied by others, to indicate the philosophical character of Marx's main theory about historical development since the Middle Ages. It is used here in preference to Marxism, because Marxism is a house with several rooms. The Marxism of Marx's early writings consists of the loosely formulated views of a romantic idealist, a utopian socialist with a somewhat anarchistic vision of the future. Then followed a period of just over twenty years, from Marx's first collaborative work with Engels in 1845 to the publication of the first volume of *Capital* in 1867, when Marx and Engels produced and elaborated the theory that set out law-like generalizations about economic and political development. Marx's later years, until he died in 1883, were years in which he kept adding refinements and qualifications to his doctrine in the light of further study and further events, particularly the political upheavals in France. And in the long period since his death his various followers have added to the whole corpus of Marxist theory in significant but not entirely consistent ways, with the tendency of many scholars since the 1960s being to play down the importance of dialectical materialism and to revert to the idealism of Marx's early years.

It is not my task to assess these developments, but in the context of this chapter it is fair to say that dialectical materialism is the version of Marxism for which predictive value, and thus scientific status, was and can be claimed.

Its character has been so thoroughly explained in scores of books that the briefest sketch will suffice in this chapter. The argument is that the driving force of historical development in all societies is economic. The pattern of production in any period determines the relations between classes, which are themselves defined in terms of their relationship to the system of production, and the relations between classes determine the distribution and structure of social and political power. In agricultural societies the land owners were inevitably the wealthiest class and their economic position enabled them to dominate the other classes, not only economically but also socially and politically. As industrial production grows in scale and comes gradually to exceed agriculture in its contribution to the national economy, so the new class of industrial entrepreneurs – the capitalist class – comes to grow in wealth and influence. There is a transitional period during which the land owners still control the main levers of political power even though their economic power is slipping away, but there inevitably comes a time when the pressures of the capitalist class burst the chains of a land-owner-dominated regime and lead to the seizure of political power by the capitalists and their agents. This process was described by Marx and Engels as the bourgeois revolution.

Most of their examples were drawn from the history of England, because England was economically more advanced than any other country at the time they were studying and writing. In England the industrial developments of the last forty years of the eighteenth century, which were themselves the consequence of significant technological developments such as Watt's construction of the world's first steam engine in 1776, led to a transitional period in the first thirty years of the nineteenth century when the new bourgeoisie had acquired a measure of economic dominance but Parliament and the Cabinet were still dominated by land owners and their agents. This changed with the great parliamentary Reform Act of 1832, which gave bourgeois interests a controlling role in the political system and led to a series of reforms designed to help the development of industry and trade.

The Poor Law Amendment Act of 1834 abolished the age-old system whereby parishes had looked after their poor, thus releasing a flood of unemployed people who were forced to leave their villages to find work in the growing industrial areas. The introduction of limited liability enabled investors to shield their personal and family possessions from the consequences of industrial bankruptcy. The repeal of the corn laws in 1846 abolished protection for British agriculture and enabled cheap food to be imported for the industrial workforce. The opening of the higher ranks of the public service to entry by competitive examination ended the system whereby the land-owning classes had been able to put their younger sons into comfortable positions in the bureaucracy. One by one, reforms were passed that turned Britain into a land dominated by capitalists and capitalist interests.

How would this be changed? It would be changed because the system contained within itself the seeds of its own destruction. New methods of large-scale factory production were congregating large numbers of exploited workers into situations in which they would combine for their defence. Industrial competition would force capitalists to hold down wages, so that the workers would see themselves getting poorer. The trade cycle would produce large-scale unemployment. The more enlightened of the workers would educate their brethren in the need for revolt against the system. An understanding of the laws of historical development – that is, an understanding of Marxism – would enable the organized workers to recognize a revolutionary situation when mass unemployment or warfare produced a crisis, and to seize power from the capitalists and the capitalist state. The revolutionary workers would then institute a limited period of proletarian dictatorship to reorganize the economic system, which would usher in a period of socialism based upon the common ownership of the means of production, distribution and exchange. The state would then wither away, in its coercive forms, and the government of persons would be replaced by the administration of things.

Now, this programme was presented by Marx and Engels as inevitable. They had lived through the bourgeois revolution, they had understood the dynamic of history, and they predicted that – though not exactly when – the system would be transformed by the proletarian revolution. Britain was leading the way, but the British example would be followed by other countries as they too became industrialized. In the Preface to the German edition of *Capital*, Marx said plainly that the path followed by Britain would inevitably be followed by Germany also, only a little later. The British developments 'must re-enact on the continent':

> 'Intrinsically', declared Marx, 'it is not a question of the higher or lower degree of development of the social antagonisms that result from the natural laws of capitalist production. It is a question of these laws themselves, of these tendencies working with iron necessity towards inevitable results. The country that is more developed industrially only shows, to the less developed, the image of its own future'.
>
> (Tucker 1978: 296)

Now, this is without question a deterministic view of historical development. Marx wrote repeatedly of the *natural laws* of development, of the *necessary* relationships between economic and political power, of the *inevitability* of historical change on the lines he mapped out. In this period of his life Marx was a positivist. In his later years he qualified his predictions with various refinements and words of caution. In intellectual terms this is interesting, but in practical terms it made little difference. It was the positivist theory, the grand design, that inspired generations of communists in numerous countries, imbued with the confidence that they understood the dynamics of social development and would be ready to strike a revolutionary blow when the time was ripe.

As a theory, it had much of the character of a theory in those natural sciences, like astronomy, in which no experiments under controlled conditions can be carried out. Careful study of economic and political events that had taken place led to conclusions about their interrelationships and the construction of a model, on the basis of which predictions were made about future social and political developments. The weakness of the theory is that most of the predictions have been falsified by subsequent events. Large-scale unions of industrial workers were certainly formed, but instead of attempting to overthrow the capitalist system they bargained for increased wages and better working conditions within the system. Their bargaining was largely successful, with the result that the living standards of workers improved and the prediction of progressive impoverishment was invalidated. Not one of the advanced industrialized societies has produced a communist revolution. When revolutions took place, they did so in Russia, which was only in the early stages of industrialization, and in the largely agricultural societies of Yugoslavia, Albania, China and Cuba. As a scientific and therefore predictive theory, dialectical materialism has been proved to be a failure.

Nobody since Marx and Engels has attempted to construct a science of politics on such a grand scale.

THE BEHAVIOURAL MOVEMENT

The next attempt to introduce scientific methods into the study of politics started in a very different fashion, using statistical data about individual behaviour as the building blocks of theory instead of the historical experiences of national societies. The object of the behaviouralists has been to frame testable hypotheses about political behaviour on the basis of these data, which if validated by further empirical research could be turned into law-like generalizations which would have the status of empirical theories unless and until they were invalidated by later studies. This is the method of the natural sciences, as explained most clearly by Karl Popper in *The Logic of Scientific Discovery* (Popper 1959) and subsequent books.

The particular trigger that set the behavioural movement going was the introduction of sample surveys and their application to voting behaviour. The technique of the sample survey was developed by social psychologists, not by political scientists, and was first used in political research by three sociologists who organized a survey of voting behaviour in the presidential election of 1940 in a small town in upstate New York (see Lazarsfeld et al. 1944). The study was copied in another area in 1944 and has been repeated, in an increasingly elaborate form, in every presidential election since that date. Similar studies were made of voting in the British general election of 1950 (see Birch and Campbell 1950; Milne and Mackenzie 1954; Benney et al. 1956); these also have been replicated, with larger and then national samples and more complex questionnaires, in every succeeding British general election. (For national surveys, see Butler and Stokes 1969; Sarlvic and Crewe 1983.)

The first object of these studies was to correlate voting behaviour with demographic variables such as the age, sex and occupation of the voters; the second was to analyse the behaviour of the floating voters and to explore their reasons for changing their vote; the third was to uncover the opinions of electors on a range of policy issues and to study the relationship between opinions and behaviour. Studies of this kind were followed by a content analysis of newspaper coverage of the elections (see Birch et al. 1956) and by studies of the impact of televised political propaganda on political knowledge, political opinions and voting behaviour (see Blumler and McQuail 1968).

The consequence of this type of research, which has been carried out in most western societies, is that we know much more about elections than it was possible to know before sample surveys were used. Historians who have written about earlier elections have produced informed judgements about why this party lost ground and that leader won widespread support, but they do not actually know why those developments took place, so their judgements are always liable to be contradicted by other historians. In respect of contemporary elections, we do actually know why electors behaved as they did. However, these empirical studies are scientific in the sense that they use precise quantitative methods rather than in the sense that they have yielded predictive generalizations that have changed our understanding of the electoral process. Campaign managers have certainly learned something from the studies, and campaigns are more professionally organized than they were in the past, but betting on election results is still a risky business. After the event, scholars can explain why the results went the way that they did. Before the event, there is always an element of guesswork involved in predictions. It can be said that if electors turn against one of the parties in key areas of policy, then that party is likely to lose votes; but this is a generalization that was commonly made before election surveys were introduced.

Following this beginning, quantitative research methods were extended from electoral behaviour to the behaviour of legislators (see MacRae 1958; Wahlke and Eulau 1959; Wahlke et al. 1962; Miller and Stokes 1963); to the behaviour of judges (see Schubert 1959, 1963); to the behaviour of state representatives at meetings of the United Nations; to the formation of Cabinets; to the behaviour of municipal politicians and group spokesmen; and to several other types of political behaviour.

If we ask what kinds of generalization have emerged from all this research, the answer is that we have been given empirical generalizations about particular political systems. From American electoral studies, we have learned about the loosening of party loyalties and the growth of single-issue voting. From British electoral studies, we have learned about the decline of the alignment between class status and voting behaviour. From American studies of the influence of television, we learn that American voters tend to watch only those programmes that favour their party or their preferred policies, and that the effect of the exposure is to reinforce existing views. From similar studies in Britain, we learn that viewers do not discriminate in this fashion and that repeated exposure to any one politician is more likely to increase scepticism about this person than support for him or her. We learn about party loyalty in the British Parliament and its relative weakness in the US Congress. We learn about how many representatives in American state assemblies see themselves as delegates of their constituents and how many, in contrast, see themselves as trustees for the public welfare. We learn about the structure of political influence in American cities, as discussed in earlier chapters. (For useful compendiums of behavioural research articles, see Eulau et al. 1956; Eulau 1966.)

Three things can be said about the empirical data and generalizations produced by this type of research. One is that they have added very greatly to our store of knowledge and understanding about political behaviour and processes in western systems of government, and have produced a number of low-level theories and descriptive generalizations. A second comment is that they involve only a little deviation from the conceptual frameworks used in mainstream political science. The research methods differ, but the general framework remains much the same. The techniques used by Dahl and his colleagues to measure political influence within a community were novel, but their result was a descriptive generalization about one city rather than a scientific law. The proposition that any American city with a plurality of interest groups is likely to enjoy a pluralistic dispersal of political power is not trivial, but it is too tautological to have a status similar to that of propositions in the natural sciences. Other empirical generalizations arising from behavioural studies have thrown extra light upon familiar questions rather than suggesting a new set of questions. The third point is that empirical research has tended to reinforce the assumption of mainstream political scientists that the most important variable in politics is the national variable. American and British television viewers, to take only one example, react in different ways when faced with political propaganda on the screen, and the differences between the two nations appear to be greater than the differences between sexes or classes within each nation. There is little support from these studies for the hope sometimes expressed that more scientific research methods might yield generalizations of more universal validity.

NEW MODELS AND FRAMEWORKS

A very different development of the 1950s and 1960s was the introduction of new models and conceptual frameworks. One of these was games theory, being a mathematical model-making approach to games and tactics in situations of conflict between a limited number of players. Distinctions were drawn between two-person games and multi-person games, for which the mathematics are different; and between zero-sum games, in which one player wins what the others lose, and non-zero-sum games, in which there is either an overall gain or an overall loss. Games theory does not involve any generalizations about politics, it should be stressed. It is based upon certain strict assumptions about the rationality, knowledge and objectives of the players and it tells the scholar how to assess the probable consequences of various possible tactics by the players. If the result of the use of the model (for it is a model rather than a theory) has explanatory value in one situation, this may yield a prediction about what is likely to happen if the situation is exactly repeated, but it would be difficult to point to any general laws of predictive value arising from the application of games theory to domestic politics. In international relations it has been of greater value, leading to various generalizations that are usually grouped under the heading of strategic theory.

Another and rather different model goes under the name of public choice theory. This is a theory about how to assess the efficiency of the systems for providing public services which differs from the traditional methods used in the study of public administration, which adopt institutions as the main units of analysis. Public choice theory starts with the individual citizen, viewed as a consumer of public goods and services rather than as a participant in politics, and regards society as a collection of consumers who are rational and egoistical. Their aim is to increase their individual satisfactions at minimum cost, and the public interest is defined in a Utilitarian manner as the maximization of individual satisfactions.

The unit of analysis favoured by public choice theorists is the 'provision system' for the service being studied, which may include participation by national, regional and local government bodies and also by private suppliers of services. The institutional arrangements are regarded not as given but as variables. It may be that a provision system could be made more efficient, in the sense of increasing consumer satisfactions or maintaining them at lower cost, by changing the institutional arrangements. A common conclusion of public choice studies is that services are better provided on a local than on a regional basis, because consumers tend to favour neighbourhood police forces, school boards and so forth. Another common conclusion is that services like rubbish collection could be made more efficient by privatization, with the municipality putting them out to tender. Despite its title, however, public choice theory is not so much a theory about public administration as a methodology for studying it, albeit a methodology with so many built-in assumptions that its application to various problems tends to yield a pattern of somewhat similar conclusions.

Both games theory and public choice theory are forms of what can best be described as rational-actor models. The assumptions are the same as those made by most theoretical economists; that the players in a situation are entirely rational in their pursuit of measurable objectives, that they are possessed of equal knowledge about the alternatives available, and that their moves can be mapped without considering questions of emotion or moral values. Some theories about political behaviour by economists, notably Anthony Downs and Mancur Olson, have already been discussed in Chapter 9. Another theory or model is that put forward by Albert Hirschman under the title of 'exit, voice and loyalty' (Hirschman 1970). In this book the author posits an actor faced with a decline in the performance of his favourite company or political party and suggests factors that might lead him to decide between his alternatives of switching to a rival company or party (exit) and staying with it while trying to improve it (voice).

There is an interesting question about how extensively rational-actor models can profitably be used in the study of political behaviour. Some writers have suggested that there are a wide range of political activities which can be analysed in this way, while other writers are more sceptical.

My own position is one of moderate, but not complete, scepticism. I do not believe that the value of rational-actor models in political science can ever approach the value they have had in traditional economic theory. The analysis of economic behaviour in terms of this type of model has two advantages over the analysis of political behaviour in similar terms. The first is that, although 'economic man' is an abstraction, a sufficient number of people in advanced capitalist societies behave roughly in the manner of 'economic man' for the theoretical models devised by economists to have considerable explanatory power. The second advantage is that most of the costs, benefits and profits of economic action can be reduced to the same standard of measurement.

In the case of political behaviour there are competing versions of 'political man', each unsatisfactory in different ways. The hedonistic person of Utilitarian theories is only of limited value because the assumptions on which this abstraction is based are over-simplistic. The power-seeking person of some theorists is clearly unrealistic, if intended as a representation of the ordinary citizen; he/she might do for a tiny minority of politicians, but where numbers are so small this kind of approach loses much of its advantage because the idiosyncratic variations of particular individuals fail to cancel one another out. The most plausible abstraction is probably the influence-seeking individual, but this has limitations. The Downsian theory of why people vote revolves around the assumption that 'political man' is an influence-seeking creature, and the explanatory value of this theory is not at all great. There are undoubtedly some people who go to the polls only when they think their vote has a reasonable chance of influencing the result, and it is sometimes possible to trace a slight statistical relationship between turnout and marginality. But in most political systems the difference in turnout between marginal seats and safe seats in national elections is so small that it is evident that Downs's theory contributes very little to our understanding of the question. And this is not because Downs's logic is faulty but because his original premise does not hold good for the majority of electors.

The other problem about analysing political behaviour in this way is that the costs and benefits of political action cannot easily be reduced to a common unit of measurement, if indeed they can be measured at all. The difficulties of measuring happiness clearly weaken the value of the Utilitarian model for empirical research (though that does not of course affect the value of Utilitarianism as a normative theory). The difficulties of measuring power and influence are very great, as has been amply demonstrated by community power studies and the methodological controversies to which they have given rise.

For these reasons and others it seems unlikely that the economic approach to the study of politics will ever cover such a wide range of problems as the historical or sociological approaches. However, so long as its limitations are recognized, the economic approach has advantages which claim our attention. It is clear and logical, and its models yield hypotheses which can to some extent be tested against evidence. Even if the evidence is unclear or the hypotheses are invalidated, the analysis may clarify the problem by illuminating the relationships that are under investigation. The use of economic models therefore offers some prospect of intellectual progress, even though they can be usefully applied only to certain areas and aspects of political behaviour.

In logical (though only partly chronological) terms, the movement towards a science of politics can be divided into three phases. The first phase of the movement was the use of quantitative methods to analyse individual behaviour in political situations and the second phase was the construction and use of rational-actor models. The third phase was an ambitious attempt to build a large-scale conceptual framework known as systems theory. Taken from the biological sciences, first formulated as a theory of politics by David Easton in the 1950s (see Easton 1953), and developed by Gabriel Almond and others, the main thrust of systems theory was to replace the state and its institutions as the central subject of political analysis by the political system and its processes. That is to say, the focus of study shifted again, from institutions in mainstream political science and individual behaviour in the first two behavioural phases to political processes in the systems-theory phase.

In the model that is central to systems theory, representative institutions such as elections, parties and pressure groups are replaced by the process of articulating and aggregating interests and values. The advantage of this change, it was claimed, was to provide a more suitable language for the analysis of politics on a comparative and international basis. Instead of talking about the US Congress or the British or French Parliaments, which have had no precise equivalents in communist party states or in developing countries, scholars should talk about the processes of articulation and aggregation, which occur in all political systems, democratic or dictatorial, national or international. Similarly, talk about administrative institutions should be replaced by talk about policy implementation, and the circular nature of all political systems should be indicated by the concept of feedback (borrowed from electrical engineering), meaning the process whereby the implementation of policies in one period leads to the articulation of revised demands in the following period. In outline, the political system can then be portrayed as composed of inputs (articulated and aggregated) into a 'black box' where authoritative decisions are made, outputs from the black box in the form of policies, and feedback from the society that is affected by the policies. The model is commonly summarized in the diagrammatic form shown in Figure 1.

This model (Figure 1) has some fairly obvious merits and most political science students in the English-speaking world are probably introduced to it at some stage of their studies. It tells the student what to look for when

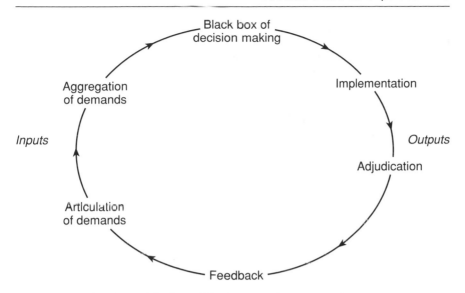

Figure 1 The basic model of a political system in systems theory

studying a system with unfamiliar institutions. It has the merit of emphasizing the circularity of the political process. At the same time, it has certain
limitations. One is that the model does not have any logical place for the
source of political authority. It is all very well to say that decision making
within the black box results in the authoritative allocation of values for
society, that is, that it produces authoritative policies, but what makes them
authoritative? There is no place in this model for the crown, as the source of
authority in Britain and other monarchies, or for the constitution as the
course of authority in the United States and some other republics. Easton
has tried to cope with this by adding public support on the input side of the
model, but support for the system does not have the same logical status as
the demands for policy changes that constitute the main inputs and in any
case it cannot encompass the crown and the constitution.

Another weakness of the model is that it has no place for a bill of rights
or for a body like the US Supreme Court. The work of the lower courts
comes under the heading of adjudication, but the US Supreme Court (and
its equivalent in other countries) has the power to put aside decisions and
laws emanating from the black box. This weakness further illustrates the
point that it is impossible to explain a political system adequately without
indicating the status and role of the key institutions that shape it.

Yet another weakness of the central model of systems theory is its democratic bias. The arrows point in only one direction, from the public through
the articulation of public demands to the decision makers. In practice many

policy changes, and by some definitions most policy changes, originate within the executive organs of government, either within the cabinet or within the bureaucracy. It is common for bureaucrats to persuade ministers of the need to modify policies or levy extra taxes, for the ministers to persuade elected representatives of this need, and for the elected representatives to sell the idea to the voters. In such cases the arrows would have to be reversed, which would make nonsense of the section of the diagram labelled inputs. In dictatorial systems of government, the great majority of policy initiatives originate with the central executive, so that the input side of the model is relatively unimportant. This fact somewhat undermines the claim made for the model that it provides a better basis than institutional analysis for the study of all political systems.

Taken together, these weaknesses considerably limit the utility of systems theory when applied to the study of politics. It offers a different language from the conventional language of mainstream political science and this has the merit of forcing students to think some things out afresh. However, the framework it offers is not really an improvement on more conventional frameworks and it certainly does not live up to the rather large claims that were made for it in the heyday of the search for a science of politics. Easton himself said this about it:

> When my volume, *The Political System*, was first published, there was a transparent need to argue the case for the construction of empirically oriented general theory in political science. It is an index of the gargantuan strides that have been made in the development of political science as a discipline that what was then an entirely appropriate subject for intense discussion has now come to be taken for granted.
>
> (Easton 1965: 3)

Easton went on to explain that by an empirically oriented theory he meant one 'that, in principle, can be reduced to testable propositions' (Easton 1965: 13). Now, what has to be emphasized is that systems theory can not be reduced to testable propositions. Certain of the rational-actor theories mentioned above can be so reduced, but systems theory cannot be. It is true that in a later book Easton put forward some tentative attempts to generalize about the persistence or non-persistence of political systems, but he was not able to specify clear rules about how much change in a system can be accepted before it can be said not to have persisted. At one point he even suggested that there was something called the British political system that had persisted from the time of the Anglo-Saxon warlords to the twentieth century (Easton 1965: 84). It was this kind of theorizing that led Dowse and Hughes to observe that 'system non-persistence seems a highly elusive concept. The problem is that if everything may change and yet the system in some sense persists, what is the sense in which it may be said to persist?' (Dowse and Hughes 1986: 74). It must be concluded of systems theory that it offers a different language for the analysis of politics, but not a scientific theory about politics or even a set of testable hypotheses.

It follows that the modern search for a science of politics has not produced anything as ambitious as the Marxist theory of dialectical materialism. It has certainly come nowhere near validating the claim made by one writer (one among several, it should be added), that scientific predictions 'would appear to be as feasible in politics as in physics' (Sibley 1967: 60). However, it has had the advantage of bringing political scientists into cooperation with social psychologists and sociologists and thus opening the windows of the discipline to the ideas and methods generated by allied disciplines. A valuable summary of the work done on the frontiers (or common territory) of political science and sociology will be found in Dowse and Hughes, *Political Sociology* (1986).

The search has also had the merit of forcing political scientists to think carefully about the relationship between their work and their own political values. The claim of most political behaviouralists is that the scientific methods they have adopted force them to be more nearly value-free in their analyses than most mainstream political scientists have been. They have assumed that facts can and should be separated from values, which is a contention strongly supported by some schools of philosophy but strongly opposed by others. The modern philosophical movement which has supported it most strongly is logical positivism, which happened to flourish just at the time that the search for an empirically based science of politics was getting under way. Herbert Simon declared in his famous book on *Administrative Behaviour*, first published in 1945, that 'the conclusions reached by a particular school of modern philosophy – logical positivism – will be accepted as a starting point' (Simon 1976: 45). In view of this, it will be appropriate in this chapter to indicate the central features of this philosophical outlook.

LOGICAL POSITIVISM

This philosophical movement started in Vienna in the 1930s and moved to England, where it was developed with such vigour that it came to dominate British philosophical thought for a generation. While it was never so dominant in the United States it was certainly influential there, partly because Rudolf Carnap moved from Vienna to Chicago and took his ideas with him, partly because American theorists were influenced by theorists in Oxford.

If David Hume can be regarded as the father of positivism, as was suggested above, he can also be regarded as the grandfather of logical positivism. The most central of the logical positivists' beliefs was the acceptance of Hume's division of theory into three categories, namely analytical theory, empirical theory, and moral or normative theory. A proposition is analytical if, like the theorems of mathematics or the propositions of formal logic, it is necessarily true. In the words of A. J. Ayer in *Language, Truth and Logic*, first published in 1936 and still in print in 2004, 'a proposition is analytic when its validity depends solely on the definitions it contains' (Ayer 1946: 78). Such a proposition is devoid of factual content and cannot be either confirmed or invalidated by empirical data. It is true if the logic is correct and false otherwise. It is helpful because it demonstrates and encapsulates certain necessary connections and relationships.

An empirical proposition, on the other hand, is a proposition about factual matters that can be verified by observation. This verification principle can be expressed in either a strong or a weak form. According to the strong form, a proposition can be verified only 'if its truth could be conclusively established in experience' (Ayer 1946: 37). In Ayer's view, and here too he follows Hume, this is asking too much. As we cannot know what the future holds, it is unreasonable to demand or to claim complete certainty for an empirical proposition. Ayer prefers the weaker form of the principle, which demands only 'that some possible sense-experience' should be relevant to the task of establishing the truth or falsehood of the proposition (Ayer 1946: 31). Empirical propositions, in this view, can be invalidated by contrary experiences and evidence but can only be probably or provisionally or substantially verified by experiences and evidence that are compatible with the proposition.

In addition to the two categories of analytical propositions and empirical propositions, there are also metaphysical propositions and ethical judgements. Metaphysical propositions, such as have been the common concern of many schools of philosophy, are 'neither true nor false but literally senseless' (Ayer 1946: 31). This implies that much philosophical speculation has always been a waste of time, and Ayer makes it quite clear that this is his view: 'The traditional disputes of philosophers', he asserts, 'are for the most part as unwarranted as they are unfruitful' (Ayer 1946: 33).

Ethical judgements are by no means senseless, but they have to be seen as the expression of personal emotions which cannot be justified or falsified in any objective way. A personal judgement cannot be justified by showing that it is commonly approved of, because there are some actions that are commonly approved of that may, nevertheless, be condemned as wrong by someone who holds a contrary view, as everyone is entitled to do. Nor can they be justified by showing that if everyone behaved in the way approved of by the person making the judgement, this would be likely to increase the sum total of human happiness, because there is no logical equivalence between the sentence 'x is good' and the sentence 'x is pleasant' (see Ayer 1946: 104–5). We simply have to accept that ethical judgements are in a category of their own and can never be proved true or false. Ayer explained his position as follows:

In saying that a certain type of action is right or wrong, I am not making any factual statement, not even a statement about my own state of mind. I am merely expressing certain moral sentiments. And the man who is ostensibly contradicting me is merely expressing his moral sentiments. So there is plainly no sense in asking which of us is in the right. For neither of us is asserting a genuine proposition.

(Ayer 1946: 107–8)

Ayer describes this philosophical outlook as radical empiricism, and it is this empiricism that the logical positivists who dominated British philosophy from the 1940s to the 1960s had in common with the mainly American scholars who were seeking a science of politics in the same period. One of the central points on which they were agreed was the strict separation and independence of facts and values, as summarized in what became a catchphrase of the period, 'an "is" cannot lead to an "ought"'. If I observe that it is a bad thing that so many people in Ethiopia are starving, this is a conjunction of two quite independent propositions; the empirical proposition or assertion that many Ethiopians are starving and my personal ethical judgement that starvation is bad. Similarly, if I observe that it is a pity electoral turnout in the United States is low, this is a conjunction of an empirical assertion about electoral behaviour and a personal judgement that low turnouts are undesirable. Political scientists, to be scientific, should discover the facts and eschew the ethical judgements.

There is a good deal more to logical positivism than this, particularly the later development of linguistic analysis, but enough has been said to indicate its relevance for the attempt to create a science of politics. As a philosophical school, it had both a significant merit and two significant limitations. Its merit was to offer a simple guide to clear thinking, particularly useful in a period when fascist and communist movements were justifying brutal dictatorships in terms of complex ideologies. In Britain it brought philosophical thinking within the reach of the ordinary non-graduate citizen, as evidenced by the fact that Ayer's book became a runaway best seller and another logical positivist became a popular radio personality.

One of its limitations was that it contained no account of historical explanation, which is not mentioned at all in Ayer's book. Clearly, historians are making statements about the past that are based upon evidence but are not quite the same as the empirical generalizations produced by scientists, and the whole question of historical explanation (to be discussed in Chapter 17) was ignored by the logical positivists. Another limitation was its refusal to distinguish between various types of personal judgement. There are important differences between the statements 'I don't like plum pudding', 'I don't like Picasso's paintings', and 'I don't like to see human beings tortured', and it is really not good enough to reduce them all to examples of personal sentiments that cannot usefully be argued about. They may have a similar logical form, but there are more things to say about them than that. And in the end these limitations made logical positivism a passing phase in the history of philosophy, for it ascribed too limited a role to that discipline to satisfy academic philosophers for more than one generation.

A CONCLUDING NOTE

The only possible conclusion to this chapter is that political scientists have failed in the attempt to remodel the discipline on the lines of the natural sciences and to produce anything resembling a comprehensive science of politics. However, there is an old adage to the effect that it is better to travel hopefully than to arrive, and it seems to be applicable in this case. The search for scientific methods has produced a number of interesting ideas and a mass of valuable data about political behaviour in various circumstances. (For a valuable guide, see Kavanagh 1983.) For this reason, we should appreciate its contributions, despite the fact that it also produced a certain amount of useless theorizing and a great many extravagant claims.

It can therefore be seen as unfortunate that in the United States it divided the political science profession, with university departments split down the middle between behaviouralists and the rest. In 1968 J. Roland Pennock said that in the previous twenty years:

> a large, productive, and able group (including the bulk of the recognized leaders of the profession) has more or less self-consciously as a group attempted to revolutionize our discipline, and that many (though by no means all) of the members of the profession who did not identify with them have resisted vigorously and sometimes bitterly what they often saw as a Philistine onslaught.
>
> (Pennock 1968: 40)

Political theorists, in particular, resented Dahl's much-publicized declaration that 'in the English-speaking world . . . political theory is dead' and that its students, like literary critics, are 'reduced to living off capital – other people's capital at that' (Dahl 1958: 89).

Given this kind of attack, and given that the behaviouralists and model-builders were ultimately unable to achieve their wider ambitions, an academic reaction to their work was probably inevitable. It came in the 1970s and 1980s, in the form of attacks from political theorists of the left, the right, and even (to some extent) the centre. In so far as such theorists have a common philosophical position, it is that they prefer historicism to positivism. There are several alternative schools of thought that will be identified, together with the concept of historicism, in the following chapter.

Chapter 17

Against a science of politics: values, historicism and hermeneutics

The attempt to create a science of politics, so popular in the 1950s and 1960s, has met with heavy criticism in later years. One line of attack has been that the claims of the behaviouralists to be value-free in their research were actually false claims, so that the result was to promote the author's values without any admission by the author that this was being done and without any reasoned normative arguments to justify the values. A second line of attack has been the claim that the values secretly promoted by the behaviouralists and model-makers are undesirable values. A third and much more basic line of attack has been the claim that it is a philosophical error to suppose that political behaviour can be properly explained in terms of empirical generalizations similar in form to those of the natural sciences. Each of these lines of criticism will now be examined.

BEHAVIOURALIST VALUES

The proposition that the work of political behaviouralists only pretends to be value-free was made as early as 1962 by Leo Strauss, arguably the most eminent American political theorist of his generation: 'The alleged value-free analysis of political preference', he declared, 'is controlled by an unavowed commitment to ... a particular version of liberal democracy' (Strauss 1962: 326). Charles Taylor reached a similar conclusion in a more detailed and careful study of the work of leading behaviouralists (in particular, S. M. Lipset) published in 1967. Empirical studies of politics, he asserted, are based on conceptual frameworks which include some factors and exclude others; some of the excluded factors would be thought highly relevant by scholars approaching the same set of actions or recorded opinions with a different conceptual framework; and the choice of one framework rather than another is 'inextricably connected to a certain set of values' (Taylor 1967: 39).

Each possible framework of explanation contains or implies a 'value-slope', making some generalizations and evaluative conclusions more likely than others, and the only way in which empirical scholars can avoid this kind of bias is by sticking to 'the narrow-gauge discoveries which, just because they are, taken alone, compatible with a great number of political frameworks, can bathe in an atmosphere of value neutrality' (Taylor 1967: 40–1, 57). More tolerant than Strauss, Taylor commends the attempt to avoid bias, but believes that attempts to make generalizations that are significantly more ambitious than 'Catholics in Detroit tend to vote Democrat' are bound to involve the scholar in some kind of normative position.

Another careful analysis of the work of leading behaviouralists, this time focusing on Robert Dahl, was made by Quentin Skinner in 1973. He demonstrated that Dahl and his colleagues, hard though they try to be value-neutral, end up by describing the situation they analysed as democratic, which is necessarily to commend it, even though this involves using a particular definition of democracy which attaches little value to public participation (see Skinner 1973).

Other theorists have joined in the attack, and in 1976 R. J. Bernstein summarized it by saying that 'when we examine those empirical theories that have been advanced, we discover again and again that they are not value-neutral, but reflect deep ideological biases and secrete controversial value positions' (Bernstein 1976: 228). And it is impossible to read all these criticisms without concluding that their main thrust is justified.

The second line of attack has insisted not only that the work of the behaviouralists and economic model-builders embodied political values that were largely covert, but also that these values are undesirable. The lead in this was also taken by Strauss, who produced a veritable broadside against what he called 'the new political science'. This science, he alleged, strengthened:

> the most dangerous proclivities of democracy. . . . By teaching in effect the equality of literally all desires, it teaches in effect that there is nothing that a man ought to be ashamed of. . . . By teaching the equality of all values, by denying that there are things which are intrinsically high and others which are intrinsically low . . . it unwittingly contributes to the victory of the gutter.
>
> (Strauss 1962: 326)

This was clearly an attack from the right, but it was quickly followed by attacks from the left. It is a characteristic of divisions within the discipline of political science that the scientists have tended to be in the political centre whereas their critics have tended, with a few exceptions, to be either conservatives or radicals. One attack from the left was published in 1963. In this, Graeme Duncan and Steven Lukes argued that the empirical theorists of democracy had been led by their fear of totalitarian dictatorship to be unduly worried about ideological conflict and to place their highest value on a consensual political system in which most citizens were content to choose between rival teams of leaders every few years. In this way, it was said, they were implicitly rejecting the participatory values elaborated (in different ways) by Rousseau and J. S. Mill and were led to a defence of political apathy. Not only did this slant destroy their claim to neutrality, but also it was an undesirable slant with conservative implications (see Duncan and Lukes 1963).

This article was followed by a rather more radical critique by Christian Bay, who broadened the attack to include economic model-builders as well as empirical theorists of democracy. Much behavioural literature, he suggests, is 'profoundly conservative', not in the traditional way that Strauss was a conservative but in the sense that it contains an 'antipolitical dimension'. This dimension is the assumption that American politics 'is and must always remain primarily a system of rules for peaceful battles between competing private interests, and not an arena for the struggle toward a more humane and more rationally organized society' (Bay 1965: 44).

In the following year J. L. Walker joined the attack, declaring that empirical theorists of democracy had abandoned the basic ideals of what he calls the 'classical theory of democracy'. This is a highly elusive concept, but Walker describes it as 'the familiar doctrine of popular rule, patterned after the New England town meeting' (Walker 1966: 285). The behaviouralists have replaced popular participation by 'stability and efficiency as the prime goals of democracy'. By doing this, they had incurred the danger of becoming 'sophisticated apologists for the existing political order' (Walker 1966: 289).

It cannot be denied that there is some substance in these criticisms. Even the work of Robert Dahl, so careful that it escapes most of them, has been described by Skinner as involving 'an act of political conservatism' in that it 'serves to commend the recently prevailing values and practices of a political system like that of the United States, and it constitutes a form of argument against those who have sought to question the democratic character of those values and practices' (Skinner 1973: 303–4).

Despite this, it is possible to question how damaging the criticisms are. There is not much cash value in Bay's wish that people should struggle for a 'more humane and rationally organized society'. Logical positivists could quite reasonably describe this as 'a hurray phrase', with no clear meaning. The New England town meeting that Walker takes to be a desirable model is not a viable model for government in the modern state, particularly if we are discussing a state with over two hundred million citizens. It might well be argued that it is more helpful to base one's ideals on a model that is actually viable in the modern world than to hanker constantly after a dream that has been outmoded by history.

More generally, the suggestion that writers who do not criticize an existing system of government are implicitly defending it, and can therefore be charged with conservatism, implies that political scientists should all be engaged in furthering ideological positions. Any decent university library contains hundreds of books, written by liberals and social democrats, that analyse systems of government and public administration without subjecting them to ideological criticism. Are all these liberals and socialists to be classified as conservatives because they did not think it appropriate to impose their personal political views on their material? It would be a sad day for political science if this were to become the rule.

THE TROUBLE WITH POSITIVISM

The third line of attack is more philosophical and more important. It is an attack on positivism itself, rather than on particular examples of research inspired by positivist beliefs. The logic of positivism is that social and political behaviour is determined by the interaction of objective factors that can be identified, so that if a particular combination of factors is repeated, the resulting behaviour can be predicted. The relationship between the factors and the behaviour can be expressed in law-like generalizations similar in form to those by which progress is made in the natural sciences. For this to be true, the social and political laws must be universally valid, like those of the natural sciences. They may be probabilistic, to allow for eccentricities of behaviour, but they must not vary in an unpredictable way over space or time.

Now, in practice, a great deal of social and political behaviour varies from one community to another and varies unpredictably over time even within the same community. If it is variable and unpredictable it cannot be bound by scientific laws. To illustrate the point, let us suppose that a shipping company plans to build a new cruise liner and appoints a naval architect to advise on the structural and external design of the vessel and a sociologist to advise on the internal design and fittings. Both advisers would rely partly upon the experience of existing cruise liners when formulating their advice. The naval architect would use laws about the relationships between a ship's displacement, hull design, engine power and stability. If these laws had been arrived at correctly, they would be correct for all ships and all periods.

The sociologist, in contrast, would find that the ideal arrangements for internal design would vary according to the nationality of the expected passengers. American passengers like to be offered lectures and religious services, so that an auditorium and some chapels would be desirable. British passengers like to gamble and French passengers to play bridge, so these tastes must be catered for. Italian passengers have no objection to noise and would expect to have loudspeakers in each cabin to tell them about the day's activities. There is no formula that indicates the ideal arrangement for a national mixture of passengers. Judgement and even guesswork is required, not the application of scientific laws.

In addition to this problem, there are variations over time in the tastes of passengers. In the 1950s there was a general demand for accommodation to be divided strictly into classes, each with its own set meals, whereas today the fashion is for one-class ships, though with variable prices in the restaurants.

However, there was no scientific way of predicting in the 1950s when, or even if, this change in fashion would take place.

This example has a clear parallel in the problems of studying comparative government. It is useful to study similar systems of government side by side, or one after another, because the student gets to know what to look for and the differences between countries raise interesting questions for exploration. However, the number of cross-national generalizations with predictive value that have emerged from a century of studies in comparative government is very small. Where significant constitutional similarities exist it may be possible to generalize about institutional arrangements that are made appropriate, as in K. C. Wheare's classic study of the institutional requirements of federal systems (see Wheare 1946). However, it is much more difficult to produce worthwhile generalizations about political behaviour. It could be said that a federal constitution requires a supreme court to settle conflicts of jurisdiction between the national and the state governments, but it is not possible to predict what judgements different courts will reach. In the 1870s, for example, it was not possible to predict that judicial decisions in the United States would make that federation progressively more centralized whereas judicial decisions in Canada would make that federation progressively less centralized.

The obvious difficulties of making cross-national generalizations about political behaviour have led students to concentrate on the more modest task of making generalizations that are confined to particular countries. Even these tend to vary over time, however, and thus not to have much predictive value. The safest kind of generalization to make is one about voting behaviour, because there are so many actors that individual peculiarities tend to cancel one another out. However, there are unpredictable changes in voting behaviour. It was true for about a century that most white voters in the southern states supported the Democrats because of memories of the civil war, but it has ceased to be true since the 1970s. It was true from the 1930s until the late 1960s that the great majority of Scottish industrial workers voted Labour, but it ceased to be true in the early 1970s when many of them switched to the Scottish National Party. Such generalizations often have explanatory value while they are true, but there is nothing scientific about a law stating that a given body of voters will behave in such and such a way until they change their minds.

These objections to positivism apply to all forms of social behaviour, but are particularly relevant to political behaviour because full-time politicians are few in number. Economic laws depend for their validity on the predictability of economic behaviour by vast numbers of consumers, merchants and industrialists. That they are somewhat unreliable, and thus not to be equated with the laws of natural science, is made clear by the repeated failures of economic policy that occur. Nevertheless, at least the number of actors involved is large enough for individual quirks and miscalculations to cancel out. The same might be said, though less certainly, about certain types of sociological generalization, such as those about the factors influencing divorce rates and suicide rates. In each case millions of people are involved, so that individual peculiarities are submerged in the mass and statistical correlations are based on large numbers. However, in the realm of politics the mass of people do little apart from voting and joining pressure groups, while governmental decisions are made by a handful of political actors whose personal ambitions and peculiarities often affect the decisions that emerge from their interaction. When we study the behaviour of Cabinet ministers we are not dealing with a random sample of a sizeable population, only with a limited number of rather unusual individuals.

All experience indicates that the behaviour of leading figures in political situations is only influenced, not determined, by objective factors such as their age, sex, class and economic circumstances. Political leaders have motives, emotions and personal ideals that influence their behaviour in ways that cannot always be predicted. Their perception of the options open to them in any given situation may not be identical with the perception that observers have of their options, and their choice is a personal decision. It follows that each political move is a unique event that cannot be understood simply as the consequence of the interaction of objective factors, important though these factors may have been. Political actors have intentions, and a full explanation of the event must include an account of the intentions of the actors.

Now, political scientists who study a succession of unique events are doing something closely akin to the work of historians, who also study a succession of unique events, for there is no philosophical difference between a unique event that took place two hundred years ago and one that occurred two months ago. The student of very recent events may have the advantage of being able to interview participants, but he lacks the historian's advantage of having access to diaries and letters. These are practical details that only marginally affect the character of the explanation that is given, and the essential point is that explanations by political scientists have much more in common with historical explanation than with scientific explanation.

Admittedly, there is one philosopher of history who minimizes the difference between the two types of explanation. Carl Hempel asserts that whenever historians point to a causal relationship between two events they are relying on unstated 'covering laws' which have the character of scientific generalizations. Thus, if it is said that a prime minister called an early election because the polls showed that his or her party had a substantial lead, the historian is relying on two covering laws, namely that opinion polls are reliable guides to voting behaviour in subsequent elections and that prime ministers always put electoral victory above other considerations. However, most philosophers of history would say that Hempel's covering laws are not scientific laws at all, but merely appeals to common sense and common experience that may not hold good in every situation. To understand conventional views about historical explanation, it will be helpful to explain the concept of historicism.

HISTORICISM

Whereas positivism is derived from a combination of French rationalism and British empiricism, historicism has its origins in German romanticism. It is not so clear a concept as positivism, for it has been used to label two theoretical tendencies that are actually very different in character. One of these is defined by the *OED* as the 'tendency to regard historical development as the most basic aspect of human existence', the other as the 'belief that historical events are governed by laws'. This difference is itself best explained in historical terms.

The writer who has the best claim to be regarded as the father of the first type of historicism is J. G. Herder, who was also the father of the theory of nationalism. Writing in the 1770s and 1780s, Herder reacted not against positivism, for that had not yet been developed, but against the universalist assumptions of the theorists of the Enlightenment that were later to be taken for granted by positivists. Friedrich Meineche captured these well when he said that Enlightenment thinkers regarded individuals as rather like leaves in a forest, all separate but all predictably moved in the same direction by the wind. Herder's view of human behaviour was both more communalistic and more particularistic. People belonged to national groups, or *volks*, each of which had its own traditions, habits and values.

It was wrong of Enlightenment thinkers, who were mainly French, to believe that everyone in the world would behave (or ought to behave) like French people. On the contrary, Germans behaved like Germans and Italians like Italians. To understand their behaviour it was necessary to understand the history, traditions and values of their societies. And to understand the significance of historical events, it was Herder's view, as summarized by F. M. Barnard, that 'the historian had to re-live the past, to reconstruct and re-think for himself its thoughts and feelings, and thus to recapture the spirit of the age which he was studying' (Barnard 1965: 110).

This is the essence of the first type of historicism, as is the belief, also expressed first by Herder, that national sets of values have to be understood and accepted for what they are, there being no universal set of values by which national values can be assessed. As Berlin has put it, Herder believed 'not merely in the multiplicity but in the incommensurability of the values of different cultures and societies', so that notions about an ideal society 'are intrinsically incoherent and meaningless' (Berlin 1965: 54). One implication of this kind of view is that the task of the historian who studies cultures other than his own is a difficult one of interpretation and understanding. At the end of the eighteenth century J. G. Fichte continued where

Herder left off, giving this kind of approach a more overtly nationalist slant by stressing the importance of language in forming a national culture and then asserting that the German language was more pure and therefore better than other European languages. Fichte also took the view that history could be seen as in some sense the unfolding of divine will.

Fichte's ideas about a divine will are rather confusing, but they can perhaps be seen as a step towards the more elaborate theories of Hegel, who developed the view that the sequence of historical events in the life of a nation, which proceeds by a dialectical process of resolving contradictions, should be seen not as random but as the manifestation of the world-historical spirit as it unfolded. There is reason in history, declared Hegel: 'That history . . . is founded on an essential and actual aim, which actually is, and will be, realised in it – the Plan of Providence; that, in short, there is Reason in History, must be decided on strictly philosophical grounds' (quoted Popper 1962: 45). This attitude is at first sight mystifying, and there is no space in this book to attempt an explanation of it in philosophical terms. Its relevance to political science is not direct, for few political scientists take it seriously, but indirect, in that it played a significant role in forming Marx's ideas about dialectical materialism.

That the march of historical events had an inner logic was a fundamental constituent of Marx's thought, but instead of identifying the driving force of historical development as a world-historical spirit Marx identified it as the changing character of the economic system and the relations of classes to the means of production. There was indeed an inevitability about historical progress, according to the theories of the mature Marx and Engels, and it could be explained in terms that were not at all mystifying. The way they explained it has been summarized in the previous chapter. In Popper's early writings, this theory is said to be a form of historicism, closely related to Hegel's historicism and equally mistaken. (For Popper's attacks on this form of historicism, see Popper 1957, 1962.) The cause of human history is strongly influenced by the growth of human knowledge, declared Popper; we cannot predict the future growth of knowledge; and therefore we cannot predict the future course of history. It was put as simply a matter of logic.

Almost all contemporary scholars would agree that theories of historical inevitability are misleading, and this is no longer a real issue. The question that Popper's work raises is whether he was correct in calling Marx's theories a form of historicism. There was clearly an historical link, sketched out in the barest terms in the previous paragraphs, between the ideas of Herder and the ideas of Marx and Engels, but their beliefs were so totally different that it seems unhelpful to place too much emphasis on this. Because the link existed, it is not entirely unreasonable to describe dialectical materialism as a form of historicism, but if this nomenclature is used it is essential to distinguish between Herder's emphasis on understanding the spirit of the age in historical interpretation, which might be labelled historicism type A, and Marx's scheme of predictable historical development, which could be labelled historicism type B.

For my part, I would prefer to reserve the term historicism for Herder's version and to regard dialectical materialism as a form of positivism, as explained in Chapter 16. Theories of historical inevitability will be ignored in what follows, not only because it is confusing to describe them as examples of historicism but also because they are in practice quite unhelpful as a guide to the real world. Dialectical materialism, which is by far the most ambitious of them, has been shown to be wrong as a guide to practice. Other more modest attempts to predict the future have repeatedly been falsified by events. Nobody in the 1970s, to take only the most recent and obvious example, predicted that the Cold War would be over by 1989 or that the Soviet Union would have disintegrated by the beginning of 1992.

If we assume that the political scientist's task is to make sense of historical events and developments, what methodological conclusions follow from the assumption and what can be learned from the philosophy of history? One lesson that historicists draw is that cross-national analysis of political behaviour is an exercise fraught with difficulties. To understand political behaviour in a period different from that of the writer it is necessary to understand 'the spirit of the age', meaning the whole bundle of assumptions, traditions and values that shaped behaviour in that period. It is said to be equally true that to understand political behaviour in a society different from that of the writer it is necessary to understand the assumptions, traditions and values of that society. This can be done by the scholar who studies each country separately and acquires insights into each country's political culture, its assumptions about political authority and leadership, its beliefs about public participation in politics and individual rights, its readiness to tolerate some forms of corruption but not others. However, cross-national surveys rarely give full weight to national differences of political culture, and cross-national indexes are apt to conceal them. Most scholars who regard themselves as historicists believe that the whole field of comparative government has to be regarded with suspicion.

Another lesson that historicists draw is the difficulty of tracing cause and effect when studying political decisions. The study of historical documents like diaries, memoirs and letters reveals that political actors not only have a variety of motives but also differ in their appreciation of the significance and probable consequences of their actions. The academic historian is customarily cautious about drawing the conclusion that one event or development caused another, because his studies have taught him that between the first event and the second there were a number of individual decisions based upon mixed motives and imperfect understandings of the situation, so that the second event often appears to the scholar to have been as much a matter of chance as a matter of causal determination. It is argued that political scientists who draw conclusions about the causal relationships between very recent events are apt to be over-rational in their assumptions about the behaviour of the individuals who shaped the events.

For similar reasons, historicists deplore the use of economic models in political science. The models are based upon assumptions about the rationality and single-mindedness of political actors that are unwarranted, it is said. A study of history teaches one that people are not always rational about politics and often act from a mixture of motives. They may be calculating their personal advantage when they make decisions, but they may also be influenced by a sense of duty or an attachment to tradition. That they may have a confused sense of duty or a misunderstanding of tradition makes the assessment of their motives, and thus the prediction of their behaviour, even more difficult.

There are, of course, differences between historicists. Recent British thinking about historiography has been greatly influenced by the writings of R. G. Collingwood and Michael Oakeshott, who were philosophical idealists. Collingwood has said that 'all history is the history of thought' (Collingwood 1939: 110), meaning not that all history is intellectual history but that the essential task of the historian is to reconstruct what was going on in the minds of key political actors when they acted in the way that they did. Economic and social factors are deemed irrelevant unless the actor in question can be shown to have been influenced by his or her knowledge of them. Oakeshott has decried the tendency of political scientists (and some historians) to engage in a backwards look at history, assessing what happened in the light of what came later. The scholar should stick closely to the facts as they happened, not fit them into a scheme of his own. One should not say that 'the Pope's intervention changed the course of events', because the Pope's intervention was part of the course of events. One should not say that 'the effect of the Boer War was to make clear the necessity for reform in the British Army', because the Boer War was followed by all sorts of events and the reforms in the British Army had all sorts of antecedents (see Oakeshott 1962: 147–54).

This understanding of historical method is, however, not the only kind of understanding available. French historians of the 'annales school' look for historical examples of changes in material culture and social structure. Historians in the Marxist tradition look for changes in the structure of the economy that were followed by changes in the relationships between social classes. It is important to learn from the criticisms and contributions of historicists, but better not to become trapped in one particular view of the philosophy of history.

HERMENEUTICS

This is an ancient concept, much older than historicism, that suddenly came into fashion among political theorists in the 1980s. The fashion may or may not be long lived, but the concept deserves our brief attention because it illuminates certain trends in post-structural and post-modern scholarship.

The *OED* defines hermeneutics as 'the art or science of interpretation, especially of Scripture'. The term carries with it the connotation of a text that is not simple or self-explanatory, but needs sympathetic and constructive interpretation to make its significance clear, to 'bring to light an underlying coherence or sense' (Taylor 1985: 15). It also carries with it the connotation of a particular audience for whom the interpretation is made; an audience using a particular language and living in a particular culture at a particular period of history. For hermeneuticists concerned with literary criticism – and the concept has become fashionable in this branch of scholarship as well as among political scientists – it is a mistake to think of a definitive interpretation of a text as if it were good for all time. Hermeneuticists are to some extent audience focused, emphasizing the act of explaining the significance of a text (or a body of texts, or a set of recorded actions) in such a way that the understanding of it by a particular audience will be enhanced.

The view that a hermeneutic approach is the best approach to the study of human social behaviour is associated with the name of Wilhelm Dilthey, a German historian and social philosopher who wrote in the later decades of the nineteenth century and the first decade of the twentieth century. He believed it to be a mistake to assume, as Comte had done, that the social sciences could be modelled on the natural sciences. Because human behaviour is purposive behaviour, it could properly be understood only by understanding what people believed they were doing and what questions they were responding to. For this reason, biographies may provide better insights into the past than more formal works of historiography. Dilthey emphasized the importance of *verstehen* in interpreting human behaviour, this being a German word that has no exact equivalent in English and is best translated as sympathetic and insightful understanding.

This outlook is entirely compatible with the outlook of Idealists like Collingwood and Oakeshott, but whereas they were concerned simply with the interpretation of historical events, as one followed another, Dilthey claimed that *verstehen* was the appropriate method for the entire range of human studies, including the study of social and political systems as whole working systems of relationships. Dilthey also believed that, as the categories we use to explain behaviour undergo subtle changes over time, history would have to be re-written for each generation. This would have the further advantage that it would enable the historian to assess the contemporary consequences of what had happened. Interpretation in the human studies should mean not only an assessment of the meaning of events in their own time but also, as H. P. Rickman put it in his introduction to one of Dilthey's works, 'an assessment of these events in the light of the historian's own age, that is, in terms of their consequences in time' (Dilthey 1961: 50). Dilthey, that is, encouraged the 'backwards look' at history that Oakeshott has dismissed as unhistorical, but which most social and political scientists believe to be illuminating and useful.

A contemporary hermeneuticist is the German philosopher, H. G. Gadamer, of whom it has been said that 'for him, the purpose of hermeneutics is not to put forward rules for "objectively valid" understanding but to conceive understanding itself as comprehensively as possible' to understand 'more deeply, more truly' (Palmer 1969: 215). The contemporary move towards hermeneutics in various branches of scholarship can therefore be itself interpreted as a move towards a more humane and subjective, perhaps even romantic, approach to study, as distinct from the emphasis on rationality and objectivity that characterized scholarship in earlier post-war decades.

The emphasis on the meaning and purpose of human actions is repeated in the work of all social theorists who are sympathetic to hermeneutics. Thus, Taylor points out that for political behaviouralists a vote for a motion is simply that, a vote to be counted, whereas for hermeneuticists there is much more to explore: 'in voting for the motion I am also saving the honour of my party, or defending the value of free speech, or vindicating public morality, or saving civilization from breakdown' (Taylor 1985: 29). Ball has asserted that in practice political scientists are constantly engaged in the interpretation of actions, but that many of them do it less well than they should because of their commitment to a more scientific mode of explanation that requires them to downplay their interpretive skills in favour of using measurable data (see Ball 1987: 97–104).

Oakeshott, though he never described himself as a hermeneuticist, revealed his sympathy with this approach when discussing the ideal syllabus for courses in foreign or comparative government. He said that a foreign system of government could be regarded as a text to be interpreted, and he deplored the fact that most universities emphasized courses on the Soviet system in their undergraduate syllabus, because this was a peculiarly difficult text to understand: 'Why should a School of Politics go out of its way to choose for undergraduate study particularly obscure and corrupt "texts" ... when well-edited "texts", like the politics of France or Sweden or the USA or Spain, are available?' (Oakeshott 1962: 332).

In contemporary work in political science, a sympathy with the hermeneutic approach has led some scholars to emphasize the significance of what an older generation of scholars would regard as anecdotal evidence. If the concern is with welfare policies, for instance, a mainstream scholar would tend to concentrate on party programmes, welfare legislation, and the administration of welfare services; a behaviouralist might correlate patterns of welfare expenditure with social variables such as gross national product per head; and a radical hermeneuticist might be concerned to show how the services appeared to the actual clients, using long interviews with a single mother on welfare to gain understanding of her problems and attitudes to the system. Some would describe studies of this latter kind as 'counter-hegemonic', in that they view government from the bottom up, through the eyes of those on whom government acts, rather than from the top down, tracing the behaviour of people in power. Another way of describing them would be as attempts to provide contemporary 'genealogies', in the sense of the term used by Foucault, as explained in Chapter 12. They are perhaps best regarded not as alternatives but as supplements to institutional and behavioural analyses, adding an extra dimension to our understanding of the situation.

IN CONCLUSION

It is evident that in recent decades the divisions of methods between students of politics have involved philosophical disagreements of some importance. On the whole, this should be welcomed as stimulating and educative. It may seem unfortunate if academic departments become divided over methodological questions, but sensible scholars are generally able to handle such disagreements in an amicable fashion. What is important is to realize that differing approaches complement one another. It is one of the great merits of political science as a discipline that its students are expected both to be numerate and to be literate, and in addition to have some capacity for philosophical reflection. There are very few academic disciplines for which this claim could be made. Any attempt to impose methodological orthodoxy on the subject is therefore best resisted.

The source of most of the philosophical controversy has been the positivist claim that the study of politics, if based upon scientific methods, can become a predictive science. This claim is now pretty well exhausted. It has been thoroughly attacked by normative theorists, and in any case it has not worked. Political scientists have displayed only a very limited ability to predict the future, not noticeably greater than some journalists and other commentators. An ironical example of this was provided by the student protests and riots of the late 1960s and early 1970s, when political science professors were often unable to predict how their own students would behave in the following month. After the event they were perhaps better than other scholars in explaining why the disturbances had occurred, but before the event they were not conspicuously better in foreseeing when or how they would occur.

Disappointing though this has been to some scholars, it should not be used to condemn behavioural research. The real object of all the social sciences is explanation, not prediction, and many of the behavioural studies have had considerable explanatory value. They have added greatly to our knowledge of how the political process operates, and it would be flying in the face of the evidence to pretend otherwise.

The claim that political science can be and should be value-free has also taken a considerable beating in recent years, almost as much as the claim that it can be a predictive science. The normative theorists have won this particular controversy. This is not too damaging to the discipline, however, for very few mainstream political scientists ever made the claim. We have to face the fact that in the English-speaking world most books and articles on political science are written by liberal democratic authors about the politics of liberal democracies for readers who are themselves mostly liberal democrats. In these circumstances it does not matter too much if the authors exhibit liberal democratic values. It is better if they admit this, of course, rather than pretend to an Olympian detachment. But what is important is not whether authors try to be value-free or are openly committed but whether they are honest and fair-minded in the presentation of their material. Skilled readers can usually tell when authors are deliberately slanting their arguments and presenting only those facts that support their side of the case, and it is certainly one of the objects of an education in political science to impart this kind of skill to students.

There are, of course, differing emphases possible within a commitment to liberal democracy, and differing degrees of satisfaction with existing systems of democratic government. The claim of many critics is that the majority of writers are too complacent about the level of public participation in politics. This is a reasonable point or view, though the way it is presented is often questionable. It is no use appealing to a supposed classical theory of democracy, for in fact there is no such thing, only a variety of differing theories. It is equally useless to lament the passing of the New England town meeting, for population growth, urbanization and the increased centralization of government have combined to make that kind of institution irrelevant to modern needs. The case for greater participation needs to be based on an examination of the various options that are viable in the modern state, and these have been discussed in Chapter 9.

Finally, and more generally, I believe that all who write about politics and all who teach political science or civics should pay more attention than seems to be common to the conceptual confusions that are so evident in much political debate. A study of politics may or may not make people wiser than their contemporaries and it may or may not make them better at predicting the future, but it ought to add clarity to the way they present their arguments. It is to the object of promoting clarity that this book has been devoted.

References

Agar, H. (1950) *The Price of Union*, Boston, MA: Houghton Mifflin.

Aiken, H. D. (1956) *The Age of Ideology*, New York: New American Library.

Almond, G. and Verba, S. [1963] (1965) *The Civic Culture*, Boston, MA: Little, Brown.

Arendt, H. (1968) *Between Past and Future*, New York: Viking Press.

Ayer, A. J. (1946) *Language, Truth and Logic*, 2nd edn, London: Gollancz.

Azpiazu, J. (1951) *The Corporative State*, St Louis, MO: Herder.

Bachrach, P. [1967] (1969) *The Theory of Democratic Elitism*, London: University of London Press.

Bachrach, P. and Baratz, M. S. (1962) 'The two faces of power', *American Political Science Review*, 56: 947–52.

—— (1970) *Power and Poverty*, New York: Oxford University Press.

Ball, T. (1983) 'The ontological presuppositions and political consequences of a social science', in D. R. Sabia and J. T. Wallulis (eds) *Changing Social Science*, Albany, NY: State University of New York Press.

—— (ed.) (1987) *Idioms of Inquiry*, Albany, NY: State University of New York Press.

—— (1988) *Transforming Political Discourse*, Oxford: Blackwell.

Barker, E. [1915] (1928) *Political Thought in England: 1848–1914*, London: Oxford University Press.

—— (1942) *Reflections on Government*, London: Oxford University Press.

—— (ed.) (1947) *The Social Contract*, London: Oxford University Press.

Barnard, F. M. (1965) *Herder's Social and Political Thought*, Oxford: Clarendon Press.

Barry, B. (1965) *Political Argument*, London: Routledge & Kegan Paul.

—— (1970) *Sociologists, Economists and Democracy*, London: Collier Macmillan.

—— (2001) *Culture and Equality: An Egalitarian Critique of Multiculturalism*, Cambridge, MA: Harvard University Press.

Bassett, R. (1935) *The Essentials of Parliamentary Democracy*, London: Macmillan.

Bay, C. (1965) 'Politics and pseudopolitics: a critical evaluation of some behavioural literature', *American Political Science Review*, 59: 39–51.

Benn, T. (1987) 'British politics, 1945–1987', in P. Hennessy and A. Seldon (eds) *Ruling Performance: British Governments from Attlee to Thatcher*, Oxford: Blackwell.

Benney, M., Gray, A. P., and Pear, R. H. (1956) *How People Vote*, London: Routledge & Kegan Paul.

Bentham, J. (1838–43) *Works*, ed. J. Bowring, Edinburgh: William Tait.

Berelson, B., Lazarsfeld, P., and McPhee, W. (1954) *Voting*, Chicago, IL: University of Chicago Press.

Berlin, I. (1965) 'Herder and the enlightenment', in E. R. Wasserman (ed.) *Aspects of the Eighteenth Century*, Baltimore, MD: Johns Hopkins University Press.

—— (1969) *Four Essays on Liberty*, Oxford: Oxford University Press.

Bermeo, N. (2003) *Ordinary People in Extraordinary Times*, Princeton, NJ: Princeton University Press.

Bernstein, R. J. (1976) *The Restructuring of Social and Political Theory*, New York: Harcourt, Brace, Jovanovich.

Birch, A. H. (1959) *Small-Town Politics*, London: Oxford University Press.

—— (1964) *Representative and Responsible Government*, London: Allen & Unwin.

—— (1971a) *The Nature and Functions of Representation*, Exeter, UK: University of Exeter.

—— (1971b) *Representation*, London: Pall Mall Press and Macmillan.

—— (1975) 'Some reflections on American democratic theory', *Political Studies*, 23: 225–31.

—— (1977) *Political Integration and Disintegration in the British Isles*, London: Allen & Unwin.

—— (1984) 'Another liberal theory of secession', *Political Studies*, 32: 596–602.

—— (1989) *Nationalism and National Integration*, London: Unwin Hyman.

—— (1990) *The British System of Government*, 8th edn, London: Unwin Hyman.

—— (1998) *The British System of Government*, 10th edn, London: Routledge.

Birch, A. H. and Campbell, P. (1950) 'Voting behaviour in a Lancashire constituency', *British Journal of Sociology*, 1: 197–208.

Birch, A. H., Campbell, P., and Lucas, P. G. (1956) 'The popular press in the British general election of 1955', *Political Studies*, 4: 297–306.

Bissoondath, N. (1994) *Selling Illusions: The Cult of Multiculturalism in Canada*, Toronto: Penguin.

Blumler, J. G. and McQuail, D. (1968) *Television in Politics: Its Uses and Influence*, London: Faber.

Bosanquet, B. (1899) *The Philosophical Theory of the State*, London: Macmillan.

Bottomore, T. B. (1966) *Elites and Society*, Harmondsworth: Penguin.

Breton, R. (1986) 'Multiculturalism and Canadian nation-building', in A. Cairns and C. Williams, *The Politics of Gender, Ethnicity and Language in Canada*, Toronto: University of Toronto Press.

Brotz, H. (1980) 'Multiculturalism in Canada: a muddle', *Canadian Public Policy*, 6: 41–6.

Brown, C. (1984) *Black and White Britain*, London: Heinemann.

Brown, P. A. (1918) *The French Revolution in English History*, London: Allen & Unwin.

Bryce, J. (1920) *Modern Democracies*, New York: Macmillan.

—— (1939) *Bryce's American Commonwealth: Fiftieth Anniversary*, ed. R. C. Brooks, New York: Macmillan.

Buchanan, A. (1991) *Secession: the Morality of Political Divorce from Fort Sumter to Lithuania and Quebec*, Boulder, CO: Westview Press.

Bullock, A. and Shock, M. (eds) (1956) *The Liberal Tradition*, London: Black.

Burke, E. (1921) *Selections*, Oxford: Clarendon Press.

Butler, D. and Stokes, D. (1969) *Political Change in Britain*, London: Macmillan.

Cable, J. (1981) *Gunboat Diplomacy*, London: Macmillan.

Calhoun, J. C. [1853] (1943) *Disquisition on Government*, New York: Peter Smith.

Cam, H. C. (1963) *Liberties and Communities in Medieval England*, London: Merlin Press.

Cammack, P. (1994) 'Democratization and citizenship in Latin America', in G. Parry and M. Moran (eds) *Democracy and Democratization*, London: Routledge.

Carter, A. (1979) *Authority and Democracy*, London: Routledge & Kegan Paul.

Cassinelli, C. W. (1961) 'Political authority: its exercise and possession', *Western Political Quarterly*, 14: 635–46.

Castells, M. (1997) *The Power of Identity*, Oxford: Basil Blackwell.

Citizens' Forum (1991) *Citizens' Forum on Canada's Future*, Ottawa: Canadian Government Publishing Center.

Cobban, A. [1929] (1960) *Edmund Burke and the Revolt Against the Eighteenth Century*, 2nd edn, London: Allen & Unwin.

Collingwood, R. G. (1939) *An Autobiography*, Oxford: Oxford University Press.

Cook, T. E. and Morgan, P. M. (1971) *Participatory Democracy*, New York: Harper & Row.

Cooper, B. (2004) *New Political Religions; or, An Analysis of Modern Terrorism*, Columbia, MO: University of Missouri Press.

Cox, A., Furlong, P., and Page, E. (1985) *Power in Capitalist Societies*, Brighton: Wheatsheaf.

Cranston, M. (1962) *Human Rights Today*, London: Ampersand.

Crewe, I. (1982) 'The Labour Party and the electorate', in D. Kavanagh (ed.) *The Politics of the Labour Party*, London. Allen & Unwin.

Crouch, C. (1979) *The Politics of Industrial Relations*, Glasgow: Fontana/Collins.

Dahl, R. A. (1956) *A Preface to Democratic Theory*, Chicago, IL: University of Chicago Press.

—— (1958) 'Political theory: truth and consequences', *World Politics*, 2: 89–102.

—— (1961) *Who Governs?*, New Haven, CT: Yale University Press.

—— (1967) *Pluralist Democracy in the United States*, Chicago, IL: Rand McNally.

—— (1970) *After the Revolution?*, New Haven, CT: Yale University Press.

—— (1971) *Polyarchy*, New Haven, CT: Yale University Press.

—— (1982) *Dilemmas of Pluralist Democracy*, New Haven, CT: Yale University Press.

—— (1985) *A Preface to Economic Democracy*, Berkeley, CA: University of California Press.

Dawson, R. E. and Prewitt, K. (1969) *Political Socialisation*, Boston, MA: Little, Brown.

Deutsch, K. W. (1953) *Nationalism and Social Communication*, New York: Wiley.

Dilthey, W. (1961) *Meaning in History*, London: Allen & Unwin.

Doherty, B. (1999) 'Paving the way: the rise of direct action against road-building and the changing character of British environmentalism', *Political Studies*, 47: 275–91.

Downs, A. (1957) *An Economic Theory of Democracy*, New York: Harper.

Dowse, R. E. (1978) 'Some doubts concerning the study of political socialisation', *Political Studies*, 26: 403–10.

Dowse, R. E. and Hughes, J. A. (1986) *Political Sociology*, 2nd edn, New York: Wiley.

Duncan, G. and Lukes, S. (1963) 'The new democracy', *Political Studies*, 11: 156–77.

Dunn, J. (1972) *Modern Revolutions: an Introduction to the Analysis of a Political Phenomenon*, Cambridge: Cambridge University Press.

—— (1989) 'Revolution', in T. Ball, J. Farr and R. L. Hanson (eds) *Political Innovation and Conceptual Change*, Cambridge: Cambridge University Press.

—— (1990) *Interpreting Political Responsibility*, Cambridge: Polity Press.

Dworkin, R. (1978) *Taking Rights Seriously*, Cambridge, MA: Harvard University Press.

Easton, D. (1953) *The Political System*, New York: Knopf.

—— (1965) *A Framework for Political Analysis*, Englewood Cliffs, NJ: Prentice-Hall.

Edwards, A. (1994) 'Democratization and qualified explanation', in G. Parry and M. Moran (eds) *Democracy and Democratization*, London: Routledge.

English, R. (2003) *The History of the IRA*, Oxford: Oxford University Press.

Eulau, H. (ed.) (1966) *Political Behaviour in America: New Directions*, New York: Random House.

Eulau, H., Eldersveld, S. J., and Janowitz, M. (1956) *Political Behaviour: a Reader in Theory and Practice*, Glencoe, IL: Free Press.

Evans, M. (1972) 'Karl Marx and political participation', in G. Parry (ed.) *Participation in Politics*, Manchester: Manchester University Press.

Fainsod, M. (1953) *How Russia is Ruled*, Cambridge, MA: Harvard University Press.

Farr, J. (1989) 'Understanding conceptual change politically', in T. Ball, J. Farr and R. L. Hanson (eds) *Political Innovation and Conceptual Change*, Cambridge: Cambridge University Press.

Feiling, K. (1963) *A History of England*, London: Macmillan.

Feinberg, J. (1980) *Rights, Justice, and the Bounds of Liberty*, Princeton, NJ: Princeton University Press.

Fekete, L. (2004) 'Anti-Muslim racism and the European security state', *Race and Class*, 46(1): 3–29.

Fetzer, J. S. and Soper, J. R. (2005) *Muslims and the State in Britain, France and Germany*, Cambridge: Cambridge University Press.

Foucault, M. (1980) *Power/Knowledge*, ed. C. Gordon, New York: Pantheon.

—— (1983) 'The subject and power', Afterword to H. L. Dreyfus and P. Rabinow (eds) *Michel Foucault: Beyond Structuralism and Hermeneutics*, 2nd edn, Chicago, IL: University of Chicago Press.

Fox, H. (1999) 'The Pinochet case no. 3', *International and Comparative Law Quarterly*, 48: 687–702.

Fukuyama, F. (2006) 'Identity, immigration, and liberal democracy', *Journal of Democracy*, 17(2): 5–20.

Gallie, W. B. (1955–6) 'Essentially contested concepts', *Proceedings of the Aristotelian Society*, 56: 167–98.

Gannon, K. (2005) *I Is for Infidel*, New York: Public Affairs.

Gaventa, J. (1980) *Power and Powerlessness*, Urbana, IL: University of Illinois Press.

Gibbins, R. and Ponting, J. R. (1986) 'An assessment of the probable impact of Aboriginal self-government in Canada', in A. Cairns and C. Williams (eds) *The Politics of Gender, Ethnicity and Language in Canada*, Toronto: University of Toronto Press.

Gibbs, B. (1976) *Freedom and Liberation*, London: Sussex University Press.

Giraud, M. (2000) 'Cultural identity and migrations', in R. Hudson and F. Reno (eds) *Politics of Identity*, Basingstoke: Palgrave.

Gottschalk, L. (1954) 'A professor of history in a quandary', *American Historical Review*, 59: 273–80.

Gray, J. (1998) *False Dawn: The Delusions of Global Capitalism*, London: Granta.

Green, T. H. (1881) *Liberal Legislation and Freedom of Contract*, London: Longmans, Green.

—— [1882] (1941) *Lectures on the Principles of Political Obligation*, London: Longmans, Green.

Grove, J. W. (1999) 'The face of science at the end of the twentieth century', *Queen's Quarterly*, 106: 383–92.

Hagen, W. W. (1999) 'The Balkans' lethal nationalisms', *Foreign Affairs*, 78(4): 52–64.

Hamilton, A., Jay, J., and Madison, J. [1787] (1901) *The Federalist*, New York: The Colonial Press.

Hanson, R. L. (1985) *The Democratic Imagination in America*, Princeton, NJ: Princeton University Press.

Hart, H. L. A. (1979) 'Between utility and rights', in A. Ryan (ed.) *The Idea of Freedom*, Oxford: Oxford University Press.

Held, D. (1991) 'Democracy and the global system', in D. Held (ed.) *Political Theory Today*, Stanford, CA: Stanford University Press.

Herold, J. C. (ed.) (1955) *The Mind of Napoleon*, New York: Columbia University Press.

Herzog, D. (1991) 'Review of T. Ball, *Transforming Political Discourse*', *Political Theory*, 19: 141–2.

Hirschman, A. O. (1970) *Exit, Voice and Loyalty*, Cambridge, MA: Harvard University Press.

Hobbes, T. [1651] (1985) *Leviathan*, Harmondsworth: Penguin.

Hobhouse, L. T. [1911] (1964) *Liberalism*, New York: Oxford University Press.

Holcombe, A. N. (1950) *Our More Perfect Union*, Cambridge, MA: Harvard University Press.

Horowitz, D. (1953) *State in the Making*, New York: Knopf.

Hunter, F. (1953) *Community Power Structure*, Chapel Hill, NC: University of North Carolina Press.

Huntington, S. (1996) *The Clash of Civilizations and the Remaking of World Order*, New York: Simon & Schuster.

Jennings, J. (2000) 'Citizenship, republicanism and multiculturalism in contemporary France', *British Journal of Political Science*, 30: 575–98.

Jessop, B. (1982) *The Capitalist State*, Oxford: Blackwell.

Jones, P. (1989) 'Re-examining rights', *British Journal of Political Science*, 19: 69–96.

Juergensmeyer, M. (2003) *Terror in the Mind of God*, Berkeley, CA: University of California Press.

Kallen, E. (1982) *Ethnicity and Human Rights in Canada*, Toronto: Gage.

Karatnycky, A. and Ackerman, P. (2005) *How Freedom Is Won: From Civic Resistance to Durable Democracy*, New York: Freedom House.

Kavanagh, D. (1983) *Political Science and Political Behaviour*, London: Allen & Unwin.

Keating, M. (1996) *Nations Against the State*, London: Macmillan.

Kedourie, E. (1961) *Nationalism*, London: Hutchinson.

Kepel, G. (2002) *Jihad: The Trail of Political Islam*, Cambridge, MA: Harvard University Press.

Klausen, L. (2005) *The Islamic Challenge: Politics and Religion in Western Europe*, Oxford: Oxford University Press.

Kringas, P. (1984) 'Really educating migrant children', in J. Jupp (ed.) *Ethnic Politics in Australia*, Sydney: Allen & Unwin.

Krislov, S. (1974) *Representative Bureaucracy*, Englewood Cliffs, NJ: Prentice-Hall.

Landauer, C. (1983) *Corporate State Ideologies: Historical Roots and Philosophical Origins*, Berkeley, CA: Institute of International Studies.

Laponce, J. A. (1987) *Languages and their Territories*, Toronto: University of Toronto Press.

Laqueur, W. (1987) *The Age of Terrorism*, Boston, MA: Little, Brown.

Laski, H. J. (1928) *The Development of the Representative System in our Times*, Geneva: Inter-Parliamentary Union.

Lasswell, H. D. and Kaplan, A. (1950) *Power and Society*, New Haven, CT: Yale University Press.

Latham, E. [1952] (1965) *The Group Basis of Politics*, New York: Octagon.

Lazarsfeld, P., Berelson, B., and Gaudet, H. (1944) *The People's Choice*, New York: Columbia University Press.

Lerner, M. (1957) *America as a Civilization*, New York: Simon & Schuster.

Lewis, B. (1990) 'The roots of Muslim rage', *Atlantic Monthly*, 266(3): 47–60.

—— (1993) *Islam and the West*, New York: Oxford University Press.

—— (1995) *Cultures in Conflict*, New York: Oxford University Press.

Lindblom, C. E. (1959) 'The science of muddling through', *Public Administration Review*, 19(4): 79–88.

—— (1965) *The Intelligence of Democracy*, New York: Free Press.

Lindsay, A. D. [1929] (1935) *The Essentials of Democracy*, London: Oxford University Press.

Linz, J. and Valemzuela, A. (eds) (1994) *The Failure of Presidential Democracy*, Baltimore, MD: Johns Hopkins University Press.

Lively, J. (1983) 'Paternalism', in A. P. Griffiths (ed.) *Of Liberty*, Cambridge: Cambridge University Press.

Lo Bianco Report (1987) *National Policy on Languages*, Canberra: Australian Government Publishing Service.

Lowell, A. L. (1896) *Governments and Parties in Continental Europe*, London: Longmans, Green.

—— (1908) *The Government of England*, New York: Macmillan.

Lukes, S. (1974) *Power: a Radical View*, London: Macmillan.

Luttwak, E. N. (1999) 'Give war a chance', *Foreign Affairs*, 78(4): 36–44.

McKenzie, R. T. (1955) *British Political Parties*, London: Heinemann.

—— (1982) 'Power in the Labour Party: the issue of intra-party democracy', in D. Kavanagh (ed.) *The Politics of the Labour Party*, London: Allen & Unwin.

Mackenzie, W. J. M. (1971) *The Study of Political Science Today*, London: Macmillan.

MacRae, D. (1958) *Dimensions of Congressional Voting*, Berkeley, CA: University of California Press.

Mamdani, M. (2004) *Good Muslim, Bad Muslim*, New Delhi: Permanent Black.

Mandelbaum, M. (1999) 'A perfect failure: NATO's war against Yugoslavia', *Foreign Affairs*, 78(5): 2–8.

Manning, D. J. (1968) *The Mind of Jeremy Bentham*, London: Longmans.

Marx, K. [1843] (1964) *Critique of Hegel's Philosophy of Right*, in T. B. Bottomore (ed.) *Karl Marx: Early Writings*, New York: McGraw-Hill.

Marx, K. and Engels, F. [1846] (1970) *The German Ideology*, New York: International Publishers.

Meisel, J. H. (1962) *The Myth of the Ruling Class*, Ann Arbor, MI: University of Michigan Press.

—— (ed.) (1965) *Pareto and Mosca*, Englewood Cliffs, NJ: Prentice-Hall.

Michels, R. (1930) 'Authority', in *Encyclopedia of the Social Sciences*, vol. 2, New York: Macmillan.

—— [1911] (1962) *Political Parties*, New York: Free Press.

Milbrath, L. W. (1965) *Political Participation*, Chicago, IL: Rand McNally.

Miliband, R. (1964) 'Mills and politics', in I. L. Horowitz (ed.) *The New Sociology*, New York: Oxford University Press.

—— (1969) *The State in Capitalist Society*, London: Weidenfeld & Nicolson.

—— (1983) *Class Power and State Power*, London: New Left Books.

—— (1984) *Capitalist Democracy in Britain*, Oxford: Oxford University Press.

Mill, J. S. [1848] (1963) *Principles of Political Economy*, in *Collected Works of J. S. Mill*, vols 2 and 3, Toronto: Toronto University Press.

—— [1859] (1946) *On Liberty*, Oxford: Blackwell.

—— [1861] (1946) *Considerations on Representative Government*, Oxford: Blackwell.

—— [1873] (1924) *Autobiography*, London: Oxford University Press.

Miller, W. E. and Stokes, D. E. (1963) 'Constituency influence in Congress', *American Political Science Review*, 57: 45–56.

Mills, C. W. (1956) *The Power Elite*, New York: Oxford University Press.

Milne, A. J. M. (1962) *The Social Philosophy of English Idealism*, London: Allen & Unwin.

Milne, R. S. and Mackenzie, H. A. (1954) *Straight Fight*, London: Hansard Society for Parliamentary Government.

Minogue, K. R. (1967) *Nationalism*, London: Methuen.

Morris-Jones, W. H. (1954) 'In defence of apathy: some doubts on the duty to vote', *Political Studies*, 2: 33–7.

Mosca, G. [1896] (1939) *The Ruling Class*, New York: McGraw-Hill.

Naisbitt, J. (1995) *Global Paradox*, London: Nicholas Brealey

Nickel, J. W. (1987) *Making Sense of Human Rights*, Berkeley, CA: University of California Press.

Nordlinger, E. A. (1981) *On the Autonomy of the Democratic State*, Cambridge, MA: Harvard University Press.

Nugent, N. (1991) *The Government and Politics of the European Community*, 2nd edn, London: Macmillan.

Nye, J. S. (1999) 'Redefining the national interest', *Foreign Affairs*, 78(4): 22–35.

Oakeshott, M. J. (1933) *Experience and its Modes*, Cambridge: Cambridge University Press.

—— (1962) *Rationalism in Politics*, London: Methuen.

O'Farrell, C. (1989) *Foucault: Historian or Philosopher?*, London: Macmillan.

Offe, C. (1972) 'Political authority and class structures: an analysis of late capitalist societies', *International Journal of Sociology*, 2: 73–108.

—— (1975) 'The theory of the capitalist state and the problem of policy formation', in L. N. Lindberg, R. Alford, C. Crouch and C. Offe (eds) *Stress and Contradiction in Modern Capitalism*, Lexington, MA: D. C. Heath.

—— (1980) 'The separation of form and content in liberal democratic politics', *Studies in Political Economy*, 3: 5–6.

Ohmae, K. (1995) *The End of the Nation-State: The Rise of Regional Economics*, London: HarperCollins.

Oliver, D. (1989) 'The parties and Parliament: representative or intra-party democracy', in J. Jowell and D. Oliver (eds) *The Changing Constitution*, Oxford: Clarendon Press.

Olson, M. (1965) *The Logic of Collective Action*, Cambridge, MA: Harvard University Press.

—— (1982) *The Rise and Decline of Nations*, New Haven, CT: Yale University Press.

O'Sullivan, N. (2004) *European Political Thought since 1945*, Basingstoke: Palgrave.

Padover, S. K. (1963) *The Meaning of Democracy*, New York: Praeger.

—— (ed.) (1969) *Thomas Jefferson on Democracy*, New York: Greenwood Press.

Palmer, R. E. (1969) *Hermeneutics*, Evanston, IL: Northwestern University Press.

Panitch, L. (1979) 'The development of corporatism in liberal democracies', in P. C. Schmitter and G. Lehmbruch (eds) *Trends Towards Corporatist Intermediation*, Beverley Hills, CA: Sage.

Pape, R. A. (2005) *Dying to Win: The Strategic Logic of Suicide Terrorism*, New York: Random House.

Parekh, B. (2000) *Rethinking Multiculturalism: Cultural Diversity and Political Theory*, Cambridge, MA: Harvard University Press.

Parry, G. (1969) *Political Elites*, London: Allen & Unwin.

—— (ed.) (1972) *Participation in Politics*, Manchester: Manchester University Press.

Pateman, C. (1970) *Participation and Democratic Theory*, Cambridge: Cambridge University Press.

—— (1980) 'The civic culture: a philosophic critique', in G. A. Almond and S. Verba (eds) *The Civic Culture Revisited*, Boston, MA: Little, Brown.

Paul, E. F., Paul, J., and Miller, F. D. (eds) (1984) *Human Rights*, Oxford: Blackwell.

Pennock, J. R. (1968) 'Political philosophy and political science', in O. Garceau (ed.) *Political Research and Political Theory*, Cambridge, MA: Harvard University Press.

Peters, R. S. (1958) 'Authority', *Proceedings of the Aristotelian Society*, 32: 207–24.

Pitkin, H. F. (1968) 'Commentary: the paradox of representation', in J. R. Pennock and J. W. Chapman (eds) *Representation*, New York: Atherton Press.

—— (1988) 'Are freedom and liberty twins?', *Political Theory*, 16: 523–52.

—— (1989) 'Representation', in T. Ball, J. Farr and R. L. Hanson (eds) *Political Innovation and Conceptual Change*, Cambridge: Cambridge University Press.

Plamenatz, J. (1949) *The English Utilitarians*, Oxford: Blackwell.

—— (1973) *Democracy and Illusion*, London: Longman.

Polsby, N. (1963) *Community Power and Political Theory*, New Haven, CT: Yale University Press.

—— (1979) 'Empirical investigations of mobilization of bias in community power research', *Political Studies*, 27: 527–41.

Popper, K. R. (1957) *The Poverty of Historicism*, London: Routledge & Kegan Paul.

—— (1959) *The Logic of Scientific Discovery*, London: Hutchinson.

—— [1945] (1962) *The Open Society and its Enemies*, 4th edn, vol. 2, London: Routledge & Kegan Paul.

Porter, J. (1965) *The Verticle Mosaic*, Toronto: University of Toronto Press.

—— (1975) 'Ethnic pluralism in Canadian perspective', in N. Glazer and D. Moynihan (eds) *Ethnicity: Theory and Experience*, Cambridge, MA: Harvard University Press.

—— (1979) 'Melting pot or mosaic: revolution or reversion', in J. Porter (ed.) *The Measure of Canadian Society*, Toronto: Gage.

Poulantzas, N. (1973) *Political Power and Social Class*, London: New Left Books and Speed and Ward.

—— [1978] (1980) *State, Power, Socialism*, London: Verso.

Preece, J. J. (2005) *Minority Rights*, Cambridge: Polity Press.

Rees, J. C. (1960) 'A re-reading of Mill on liberty', *Political Studies*, 8: 113–29.

Reno, F. (2000) 'Caribbean identities in Europe: a comparative perspective', in R. Hudson and F. Reno (eds) *Politics of Identity*, Basingstoke: Palgrave.

Rex, J. (1996) *Ethnic Minorities in the Modern Nation State*, London: Macmillan.

Richardson, A. (1983) *Participation*, London: Routledge & Kegan Paul.

Riker, W. H. and Ordeshook, P. C. (1968) 'A theory of the calculus of voting', *American Political Science Review*, 62: 25–42.

Rodman, P. W. (1999) 'The fallout from Kosovo', *Foreign Affairs,* 78(4): 45–51.

Ronen, D. (1979) *The Quest for Self-Determination*, New Haven, CT: Yale University Press.

Rose, R. (1976) *The Problem of Party Government*, Harmondsworth: Penguin.

Rose, R. and Peters, G. (1978) *Can Government Go Bankrupt?*, New York: Basic Books.

Rousseau, J. J. [1762] (1913) *The Social Contract*, London: Dent.

Roy, O. (1994a) 'Islam in France: religion, ethnic community or social ghetto?', in B. Lewis and D. Schapper (eds) *Muslims in Europe*, London: Pinter.

—— (1994b) *Globalised Islam*, London: Hurst.

Runciman, W. G. (1963) *Social Science and Political Theory*, Cambridge: Cambridge University Press.

Runnymede Trust (2000) *The Future of Multi-Ethnic Britain*, London: Profile Books.

Ruthven, M. (2002) *A Fury for God: The Islamist Attack on America*, London: Granta.

Sabine, G. H. (1937) *A History of Political Theory*, London: Harrap.

Samuel, H. (1902) *Liberalism*, London: Richards.

Sarlvic, B. and Crewe, I. (1983) *Decade of Dealignment*, Cambridge: Cambridge University Press.

Sartori, G. (1987) *The Theory of Democracy Revisited*, Chatham, NJ: Chatham House.

Schaar, J. H. (1981) *Legitimacy in the Modern State*, New Brunswick, NJ: Transaction Books.

Schattschneider, E. E. (1960) *The Semisovereign People*, New York: Holt, Rinehart & Winston.

Schmidt, D. C. (1989) *Citizen Lawmakers*, Philadelphia, PA: Temple University Press.

Schmitter, P. C. and Lehmbruch, G. (eds) (1979) *Trends Towards Corporatist Intermediation*, Beverley Hills, CA: Sage.

Schubert, G. A. (1959) *Quantitative Analysis of Judicial Behaviour*, New York: Free Press.

—— (ed.) (1963) *Judicial Decision-Making*, New York: Free Press.

Self, P. (1985) *Political Theories of Modern Government*, London: Allen & Unwin.

Sennett, R. (1980) *Authority*, New York: Knopf.

Shonfield, A. (1965) *Modern Capitalism*, London: Oxford University Press.

Simon, H. A. (1957) *Models of Man*, New York: Wiley.

—— [1945] (1976) *Administrative Behaviour*, 3rd edn, New York: Free Press.

Simon, R. (1982) *Gramsci's Political Thought*, London: Lawrence & Wishart.

Skinner, Q. (1973) 'The empirical theorists of democracy and their critics', *Political Theory*, 1: 287–306.

—— (1983) 'The idea of negative liberty: philosophical and historical perspectives', in R. Rorty, J. B. Schneewind and Q. Skinner (eds) *Philosophy in History*, Cambridge: Cambridge University Press.

—— (1989) 'Language and political change', in T. Ball, J. Farr and R. L. Hanson (eds) *Political Innovation and Conceptual Change*, Cambridge: Cambridge University Press.

Smith, A. (1995) *Nations and Nationalism in a Global Era*, Cambridge: Polity Press.

Spotts, F. and Wieser, T. (1986) *Italy: a Difficult Democracy*, Cambridge: Cambridge University Press.

Strange, S. (1996) *The Retreat of the State*, Cambridge: Cambridge University Press.

Strauss, L. (1962) 'An epilogue', in H. J. Storing (ed.) *Essays on the Scientific Study of Politics*, New York: Holt, Rinehart & Winston.

Talmon, J. L. (1955) *The Origins of Totalitarian Democracy*, London: Secker & Warburg.

Taylor, C. (1967) 'Neutrality in political science', in P. Laslett and W. G. Runciman (eds) *Philosophy, Politics and Society: Third Series*, Oxford: Blackwell.

—— (1979) 'What's wrong with negative liberty', in A. Ryan (ed.) *The Idea of Freedom*, Oxford: Oxford University Press.

—— (1985) *Philosophy and the Human Sciences*, Cambridge: Cambridge University Press.

—— (1999) 'Democratic exclusion (and its remedies?)', in A. C. Cairn, J. C. Courtney, P. Mackinnon, H. J. Michelmann and D. E. Smith, *Citizenship, Diversity and Pluralism*, Montreal: McGill–Queen's University Press.

Trudeau, P. (1977) *Federalism and the French Canadians*, Toronto: Macmillan.

Truman, D. (1951) *The Governmental Process*, New York: Knopf.

Tucker, R. C. (ed.) (1978) *The Marx-Engels Reader*, 2nd edn, New York: Norton.

Van Dyke, V. (1982) 'Collective entities and moral rights: problems in liberal-democratic thought', *Journal of Politics*, 44: 21–40.

—— (1985) *Human Rights, Ethnicity and Discrimination*, Westport, CT: Greenwood Press.

Wahlke, J. C. and Eulau, H. (eds) (1959) *Legislative Behaviour: a Reader in Theory and Research*, New York: Free Press.

Wahlke, J. C., Eulau, H., Buchanan, W., and Ferguson, L. C. (1962) *The Legislative System*, New York: Wiley.

Waldron, J. (1987) *Nonsense Upon Stilts*, London: Methuen.

Walker, J. L. (1966) 'A critique of the elitist theory of democracy', *American Political Science Review*, 60: 285–95.

Walzer, M. (1997) *On Toleration*, New Haven, CT: Yale University Press.

Waters, M. (1995) *Globalization*, London: Routledge.

Weinfeld, M. (1981) 'Myth and reality in the Canadian mosaic: "affective ethnicity"', *Canadian Ethnic Studies*, 13: 80–100.

de Wenden, C. W. (2003) 'Multiculturalism in France', *International Journal on Multicultural Societies*, 5(1): 77–87.

Wheare, K. C. (1946) *Federal Government*, London: Oxford University Press.

—— (1955) *Government by Committee*, Oxford: Clarendon Press.

Wiley, N. F. (1967) 'The ethnic mobility trap and stratification theory', *Social Problems*, 15(2): 47–59.

Wilson, D. (1999) 'Exploring the limits of public participation in local government', *Parliamentary Affairs*, 52: 246–59.

Winch, P. (1958) *The Idea of a Social Science*, London: Routledge & Kegan Paul.

Woodward, E. L. (1934) *French Revolutions*, London: Oxford University Press.

Index of concepts

General index